Ellen Chennells

Recollections of an Egyptian Princess

Ellen Chennells

Recollections of an Egyptian Princess

ISBN/EAN: 9783337168520

Printed in Europe, USA, Canada, Australia, Japan

Cover: Foto ©ninafisch / pixelio.de

More available books at **www.hansebooks.com**

RECOLLECTIONS

OF

AN EGYPTIAN PRINCESS

BY

HER ENGLISH GOVERNESS

BEING

A RECORD OF FIVE YEARS' RESIDENCE AT THE COURT OF ISMAEL PASHA, KHÉDIVE

NEW EDITION

WILLIAM BLACKWOOD AND SONS
EDINBURGH AND LONDON
MDCCCXCIII

INTRODUCTION.

VERY soon after my arrival in Egypt, I had occasion to observe that the opinion prevalent among Mahometans was, that it was a disgrace to any woman for her face to be seen, or her name to be heard, beyond the walls of the harem. Every book published in London or Paris was immediately procured in Cairo, and great displeasure was manifested when (as occasionally happened) some distinguished visitor to the harem gave her impressions to the world at large.

I had always been in the habit of keeping a journal when travelling or residing in foreign countries, and as I wrote openly it soon attracted the notice and disapprobation of my pupils. "Was I going to publish a book?" they asked. I said, "No; but as everything was new and strange to me, I wished to write down my impressions while still fresh, to assist my memory in later years." After a time they seemed satisfied, and had full confidence in me. Indeed the young Pasha often gave me information.

When I left Egypt in the autumn of 1876, all I possessed was invested in Egyptian bonds, bought in at prices ranging from £80 to £30. They kept falling! falling! falling! Turkish bonds had already ceased payment, and Egyptian seemed likely to follow suit! They actually went down to £25!

My Anglo-Egyptian friends strongly advised me to publish my journal, and I revised it for that purpose. But Mr Goschen went out to Egypt and set the finances in order, the Khédive Ismaël Pasha was deposed, and the English occupation began. The bonds were safe, though the interest was reduced.

Several years have passed: of the four children whom we educated, three are dead—first the Princess, and a few years later Shefket, the Abyssinian boy, and last of all the beautiful Kopsès Hanem! Ibrahim Pasha (the son) is with his father at Emirghian, their palace on the Bosphorus, where, like the unwary fly in the fable of "The Spider and the Fly," "They went in, but can't get out again," and will probably be heard of no more.

Under these circumstances there is no one left to feel aggrieved at my publication, and I have spoken ill of none.

ELLEN CHENNELLS.

CONTENTS.

CHAPTER I.

Introduction—Arrival in Egypt.   1

CHAPTER II.

First visit to the Pyramids—Enter the Third and the Great Pyramid—The Princess first to go in—Torment of insects at Choubrah; mosquitoes, sand-flies, wasps, &c.—Dogs and cats—Prevalence of ophthalmia—Ramadan—Sufferings of the Arabs during the fast—Fine climate of Cairo in the winter—Length of day—Temperature—Building everywhere going on.   12

CHAPTER III.

Bairam—First visit to the harem—Gorgeous dresses of the slaves—Visit the Queen-Mother at Kasr-el-Ali—Shaheen's views of morality—Roses at Christmas—Second visit to the Pyramids—Inundation subsided, and succeeded by green crops—Procession of the Mahmal—First ride on a dromedary—Cruelty of the Arabs to horses and asses.   22

CHAPTER IV.

Proposed journey up the Nile—Frequent postponement—Original party greatly increased in numbers—Final departure—Excursion to Sakkara—The Serapeum—Tombs of Ti and of Ptahhotep—Donkey-riding—The "Flying Dutchman"—Proceed on our voyage—Inconvenient separation from our effects—Stop at Feshna for the night—Arrive at Minieh, and stop at the palace—Voyage delayed—Arrange my pupil's studies—No walking at Minieh—Flat-bottomed boats pass down the river loaded with forced labourers—Animated appearance of the river, ... 32

CHAPTER V.

At Minieh—Voyage still delayed—How we spent our time—Belief of the ancient Egyptians—A woman's name never mentioned out of the harem—Sudden return to Cairo—Death on the river, ... 44

CHAPTER VI.

Sight-seeing—Whirling dervishes—Howling dervishes—Visit to the petrified forest—To the opera—Harem boxes—No English church at that time in Cairo—Service held in the New Hotel—Visit received from some Mahometan ladies—Invitation to a wedding—Translation of the letter into English—Shem-el-Nesseem—Khamseen winds, ... 51

CHAPTER VII.

The Viceroy and harem remove to Gezireh—We drive there daily—Great heat—Sand-storms—Receive some Arab sheikhs at dinner—"Moulid-el-nebbee"—"Doseh"—Removal to Alexandria—Daily visits to Ras-el-Tin—Departure for Constantinople - Voyage thither, ... 63

CHAPTER VIII.

The Mahroussah off Stamboul—Entrance into the Bosphorus—Port-holes closed—Landing at Emirghian—Description of palace and grounds—Our house on the hillside—Steamers on the Bosphorus—First visit to Pera and Galata—Impediments to progress—Turkish time—First visit to St Sophia—Climate of Constantinople—Harem—Caïques—Turkish cemetery at Scutari—Ascent from Kadikeui, ... 75

CONTENTS. ix

CHAPTER IX.

On the Bosphorus—Mustapha's house—Roumeli-Hissar—Anniversary of the Sultan's accession—Illuminations—Tramway in Stamboul—Separate omnibuses for harem—We make the circuit of the walls of Constantinople—Frequent change of temperature—Turkish money—Turkish language, . . 87

CHAPTER X.

Picnic to the Forest of Belgrade—Sudden appearance of the cook at dinner—The Viceroy returns to Egypt—Unexpected departure of the Pasha and his household—Am at first left unprovided for—Great improvement in affairs—Weather in August—Slave children—Candili—Charming residence there —Railway from Constantinople to the Seven Towers—Miss the station—Euphrates Valley scheme, . . . 99

CHAPTER XI.

Turkish and Greek boatmen—Sudden irruption of eunuchs into our little garden—Cliff walk on the Bosphorus—Dogs—Unexpected return of the Pasha and his suite—Excursion to Eyoub— Curiosity of Turkish women—Buffaloes in the water—View from the cemetery at Eyoub—Tobacco monopoly—Candili— A Persian nurse's ideas about a bedstead—British cemetery at Scutari, ... 112

CHAPTER XII.

Beicos—The Giant's Mountain—The Pasha's taste for building— Greek boatmen—Leave the Bosphorus—Crowded state of the Masr—Voyage—Story of a pilgrimage to Mecca—Arrival off Alexandria—Go to the Hôtel de l'Europe—Journey to Cairo— We are sent to the New Hotel—Lessons at the harem begin, my pupil being shut up, ... 122

CHAPTER XIII.

Palace of Abdeen—Difficulties with harem carriage—I remonstrate —Am provided with another—Arab weddings—We leave the New Hotel and return to Choubrah—Eunuchs—Constant interruptions from the slaves—Baïram, ... 134

CHAPTER XIV.

Opera—Four royal marriages announced as to take place during the winter—Old Cairo, Nilometer and Mosque of Amrou—Procession of the Mahmal—Mosque of Sultan Hassan—Drive to Heliopolis—Weather changes—Cold and wet—Funerals—Departure of the pilgrims for Mecca—We are told we are to leave Choubrah—Remove to the New Hotel—Arrival of two of the Princes from England—Curious instance of forgetting one's own language—Photography in the harem—Royal trousseaux—Wedding *fêtes* begin—Marriage contracts, . . 146

CHAPTER XV.

Races—Ball at Gezireh—Wedding *fêtes* begin—Dinners—Provisions given to the poor—Procession of the bride on the third evening—Dancing in the harem—The bride is brought out fainting—Weight of the ornaments—Christy Minstrels—Sudden death—Great difference in the treatment of Europeans during the last twenty years, ... 159

CHAPTER XVI.

Excursion to Toura—Death in the hotel—My pupil is betrothed—Turkish comedians brought in blindfolded—The second betrothal takes place—Quail-shooting near the Pyramids—We return to Choubrah—Bookcase turned into a meat-cupboard—Sprain my ankle—Court moves to Gezireh—We are ordered to Constantinople, ... 170

CHAPTER XVII.

Departure for Alexandria—Harem travel the same day—Consequent delay—Arrive too late for the boat—Hotels crowded—Proceed in the Mahalla to Constantinople—We are ordered to Therapia—Go to the Hôtel des Ambassadeurs—Remove to Emirghian—Lessons in the harem—*Fête* at the palace given to the Sultane Validé, ... 184

CONTENTS.   xi

CHAPTER XVIII.

Arrival of the Sultane Validé—Illuminations—The Sultan visits Emirghian—Etiquette on the occasion—Signs of departure—Leave Turkey on the Dakahlieh—Obstructions to the view on deck—Stop at Gallipoli—At Dardanelli—Mitylene—Smyrna—Stay there twenty-four hours—Great heat—Go ashore towards evening—Leave Smyrna—Stop at Scio—At Syra—Land—Fine position of the town—Well built and well paved—Town dates only forty years back—Continue our voyage—Arrival at Alexandria, ... 196

CHAPTER XIX.

Arrival at Alexandria—Go to the Hôtel de l'Europe—Khédive and harem not yet come—Preparations for illuminating the town—The hotel is photographed—Khédive and harem go to Cairo—Return of my pupil—I begin lessons at Ramleh—Shaheen's story—Generosity of the second Princess—Our party diminishes—We are ordered to Cairo—Go to the New Hotel—Remove to the Palace of Gezireh—Description of it—Kiosk in the garden, ... 206

CHAPTER XX.

Harem at Gezireh—Daily lessons there—Departure of his Highness and the harem from Gezireh to Abdeen—I remain at Gezireh—Again difficulties about a carriage--October a trying month in Egypt—Ramadan begins—Sudden removal to Choubrah—French cook and Arab sentinel — Locks and keys — Mixed nationalities among us—Copper coinage—Popular superstition concerning Baïram commencing on a Friday, . . . 218

CHAPTER XXI.

Weather—I go to the New Hotel—Customs in the harem—Different opinions of the same thing—Constant difficulties with the harem carriage—The driver is bastinadoed—Treatment of new-born infants—European servants in the harem—Invalids in the hotel—Death of one—Strange story, ... 230

CHAPTER XXII.

Dust-storms and rain—Unceremonious hour for paying a bill—Marriage of the Princess—Panic in the chief saloon—Intrusion of Arab women—Going home of the bride—Dine at Aurique's, and afterwards drive out to see illuminations—Meet a funeral car—Marriage of the adopted daughter—Concert at Kasr-el-Nil—First visit to the two brides, ... 242

CHAPTER XXIII.

Visit the (so-called) school of the third Princess—Excellent arrangements—Presents received—Persian shawls—Am summoned to take up my abode in the harem—Go, but return to the hotel—Excellent police of Cairo—Burglary committed by Greeks—Finally take up my residence in the harem—My apartments—Go to the opera attended by a eunuch—Want of employment in the harem, ... 254

CHAPTER XXIV.

Curious superstition about brides—Fantasia in the harem—Again visit the Pyramids—Photography in the harem—Summer heat begins—Amusements in the harem, ... 266

CHAPTER XXV.

Married life in the East contrasted with that in England—Amusements in the harem—Distinction between the white and black slaves—Sudden appearance of eunuchs in my room—Removal to Alexandria—Story of the diamond buckle—Family life on the Canal—I make a new acquaintance, . . . 278

CHAPTER XXVI.

Go to reside in the palace at Ramleh—We read a great deal—Dinner-party at the harem—Am taken ill—Remove to Koum-el-Dikke—Maltese cook—Arab funeral—Corpse objects to be buried—Return to the harem—Son born to Tewfik Pasha, . 291

CONTENTS. xiii

CHAPTER XXVII.

Return to Cairo—Nuisance of cats in the harem—Purchase of slaves—Two negresses whipped—Bézique—English groom complains of being robbed—Illness in the harem—Accident while driving The "dada's" leg is broken—Blind doctor attends—Disastrous result—Ramadan, ... 303

CHAPTER XXVIII.

Ramadan in the harem, 315

CHAPTER XXIX.

The Night of Power at the Mosque—Baïram—The Prince and Princess leave for a time—Candle-stealing—Discover the thief—Transit of Venus—Slight shock of earthquake, . . 329

CHAPTER XXX.

Kourban Baïram—Arab saddles—Donkey-ride to Heliopolis—Ball at Gezireh—Dinner-party at the harem—Particularly fine spring—Many donkey-rides—Readings with my pupil—Difficulty of procuring books unless specially ordered from Europe—Good disposition and unselfishness of the Princess—Cicolani's garden—"Doseh"—Am taken ill, . . . 340

CHAPTER XXXI.

Remove to the Hôtel d'Orient—Remain there a fortnight—Return to the palace—Three weddings in the harem—The Prince is to go to Europe—Departure—We go to Ramleh—I am taken ill, 352

CHAPTER XXXII.

Illness of the Princess—Her death, . . 360

CHAPTER XXXIII.

Funeral of the Princess—Conclusion, . . 370

PORTRAITS.

PRINCESS ZEYNEB, ... *Frontispiece*

PRINCE IBRAHIM AND THE PRINCESS ZEYNEB, *To face p.* 102

KOPSÈS,   ,,   ,, 276

RECOLLECTIONS

OF

AN EGYPTIAN PRINCESS.

CHAPTER I.

Introduction—Arrival in Egypt.

WHEN I accepted the post of instructress to the Khédive's daughter, the Princess Zeyneb, it was beginning quite a new life, and I was anxious to obtain every possible information before undertaking the duty. All that I heard tended to encourage me.

Some five years earlier, the Khédive Ismael had engaged an English gentleman (General Maclean, a retired Indian officer) to undertake the education of his fourth son, Prince Ibrahim. The General was a married man, and his wife and family accompanied him to Egypt. He was lodged in a house in the vicinity of the palace, and the young Pasha spent several hours with him daily.

The wife and eldest daughter of the General went occasionally to the palace to pay their respects to the mother of their young charge; and this lady, the second wife of the Khédive, was so much pleased with Miss Maclean that she asked her to undertake the education of her daughter, which Miss Maclean consented to do.

Harem influences and surroundings are not favourable to the development of young children, either in mind or body, and it was therefore settled that the young Princess should, with her brother, pass the whole day at the General's house and with his family.

They came early, often before 8 A.M., and remained until evening. They were always accompanied by two children, a boy and girl, their companions in study and their playmates in recreation. Had the Khédive sought through all the Ottoman dominions he could not have found two children more suitable for the position in which they were placed. The boy was Abyssinian, the girl Circassian; both were faithful, honest, and truthful.

This system of education had gone on for five years, when it was interrupted by the departure from Egypt of the General and his family.

A new educational staff was formed, new with the exception of a young Oxford graduate, Mr Michell, who had come out during the last year of the General's stay, to teach the Pasha Greek and Latin, and to prepare him for Oxford, to which university the Khédive then intended sending his son.

The General's place was to be filled by Mr Freeland (also an Oxford man). He was married, and accompanied by his wife and three little children.

In October 1871 we were all established in a charming house in the Choubrah Road, which is the fashionable drive of Cairo, and is a beautiful avenue of acacias and sycamores, extending three or four miles. The house was spacious and handsomely furnished, with every possible convenience. We had all our separate suites of apartments, so as to enjoy privacy and social life at the same time.

On the second morning after my arrival at Choubrah, at a little before nine, our dragoman, Shaheen, came to tell me that the Princess was just driving up. She came in an English carriage, driven by an English coachman. An English groom sat by the coachman; and two tall Arabs in flowing white robes, and carrying long sticks in their hands, preceded the carriage as runners (or *syces*, as they are called in Arabic)—a by no means unnecessary precaution, as progress is continually impeded by camels, donkeys, water-bearers, and even pedestrians, there being no footpath. The road is soft sand, no noise is made either by animals or wheels, so that these runners are very necessary to clear the way for a carriage when driven rapidly.

The Princess was accompanied by Zohrab Bey, an Armenian physician, and a prettily little Circassian girl named Kopsès, the sharer of her studies and amusements, of about the same age as the Princess, or perhaps a little older. The latter came shyly to me, and Zohrab Bey stayed some time, that she might become familiarised with me. She was rather short in stature; but her face was very pretty—regular features, soft brown eyes (which she had a trick of screwing up), and long eyelashes, well-shaped head, and very good hair. Beauty is the all-important qualification among oriental women, and notwithstanding the personal advantages I have mentioned, which were undeniable, the Princess was in childhood considered plain. On account of ill health, she was rather backward in her studies, and was painfully conscious of her own deficiencies. Gentle and timid to a fault, she was of a character that developed late, and required great encouragement. Her admiration for her little companion was unbounded, and without a shade of jealousy. The latter was indeed a remarkable child, and well worthy the love of her little mistress. She was also small in stature, but slim and agile as a young fawn. She excelled in everything that she attempted, and learned all that she was taught with ease and exactness; but it would have been a false kindness to cultivate her powers according to their capability, at the risk of exciting ill-feeling on the part of the Princess, on whom she was wholly dependent. She was very lively, but wonderfully reticent in all concerning the inner life of the harem. She had the greatest influence over her little mistress, but it was always exercised for good.

Ibrahim Pasha had also a young companion, who shared his studies and amusements; Shefket, an Abyssinian boy, a year or two older than the Pasha, equally reticent and truthful as Kopsès. But there was this difference between the two children, that with the best intentions, Shefket was not able to keep pace with the young Pasha, whose intellect was remarkably acute. Shefket was light and active, and excellent in all athletic sports, as I had often occasion to see. He, as well as Kopsès, was a universal favourite with all the masters who had to do with the children.

When the lessons were over, the children played together in the large garden belonging to the house, and were generally joined by some of us. As there were a good many hours in the day devoted to lessons, we chose those games which involved running and bodily exercise. The Princess joined in them most heartily, and though she never gained the palm herself, she was quite as much delighted when the victory fell to Kopsès or Shefket.

For the first week or so, Zohrab Bey accompanied the Princess each morning to Choubrah; and then considering her sufficiently familiarised with me, he gave up the charge to Lolla Jani, a Greek, who held the (to us) extraordinary post of outer nurse, if I may so call it, to the Princess, and who was responsible for her safety everywhere beyond the gates of the harem. When the Princess came with this man, I observed that the blinds of the carriage were closely drawn down.

Though the brother and sister came from the same palace, they were always in separate carriages, and had separate attendants. It was the Eastern etiquette that, however nearly connected, they should be strangers to each other out of doors. Manners and customs have become so modified in Egypt during the last few years, by the increasing influx of Europeans, that it is difficult to say what further changes may take place; but though I saw a marked difference during the five years of my residence in Egypt, this custom still prevails, that husband and wife, brother and sister, are never together out of doors.

This was also the first instance in which a young Mahometan princess had been brought up without the harem walls, and in an English family. She was now twelve years old, and this training had already gone on for five years. Soon I was told she would be "shut up" in the harem, and although I dreaded the event, I felt that in a Mahometan country it could not be otherwise. The two girls were as yet perfect children, as much so as any English girls of that age. The Princess was shy to strangers, but very amiable and prepossessing to those whom she knew. Although not quick at lessons, she had much natural shrewdness, and quick observation. As children in their mother's harem, Ibrahim Pasha, though a year younger than his sister, was put first in everything; but in the English household into which the little creatures were brought at the ages of six and seven, the European custom was at once introduced, and the young lady had due precedence. I am told this created great astonishment, but the regulation was adhered to.

After a short time Mrs Freeland and I paid a visit of ceremony to the mother of the Princess, who was living at the Khédive's palace at Abdeen, at the southern extremity of Cairo. The great object of European ladies, either at Constantinople or Cairo, is to get an introduction to the harem, but once visited the charm is generally broken. On *fête* days the impression is gorgeous; the magnificent dresses, the splendid apartments, the flashing of jewels, the open courts with the feathery palms, and the sound of falling waters, all produce a delightful effect. But on ordinary visits you were struck with the entire absence of anything to promote amusement or mental occupation. No books, music, or any little feminine work lying about. The windows might look out on a garden, but there was sure to be a high wall which shut out all outer life.

The Khédive, to do him justice, was anxious to raise the position of women; he founded schools for girls, he endeavoured to promote education in his own harem, and gave much greater liberty and means, both of recreation and instruction, to its inmates, than any sovereign had done before him.

Ismael Pasha had four wives, the full proportion allowed by the Koran. To the first and second he was married when quite young, and to the third soon after his accession. These three ladies lived with him in the same palace. They, of course, had separate suites of apartments, but they lived in perfect amity, as I had full opportunity of knowing later. I once said what a wonderful thing it was for three wives to live together like affectionate sisters, but I was answered immediately, "That is because his Highness never shows any preference for one more than the others; if one is favoured to-day, the others have their turn to-morrow." I thought him a wonderful man to keep the balance so even, and I think most people will be of my opinion.

These ladies were called by Europeans the first, the second, and the third Princess; and by Mahometans the *Buyuk Hanem* or Great Lady, the *Ortangi Hanem* or Middle Lady, and the *Kutschuk Hanem* or Little Lady. These last were the titles given them inside the harem, but by the European and Levantine visitors their titles were numerically arranged. The first Princess (or *Buyuk Hanem*) had two lovely daughters, the eldest of whom was already married and had two children, the second still under her father's roof. The second Princess (or *Ortangi Hanem*) had had six children, the eldest of whom was the Khédive's firstborn son, and, had he lived, he would have been the heir, but to the inexpressible grief of the parents he and three others died in childhood. Two were left, Ibrahim and Zeyneb (the two placed under our charge), but in infancy they were both so delicate that there seemed little hope of rearing them. Ismael Pasha was then with his harem on the Bosphorus, and the services of Dr Zohrab, an Armenian physician practising at Constantinople, were called in. The children improved so rapidly under his care that Ismael Pasha asked him to give up his practice and enter permanently into his service, which after some consideration Dr Zohrab agreed to do, under certain conditions. One of these conditions was, that he should have as free access to his patients as he would have in a European household, and of course this implied free access to the harem, at all hours, without the intervention of eunuchs.

This was an unprecedented thing, but Ismael Pasha was an enlightened man; he doubtless knew that harem habits were not favourable to the development of infant life, but he could not overturn the institutions of ages, and he had full and just confidence in his physician. The mother, a beautiful little woman, had been overwhelmed with grief at the loss of so many children, and could not sufficiently express her gratitude to the man who had saved the lives of the two remaining.

The third Princess was childless, but she had the privilege of adopting one, so she selected a lovely little Circassian girl, chosen of course for her early promise of beauty. It may be wondered perhaps why she did not choose a boy, since the possession of a son is so much more coveted than that of a daughter. She could have done so, if the Viceroy had had any *motherless* son at that time; but though there were other sons, the mothers were all living, and the tie of mother and child is held so sacred that the two are never separated. The presence of an additional rival might have been objected to by the other wives, so the third Princess chose a little girl, who could always remain with her.

The Khédive had other sons and daughters, but they did not reside under the same roof. As is well known at Cairo, there are other harems in which the favourites reside; and when a son or daughter is born to the Khédive, mother and child are at once removed to the palace of the *Validé* (mother of the sovereign). If a son, a separate establishment is provided for him when he is old enough, and he holds equal rank with the son of a wife, the Mahometan law making no distinction in such a case. A few years ago the Khédive, as is well known, purchased from the Sultan the right of primogeniture in the succession of his own royal house, in contradistinction to the rule which had hitherto prevailed of the eldest male of the family succeeding to the throne. When primogeniture was established in Egypt, Tewfik Pasha, the eldest surviving son, was at once named heir-apparent, and his mother was elevated to the dignity of fourth wife, and was called the fourth Princess, or, in Turkish, *Deurtundju Hanem*. This lady did not, however, live with the Khédive, but resided with her son, taking her due place with the other wives on all State occasions.

Thus it will be seen that although there were other sons and daughters, the domestic circle under the roof of his Highness, at the time of which I write, was limited to the three wives, the Princess Fatma (the unmarried daughter of the first Princess), and Ibrahim Pasha and his sister the Princess Zeyneb, children of the second Princess. These breakfasted, lunched, and dined with his Highness *en famille*. But the young Pasha and the Princess Zeyneb, being engaged with their lessons, enjoyed that privilege only on Fridays and Sundays. The advantages thus obtained by the children of the wives is obvious; they were in daily close intercourse with their father. The Princess Fatma had a Levantine governess residing in the harem with her; but the Princess Zeyneb was the only instance of a daughter brought up outside the harem. Ibrahim Pasha being the only boy, was considered the joint property of the three wives—he had three mothers, so to speak, instead of one. The Pasha had frequently accompanied his father on his different journeys, and had visited with him almost every Court in Europe. On occasion of the Khédive's visit to England in 1869, he had been lodged with his father in Buckingham Palace, attended by Zohrab Bey and by Shefket.

I have said that Zohrab Bey was an Armenian physician, and that at first he usually brought the Princess to us. His presence was always very welcome, for he almost seemed like a fellow-countryman. At the early age of nine he had been taken to Scotland, where he remained seventeen years, and studied medicine at the College of Aberdeen. He was an enthusiastic admirer of Burns and Scott, and spoke English without the slightest foreign accent; rather like an educated Scotsman. He was a kind-hearted man, and was constantly appealed to by the numerous English *employés* of his Highness, who, not understanding Turkish or Arabic, had recourse to him in any difficulty in which they might be placed. He held a regular *levée* every morning, and as he always found it extremely difficult to say "No," he would promise much more than he was able to perform, and got himself into many difficulties in consequence.

The Princess and her companion passed the whole morning with me; but in the afternoon she studied Turkish and Arabic, on alternate days, with her masters, Mustafa Effendi and Sheikh Ali. At first I always remained in the room during their lessons, until one day Zohrab Bey told me he had something very serious to say to me: that the Turkish and Arabic masters took it extremely amiss that I should think it necessary to be present at their lessons; that they did not require to be present at mine, and that they considered it an affront offered to them. I replied that I had no idea of offending, that I was acting according to the customs of my country; but that I would discontinue doing so, since they took it so much amiss. After that I sat in my own room adjoining, with the door open between us; but as open doors are universal in the East, no offence was taken at this.

Our household consisted of Mr and Mrs Freeland, with their three children and two nurses, the young Oxonian Mr Michell, and myself. Our servants were—first, Shaheen, the dragoman, who spoke English indifferently; Hussein, the table-man (or footman as we should say); Ali the cook, and his satellite in the kitchen; and two *ferashes*, whose business was that of housemaids, and whose duties were most indifferently performed. Their idea of sweeping was to make a great dust, get all the sweepings into a corner, and then tuck them under the carpet; their notion of making a bed was to turn down the sheet, dust it with a feather broom with which they had previously dusted the furniture, and then cover it up again. After this they would empty your bath and basin out of the window, take your sponge or towels to wipe up any slop they might make, and having devoted perhaps five minutes to the entire performance, Mohammed would triumphantly inform me that my room was "finish"!

I am far from saying that all Arab servants are like these; I have known many since who with careful training make excellent attendants; but we had this disadvantage with the *ferashes*, that their wages were paid by the *Daïra* of his Highness and not by us. By complaint we could have caused them to be dismissed; but we should have had others of the same stamp in their place, and thus have gained nothing by the exchange. Those servants whom we paid ourselves, and who were consequently dependent on us, gave us no cause of complaint. There never was a better servant than Hussein, clean, active, and respectful. Ali the cook, who was also paid by us, was a good servant and made capital dishes. He was a very handsome man, of a tall commanding figure, and looked so picturesque as he stood receiving orders for dinner that his mistress longed to sketch him, and did so, I believe, one day, though I never saw the result.

Up to the middle of November the heat was great, but after that we had many weeks of glorious weather—ten hours of uninterrupted sunshine every day. The garden was in perfection, full of roses and other flowers, and all the trees in the avenue were in full leaf. The only drawback to us strangers was the myriads of mosquitoes and sand-flies, which were at first almost intolerable; but after two or three years I became accustomed to them, and at last ceased to notice them altogether.

CHAPTER II.

First visit to the Pyramids—Enter the Third and the Great Pyramid—The Princess first to go in—Torment of insects at Choubrah: mosquitoes, sand-flies, wasps, &c.—Dogs and cats—Prevalence of ophthalmia—Ramadan—Sufferings of the Arabs during the fast—Fine climate of Cairo in the winter—Length of day—Temperature—Building everywhere going on.

Early in November we made an excursion to the Pyramids. It was all arranged by Zohrab Bey, who was to meet us there with the Prince and Princess. Six A.M. was the hour fixed upon for our starting, and as this involved getting up before five, there was some consultation among us as to who could be the best depended upon for waking. It was settled that I was the earliest riser of the party, so I undertook to rouse them all in time. After sleeping some hours I awoke, and having lighted a match discovered that it was ten minutes to one! This was rather too soon, so I again fell asleep, and was awoke in a panic by Mrs Freeland at my door, telling me that it wanted a quarter to six, she being in an equal panic, thinking she had slept through my call! We scrambled up, and as the carriage came punctually at six, felt very much ashamed of ourselves for being so late. At about twenty minutes to seven we started. The morning was delightful, clear, and invigorating. We had a kind of brake, or *char-à-banc*, very high above the dust, drawn by four horses, and the driver rode postilion. There was room for eight or ten persons, but we were only four, Mr and Mrs Freeland, myself, and a gentleman whom we called for *en route*. He kept us waiting a short time, and we afterwards ascertained from his own confession that he had only just got out of bed when the carriage drove up.

We crossed a bridge of boats over the Nile, and passed the Khédive's palace at Ghizeh, and then drove through a shady avenue of acacias, very cool and refreshing. By the side of us wound an old branch of the Nile, and gradually the waters widened, until we seemed for some miles to be going along a causeway with a wide lake on each side of us. This is occasioned by the inundation of the Nile, and we were told that a few months later it would be all green land, and afford excellent snipe-shooting. This road led us straight up to the Great Pyramid, and the water accompanied it on each side, ceasing at about a hundred yards from the base. The Pyramids are built on rocks which rise up in the centre of the interior, so that no inundation can ever reach the tombs therein. The road had been constructed two years before to enable the Empress of the French to visit the Pyramids. Before that time there had been a road for camels and asses, but the inundations often covered it, or part of it; so that travellers who visited the Pyramids when the waters were out had to ford the stream, or to be carried on the shoulders of the Arabs. Every now and then, a rising ground like a little island stood out in this watery world. It was covered with mud-huts, and as our carriage drove up the causeway Arabs plunged from them into the water, hastily drawing up their dress to keep it dry, and shaking it down upon landing. They then ran alongside the carriage so as to offer their services on our arrival.

As we came up the ascent at the foot of the Great Pyramid, and drove up to the kiosk where we were to dine, we found that we were the first to arrive. About a quarter of an hour after, the Princess with Kopsès and Zohrab Bey drove up. Soon after Ibrahim Pasha, accompanied by Mr Edward Zohrab and Shefket, with Mr Michell on horseback, were seen approaching. This completed our party, and the arrival of the young Pasha brought every Arab man, woman, and child in the vicinity around us. Mr Freeland prepared at once to ascend the Great Pyramid, but the rest of us remained with the Princess and her brother. It was amusing, however, to watch the ascent. At first they walked sideways, but when at a certain distance, began to mount straight up. A number of Arabs had accompanied Mr Freeland; one was pushing him from behind, two others in front dragging him up by the arms. Altogether it did not look pleasant. While I stood looking on, Mrs Freeland came to tell me that they were all starting to see the Sphinx. It was only a few minutes after nine; the heat was already great, though I was astonished to find such a charming pure air in the desert as greatly to temper the heat. We went to the Sphinx, of which little more than the gigantic head rises out of the sand. A man climbed up to the ear, which gave us a good idea of its proportions, as he looked a mere pigmy upon it. The Princess and her little companion were delighted with everything. I found later they always were with all open-air excursions. They ran about just like English children, and their merry peals of laughter were chorussed by all around.

We went on to the Third Pyramid, which it was intended we should explore. The heat was great, and the young Pasha had loitered behind us; so the Arabs laid hold of him, as they do with great people, as if they had not the free use of their limbs. He, however, shook them off, and mounting a horse which had been prepared for him, galloped on to the Third Pyramid. As we came up we met him riding away; he did not like the appearance of the entrance, which certainly was far from inviting. We ladies stood outside for a minute debating whether we should go in, when the Princess, who had made up her mind on the subject, suddenly disappeared down the opening with surprising alacrity. Of course we all followed immediately, Mrs Freeland and I, Kopsès, Mr Michell, Edward Zohrab,[1] and Shefket, and goodness knows how many Arabs! Some carried bits of candles; some dragged us along—and their help was needed! Sometimes we were in passages about three feet high, crawling like reptiles, sometimes going down steep inclines equally low, composed either of smooth slippery stone or of huge boulders, so that when you put out one foot you might have a yard to stretch before you had anything to plant it on. Sometimes you emerged into large chambers, where was some great sarcophagus, now empty. You were always going up, or down, and generally on all-fours. At last we again came out in the daylight, and I cannot say I was sorry. One ought to have a particular dress for such occasions, as when one goes down into mines; but to enter the Pyramids in a crinoline and in a fashionable high bonnet was quite a mistake. I must say these Bedouin Arabs are a fine race of men, tall athletic fellows with intelligent countenances; and though in such close proximity, with an entire absence of fresh air, there was nothing more unpleasant than might have arisen in a London ballroom.

We had explored the Third Pyramid, but our labours were not over. Mr Michell, who had made weekly visits to the Pyramids ever since his arrival in Egypt, now led us to Colonel Howard Vyse's tomb, so named as that gentleman had been the first to discover it. As we approached, Mr Freeland appeared at the opening, emerging at full length, and presently after Zohrab Bey and the young Pasha. This tomb pleased me better than any. It was not so difficult of access, and though there was plenty of crawling, it was on a level, and now and then there was a little daylight. There was one chamber which was exceedingly curious; it had a series of pictures

[1] Now Sir Edward Zohrab.

in bas-relief of culinary and other domestic operations, field-work, &c., and the owner at the beginning of each picture, much larger, as befitted his dignity. When we came out of this tomb it was one o'clock, and we had been nearly four hours walking and exploring, so we went back to the kiosk and had luncheon. How fresh and charming it was! seated in a comfortable breezy room, with an excellent luncheon to which our exertions made us do full justice, looking on one side at the Great Pyramid with a picturesque group of Bedouin Arabs at the foot of it, behind them the desert; and on the other side the inundations of the Nile, the little islands dotted about in the water, and the long causeway stretching through it.

We had not long finished luncheon when the Princess begged to go into the Great Pyramid, so off we started again. The entrance is considerably above the base. The object of the founders of these Pyramids seems to have been, first, to secure for themselves a burying-place where neither air nor water could penetrate, and for this purpose the tomb was constructed in the solid rock; and next, to make the entrance and passages so tortuous and difficult, that it would be almost impossible to penetrate into them. As the Great Pyramid is the most important of all, so much more difficult are the passages. This, however, only added to the fun and merriment of the young girls, and their laughter was contagious. I had three Arabs to myself, and was carried through all without any resistance on my part; but upon comparing notes afterwards with the other ladies, I found I had not been more helpless than they. I should have liked it better if we had not had the whole population with us; but as it is not often that a prince and princess visit the interior of the Pyramids, all thought they had a right to assist in the ceremony. It was twenty minutes past three when we came out, and then commenced the settling with the Sheikh, who always accompanies the Bedouins, and keeps strict order with them, sternly prohibiting their receiving any private *backsheesh* which they try very hard to obtain when he is not looking at them. When the settling was finished, the horses were put to the carriages, and we drove back to Choubrah after one of the most enjoyable days I had ever spent in my life.

At this time (early in November) the temperature at mid-day was about 75° in the shade, and 105° in the sun; but the nights were getting cooler. The plague of mosquitoes still continued; the sand-flies were, if possible, worse, because they are equally venomous, and so tiny that no net can protect you from them. Then we had large wasps as big as hornets; their sting was said to be very painful, but though we had such numbers, I don't remember any of us being ever stung. Upwards of seventy were one day killed in my room. There were windows to the west and one to the north, and the wasps, it seems, had been in the habit of flying in at one side and going out at the other. There was rather a strong breeze, and I had shut the north window. Soon after, my attention was attracted by swarms of these insects crawling up and down the window, vainly seeking their usual means of exit, their numbers constantly reinforced by others. An indiscriminate slaughter was made, and luckily no one was stung; but it was not until some time after this that the plague ceased. Insects were not our only tormentors, dogs and cats also abounded. They are not domestic animals in Egypt, but run wild, hiding themselves in the houses (if they can get in) at the approach of winter. The Arabs were always leaving the doors open, even when the evenings became cold; and it was no uncommon thing, when we came out from dinner, to find two or three dogs lurking about the hall or drawing-room, or rushing past you on the staircase as you ascended to your bedroom. At first it was difficult to sleep at night, on account of the incessant barking. They (the dogs) seem to have a general law among themselves, assigning certain quarters to each troop, and the entrance of a strange dog on their territory is resented by the whole pack. They raise dismal howls and chase the intruder until he succeeds in making his escape. Sometimes a hunted dog would, through an open door, rush into our house, and some of his pursuers after him, and we were awoke by the skirmishing just outside our bedroom doors. At first sleep seemed out of the question in this country, so many were the interruptions; but I got accustomed to them in time, and slept peacefully without heeding any noise.

I had learned in my school-books that rain never fell in Egypt, but I found this a mistake, as owing to the millions of trees planted by Mohammed Ali and his son Ibrahim Pasha, rain frequently falls on the coast, and is by no means uncommon during the winter in Cairo. These trees are mostly acacias, sycamores, planes, and cotton-trees; there seems no limit to the productiveness of the country, as the sands have only to be irrigated and the desert becomes a garden.

I was startled, as every one is, by the number of blind people I met with in the roads and in the streets. It was generally among the poorer classes, but the rich are by no means exempt. What causes this frightful scourge of ophthalmia seems by no means certain; whether the sand, the glare, or the insects, or all combined. Mrs Freeland's children were all attacked with it, one after the other. It begins with redness, then a copious discharge, and on the third day the eyes are totally closed, and the patient sees nothing. It was curious to observe the different manner in which the children bore this sad infliction. Little Bessie, who was a year and a half old, never uttered a murmur, but sat in the nurse's arms such a picture of patient resignation as melted the hearts of all who saw her. Tony, a pretty little fellow between three and four, was frantic with grief at his loss of sight, and doubly wrung his mother's heart, as she found her inability to soothe him. Poor Tony's religious belief had been sorely tried by the mosquitoes, and he had earnestly asked his mother whether God had really sent them, and now this deprivation of sight shook him still further. The children got well, however, in a short time, but the agony of the parents during the infliction was not easily forgotten.

On the 14th of November began the fast of Ramadan, and though of course we did not keep it, we could not be indifferent to its effect on all our Arab servants. No food, and, what is almost worse in a hot climate, no water passed their lips from a couple of hours before sunrise until sunset, when a little coffee was drunk, a cigarette smoked, and as soon as it could be prepared, some light food eaten, the principal meal taking place after midnight, as a preparative for the long fast of the next day. It was of course doubly trying to our servants, because they had to cook our food, and to wait at table and see us eat. Had they been in a Mahometan household they would probably have dozed away half the day; but the Prince and Princess came to their lessons all the same, and therefore the servants' work must go on as usual. If the royal children did not come on any day, we found a good deal of difference, and meal-times would approach without any preparation for them. Hussein, our "table man," being very young, was probably keeping his first fast, and he moved about like a ghost. He was naturally very active, and a short time before I used to meet him walking briskly through the hall with a heavy lamp in each hand, which he carried as lightly as if they were chamber candlesticks; now, I was always expecting to hear a grand crash, and to find that he had fallen under the weight of one of them.

As the weather became cooler we generally made some excursion, particularly on Fridays, when our pupils did not come to us. It was their Sabbath, so they left us free, and Sunday being ours, we had thus two holidays in the week. This, however, only lasted while we lived at Choubrah, which was two miles from the palace at Abdeen. At other places, when the children were close at hand, they would come to us much as usual, only they did no lessons.

One night towards the end of November I woke up with cramp, occasioned by the cold. I was lightly clad, and had no woollen coverlets on the bed. So, feeling unable to go to sleep without additional wraps, I got up to seek them. My bedroom faced the north, but the sitting-room adjoining, the west; and going into it to seek for a wrap, there was such a magnificent flood of light from the moon that I stood for some time at the window looking down upon the avenue, perfectly charmed with the scene. It was then about five, and at twenty-three minutes to six the gun fired to announce the dawn. The commands of the Koran are to abstain from food or drink during Ramadan from sunrise to sunset. They are not to wait for the rising of the sun, but to abstain "from the moment there is sufficient light to distinguish a black thread from a white." The gun is supposed to fire at that moment. At 6 A.M. it was sufficiently light for me to look at the thermometer hanging out of my bedroom window, which was 51°, and at twenty-three minutes to seven the first rays of the sun lighted up the stems of the acacia-trees opposite to my window, being just an hour after the firing of the gun at dawn. I timed the sunset on that evening, and found the length of day to be ten hours and nine minutes. What a change from the gloomy dark month of our northern climates! I was never tired of watching the glorious sunrise, and witnessed it every morning throughout the year during my stay in Egypt until I lived in the harem, and then it was shut out by high walls! During this first winter in Egypt I found a silk dress too warm for me in the middle of the day, though I could well have borne an extra light shawl or jacket in the mornings and evenings; but in succeeding winters, when I got more acclimatised, I was glad of a woollen dress during three or four months. But I never wished for a fire, nor did I ever see one during the first winter.

The Ezbekeah Gardens were very different then to what they have since become. At that time they were a pleasant and quiet resort where one could walk or sit unmolested for an hour or two. There was, and *is*, a rockery, something like that in the Bois de Boulogne; a cascade, a cavern, and paths in and out. There was a belvedere constructed of the stems of palm-trees, some of which served as columns to support the edifice, and others of smaller size formed a circular roof, radiating from the centre. Comfortable seats were scattered all over the garden, but the Arabs seemed to think them especially placed for their convenience, and were generally found on them asleep, stretched at full length. All round the gardens handsome houses were being built in the style of the Rue de Rivoli, with arcades. Then, however, all was unfinished, and fine dust almost blinded you as you passed. Now they are nearly all completed, and a handsome European quarter is in close proximity to the oriental city; a broad road is constructed from the Ezbekeah to the Citadel, in place of the narrow tortuous way through the Mouskee; and streets, roads, and detached villa residences are multiplying between the Ezbekeah and the Nile. The chief drawback is that the rents are enormously high, and to new-comers living appears equally so; but this is really not the case, as I know from old residents that if you can speak a little Arabic, and market for yourself, you will find everything as moderate and good as in most European capitals. This experience, however, may perhaps be dearly purchased.

CHAPTER III.

Baïram—First visit to the harem—Gorgeous dresses of the slaves—Visit the Queen-Mother at Kasr-el-Ali—Shaheen's views of morality—Roses at Christmas—Second visit to the Pyramids—Inundation subsided, and succeeded by green crops—Procession of the Mahmal—First ride on a dromedary—Cruelty of the Arabs to horses and asses.

On the 12th of December, at sunset, the gun fired, announcing the close of the long fast of Ramadan!

The Princess had brought me a message two or three days before, to the effect that we (Mrs Freeland and I) were expected at the palace of Abdeen on the first day of Baïram, between ten and eleven o'clock *à la franque*. It was the first cold day I had known in Egypt: a keen south-east wind, the coldest in winter, and the hottest in summer. We had an open carriage, for it was extremely difficult then to procure any other—that is to say, among hired vehicles; and we had a very indifferent one, with a pair of sorry horses, at the rate of three guineas the day. At the Baïram all carriages are charged double and treble the usual price; but, as a general rule, we paid more than other people (that is to say, than old residents), because our dragoman considered it a necessity of our position. When we grumbled at any charge, he would say reprovingly, "Highness's people!—everybody expect!—looks well!" and in our ignorance we then submitted.

At daybreak the Khédive went to the mosque of Mohammed Ali, up by the Citadel, and a salute of twenty-three guns announced when he went in, and was repeated when he came out. Then began his *levée* at the Citadel; and after having paid their respects to him, the chief dignitaries hurried off to present their salaams to the Queen-Mother (*Validé Effendemiz*, literally Mother of our lord) and to the Princesses, wives of his Highness. The princes of the blood were allowed the privilege of entering the presence of these ladies; but the great dignitaries, ministers, pashas, and beys, merely sent a message to each lady through the chief eunuch, asking permission to lay their heads in the dust at her feet, and receiving a gracious reply in return.

We left Choubrah at ten, and our drive through the town presented a most animated spectacle. The large square in front of the palace of Abdeen was lined with soldiers. We drove through into an inner court, where we were received by several eunuchs, who assisted us out of the carriage, not in the way customary in Europe, but rather as persons who had lost the use of their limbs; a great honour, as we afterwards found. They escorted us across an inner court to the entrance of the harem, and there gave us over to the attendants. Our eyes were dazzled by what we saw. Could those gorgeously dressed ladies who came forward to meet us be slaves, of whom we had heard so much? The word *slave* has a very different acceptation with us from what it bears in the East. There is no degradation implied there in the term. Those belonging to a great harem have generally been there since their early childhood; they have no recollection of their previous life; they have grown up with the family, and identify themselves with it. They are confined, it is true, within four walls, but they are allowed a degree of liberty within those walls astonishing to our habits. The menial work of the harem is mostly done by the black slaves; and they, with few exceptions, are kept quite in the background.

We were in a spacious saloon, richly furnished in the French style, lined with looking-glasses, couches, sofas, and chairs, covered with yellow damask satin, hangings of the same at the windows, and numerous doors that led from this saloon into inner apartments; making it cool and pleasant in summer, but rather draughty in winter. Rich thick carpets on the ground, large lustres hung from the ceiling, and girandoles from the walls.

Two or three ladies sat by us, but as we knew no Turkish, conversation was out of the question. We felt that we cut a very indifferent figure amid all this splendour, for we wore plain dark silk dresses, and the ladies about us were in the richest silks and satins, of brilliant colours, and with long trains. They were all in European costume, as that was already generally adopted in the Khédive's harem. Presently some one came to conduct us into the presence of the Princesses. The messenger was a Levantine lady, who spoke French, and who led us up a spacious staircase to an upper storey, identical with the one we had left, and we then found ourselves in the "presence chamber."

The four wives of the Khédive were seated at a short distance from each other; they were magnificently dressed, and blazing with jewels. We were presented to each in turn, and each had something pleasant to say to us, which was duly translated by the lady who officiated as interpreter. My pupil had taught me a Turkish sentence to say to her mother—"*Baïram cherifiniz moubarek olsoun! Allah nidjé senderi yettich dursin!*" (May Baïram be fortunate to you! May Allah grant you many of them!);

and I thought I had it by heart, but I broke down in the middle of it. The Princesses laughed and took it in very good part, so after about ten minutes' stay we rose and took our leave.

We were escorted down-stairs by the lady who officiated as interpreter, and again seated on a divan in the saloon which we had first entered. As the European visitors had not yet arrived, this lady kindly stayed with us, and answered the inquiries which we made respecting all we saw. "Who were these splendidly dressed ladies around us?" They were all slaves, our informant told us, only the four Princesses, wives of his Highness, and two younger ladies near them, who were his daughters, were exceptions; all the rest were slaves, and almost all Circassians. Their dress was a mixture of European and oriental fashions, being generally looser than those worn by us. When we first entered this saloon we had been presented with tiny cups of coffee. The drinking-cups are the shape of an egg, but they are presented in little stands in the form of an egg-cup, made of gold, and set with jewels. Before we left the harem a delicious beverage was handed to each of us in gold cups, and presented on gold salvers. We were then escorted to the door, and across the inner court, and made over to the eunuchs.

The next thing was to drive to the residence of the Queen-Mother, who lived in a palace on the banks of the Nile, which struck us as handsomer and at the same time more oriental than Abdeen. After crossing the inner courts, we found ourselves in an arcade which stretched across the garden, and was raised some feet above it. Trellis-work enclosed the sides, covered with vines and creeping plants. This arcade formed a covered way from the palace to the gates, protecting from the heat of the sun, and affording always a cool promenade. Two eunuchs escorted us along the whole length, and led us into the palace, where we were received by the attendants, as at Abdeen, but there was an indefinable something which looked more Eastern. The inmates were as richly dressed, but the cut of the garments was different. They led us up to one of the numerous couches with which the saloon was filled, but they themselves sat preferably on low seats about a foot from the ground. Coffee and pipes were brought and handed to us. Formerly it was *de rigueur* to accept the pipe, but European visitors had become frequent in the harems, and the inmates soon saw that their visitors were unaccustomed to smoking, so that declining the pipe gave no offence. I did not know this then, so I took the pipe, which was about five feet long, and the attendant rested the bowl on a silver plate in front of me. Mrs Freeland sat placidly puffing her pipe as if it were her everyday solace, though she had never had one in her mouth before; but I held the tube between my lips for some time, wondering how such a thing could give either pleasure or pain, when a slave crossed the room, and turning the bowl, I found that I had been holding it downwards! I never tried smoking after that; and further intercourse in the harem soon taught me it was not taken amiss to refuse the pipe.

We were soon sent for into the presence of the Queen-Mother. She was not dressed in European costume; but it being a cold day, she had a beautiful Persian shawl wound round her body. She received us with a mixture of dignity and courtesy that struck us much. She looked very pleasantly at us, asked us a few questions, and then we came out again into the large saloon which we had first entered. Here we had to drink the "sweet water," and try to go through a little conversation; and then we were conducted to the door, and again placed in charge of the eunuchs. As we were walking through the arcade to the gates of the palace, I said, "I'm so glad we came here:

this is capital—much more Eastern than the other," when I heard an explosion of laughter behind me, and, looking round, perceived that it came from one of the eunuchs. I found that he understood English, and that he was so transported with delight at having caught the sense of my words, that he could not contain his joy. There was nothing to laugh at, but his mirth was so infectious that we joined in it heartily, and came away quite exhilarated at the success of our visits to royalty.

This was the first wintry day we had felt in Egypt,— cold wind and no sun.

On the second day I had a visit from my pupil, accompanied by Zohrab Bey. It was a visit only, for during Baïram no lessons were done. The Princess was magnificently dressed in black velvet, made in the last Parisian fashion. The trimming was of white ostrich feathers; a diamond brooch, which, with the pendants attached to it, was as large in circumference as an orange, sparkled on her chest. She wore diamond earrings, a clasp of the same precious stones at the waist, black velvet boots with diamond buckles, and a velvet hat with the same feather trimming as on the dress. She had a weary look, as if all this adornment did not add to her happiness, and taking my hand, she asked me to go up-stairs with her and read a story to her! She sat by with rapt attention while I read, until Zohrab Bey's voice was heard, calling out that there were more visits to pay.

I had received a letter asking me to call on Lady Dudley, who, with her husband (Lord Dudley), was then the Khédive's guest, and was lodged in a palace near us. When the Princess was gone, I walked to Kasr-el-Nuss, taking Shaheen, our dragoman, with me. He pointed out a large house on our way, and said, "One great English pasha (the Maharajah Dulep Singh) once lived there; he marry Arab lady, take her away to England." I thought it a good opportunity to instil a little morality, so I said, "You know, Shaheen, that in England a man can have only one wife, and he is thought very wicked, and is severely punished by the law, if it is found out that he has two."

"Yes, missus," said Shaheen, "me know. Not English custom here. Man marry one wife, two wife, three wife,—many as he can keep."

"But I hope, Shaheen, you have only one wife?"

"Me only two wife now, missus; me can't afford more, just yet."

"And where are your two wives, Shaheen?"

"One wife up First Cataract—my home; other here at Cairo."

"And how long is it since you have seen the first?"

"Long time, missus,—four, five year. Me want much go and see her."

During Christmas we had glorious weather, ten hours of uninterrupted sunshine almost every day; the thermometer at sunrise was generally about 42°, but for three or four hours in the middle of the day it would be 65° in the shade, and 80° in the sun. In the house the temperature was wonderfully equal throughout the twenty-four hours, varying from 60° to 65°, so that in the middle of the day it was warmer out of the house than in it. The garden was in perfection, full of roses and other flowers. The beautiful *Poinsettia pulcherrima* was as brilliant as ever; and the acacias in the avenue were in full leaf. The only drawback to the pleasure of walking in the garden was the sandy paths, which were deep and heavy.

At the close of the year I spent another day at the Pyramids. It was not quite two months since my first visit, but the drive was quite changed. Where the inundation had covered the land and all had seemed a vast lake, were now green crops. Some of our party, upon arrival, at once ascended the Great Pyramid; but as it did not appear to me that the ascent was worth the trouble and exertion, I remained in the carriage, surveying all the surrounding objects through my glass, which I certainly should not have been allowed to do so leisurely and calmly had I been at the top. As it was, I was surrounded by Arabs, who could not understand why I should prefer remaining at the bottom to going up with my friends. Was I ill? was I weak? if so, any number volunteered to carry me up and down again in the shortest possible time. I declined these tempting proposals, and then an Arab offered for a small gratuity to go up to the top and down again in ten minutes, I holding watch in hand. This offer was also declined, and then, with one accord, they all declared they would remain by me and take care of me until my party came down from the Great Pyramid. There was not the slightest occasion for such care, since every one going to the Pyramids is as safe as in the hotel; but of course they expected *backsheesh* for such care, and I had no remedy but to thank them. Two or three carriages drove up, and their occupants mostly ascended forthwith; but in one was a lady, who, not liking the appearance of the mount, said she would prefer *ascending inside*, supposing there was some way of doing so; and the Arabs, misunderstanding her, readily undertook to conduct her. Of course she soon found out her mistake, and then contented herself with sitting outside as I had done.

In the beginning of January I went to see the procession of the Mahmal, or of the pilgrims accompanying the holy carpet to Mecca. The Khédive goes in person always to assist in the ceremony at starting. Awnings are erected in a large space just below the Citadel, and chairs of state are placed under them for his Highness and chief dignitaries. These open tents are far the best places from whence to see the procession, if by favour you can get to them. It is necessary, however, to be very early, as the space is limited, and soon filled. When the Khédive (or perhaps one of his sons whom he may depute to officiate for him) has driven up and taken his seat, the procession is formed, and files past him. It takes, I think, about half an hour to pass. First come several regiments of infantry, carrying little pennons (magenta and green) on their lances, then come the camels carrying the holy object, the sacred carpet, in a sort of box, and followed by two or three other camels, on the last of which is seated a sheikh, naked from the waist upward, who rolls his head incessantly, and is said to do it all the way to Mecca. He certainly began well, every time I saw him; but as he is enveloped in clouds of dust very soon after he leaves the city, his movements are happily veiled. After him come hundreds of camels, bearing the numerous pilgrims, whose numbers are always to be counted by thousands. They pass slowly through the town, amid crowds of people, who line the streets, the shops, and the windows, and then go out into the desert near Abbassieh, where they remain encamped for some days, and at an uncertain period, most difficult for Europeans to ascertain, they break up and proceed on their long march to Mecca.

One day as Mr Freeland and I were standing at the window looking at the motley objects which were always passing along the Choubrah Road—camels, donkeys, water-bearers, and gay carriages and horsemen—we saw a lady on a dromedary stopping at the gate, whom we recognised at a second glance as our chaplain's wife (Mrs Potter). Her husband and son accompanied her, mounted on white donkeys, and looking ridiculously diminutive by her side. Her dromedary was led by a Bedouin Arab similarly mounted. I had always had the idea that a dromedary had two humps. This is a mistake: the Bactrian camel has two humps, but the Arabian only one. The dromedary is to the camel what the race-horse is to the carthorse, the one thorough-bred and handsome, the other a mere beast of burden. The dromedary had been lent to the lady by an Armenian gentleman resident at Cairo, deservedly popular among all travellers for his hospitality, his general information, and excellent English. He had been sent by Mohammed Ali in his youth to England, where he had received a first-class education, and was afterwards employed by that ruler on many confidential and important missions. The name of Hekekien Bey will long be remembered by travellers for his genial hospitality and many amiable qualities. He kindly lent the dromedary to many ladies, myself among the number, and I had a very pleasant ride upon it, as the paces of a good dromedary are very different from those of the ordinary camels which may be had on hire. It is a pretty sight to see these gentle and docile creatures kneel down at a word for their riders to mount and dismount. I had many opportunities of witnessing this, but it is a very different thing to watch the ordinary camels that pass along the Choubrah Road. I constantly saw them lying down, and when urged to rise, they would make frightful noises, whether they were overladen or not. They seemed to protest against any burden on principle. It is generally believed that the Arab is so merciful to his beast: this is not my experience. I have seen both horses and donkeys shamefully ill-treated without any provocation; but the camel is rarely beaten, as it has a good memory for injuries, and will resent and return them.

CHAPTER IV.

Proposed journey up the Nile—Frequent postponement—Original party greatly increased in numbers—Final departure—Excursion to Sakkara—The Serapeum—Tombs of Ti and of Ptah-hotep—Donkey-riding—The " Flying Dutchman"—Proceed on our voyage—Inconvenient separation from our effects—Stop at Feshna for the night—Arrive at Minich, and stop at the palace—Voyage delayed—Arrange my pupil's studies—No walking at Minich—Flat-bottomed boats pass down the river loaded with forced labourers—Animated appearance of the river.

For a couple of months there had been continual talk of a voyage up the Nile. We were told it was to take place immediately after the Baïram. Ibrahim Pasha and his sister were to go, and all the educational staff. The Princess and Kopsès were delighted at the prospect, and were always talking of it. Bearing in mind the periodical cares of the laundry, which often made me seriously contemplate the possibility of substituting paper for linen, I begged the Princess to give me timely notice directly she heard a day named, as I had been told a few hours had been usually thought sufficient. She promised to do so, and spoke to her mother, the second Princess, about it. The latter laughed heartily at the idea of my requiring time for preparation, and I asked my pupil how they managed in the harem, so as to be ready at an hour's notice. She explained to me that there were (at that time) no wardrobes, that everything was kept in boxes; that her mother had about seventeen attendants, each of whom had the charge of certain articles of clothing, and was responsible for them. There were no books or any of the thousand knick-knacks which European ladies possess, nothing but jewels and clothes, and they were always kept in boxes, consequently ready packed. "But how about the washing?" I asked. Each of the Princesses, I was told, had a separate laundry, where washing went on daily. There was no starching, everything was ironed damp to give it the requisite stiffness; in such a climate no time was lost in drying or airing, a few minutes in the sun accomplished both. Thus there was never any accumulation of work, and as all the slaves accompanied their mistresses on any of these progresses, they could continue their daily labours wherever they might be. As with the Princesses so with the upper and immediate attendants, all of whom had slaves under them who looked after their wants. Why could not we do the same? I explained to the Princess that we had neither the conveniences she described nor those we should have in our own country— that we had only Arabs to attend to us, who knew nothing of European requirements; so she promised to let me know.

Directly after the Baïram in the middle of December, the children came one morning and announced that we were to start "bada boukra," the day after to-morrow. I instantly sent for the washerwoman, and packed up what I thought would be necessary for the voyage. The day after to-morrow came and I was ready, but the Princess came to her lessons as usual and nothing was said of our departure. This cry of "wolf!" was repeated several times, on each occasion with less and less effect, until we began to disbelieve the whole affair. In the meanwhile several travellers who had brought letters of introduction to us arrived in Cairo, and many went up the Nile. In January some of those who had only gone for a month returned, and gave us the benefit of their experience. One gentleman told us that the mornings and nights were excessively cold, and that we should do well to provide clothing for the changes of temperature. Perhaps our deferred departure was an advantage in one respect, as it enabled us to provide against all contingencies. The weather during the first half of January was rather cold—the mornings were often foggy, and rain fell on several days. This in a large well-built house was of little consequence, but on a Nile boat with small cabins and low ceilings it would be more serious.

On the 17th of January an official message was sent to us to the effect that we were to go on board that afternoon. So we again set to work to pack, and were just ready to start, when another order arrived, to tell us that our departure was delayed for a few days. But on the 20th came another order to say we were to go on board that afternoon; and after waiting some time to see if it were countermanded, we went to Boulak and to the *dahabieh*. We had been told that everything would be prepared for us, that we had nothing to provide except our own clothing. When we went on board at 4 P.M., we found that nothing was ready for us; there were no arrangements for dinner, no lamps or candlesticks, no bedroom crockery for washing—in fact, nothing but the barely furnished cabins. Luckily we had not dismissed the carriage; and having ascertained that the start would not be made on that evening, we at once returned to Choubrah to procure all that was necessary. Having made a collection, and had an impromptu dinner in our comfortable house, we returned to the *dahabieh* by moonlight between nine and ten in the evening.

Our party up the Nile was originally intended to be composed of Ibrahim Pasha and the Princess, their two companions, Shefket and Kopsès, Zohrab Bey, his nephew, Mr Freeland, Mr Michell, and myself. But the Khédive was extremely fond of his son Ibrahim, and was unwilling to be separated from him. Then the wives of his Highness had heard so much from the children of the wonders they were about to see, that they were anxious to go, so that finally our modest party swelled into a royal progress! It consisted of six large steamers and seven *dahabiehs*, and this enormous increase was the cause of the constant delay in departing. The Khédive is a most energetic man of business, and it was the hopelessness of his finding leisure for a month or more which had made us think the voyage would never come off. This immense addition to the party also affected our comforts considerably. Had the number been only those originally proposed, we should all have been together in one steamboat, as was proper and consistent; but as it was, the larger vessels were taken up by his Highness, his harem, and his general suite, and the smallest steamer was reserved for Ibrahim Pasha and the Princess. When cabins had been allotted to them, to their two companions, Shefket and Kopsès, to the Princess's French maid, and to Zohrab Bey and his nephew, there was no room left for us. A *dahabieh* was towed on behind; and we were to sleep on the *dahabieh* and spend the day on board the steamer—a most uncomfortable arrangement, as, from the moment of starting in the morning until we stopped at night, there was no possibility of getting to our cabins, whatever we might require. We scarcely found out the full discomfort of this until the second day of the voyage, when we began to realise it.

Our *dahabieh* was very small. I had the stern cabin; we had a tiny saloon; and Mr Freeland, Mr Michell, and Shaheen, the dragoman, occupied the remaining cabins. When we got up the first morning, we found all the fleet round us; but the royal party had not yet come on board. However, we went on the steamer (Azaziah) to breakfast; and immediately after we left it, our *dahabieh* fell into the rear, and we found ourselves separated from all our possessions.

At mid-day, the Khédive and the harem being on board, the signal was given for starting. The first day was not very long, for at 2 p.m. we halted at Bedresheyn, intending to visit Sakkara on the morrow.

It was rather a long process starting the next morning. First, the Princesses, wives of his Highness, drove in two carriages, escorted by several eunuchs. Then after an interval of a few minutes came a merry party on donkeys, consisting of our pupils and ourselves, Shaheen at the rear with an enormous bundle of what he called "silver" in front of him on the donkey. We passed through the ancient city of Memphis, of which no vestige remains, if I except the prostrate statue of Rameses the Great, which lies on its face in a muddy pool, and which formerly stood before the Temple of Vulcan. Our road lay through forests of palms, until we came on to the desert, and after two hours' ride we reached Sakkara, the necropolis of the ancient city of Memphis. Between these two places, the abode of the living and the dead, was formerly a lake (Acherusia), which during the inundations of the Nile became still larger, and across this lake the corpse was ferried on its way to its last resting-place. This is believed to be the origin of the Greek fable of Charon and the river Styx, which the early Greek travellers brought from Memphis and incorporated with their mythology.

A rough kind of house has been erected at Sakkara for Mariette Bey, who is making excavations on the spot by the orders of the Viceroy, and this house was given up to the ladies of the harem for the day. Spacious tents were erected for the rest of the party.

Our first visit was to the Serapeum, the tombs of the sacred bulls. The Princesses went in first with his Highness and Mariette Bey, who explained everything. After they came out, we all went in; we descended a few steps, and then walked along wide passages, lighted by three hundred candles, held by Arab boys at equal distances, and who stood immovable as statues. On each side of these passages were enormous pits, with sarcophagi, in which were interred the sacred bulls. On the walls of the long passages were tablets, inserted between each pit, on which were inscribed addresses to the divinity in the name of some visitor to the sacred object, and giving his name and the date of his visit, according to the mode of that time—that is to say, the day, month, and year of the king then reigning.

We next visited the tombs of Ti and of Ptah-hotep. The first is much the larger, but in both the walls are covered with pictures in bas-relief, many painted, and the colours still fresh. The first series represents the life, occupations, amusements, &c., of the occupant of the tomb. There are his labourers in the fields, his dancing-girls, &c., he himself being the prominent figure in every picture, distinguished as being much bigger than other people. The second series of pictures represents the death of the great man, his passage across the lake from Memphis to Sakkara. He himself presides at the passage of his own mummy across it. The third series represents the funeral gifts which at certain seasons were brought to the deceased. It was a universal custom to bring to the tomb offerings of all kinds,—bread, vegetables, parts of animals sacrificed, &c. In the tomb of Ptah-hotep he is represented as receiving these gifts in person, and as even putting his mouth to a vase. We went into a great many other tombs, but the whole ground for miles around is one vast cemetery, strewn with skulls, jaws, leg and arm bones, &c. Numerous mummy-pits have been discovered, which were probably used by the poorer classes, and there they are found in layers; but many of these pits have been closed, and are no longer allowed to be visited.

While we were at luncheon in the tent the Viceroy suddenly appeared, and said something polite to us, begging us not to rise. This was indeed rather a difficulty, as, for want of chairs, we were all squatted on the ground, with plates on our laps, in rather an undignified position.

At twenty minutes past four we again left Sakkara in the same order as we came. We ran races with each other on our donkeys, and there was nothing but laughter and merry voices to be heard. The Princess delighted in these excursions. She and her companions cantered gaily on, singing snatches of opera airs, and exchanging with voluble tongue those little passages of wit and repartee which make mixed society so attractive to young people. She had a peculiarly joyous ringing laugh, rather noisy, but so hearty and childlike that no one could help joining in her merriment. Though not particularly quick at her studies, she had great shrewdness and keen insight into character, and generally estimated at their due worth all those about her.

I said we ran races, but my donkey was a rather unsociable animal, and having once been put upon his mettle, was not satisfied with winning, but carried me on far beyond even the hearing of my companions, and then at last thought fit to slacken his pace. As I was walking thus leisurely along, I began to examine the contents of my pocket, and took out my note-book to make some entries. While thus occupied, the donkey-boy, who had run noiselessly after me on the sand, and of whose proximity I was not aware, suddenly rushed up, and with blows urged my donkey on again at full speed. He needed no such incentive. I had only time to grasp the reins, and away I went, my treasures all scattered behind me, and I shouting to the boy to desist from urging on my steed. These boys run as fast as the donkeys, and in answer to all my objurgations he only replied, "Yes missus, you very good donkey; he called 'Flying Dutchman'!" and then, to keep up the honour of the name, another blow to urge him forward. In a few minutes I was on the bank of the river, long before my companions, and then the boy had the effrontery to ask for *backsheesh* for having got me there first! It happened that Zohrab Bey and Mr Freeland had walked back to the boat, and luckily in the same track which I had taken. The former saw something gleaming in the sand, and picking it up, found it to be a pair of gold spectacles. They were duly restored to me, and were what I could least have afforded to lose.

The next morning at about half-past six I heard the steam getting up on all sides, and at a quarter before seven four large steamers passed my window, and our own speedily followed in the rear. No announcement had been made to us, and at nine I began to wonder if we were to be left all day without food, when at half-past a signal was made from the steamer to inquire if we were ready to come on board, and without waiting for our answer the steamer stopped, and the *dahabieh* was immediately alongside. Mr Freeland and I had already held a consultation as to the probable length of our fast and our capabilities of supporting it, so we stepped on board with great alacrity; but Mr Michell was left behind (though we did not know it then), and without waiting a moment the *dahabieh* immediately fell back, and we proceeded on our voyage.

The day passed monotonously; we had had no time to bring any occupation on board with us, and when we had caused the book-boxes to be unpacked, and gone through a couple of hours' lessons, we found the time hang very heavily. It was cold on deck; there was a head-wind, which would have stopped us altogether but for steam; so we remained in the chief cabins (the Pasha had one for his schoolroom, and the Princess and I the other);

and after having run about to her heart's content, and being prevented by Zohrab Bey from going on deck, the Princess at last came to me and begged me to tell her a story. She particularly delighted in tales of queens and princesses, and as I was anxious not to spoil her interest in the many charming tales of fiction which I intended her to read later on, I confined myself entirely to historical characters, chiefly those which had been mentioned in our morning reading. Like all Orientals, she was insatiable in this respect; and no sooner was one story ended than another was demanded, until lungs and imagination (or rather memory) were both at fault. But she was very thoughtful and considerate, and you had only to say you were really tired and she would desist at once.

At half-past 5 P.M. the steamers stopped for the night at Feshna, as the Viceroy wished to visit some sugar-mills which he has there.

The next morning I awoke at six as usual, but, contrary to my usual custom, did not rise immediately, and was just about to do so when a message came that all were to be on board in half an hour. Of course I was not ready, so was left on the *dahabieh*, as Mr Michell had been the day before.

As soon as I was dressed I went on deck, and saw some very pretty scenery on the east bank. Mountains came almost to the water's edge, and of various forms. They appeared to be of limestone, and were quite bare; but with groups of palm-trees interspersed at intervals, they formed a very pretty change from the hitherto flat banks. Sometimes the desert skirted the river, and then, where the inundation had covered it a couple of months back, there was beautiful green verdure. Palms were the only trees I saw, and I was told they are all date-palms in Egypt.

In spite of my interest in the scenery, I began, however, to feel a void, and knowing there was nothing whatever to eat, I asked the *reïs* to get me a little water. But when it was presented to me, I felt no temptation to drink it, it was so thick and muddy. Had we known to what we should have been exposed, we would have brought with us some preserved meat in tins, some Huntley & Palmer's biscuits, tea, coffee, and sugar, a filter, and an Etna for boiling water. But we had been told that everything would be provided for us, and this was our first experience. My powers of endurance were, however, not very severely tried, for in the course of the morning the Viceroy stopped to look at some sugar-mills, and the *dahabich* was immediately brought alongside the Azaziah. We waited about an hour and a half for his Highness, and then proceeded on our voyage. On the previous day, there being a head-wind, all the *dahabichs* we passed were drawn up close to the shore; but on this day, the wind being north, they were all in full sail, and we constantly saw the English and American flags.

At 5 p.m. we stopped at Minich, where the Viceroy has extensive sugar-mills, and it was a pretty sight to see the squadron of six steamers with the *dahabichs* in tow, all drawn up before the palace. The guns fired a royal salute, the front of the palace was lined with soldiers, who held up long awnings, only, instead of being supported overhead, they formed two walls which extended from the harem steamer to the gates of the palace. This was to enable the wives of his Highness and their suite to disembark without being exposed to the gaze of men.

In the evening Zohrab Bey told us that his Highness intended to stay two or three days at Minich; that he had many sugar-factories there, and was not satisfied with their condition; that he intended to remain until they were in full work, which might delay our voyage. In the meanwhile his Highness wished the studies to be exclusively devoted to the history of Egypt. As our own ideas were in accordance with this, there was of course no objection made on our part. Zohrab Bey, moreover, told us that there was a palace, which had been built for Ibrahim Pasha, at the southern extremity of the Viceroy's palace; that it was proposed we should have our meals and spend the day there, and return to the boats only at night. The Viceroy's palace stands on the west bank of the Nile; the steamers and *dahabiehs* were moored close to the shore, and planks were arranged to enable us to pass freely to and fro. The banks are high at Minieh, so that from the palace the view was far more extensive than from the river.

The next morning we arranged our studies, keeping the same hours as at Choubrah. Our plan was to take French one day and English the next. Of course I speak only of the Princess and Kopsès, as we had nothing to do with the gentlemen, except meeting them at meals and in hours of recreation, when we all joined together. Both the Princess and her companion were universal favourites, and every one exerted himself to please them. Of course the rank of the Khédive's daughter would have ensured this, but her sweet disposition, and thoughtfulness for all about her, made it a labour of love. Kopsès had great vivacity, and wonderful tact for so young a person: she never obtruded her opinions, but when required she expressed them with a free and independent bearing, which to our preconceived ideas was totally inconsistent with slavery. Her manner to us was quite different from her behaviour in the harem. With us she was the free outspoken member of a free community—outspoken, that is to say, in what concerned exclusively European manners and ideas; in the harem, as I afterwards had full occasion to observe, she was the quiet dignified Oriental, receiving notice from her superiors with profound respect, but without a tinge of servility.

The chief books on Egypt which we studied were, in French, Mariette Bey's 'Aperçu de l'Histoire d'Egypte' and his 'Itinéraire'; also 'L'Egypte ancienne et moderne' from the 'Histoire universelle'; and Sharpe's 'History of Egypt' in English. Then we had plenty of books on Egypt for lighter reading, for Ibrahim Pasha was fond of sending directly for any books descriptive of the country which might be published in Europe.

On one of the first days of our stay at Minich, Messrs Freeland and Michell went in a boat to the opposite shore to shoot, and as I soon found there was no walking, I accompanied them; but when I saw them carried on men's shoulders through the mud before they could be safely landed, I thought it best to return to the *dahabich*. Sometimes the river was like a sea, with large waves rolling on, and at other times it was as smooth as glass, all the vessels lying off the shore, and the sandhills on the opposite bank reflected in the water to perfection.

I saw a curious sight one morning while dressing in my cabin. I heard a strange humming noise as of many voices, and looking out, I saw a large steamer coming down the river, and behind it in tow were five immense flat-bottomed boats and two *dahabichs*. The boats were crowded with men, forced labourers from the Upper Nile, who were brought down to work on the railway which the Viceroy was constructing in Upper Egypt. There must have been some thousands.

The general view of the river, as seen from the palace windows, was very animated; *dahabichs* were constantly passing up and down, and we heard many familiar names among them. One or other of the gentlemen was always bringing us news, and though chafing at the delay of our voyage, our time passed, on the whole, not unpleasantly.

CHAPTER V.

At Minieh—Voyage still delayed—How we spent our time—Belief of the ancient Egyptians—A woman's name never mentioned out of the harem —Sudden return to Cairo—Death on the river.

Day after day passed, and we were still at Minieh. The sugar-mills were not yet in order, and his Highness would not leave them until they were. The voyage upward was still talked of, but not even the favourite term of *bada boukra* was mentioned as the date of our departure. Our time meanwhile passed with great regularity. At about eight, or half-past, we all assembled at breakfast in the palace—a party of about twelve or fourteen—as we were often reinforced by strangers who came as visitors. There was a German doctor added to our number, a very clever and amusing man, who contributed not a little to the general entertainment. After breakfast we went to lessons; we learned by rote from Mariette Bey the four epochs into which the history of ancient Egypt has been divided. First, the Ancient Empire, the age of the Pyramids, a period when the art of engraving on stones in relief rose to a perfection which has never since been attained. Then the Middle Empire, which was in existence when Abraham appeared, and to the last king of which Joseph was minister. Then came the New Empire, the age of Moses. In a voyage up the Nile the most frequent and glorious monuments belong to this epoch. Lastly, the Lower Empire, in which Egypt fell under the dominion of strangers, Greeks and Romans, to which epoch the temples of Philæ, of Edfou, of Denderah, &c., belong. These epochs are subdivided into thirty-four dynasties, and we had to portion out all the antiquities among the several dynasties to which they belonged.

This may appear dry work, but the surroundings gave them life and reality to us, and we made a sort of game of it, each submitting to cross-examination from the rest, so that we were all put on our mettle. The Princess checked off all these dates as glibly as any of us, and was highly pleased with her own proficiency. When we had had enough of the dynasties, we took to lighter reading. "This is the day for old Sharpe," she would say somewhat irreverently. A passage quoted by Sharpe from Herodotus amused her greatly: "Whenever a house was on fire, the chief care of the neighbours was to save the CATS; the men and women might be burnt in the ruins, but the cats were to be saved at all risks. When a cat died a natural death, every inmate of the house shaved his eyebrows, and when a dog died they shaved all over." This passage also interested her: "The Egyptian priests were the first to teach that the soul does not wholly die when it leaves the body. They said that after death the soul dwelt in the bodies of other animals, and was there imprisoned for its sins, and that after passing through the bodies of birds, beasts, and fishes, during a period of three thousand years, it was again allowed to take upon itself a human covering. Hence they carefully saved the dead body from decay by embalming it as a mummy, that it might be ready for the soul to re-enter when the years of punishment were at an end."

After studies were over, all played at "rounders," or at hide-and-seek (sometimes called "I spy! hi!"), anything for active exercise, of which the Princess was very fond, though her plumpness interfered rather with her speed. But Kopsès and Shefket were both remarkable for speed and agility, and she identified herself with their triumphs, as if they were her own. There was not a spark of envy or ill feeling in her composition. I think it was a happy time for all these children, though too early clouded. In the afternoon we sometimes took a boat, and went over to the opposite shore—that is to say, when we could find a landing-place sufficiently dry for us to walk ashore. The Princess did not, however, accompany us so often as I could have wished, because Zohrab Bey considered himself responsible for her safety, and would never let her go in a boat unless he was of the party. As he had a great deal to do in the way of harem-visiting, he could not always find time, so then the Princess had her choice of the palace, the steamer, or the harem.

One day, as we were seated at luncheon, a eunuch came in and told Zohrab Bey that he was wanted in the harem. "For whom?" said he; upon which the eunuch stooped down and whispered something in his ear. Zohrab Bey said he would go presently, and the eunuch disappeared. As this put the harem into my mind, I asked the Princess a question which had often occurred to me, "What was her mother's name?" for I only knew her under the appellation of the second Princess. My pupil made some unintelligible answer, and no one volunteered any information. I saw that I had committed an indecorum, so I let the subject drop. I was told afterwards that a woman's name was never mentioned beyond the harem.

The weather continued cool, which was a great blessing, as we had no mosquitoes nor any insects to speak of. As we still slept on board the boat, where the attendance was most imperfect, I shudder to think what we might have suffered had the weather been hot. The crew were there only to manage the boat, and their rough services would have been of little avail; Shaheen was a dragoman, and supposed to have nothing to do but to go on messages. He was always cheerful and civil, but very careful of over-exerting himself. So I forbade any one to enter my cabin, preferring to do all things for myself to having them continued on the footing of the first day or two.

Our *dahabieh* was drawn close under the bank, and the crew put a sailcloth up to screen them from the wind on the opposite side. The poor fellows lived and slept on deck, and being unable ever to leave the vessel, they could not warm themselves by exercise. Their contrivances to exclude the wind must have made the fore-cabins occupied by the gentlemen fearfully stuffy. For myself, my cabin being at the stern, I always got a fresh current of air passing through it, sometimes too much, and then I was obliged to call for assistance to shut the windows, which, being stiff, were beyond my powers.

One evening I was in my cabin for a few minutes, and I heard Mr Michell's voice talking to some one in the little saloon, but I did not pay any attention to what they were saying; and when I had finished what I had to do, I came out of my cabin, and heard Mr Michell say, "Shaheen, I'll tell Miss Chennells of you!" At that moment I appeared at the door, and was astonished to see Shaheen rush out of the saloon, and bolt himself in his little cabin, while Mr Michell burst into a violent fit of laughter. It was some time before I could learn the cause of all this, but when he could speak for laughing, Mr Michell told me what had passed. He delighted in drawing out the Arabs, and as Shaheen entered the cabin where he was writing, he began to ask the dragoman if he was not looking forward to seeing the wife whom he had left so many years, above the First Cataract, and whether he had no fears that she might have consoled herself in his absence? Shaheen looked very dark at this question, but said he had no fear of that; and, further stimulated by Mr Michell's apparent interest in his affairs, confided to him that, if things went on well, he hoped soon to make a third addition to his harem.

At this juncture Mr Michell uttered the threat above mentioned, and I appearing at the same moment, Shaheen at once took to flight.

We had now been three weeks at Minieh. Sometimes the river was like a sea, and I had as much difficulty to keep my equilibrium during my morning toilet as if I had really been at sea. When it was calm, the view from the palace windows was very lovely. The broad, noble river,—the opposite shore verdant to the water's edge,—the long range of Mokattam hills, of most irregular outline, and rising sometimes perpendicularly to a height of about 300 feet, the constant passing of *dahabichs* and steamboats, all made a charming scene. I have said I saw this from the palace windows; but it must be remembered that I was in a palace built for a *prince* and not for a princess! The harem was also built along the banks of the river, but no such view was open to its inmates. High walls shut out nature and the outer life: to those whose position placed them above manual labour there remained nothing but to eat, drink, and sleep! Oh, weary life! Oh, hateful system! which condemns so many thousands of God's creatures to lifelong imprisonment and mental debasement!

To do the Khédive justice, I believe he would willingly emancipate women from their present degraded position in the East; but he knows that education must precede liberty, or it will become licence. For this purpose he has founded schools for girls, the only fault to be found being that they are on so liberal a scale that the expenses are too great to enable them to be multiplied according to requirement. It is no part of the Mahometan religion to ordain polygamy and the shutting-up of women. Such things existed before Mahomet, who attempted to set some bounds to the universal licence which prevailed in his time.

The Khédive's harem is differently conducted from that of other princes. He has four wives, it is true, but these ladies are not outraged by the *presence* of other favourites, nor are the children of other mothers brought up under the same roof with them.

As the Princess was constantly asking me for stories, I told her all the Bible stories relating to Egypt; and that of Joseph and his brethren made the same impression upon her which it does upon all imaginative children. She shed tears, which she was rather ashamed of, until she saw that I was subject to the same weakness; but Kopsès, who had listened intently to every word, though without betraying any emotion, said emphatically at the end, that it was the prettiest story she had ever heard in her life! I often wished for the invention of Scheherazade, as my memory would become quite exhausted; but as the Princess always earnestly asked, "Is it true?" I never drew on imagination, but kept strictly to history.

Exactly a month from the day of our leaving Choubrah, our voyage came to an untimely end. Zohrab Bey came to us at about ten o'clock in the morning, to say that we (Messrs Freeland and Michell and myself) were to return to Cairo by special train (there is a railway into Upper Egypt) on that day at 2 P.M. The Kourban Baïram was coming on, and the Khédive's presence at Cairo was necessary. This was natural, and to be expected; the only mistake in our opinion being that we, the educational staff, had not been sent on with our pupils, while his Highness and his harem remained at Minich. It is an Englishman's privilege to grumble, and we availed ourselves most heartily of this between ourselves. Our pupils preserved the most impassible demeanour: it was his Highness's pleasure, and that was enough for them.

Packing does not take long when one's belongings are within one small cabin, and in a very short time we were

D

all ready. We were told his Highness was going up in the same train; and we had just sat down to luncheon when a messenger came to tell us to go *immediately*, as the train was about to start. So we hurried off, and, arriving at the station, found no signs of departure, and no shelter from the sun, which was then very hot. We waited about an hour, and then a message came that we were to be sent on, as his Highness was not coming on that day. At 9.30 P.M. we reached Ghizeh. Zohrab Bey had undertaken to telegraph for a carriage to meet us, but he had forgotten all about it, and we were by land four or five miles from Choubrah. It was moonlight, fortunately, and going down to the river, we found a boat which took us across, and thus saved us a couple of miles; and soon after landing we got a carriage, which conveyed us to Choubrah. It was eleven o'clock, and the household was gone to bed; but we threw up sand against the windows, and Mrs Freeland, looking out to see what was the matter, clapped her hands for joy, and hurried down to let us in, while Shaheen roused the servants and got us a comfortable supper.

Just before we left Minieh we heard a sad story. Lord Charleville, accompanied by two other gentlemen, had gone on a pleasure trip up the Nile, when one of the party died a little above the First Cataract. The body was embalmed, and the *dahabich* was returning with its sad freight, but the wind blew from the north, and they made no progress. Lord Charleville availed himself, therefore, of a steamer which was employed in towing three large barges full of forced labourers for the railway. The steamer was, however, only going a short distance, and Lord Charleville applied to the Governor of Minieh to lend him one, for which he was prepared to pay any amount. The Khédive heard of the application, and as he is never appealed to in vain for any act of courtesy which can be rendered to an Englishman, he immediately gave one, and Lord Charleville proceeded as quickly as possible to follow the first steamer, and relieve it of its sad burden. How many similar cases I heard of during my five years' stay in Egypt—of some who had come out in pursuit of health, and of others struck down when apparently in vigorous enjoyment of it!

CHAPTER VI.

Sight-seeing—Whirling dervishes—Howling dervishes—Visit to the petrified forest—To the opera—Harem boxes—No English church at that time in Cairo—Service held in the New Hotel—Visit received from some Mahometan ladies—Invitation to a wedding—Translation of the letter into English—Shem-el-Nesseem—Khamseen winds.

On our return to Cairo we determined to devote our leisure, while the weather was still cool, to sight-seeing. The first Friday we went to the whirling dervishes. I had made an attempt to see them before I went up the Nile, but unfortunately arrived just as they were filing out. We had been told the performance began at two, and we were there punctually at that hour by our watches; but different watches may not agree, and as all native performances take place according to the Arab computation of time, which varies with the hour of sunset, it is difficult to fix its exact equivalent according to our standard. We were very punctual at Choubrah, and had a great clock on the staircase which regulated the household; but the clock itself was not infallible, and who was to regulate that? The Khédive had not then introduced the custom, which he has since done, of having a gun fired from the Citadel to announce mid-day, so somebody went every day into the town and brought back the exact time from Ricci,[1] who was considered the best authority. It is curious to observe the different methods of computing time in use among different nations. The Arabs begin their day at sunset, the Persians at sunrise, the ancient Greeks at noon, the Romans, like ourselves, at midnight. The Arabs reckon their year by twelve lunar months, alternately of twenty-nine and thirty days' duration; the Copts also by twelve months, but each of thirty days' duration. All business arrangements in Egypt were made by the Coptic calendar, and the European population being numerous, there were three ways of computing the month in one country. To obviate this inconvenience the Khédive has since ordered that from a given date all payments shall be computed by the Gregorian calendar; and as money touches us all most nearly, this calendar will no doubt gradually supersede the two others.

On this our second visit to the whirling dervishes, we took care to be early, and had the satisfaction of finding when we entered that the performance had not begun. It takes place in a small building (in shape like an amphitheatre) adjoining their convent. There is an upper gallery which looks down on the performance, and also a space on the same level, outside the rails which enclose the circle for the dervishes. The building is open to any one without payment, nor is there any attempt to extract money from the visitors, except that men are in waiting outside with chairs, for which a small coin is asked, but which you are quite at liberty to refuse if you prefer standing.

At a few minutes after two, thirteen dervishes, with their chief in front, entered the circle by a private door. They all wore dark serge cloaks down to the ground, and high felt hats shaped like a sugar-loaf. They walked gravely round the circle from right to left, and the chief

---

[1] The principal watchmaker in Cairo.

seated himself on a carpet on the east side. Each dervish as he approached the carpet stopped and made a low obeisance, and when he had passed it he turned round and made another. This was done with great regularity and uniformity during three circuits, and lasted five minutes. Then there was a pause, and the next moment off went the long serge cloaks, and they appeared in full robes, chiefly white, confined at the waist and nearly touching the ground. One or two went spinning off into the centre, which they kept during the whole time, while the others revolved round the circle with the double motion attributed to the earth. But the curious thing was that they never touched each other, though their arms were extended, and their robes went swinging round like large crinolines. Each revolved in his separate orbit, like the planets whose motion they represent, never lessening or increasing the distance from one another. Their heads were on one side, their eyes fixed on vacancy, and their features expressionless as waxwork. All at once the movement ceased, each man bent down, sat on his heels, and covered his face with his hands. This pause lasted two or three minutes, then all rose simultaneously, and the revolving motion began again. Most of the men appeared in the full vigour of life, but there were two who particularly attracted my attention. One, from his snow-white hair and beard, gave the idea of old age; but he was so superior in agility to all the others, and his face was so pink and white, that we settled he must be an albino. The other was a boy of fifteen or thereabouts, who, from a peculiar twinkle in his eye as he passed us, seemed to me to consider the whole performance more from a gymnastic than a devotional point of view. He evidently looked upon the albino with admiration.

At twenty-two minutes from the time they had first started on their revolving tour they again collapsed, sank on the ground, covered their faces, wrapped their cloaks about them, and then slowly rose and left the mosque in the same order as they had entered it. A low monotonous music accompanied the whole ceremony, and the greatest order and decorum prevailed.

As we came out of the mosque we met some friends, and we agreed to drive to the so-called Tombs of the Caliphs. I say "so-called" because the real tombs are all destroyed with one exception, and the site is now covered with bazaars. The tombs which generally go by that name are without the walls, on the north-east of the town, and are the tombs of the Memlook kings of the Circassian dynasty who ruled from 1382 A.D. to the invasion of the Turks under Sultan Selim in 1517. We went out of Cairo by the Bab-el-Azab, leaving the Citadel close on our left. For miles there was nothing to be seen but tombs, all in the sand, no verdure whatever. Of course there are no roads, and somtimes the way is very bad and heavy. Here and there are large tombs, with mosques and minarets; these are of sovereigns, and we went into several. They are all in ruins; some in fair preservation—that is to say, as *ruins*—but they are not likely to remain long so, as the stones are often carted away for building purposes, and travellers recklessly break away pieces of anything that may take their fancy, to be carried home as specimens. In one of these mosques was a large lattice-screen of various patterns, which was almost perfect, and Mr P., one of our party, looked about to see if he could discover any part where it was broken or decayed, so that he might carry off a specimen. It was difficult to find, and he tried several times before he could accomplish it, but at last he succeeded in detaching a piece. I thought it such a pity that I remonstrated with him, but he replied it would all crumble away sooner or later, and he would like to have a bit of it; so he took it. Ever after, on subsequent visits, this lattice-work went by us under the name of the P. screen.

In this particular building there was a spacious courtyard, three domes, and two minarets. Two of the gentlemen went up to the top of one of the minarets, and said the staircase was in good preservation and the view from the top magnificent; but I did not try it.

Before going to the so-called Tombs of the Caliphs, we visited the family tomb of Mohammed Ali. That, of course, was not in ruins. There was a great deal of brass screen-work, painted in brilliant colours, and a man was seated near one of the tombs reciting the Koran, which, it is said, goes on constantly night and day.

We made a complete circuit of the north side of the city, all among the tombs, and re-entered it by the Bab-el-Nasr, which leads into the Mouskee, though we might have gone due south to the canal, and then turned up the Choubrah Road.

Another Friday we visited the howling dervishes, but I did not like their performance so well as the "whirlers." There are two or three sets of "howlers," but I think the best are at Old Cairo. The building is tolerably large, and the dervishes form a semicircle round their chief, who is seated, and who is a man in the prime of life, with a very curly beard, and wearing a red turban edged with green. First, each man goes up in turn to the chief, and after standing upright for some seconds, probably reciting some prayer which we could not hear, he bent his forehead to the ground, and then went back to his place. After this the chief chanted a monotonous solo, which was presently taken up by the whole party, who incessantly repeated about four bars, "Là illahà Allàh ve Mohammed resoul Allàh!" (There is but one God, and Mahomet is his prophet.) They were at first all seated on their heels, and they incessantly swayed their bodies to and fro, increasing gradually both in sound and motion. After a time the chief again gave a solo, and then the circle all rose to their feet, and swayed backwards and forwards, bending their heads almost to the ground, throwing back their long black hair (having previously divested themselves of their head-gear), and gradually increasing in violence, until their utterance became so indistinct that the noise resembled that of many broken-winded horses. I should think there were about twenty: some elderly men, who took it quietly; others became outrageous in their howls and gestures, and were obliged to be held down by their more sober companions. They foamed at the mouth, and sometimes ran forward with their heads bent down, as if they would butt somebody. A stout lady narrowly escaped being pinned to the wall by one of these enthusiasts, but his companions held him back by force. I saw a lad of about sixteen among them, who looked very roguish, and seemed particularly to enjoy holding those who had thus allowed their feelings to carry them away. The performance had, to my thinking, a very savage look, but the faces of many of the men were intelligent. It lasted altogether more than an hour, and when it was over we lingered a little outside in a pleasant court, and the chief came out and invited us to take coffee with him.

On another day we made an excursion to the petrified forest. It is about eight miles from Cairo. We rode through the Arab quarter out into the desert by the Bab-el-Nasr. This quarter is close, dark, and damp. The two first-named qualities it owes to the extreme narrowness of the streets and the height of the houses, which thus nearly exclude air and light; and the dampness is owing to the copious watering of the streets, which effectually keeps down the dust, by turning it into mud for a few hours, until the time for watering comes round again. The streets are well watered everywhere in Cairo, but in the more open thoroughfares they dry very quickly, so that the dust soon accumulates. My donkey seemed to think a crowded and narrow street just the place for a gallop, and how I escaped running down some of the children who swarmed about and never tried to get out of the way, I cannot tell. When we came out of the Bab-el-Nasr our way lay through the tombs we had visited a short time before. The desert is undulating, because sometimes the ground is rocky, and the sand drifts over it. It is very difficult to drive, though I did once subsequently; we had four horses, and yet we had hard work to get on. With donkeys it was very different, and the ride was most enjoyable; but the day was rather hot, and I suppose my donkey-boy had had enough, so he pointed to some broken pieces of petrified wood which lay about, and told me it was "finish," meaning we had come to our journey's end. Mr Michell, however, knew better, and we went a great deal farther. We measured the length of some trunks which lay half buried in sand; one was 45 feet, but there might have been a good deal more under the sand. It was far too heavy to move; the grain was perfect—it was no longer wood, but stone. We asked the donkey-boys what was the opinion among the Arabs as to how these trees came there. One of them told us that this was once a beautiful garden, and that Mahomet, passing by, asked the gardener to give him a rose, which the latter refused. Mahomet then prayed that the garden might be changed into stone, and his prayer was forthwith granted. This is very much like many of the Roman Catholic legends, and of course there was no disputing the fact, for there were the stones to prove it.

The fresh pure air of the desert makes riding a delightful exercise. When we got back to Choubrah, I had ridden seventeen or eighteen miles without feeling any fatigue, which I justly attributed to my excellent donkey;

so wishing to secure him for future excursions, I asked his name.

"Yankee Doodle," said the boy.

"Oh, he is an American, is he?" said I.

"Yes, missus; in English, Lalla Rookh!"—rather a free translation. I suppose he thought English and American two distinct languages.

I must not omit to mention our first visit to the opera. The play was "Aïda," which had been composed by Verdi expressly for the Cairo Opera. It was doubly interesting to us, as it recalled the scenes of our late voyage up the Nile. I heard this opera very many times afterwards, and liked the music better every time; but on this first occasion the scenery made more impression on me than the music. The harem boxes were a novelty to be seen in no other country. The principal one was next to the stage, on the grand tier, and opposite the Viceroy's. Four smaller ones adjoined it. The whole front of these boxes was covered with a fine network of iron, painted white, and covered with flowers in gold. It had the effect of lacework, but it was all iron, and the elaborate pattern of the flowers made it more difficult to distinguish any person or thing within the boxes so covered. The harem entrance is through a small garden, guarded by sentinels, and through which no person is allowed to pass. Once in the building, there is a separate door and staircase leading to these boxes, which communicate with no other part of the house. You can see very fairly in them, though of course the wire prevents your ever leaning forward, as is sometimes necessary when sitting in a side box.

We dined one evening with Hekekien Bey, the Armenian gentleman who had lent me his dromedary. In his early life Hekekien Bey had spent many years in England, having been sent thither according to a practice which still prevails in the family of Mohammed Ali, of choosing intelligent children and sending them to Europe to be educated. It is well known that Mohammed Ali did not learn to read or write until he was past forty. The things which he wished Hekekien Bey to learn were such as would tax the powers of four ordinary boys to acquire; but Mohammed Ali, being a man of remarkable abilities, put no limit to the capability of a boy who was to have the advantages of early instruction under the best masters. There were about ten persons at the dinner-party, but I was struck by the picturesque effect of the attendance. The waitresses were two jet-black negresses, dressed in the brilliant colours in which their race delight, with a profusion of ornaments. There was the Bedouin who had accompanied me on my dromedary ride, and his little boy, dressed like himself in long snow-white garments. The boy stood behind his master's chair; he was there to learn, and he kept immovable as a statue, except that his eyes wandered everywhere. It was a pleasant party; artists and travellers from many lands were collected together, and our host related to us many of his past experiences. We returned to Choubrah by brilliant moonlight, charmed with our visit and the picturesqueness of all we saw.

It was now getting to the middle of March. The winter had been delightful, but the hot winds had begun. We had had rain occasionally in the winter, but nothing to what I afterwards saw. Now, however, the hot winds had set in early, and very trying I found them. In a few days the wind again shifted to the north, and refreshing showers revived us. A gentleman who had lived in Egypt upwards of sixteen years, told me that the first two or three winters that he spent at Cairo he saw neither rain nor fog; the plantations, which are always increasing round the city, and indeed throughout the country, make both of more and more frequent occurrence.

At that time the English Church was not built, and divine service was performed in a large room at the New Hotel. An absurd incident took place there one day. The chaplain was often assisted by some clergyman who happened to be staying there, and on this occasion a sermon was preached by one of these clerical visitors abounding in deathbed scenes, strung together without any connection. It was always, "I stood by the bedside of a dying omnibus-conductor," &c. At the close of the sermon the Communion was celebrated, and only eight persons remained, of whom Mr Freeland was the sole gentleman. When we came out the heat was intense, and Mr Freeland left us a few minutes standing under the long portico of the New Hotel, while he went to seek a carriage. As we stood there the gentleman who had officiated came out, and addressing us, asked if he could do anything for us, to which Mrs Freeland replied that her husband was gone to get a carriage, and pointed him out as just returning. The clergyman said, "Oh! is that your husband?" and hastily walked towards him, presenting him at the same time with a tract, which Mr Freeland took with rather a blank countenance, not knowing why he was selected as "the sinner" of the congregation. I must here mention that Lord Northbrook, the new Viceroy of India in place of poor Lord Mayo, was just then passing through Cairo on his way to India, and had been one of the congregation in the morning, but not one of the communicants. In the afternoon Mrs Freeland's maids went to the service, and on their coming out were accosted by the same clergyman, who had again officiated. He asked them with whom they lived in Cairo, and after sundry other inquiries, told them he had had the Viceroy of India among his congregation that morning, that he had afterwards stayed the sacrament, and that he had presented the Viceroy with a tract which he hoped would bear fruit in India!

We had a visit one day from an English lady who had married a Turk some years previously, when the latter was *attaché* to the Turkish Embassy in England. Mrs Turabi was accompanied by two ladies, wife and daughter of a neighbouring pasha. These ladies had been two years in England, and had there acquired not only the language, but had adopted the customs of our country. On their return to Egypt they resumed the *yashmak* and *feridjee* (cloak), both of which, however, they laid aside at Mrs Turabi's request when they entered our house. The young Pasha and the Princess were gone, and the gentlemen were out riding or driving, so there was no fear of their presence being intruded on, and we talked for some time with much animation. Presently Mrs Freeland bethought herself to order coffee for the visitors, and as she kept the keys, she disappeared to give the necessary instructions. Soon after her return, as we all sat talking together, we were astonished to see our visitors suddenly extend one hand and arm, and avert their heads, with an "avaunt" air, such as one may see on the stage sometimes at some terrible apparition. Upon turning round to see the cause of this consternation, we found it was Hussein, our table-man, entering with a tray of coffee and cups. His quick eye instantly detected the gesture, and in a moment he stood with his back to the company, holding the tray, and doubtful where to deposit it. Mrs Freeland had looked upon him as a boy, and never thought his presence could excite such a commotion: however, we got him out of the room as quickly as we could, and waited ourselves on our guests.

Occasionally Mr Michell would bring one or two Arab

sheikhs to dinner, and the evening would pass absurdly enough, Mr Michell or a Coptic friend of his named Ghirghis serving as interpreter. Ghirghis spoke English very well, but in translating he always preserved the Arabic idiom, which had to us a very ludicrous effect. One day he brought to Mr Michell an invitation to a wedding. It was couched as follows, Ghirghis making a translation from the Arabic with great gravity:—

"The nightingales of pleasure warbled in the gardens of enjoyment, and the sons of merriment shone on the forehead of time, with safety. I request of your renowned help to honour me on Sunday next, the 8th of Atour 1590, at ten o'clock, hoping that enjoyment will have a turn to you."

He was very proud of his translation, and could not see in the least what there was to excite our risibility.

On the 29th of April took place the Arab *fête* of the Shem-el-Nesseem, or "Smelling of the Zephyr," as it is supposed immediately to precede the terrible *khamseen* winds, which are more or less prevalent during fifty days. I considered that we had already had these winds on several days, but I was told they were not the orthodox winds which belong to the regular *khamseen* season. From a very early hour in the morning, on this *fête*, every Arab man, woman, or child is out for the day seeking whatever country-place they can find where flowers and trees are to be met with; carriages and donkeys are in general request, and consequently dearer. This *fête* of the Shem-el-Nesseem is calculated to commence immediately after the Coptic Easter, and to last until their Whitsuntide. Certainly, immediately after this *fête* we *did* get *khamseen* winds, and terribly oppressive we found them. We were obliged to keep the doors and windows closely shut for two or three days and nights, while the outer air was like that of a furnace. Our rooms were, however, large and lofty, and we were able to keep up a tolerable circulation by having all doors of communication open, so that we suffered less than might have been expected.

CHAPTER VII.

The Viceroy and harem remove to Gezireh—We drive there daily—Great heat—Sand-storms—Receive some Arab sheikhs at dinner—"Moulid-el-nebbee"—Dosch—Removal to Alexandria—Daily visits to Ras-el-Tin—Departure for Constantinople—Voyage thither.

Early in May, as the heat was getting great, the Khédive and his harem removed from Abdeen to Gezireh. The palace of Abdeen lies rather low, and the heat is felt a good deal there. Gezireh is on the banks of the Nile, and is the summer palace of the Viceroy. It is a miniature Versailles, and consists of three or four palaces—one for his Highness, another for the reception of illustrious strangers, and a third for the harem. There is also a beautiful kiosk, in which the Princess of Wales was lodged during her visit. All these palaces are enclosed in a large garden, artistically planned and laid out. There is an extensive collection of wild beasts and of curious birds. The former are of course at some distance from the palace, though when the wind blew from their direction I have on more than one occasion scented their whereabouts. The trees in the garden are very interesting, as being so different from what we see in Europe. I noticed that the banana, like the palm, seems to grow from within, instead of from without like other trees. In the centre is a stem with a large green banner furled round it and completely enveloping it. This gradually unfurls, and is thrown back a huge leaf to the length of several feet, with a strong fibre running up the centre. At first it is all one leaf, but by degrees it splits into several narrow ribbons, which separate from the central fibre. As the leaf now hangs down, another is formed around the stem, to be also unfurled, and thus the stem rises, one leaf springing from another, and forming a graceful fringe round the parent stem.

Near the kiosk is a small lake, over which rustic bridges are constructed. There is a rockery, and winding paths; and when the Court is not there, the kiosk, the state apartments of the palace, and the gardens, are open to the public by order. The servants engaged at the palace are French, with Arabs under them, because everything at Gezireh (except the harem) is European, and would soon go to ruin if left solely to Arab supervision.

Ibrahim Pasha and his sister were placed under Zohrab Bey's charge in that part of the palace which I have mentioned as set apart for illustrious visitors. It was delightfully situated; some of the apartments looked down on the river, others on the lovely garden. The room set apart for the Pasha's study was in an angle, so that the many windows commanded views both up and down the river, and gave a side view of the garden into the bargain. In Mahometan countries the best of everything is put apart for the gentlemen, but my pupil was not then "shut up," so she came in for her full share of all good things. When studies were over, every room was free to us, and the Pasha's being a very large one and very airy, we used to have games there, it being too hot to go out of doors.

Messrs Freeland and Michell and I drove every morning early from Choubrah to Gezireh, which was not unpleasant, unless it were a *khamseen* wind, in which case it was a terrible infliction. The palace is on the western bank of the Nile, so we had to cross a fine bridge to get to Gezireh; and from about twelve to three this bridge is opened for the passage of *dahabiehs*, and necessarily closed for carriages, which sometimes causes great inconvenience. There is, of course, always the remedy of taking a boat across; but then the palace is some distance from the bridge, and no carriages are to be found at the landing-place. We usually returned to Choubrah at about half-past four or five o'clock.

One day we were seated at lessons when it became gradually very dark, and suddenly the windows burst open (they had probably been imperfectly fastened), and the whole house resounded with the slamming of doors and the crash of glass. The servants rushed in and fastened the windows and outer blinds. During this minute I looked out. The opposite shore was not visible, a whirlwind of dust seemed to rise in the air, and then we were shut up in darkness. This was a sand-storm, of which I had so often read the terrible effects when occurring in the desert. After a time a sharp shower of rain came on, and then it was comparatively cooler. Mr Freeland and I returned to Choubrah at about 5 P.M., the storm having then subsided. When we entered the house every door and window, as also shutters, had been carefully closed to exclude the heat and dust; we groped our way to the drawing-room, and there a singular sight met our eyes. Mrs Freeland and a gentleman visitor were there, each holding candles, and engaged in burning mosquitoes on the wall. At Gezireh we had scarcely any mosquitoes, the breeze from the river keeping them off, but at Choubrah we were eaten up. Mrs Freeland had, of course, been in darkness during the storm, as we had been, and being of an active turn of mind, she had ordered candles, and seated herself at her writing-table. But the mosquitoes allowed her no peace. They swarmed about her in such a way that she got up, determined upon trying to reduce their numbers. Her plan was to burn them as they settled on the walls and curtains. Some people even venture to do it on the mosquito-nets, where they are more easily seen; but it requires great dexterity not to set fire to the curtains. Mrs Freeland had capital sight, and also great dexterity, so she entered fully into the chase, and began to count her victims by hundreds, when a visitor was announced. Mr W. was not aware of our daily visits to Gezireh, and expected to find Mr Freeland at Choubrah as usual. He at once entered with spirit into the pursuit, and armed with a candle added his share to the general slaughter. But in spite of all their efforts, we were as much tormented as ever on that evening. Their name was legion, and a few hundred mosquitoes sacrificed seemed to make no appreciable difference.

About the middle of May a great festival took place called the "Moulid-el-nebbee," or celebration of the birth of the Prophet. A large space between the Ezbekeah and Boulak was covered with tents, in which all kinds of performances went on at night—whirling and howling dervishes especially. The whole Arab population is out to witness it, and travellers also make a point of seeing it. The end of it all is the *dosch*, or "treading," which is a frightful performance. Two or three hundred men are induced, either by enthusiasm or *hashish* (which produces intoxication), to throw themselves across the road to be trampled upon by a horse, convinced that if they are killed they will go straightway to Paradise without passing through any intermediate state. They are packed tightly together, so that there is not room for the horse's foot to step between them; and then the horse is led over their bodies mounted by a sheikh. Everybody goes to see this sight, which is a very horrible one, as it is impossible for many to escape either being killed or injured for life. As soon as the horse has passed over the bodies, they all (that is to say, those who are uninjured) spring up and run after the sheikh. Those who are unable to rise are quickly drawn aside. It is to be hoped that this barbarous practice will be abolished as civilisation spreads; but as Europeans hurry to see it with as much eagerness as the natives do, it will hardly be through public opinion as it at present prevails.[1]

On the evening after the *doseh* we had invited Ghirghis and an Arab sheikh to dinner; but the latter unexpectedly brought two friends with him, which rather upset Mrs Freeland's arrangements for the table, though I suppose such additions are quite in accordance with Arab ideas, as it would simply involve two additional spoons and a closer seat. One of these sheikhs wore a yellow turban and a long yellow robe; the other two were similarly attired, only in white instead of yellow. They evidently were unaccustomed to European ways of eating, and Ghirghis was their model for the use of the knife and fork. Their faces beamed with animation; it was no doubt the first time they had ever sat down to table with women, and everything was strange and amusing to them. An Oriental is naturally well-bred, so they did not laugh until they saw us laugh; but some trifling thing was too much for our gravity, and when once we began, they joined in most heartily. When they left, they thanked us through Ghirghis for a most delightful evening.

During this month the *femme de chambre* or *coiffeuse* of the third Princess was married to the *maître d'hôtel* at Ġezireh. A breakfast was given in honour of the married couple at the New Hotel; and the bride received presents from her mistress and the other Princesses, such as might be given to a lady of rank in England,—brooches, earrings, bracelets, all set with diamonds—watch, shawls,

[1] It was abolished by the late Khédive, Tewfik.

money; and, to crown all, she continued in the service, going to her mistress whenever she was sent for, so that she gained much by her marriage and lost nothing.

May was drawing to a close, and we still continued our daily visits to Gezireh. It was so much cooler there than in Cairo that we began to fear the harem would remain during the whole summer. I had been told that the Princesses always went every year to the Bosphorus, and our pupils had spoken confidently for the last two months of our speedy departure; but the long delay in our voyage up the Nile, and its untimely end, had made us incredulous, and we did not in the least believe that we should leave Egypt. But we knew that the Viceroy had palaces in the vicinity of Alexandria, and we longed for sea-breezes and a respite from the mosquitoes of Choubrah. Our departure was fixed several times, and always postponed; but at last, on the 26th, we actually started.

The heat was very great, and according to the thermometer there was little difference in the temperature of Cairo and Alexandria; but in the latter city the sea-breeze was always blowing, and there was a moisture in the air very different from the dryness of Cairo. This disagrees much with some people, but I did not feel any ill effects. There is no comparison in the interest attached to the two cities. Cairo is thoroughly oriental and picturesque, in spite of the European quarter so rapidly springing up. Alexandria has also a handsome European quarter, but the Arab streets are squalid and have nothing of the picturesque. Our pupils went with his Highness's harem to Ras-el-Tin, a palace about two miles to the west of Alexandria, built on the breeziest spot that could be found, and we were sent to the Hôtel de l'Europe on the Grand Square. It was settled that we should drive daily to Ras-el-Tin to give lessons, as until the arrival of his Highness from Cairo we could not tell how long our stay might be.

Every morning early we drove to Ras-el-Tin through the Arab quarter. The palace is built on a little peninsula, so it is open to the sea on three sides. The "school," as it was called, was a detached building on one side of an immense court, guarded by soldiers, but away from the harem and from eunuchs. It consisted of one storey only, was raised several feet above the ground, and had a broad corridor on one side, which extended the full length of the building. This was lighted by windows on the court, and formed a very good promenade and exercise-ground when it was too hot to go out. All the apartments opened into this corridor, and all had a good sea-view, but the Pasha's school-room pre-eminently so, as it commanded the sea on three sides.

Our days passed very pleasantly. We were a very united party, never interfered with one another, and enjoyed each other's society when we met. As at Minich and at Choubrah, every one tried to please the Princess, and as she was very easy to please, everybody succeeded. His Highness still remained at Cairo, and until he came we did not know how long our stay at Alexandria might be.

On the 1st of June, as we drove as usual to Ras-el-Tin, we found the whole road from the Grand Square lined with soldiers to keep the road clear for his Highness, who was expected that morning from Cairo. At 11 A.M. the cannon announced that the great man had arrived, and the Princess and her companion were immediately taken over to the harem to be present at his entry into the palace. The Pasha had already gone to meet his father at the station. As it was pleasanter at Ras-el-Tin than in the hotel, we remained there some time waiting the return of Zohrab Bey, to know what prospect there might be of an immediate departure for Constantinople. There was no beauty of scenery at Ras-el-Tin, no rocks, no picturesque bays, no hills, no verdure, but there was the fresh sea-breeze, and the constant murmur of the waves, the most soothing of all music.

Before we drove back, Zohrab Bey returned and told us that his Highness spoke of going at once to Constantinople, so that we should do well to hold ourselves in readiness to depart at an hour's notice. We had been too much accustomed to this sort of thing to lay much stress upon it: however, as we had not unpacked more than was absolutely necessary, we declared ourselves quite ready.

The following day was Sunday, and I was just on my way down-stairs to go to church, when Zohrab Bey arrived. He said that our pupils with their mother, the second Princess, would start on that day, that Mr Michell and I were to accompany them, and Mr and Mrs Freeland, with their children, were to follow in a few days by the next post-boat.

We were to be on board the Mahroussah at one o'clock. This is a splendid steam-yacht belonging to the Viceroy, and said to be one of the fastest boats built. We went on board, but our pupils had not yet arrived, so I amused myself with going over the vessel. It is divided into three parts, the stern for the Viceroy, the centre for the captain and officers, and the fore part for the crew and the soldiers. His Highness was not going with us, so the stern was appropriated to the harem, and I went over it. The chief saloon was a magnificent apartment, with seven large windows at the stern and five on each side, all of course of plate-glass. Below this saloon was a large state cabin, which was made the sleeping apartment of the second Princess, and several smaller cabins adjoining, used for her immediate attendants. Below these were again cabins, excellent in point of size and accommodation, but deficient in one thing only—air; the windows were high up, and not made to open, a most necessary precaution (though I chafed at it sadly, for I had one of these cabins), as they were only a few feet above the water, and any carelessness would have endangered the lives of all on board. No man had access to them except the eunuchs, and they were probably more amused on deck than below.

In the centre of the vessel was another upper deck, which was large, and had two charming kiosks upon it, one of which was for my Princess, who came freely on deck, and indeed spent the whole day there. On the main deck, between the stern deck and the bridge, was a square canvas awning, closed at the sides, which covered a staircase communicating with the harem. Here three or four eunuchs were always standing, sitting, or lying on couches under the awning. Of course I passed freely up and down, though I took care not to do it more frequently than was necessary; but at this early stage of my residence in the harem, I could not help thinking of what constantly occurred to me afterwards,—namely, the probable effect of the employment there of European women in various capacities. Either they must look upon us as the most abandoned of our sex, or they must think that what is harmless in us cannot be so very bad in them.

I said we were on board punctually, but it was not until 6 P.M. that we started. I went to my cabin at about halfpast nine. I looked in vain for a fastening to my door; there was no key, and no bolt, so I dragged my carpet-bag and a small box before the door to make entry more difficult, and then went to bed and fell asleep. I was soon awoke, however, by a light, and by hearing voices close to me, and upon opening my eyes found three or four persons in my cabin. I raised myself angrily, and demanded their business. They did not understand the words, but the tone was sufficient, and they all took to flight immediately. The next day the reason of their intrusion was explained to me. The second Princess had very properly sent two or three of her attendants to look into every cabin, to see that all lights were extinguished, and everything safe. They knew perfectly well which was my cabin, and could have told by the ventilator over the door if any light had been there; but curiosity prevailed, and they busied themselves in examining the contents of my cabin, and my toilet arrangements, my own presence asleep adding piquancy to the investigation, when they found themselves suddenly caught in the fact. A sound of smothered laughter accompanied their flight, which I was by no means in a state to reciprocate.

The Mahroussah went well; we made fourteen knots an hour (though I believe that is not her greatest speed). She is 400 feet long, has four engines, each of 800-horse power, and is 3550 tons burthen. A great drawback to us, however, was that two tremendous chimneys were near the centre of the vessel, so that the deck on which we passed our time lay between them. The heat was intense, and the only way of escaping in some degree from it was to remain in one of the kiosks, which did not suit the young ladies at all. They preferred walking about and asking questions concerning everything they saw. I went to pay a visit to the second Princess, who always received me very kindly. She told me she had heard I did not believe we should ever go to Constantinople, and asked me if I believed it now. She had with her a Turkish lady, who spoke a little French, and who was very kind to me on several occasions. She was called Nafia Hanem, and lived on the Bosphorus.

We had left the harbour of Alexandria at 6 P.M. on Sunday, and on the following day at 2.15 P.M. we were midway between the islands of Rhodes and Scarpanto (the ancient Carpathos). At sunset we were off Stanco (Cos). But we were not near enough to any of these islands to see more than their general outline. Speed was our object, and to that all was sacrificed. The sea was as smooth as glass, and there was no excuse for any one being ill, unless, indeed, it arose from the intense heat of the chimneys.

On Tuesday morning at seven we were off Mitylene. From that time our attention was absorbed by everything we passed. At 8.30 we were off Cape Baba, a promontory of Asia Minor. At ten minutes to ten we entered the straits between the island of Tenedos and the mainland. We were a quarter of an hour passing through the straits, and were nearer to the island of Tenedos than we had been to any land before. The chief town (probably the only one on the island) looked very picturesque. The sea was not quite so calm as on the previous day, being covered with white sparkling waves. Zohrab Bey told me he was once on a voyage to Constantinople, and at this very place a gale broke the mainmast, and so shattered the vessel that she was unable to proceed, and he was obliged to land at Tenedos, and was taken up by another boat on the following day. On a hill on the northern extremity of the island a former grand vizier was exiled, soon after bowstrung, and a monument was erected on the spot of his burial.

A quarter of an hour after we had entered the strait, we emerged from it again. The coast of Asia Minor was low, but there were mountains in the background. At 10.50 we passed the promontory of Sed-el-Bahar (the ancient Chersonesus), which forms the entrance to the Dardanelles or Hellespont, and an hour after came to the two fortresses of Europe and Asia which guard the narrowest part of the strait; here we appeared completely landlocked, no visible outlet before us. A quarter of an hour, and we came to a point on the Asiatic side called, I think, Nahara, and on this spot is a lighthouse. At 2 P.M. we were in the Sea of

Marmora—it was like enchantment, the band was playing airs from "Aïda." They were stationed round the staircase which led down into the harem; but the awning was closely drawn, even over the entrance.

Between 3.30 and 5 we were passing the Marmora Islands, the largest of which appeared to me about the size of Guernsey; there is a detached rock at some little distance out. Behind was the little peninsula of Cyzicus, also mountainous, as is indeed the whole coast, islands and mainland, more or less. After that we went nearer to the European shore, and at twenty minutes past eight we anchored near the entrance of the Bosphorus, having been $50\frac{1}{4}$ hours on our voyage. No vessel is allowed to enter the Bosphorus at night, but a small steamer was sent ashore with the third captain (as they called him) and the doctor with a bill of health, and we were told that we should land on the morrow at an early hour.

This third captain, or second lieutenant I suppose we should call him, was named Shefter, and he, as well as the pilot Suleiman, had been very kind in giving me information throughout the voyage. Both had been in England two or three times with the Mahroussah, and as they spoke a little English, they liked talking to us. Suleiman always addressed me in a loud cheery voice with "Good morning, sare!" and between him, Shefter, and Zohrab Bey, I learned the names of every point of land that we passed throughout the whole voyage; and what voyage could be more replete with interest and historical associations than one through the Grecian Archipelago to Constantinople? We all looked forward immensely to the first view of the Golden Horn, and went to bed early, determined to be on deck at sunrise, so as to miss nothing of the glorious spectacle that awaited us.

CHAPTER VIII.

The Mahroussah off Stamboul—Entrance into the Bosphorus—Port-holes closed—Landing at Emirghian—Description of palace and grounds—Our house on the hillside—Steamers on the Bosphorus—First visit to Pera and Galata—Impediments to progress—Turkish time—First visit to St Sophia—Climate of Constantinople—Harem—Caïques—Turkish cemetery at Scutari—Ascent from Kadikeui.

I had been told that we were to leave our anchorage at 6 A.M. on the Wednesday morning, but long before then I was on the bridge, having previously packed up everything in my cabin, so that I might not lose a minute when the time arrived for landing. I was met by Zohrab Bey, who told me (*apparently* with great concern) that the orders were very strict that no one could remain on the bridge as we passed Constantinople. "Could I not stay in one of the little kiosks on the deck?" I asked. "They might lock me in there if they liked, but at any rate I should see." "It was impossible," Zohrab Bey replied; "I was in the service of a Mahometan prince, and on a vessel containing his harem, and in such circumstances no woman could be allowed to show herself on deck!" I was in despair, when a bright thought occurred to me. I belonged to the harem; might I not go into the chief saloon, as his Highness was not there? Zohrab Bey was an old stager; he knew well enough what awaited me there, but he was a lover of peace, and his object was to remove me from the deck.

I had not seen my pupil, who was with her mother, so I made my way to the chief saloon. The eunuchs made no difficulty to my entering it, and I was presently after joined by a Levantine lady in the service, and by Nufia Hanem, the Turkish lady of whom I before spoke.

The windows were large, and I was enjoying the beautiful views on both sides, when, just as we were passing St Sophia, the outer shutters slowly descended, and we were left in darkness! It was like a pall thrown over me! There was no help for it. I must pass the next hour, while going through the loveliest scenery in the world, to which I had looked forward so much, as one who has lost the blessing of sight! I saw it many times afterwards, and could never do it too often. From the deck of a steamer, from a caïque, from the different heights at Scutari, at Pera, at the Seven Towers, at the top of the Golden Horn, and from the Bosphorus.

At last the vessel stopped, and I went on deck. We were off Emirghian, midway up the Bosphorus, and in front of us was the Viceroy's palace close to the water's edge. Our two Arab servants, Shaheen and Hussein, had remained behind with Mr and Mrs Freeland, and we soon found the consequence of being thus unprovided. No porters, no assistance of any kind! My trunks were in the hold with the rest of the harem luggage, but I had left a carpet-bag and some light packages in my cabin, and I went down to look after them. All had disappeared; the eunuchs had been into every cabin, and had cleared away their contents. This was of course their duty, and they had not made any distinction between my things and others'. But where were they taken? No one could tell.

The palace for his Highness, and that for his harem, were close to the water, a road only separating them from it. The whole shore of the Bosphorus on both sides is mountainous, occasionally precipitous, but generally rising gradually from the water's edge. The ground belonging to the Khédive is laid out in the English style, partaking of park and garden. When purchased by his Highness, there were houses standing at different elevations, some of which were allowed to remain, to lodge different members of his suite, and one of these was set apart for us. It was about half-way up the hill, on the northern side of the garden, but so shut in by trees that you did not see it until close upon it. You then came upon a small house one storey high, with a background of trees. This house consisted of three rooms only, with a moderate hall, and a room for a servant behind. This was formerly a *selamlik*, and the harem was behind. Upon going through the small house, you came to a steep flight of steps leading to a higher level; and there, surrounded by a wall, was another house, which had served as a harem. This consisted of two storeys, and in this Mr and Mrs Freeland, their children, nurses, and myself were to be lodged; and in addition, two schoolrooms must be provided for the Pasha and Princess. It required a great deal of management to arrange; and had we all arrived together, we should have been badly off. As it was, we were to be mixed up in the most incongruous way, and I had hard work to arrange matters for the first two or three days. The fact is, that on these royal progresses a vast number of people travel together without any one having the management. Of course the Princesses are attended to, but after them it is all a scramble; each gets the best he can for himself, and ignores all the rest. I don't know how I should ever have got my luggage but for Dick, the Pasha's English coachman, though of course it was not his business. Arrived at the house, we found nothing ready for us—the barest furniture, no table or bed linen, no water laid on or to be got. We were told we were for the present to go down to our meals to a table spread for some of his Highness's suite in the palace by the waterside. I remained in the house nearly all day busying myself with endeavouring to arrange it, with little or no help.

I have said the house in which we were put had

formerly been a harem. There was a second entrance to it besides that from the small house in front (which was occupied by Zohrab Bey, his nephew, and Mr Michell). It had an open space in front of it, which was planted with trees; and we put rocking-chairs and a table out there, which made a pleasant shady resort, though the high walls shut out all view. From the upper storey there would have been a beautiful view but for the thick foliage of the trees and those dreadful lattice-work blinds outside the windows, which impeded the view without excluding the sun.

My room had seven windows, four of which were completely blocked up by trees. It was at the eastern end of the house, and nearest to the water; and from the other three windows there was a very lovely view to the north up the Bosphorus, impeded only by the lattice-work blinds. But the windows had no cords to them, so that they were most difficult to open, and when open, very difficult to shut. They had to be propped open with sticks, and when the sticks were withdrawn, great care had to be taken, or the window would come down with a crash and some panes of glass would fly out.

My pupil did not come for the first few days, until the house was in some order, which was at last accomplished.

On the second day I relieved my labours a little by taking a walk in the grounds, and most beautiful they were. They were on the slope of the hill—clumps of trees, open grassy swards, and flower-beds, broad gravel-paths, winding about so as to make the ascent easy, and a large piece of ornamental water, with a rockery behind. Every path commanded a beautiful view, which constantly widened as each walk rose terrace-like above the last. At the foot of the hill was the Bosphorus, which like a broad river extends for about twenty miles, connecting the Black Sea with the Sea of Marmora. The width is irregular, and the outline of the coast forms numerous little bays. Emirghian is about ten miles to the north of Constantinople, but the windings of the channel prevent the latter city from being seen until you are close to it. Across the Bosphorus is the beautiful shore of Asia Minor, also hilly. At the top of the hill at Emirghian is a road to Pera, the best that has been constructed, but the Bosphorus is the great highway for all. Steamers start several times during the day from Yenimahallé to Constantinople, and *vice versa*, stopping at stated times at different stations. Some keep to the European shore, others go zigzag from one shore to the other,—tedious, if speed is your object; but agreeable if, as a stranger, you are only seeking to charm your eye and witness change of scenery.

On the third day, as I found my pupil was not coming, I went into Constantinople. The station is about five minutes' walk from the palace, and I waited there until a steamer came, which fortunately was one of the best, as it had an upper deck, from whence an excellent view is obtainable. The panorama is exceedingly fine on both sides, hills rising sometimes from the water's edge, with palaces, houses, and groves of cypress and other trees to the summit. But what struck me most was, what a magnificent road might be made along this noble channel, if in the hands of a civilised Government. Every available site by the water was taken up either by a palace or mosque, but more frequently by the wooden house of some Turk of the upper class, many of the rooms positively hanging over the water, while underneath were moored the caïques belonging to the family. I landed at the bridge at the entrance of the Golden Horn. It is a wooden structure, connecting Constantinople with the European suburbs of Galata and Pera on the northern side of the Horn. This bridge is now quite inadequate to the traffic occasioned by the steamers, and this causes great delay in landing and embarking. They start with very fair punctuality, but you may have often to wait a long while, and finally lose your steamer through inability to get over the intervening obstacles.

On this first visit, however, I had no second steamer to catch, but simply to walk ashore; so I waited patiently until I could accomplish this, amply repaid by the extraordinary scene before me. Perhaps there is no place in the world more striking to a stranger than that which presents itself on the first arrival at the bridge at Constantinople. The great variety of costume worn by the passers-by, there congregated, as in one common centre, from every nation in Europe and Asia; the city of Stamboul to the left, with all its mosques and minarets rising one above the other, and the glorious view which presents itself on every side,—all make a panorama of unequalled beauty and interest. But once off the bridge and plunged into the narrow streets of Galata, and the illusion is dispelled. In the steep ways which lead up to Pera there is no pathway. For carriages they are impassable, but horses are led or ridden up and down, and it is your business to get out of their way, not theirs to avoid you. That would, however, be a small matter, but for the many other impediments to progress. First, the way is paved with sharp pebbles, with occasional hollows full of mud and water; and it requires almost concentrated attention to avoid the sharp angles and the holes. Then there are the *hamals* (or porters) always ascending or descending with some dreadful burden on their backs, sufficient to weigh down an ox. These men are bent down, and of course see nothing: as with the horses, you must get out of *their* way, not *they* out of yours. Last of all, there are the dogs, which lie stretched across the streets, and never move for any one, unless it is to join in a body to hunt off some canine intruder that has ventured to trespass on their territory.

Once up the hill and at Pera, matters improve a little. The streets are better paved; and now and then, from an opening, you come upon a fine view. Here are all the different European embassies and the best shops. But you have to get down again, and there is no escaping the same dangers and difficulties till you reach the bridge, and again see the unequalled beauties of this grandest of all sites. I made up my mind after one visit to Galata and Pera that nothing but sheer necessity should send me there again; but then some necessity was always arising.

As the departure of the steamers (our only means of transit) is all regulated by Turkish time, we soon found that our calculations enabled us generally to arrive at the stations just after the boat had left; so we decided to keep Turkish time with our watches, while the large clock in the hall, which we had brought from Choubrah, was kept *à la franque* to regulate the lessons. On the fifth day after our arrival at Emirghian, Mr and Mrs Freeland and their children came. They had been five days on the voyage, but they had touched at several places—at Rhodes, Smyrna, &c.

The bright and at the same time cool weather, very much like what we should have in England during a fine summer, seemed to me delightful after the heat of Egypt. Then the firm soil was so different from the soft sand; but tastes do not always agree.

One day I met Dick, the Pasha's coachman, who had helped me so kindly with my luggage, and I asked him how he liked the neighbourhood.

"Oh, I don't think anything of it, ma'am," said he; "you are always going up or down steps."

F

"Why, you don't mean to say you prefer Egypt?"

"Yes, I do, ma'am," said he, "it's such a nice level country."

The second Friday after our arrival we went in a body to Stamboul, intending to visit the mosques. On the bridge, however, we separated, and Mr and Mrs Freeland and I, accompanied by our dragoman, slowly proceeded, our attention attracted by everything on our way. When we got over the bridge there appeared to be a very good road to the left, and a tramway; but as we did not know whither it went, we thought it better to walk than to enter one of the omnibuses running upon it. So we toiled up the hill, until we came to the Mosque of St Sophia, and met Mr Michell and Shefket, who were just coming out. We had been rather in doubt whether we should be admitted without an order; but Mr Michell said they had had no difficulty, and he was delighted with what he had seen, so on we went. Being Friday, it was the Mussulman Sabbath, and numbers of worshippers were coming in and going out. All devoutly took off their shoes or slippers, and went in in their stockings, carrying their shoes in their hands. The floor is covered with matting, and at intervals of a few yards there are open channels, which are, I conclude, to carry away more easily the dust and dirt that must accumulate in the building.

We took off our boots (Mr and Mrs Freeland both wore laced boots, so it was a lengthy process), and carrying them in our hands, entered in our stockings. It is a magnificent place, and we were walking slowly round, no one interfering with us or noticing us, when our dragoman, anxious to show us everything, led us across the mosque, past many groups of worshippers. Soon there were angry countenances, several persons rose and surrounded our dragoman, and insisted upon our going out. Poor Shaheen resisted, and brought forward his talisman of "Highness's people!" but it was of no use here; he was in the hands of several fierce-looking Turks, who were, I must say, very fine-looking stalwart men. One came up to Mr Freeland and took him by the shoulder; but the latter, knowing resistance to be vain, shook him off, and calmly turned round to go out. A few Turks escorted us to the nearest door, and watched us while we put on our boots. Our dragoman was of opinion that a few francs would have smoothed matters and enabled us to remain, but I think he was mistaken, and that we were in the wrong in crossing the mosque among the worshippers; had we kept to the outer circle we should have seen as well, and not interfered with those who were performing their devotions. This was my first visit to St Sophia, now for four hundred years a Mahometan mosque, and for a thousand years previous a Christian church! Will it ever become so again?

The climate of Constantinople during the month of June struck us as a good deal like that of England. During the first fortnight of our stay rain fell on six days, and the thermometer outside my window varied from 66° to 70°. An alley, with trees arching overhead, thus forming an effectual screen from sun or rain, and paved with smooth round pebbles, led from the house we inhabited to the gates of the harem, so that weather never prevented the Pasha and Princess from coming to us.

One evening I went to visit Mdlle. O. who resided in the harem with his Highness's second daughter. As I was not going to one of the princesses, I did not enter at the principal door, but at the general entrance for every one who has business in the harem. Although I was asking for a European (or more properly a Levantine), I found the rule of never mentioning a woman's name beyond the harem applied even here, for I could not make them understand whom I wanted, until I bethought myself of the Turkish term *hoja*, which signifies "teacher."

In front of the door, which was as wide as that of a coach-house, sat two eunuchs; it was opened sufficiently wide to allow you to enter, and formed thus a sort of lane to the doorway, which was only the usual size. This wide door was in order to prevent the men in the courtyard, or any passers-by through it, from seeing into the harem court when anybody went out or in, as would otherwise have been the case. When I got into the court, the spectacle which presented itself was rather singular; numbers of female faces looked down from the latticed windows, and groups stood about, some talking, others lounging listlessly. Many of them were fair as Europeans— they were mostly Georgians or Circassians; others were black as ebony, and these were for the most menial offices, as no idea of beauty is connected with them. The Circassians all wore loose dresses, mostly white, but the black women had very gaudy colours. There is a garden round the harem, surrounded by high walls, and that serves for exercise and recreation for all the slaves. It was only the princesses, accompanied by their immediate attendants and escorted by eunuchs, who had the privilege of walking in the grounds beyond the harem walls. This they usually did in the evening between five and seven; and the appearance of the eunuchs who preceded and followed them was a signal to any man to get out of the way. It was the etiquette also for ladies to turn aside, unless desired to approach. Shefket, who was then about fifteen or sixteen years old, and who had lived in the harem during his childhood, would sometimes come suddenly upon the ladies at a sharp angle which had concealed their approach. The second Princess, who was always very kind to those connected with her children, would call out, "Oh, never mind, Shefket;" but

TURKISH CEMETERY.

he knew better, and was off like a shot in the opposite direction whenever a *yashmak* came in sight.

The second Princess had kindly placed a caïque at my disposal; but as *backsheesh* is an institution in the East, I soon found that unless I gave the rowers about the same amount as a public boat would have cost, the caïque was not forthcoming when ordered. However, it was a better boat, and then there was the honour of the thing!

The first time I got into one, I was rather puzzled at the peculiar arrangement. You have to lie down in the boat with your back against the stern, and only two persons can go in one, comfortably. If you have a servant, he sits cross-legged on the little platform at the stern, against which you are leaning. This is the seat appropriated to a eunuch, when ladies of the harem go in caïques. You have to sit very quiet, and be very careful about getting in and out, for the least inadvertence may upset the boat. I enjoyed the caïques exceedingly; but my pupil never cared to go into them, which I was sorry for. It is an exceedingly pretty sight to see the caïques flitting about, with the gleaming *yashmaks* and bright *feridjees* of their occupants.

We had two rowers, one a young man, but the other, if he had only had on a bonnet and carried a corpulent umbrella, would have been the living image of Mrs Gamp; he was so portly, and his dress was just like that of a woman. He wore a sort of yellow bed-jacket, and the loose Turkish trousers, which look very like a gown.

We went one day to the Turkish cemetery at Scutari. We took the steamer from Emirghian to the bridge, and then crossed in another to Kadikeui[1] on the Asiatic side. The snowy summit of Mount Olympus was before us, but whichever side we looked, there was some new beauty to admire. We had been recommended to land at Kadikeui,

[1] The termination *keui* signifies village in Turkish.

on account of the view in ascending the hill to Scutari. After more than an hour's walk we reached the Turkish cemetery. There is nothing to divide it from other ground, the road runs through it, and on the Scutari side, on the slope of the hill, there are many *cafés* close by the tombs, and people sit among them and sip their beverage, whatever it may be. On the Scutari side the ascent is very steep, and there is no view. On the Kadikeui side the ascent is more gradual, and the view magnificent, but often behind you, so that it is necessary to turn back to enjoy it fully. We had taken some luncheon with us, and we sat down on one of the tombs, under the shade of some cypress-trees, and, facing Kadikeui, looked down on the exquisite scenery. Before us the little Bay of Kadikeui, Princes' Islands, and the Sea of Marmora. Opposite, on our right, Stamboul with its domes and minarets rising like the seats of an amphitheatre. There was plenty of movement looking down on the water, with the numerous caïques and steamers passing and repassing; but around us was a city of the dead, and during a full hour that we sat there no one passed along the public road, which was a few hundred yards from us. Then we slowly walked towards Scutari, and as we drew nearer we found *cafés* abounding among the tombs, and many people seated there, smoking and drinking. The cypresses were planted here so thickly that all view was shut out; and when the descent began (a very steep and stony one), we seemed suddenly to pass from the cemetery to the town, as there was no separation whatever between the tombs and the houses, the abodes of the dead and of the living.

When we reached the port we found the steamer would not go across for a full hour. We knew this pretty well beforehand, but as it was our first visit, we had reckoned upon finding some place where we could sit down and feast our eyes on the view. No such place was to be found; the shore was encumbered with boats and boatmen, and *cafés* of the lowest class. Our inquiries respecting the departure of the steamer brought a number of boatmen round us, who almost overturned us in their endeavours to get us into their respective boats. One offered to take us across for five piastres (about 11d.); another had a four-oared boat, and would take us for seven; then a dozen more rushed upon us, vociferating to such a degree that we turned back for shelter in the town. But the sharp pebbles and want of shade drove us back again, and at last we got a four-oared caïque, and had a delightful row across to the bridge. There we found a steamer waiting which luckily had an upper deck, and we reached Emirghian at about 6 P.M. We had been eight or nine hours walking or sitting in the open air without any feeling of fatigue. Every week we made one or two such excursions, of which the freshness and charm were indescribable; but we were yet in June, and the great heat had not begun.

CHAPTER IX.

On the Bosphorus—Mustapha's house—Roumeli-Hissar—Anniversary of the Sultan's accession—Illuminations—Tramway in Stamboul—Separate omnibuses for harem—We make the circuit of the walls of Constantinople—Frequent change of temperature—Turkish money—Turkish language.

I have observed that my room had seven windows, four of which were blocked up by trees; the remaining three, however, commanding splendid views—two to the east, across the Bosphorus and on the opposite shore of Asia

Minor, and the third up the channel towards the Black Sea. Our house was a considerable height above the water, nearly at the edge of a small platform of level ground, so that the direct descent was very steep. At the north-east corner of my room I looked out upon a small grass plot, and after about a fortnight's stay at Emirghian I saw a quantity of building materials heaped on this grass plot, and wondered what was going to be done. A little observation made it quite clear to me that a building of some sort was about to be erected there which would effectually shut out my view. I made inquiries, and was told that a house for Mustapha the cook was to be built on that spot! Now the name of Mustapha had been a bugbear to us for a long time, and for this reason: he had officiated as cook to our predecessors (General Maclean and his family); but he was employed *for* them and not *by* them, so that they had no control over him. The complaints concerning him had been so many and frequent that when we arrived it was decided a different plan should be adopted; a certain sum was to be paid monthly, and we were to employ our own cook. This plan was much more satisfactory to us; but when we left Cairo this allowance ceased, and we dismissed our cook, as we might be for an uncertain period staying at hotels. When we first arrived at Emirghian our household was not organised; when it was, we found to our dismay that Mustapha was to be our cook. I don't know whether he was brought from Egypt for that purpose, but I should think it more likely that he managed to secure himself a passage on one of the Viceroy's steamers, having previously ascertained that we had no cook with us, and then turned up just when one was inquired for. An Arab does not want much accommodation, but he wants a shelter for the night, and there was none for him. I don't know how they had managed on former occasions;

I suppose the train of followers had increased, but every dwelling-place within the grounds was occupied, and not a room was to be had in the neighbouring villages of Emirghian and Istenia. Of course the pleasure-grounds must not be disfigured by any erection, but our house was on the extreme north-east of the garden and tolerably hidden by trees. My room stood out on a little promontory, and a tiny wooden house run up on the small grassy platform I have mentioned would be quite concealed from every part of the garden, and could be an annoyance to no one but to me. I, however, complained most loudly; and my pupil, instigated by me, spoke to her mother on the subject. The second Princess was very kind. She first inquired if it was not possible to find another site for Mustapha's house, and was told there was none. She then asked how many windows there were in my room, and upon being told "seven," thought I might be contented with the remaining four. My pupil was my friend throughout, and she explained to her mother that the view from these four windows was completely blocked up by trees. The Princess then said they must be cut down, or at any rate the upper branches removed, and charged her son to see that it was done. The Pasha told me his mother's orders, and gardeners were fetched, while he stood by seeing that it was done, and I remained in my room watching the branches fall. In this way I had three other views, to the south and east, opened to me; but my northern window had to be closely shut from that time and the blinds drawn down, otherwise when Mustapha's house was finished my room would have had no privacy whatever. As the spot of ground on which it was built was very small, there was only space for one room; so another storey was built over it, with a wooden staircase on the outside, and here in the evening the men sat and smoked.

I went in a caïque to Roumeli-Hissar, where there are splendid remains of an old fortress built by Mahommed II. two years before the taking of Constantinople. I was astonished at the vastness of the ruins. There are five towers, and I went up the highest, from whence a magnificent view is obtainable. In three months this castle was finished, the walls being thirty feet thick, and high in proportion; but a thousand masons had been driven together to construct the fortress, and multitudes were associated with their labours, bringing together the necessary materials. From the highest of the towers enormous guns threw stone balls of more than six hundredweight, thus compelling every passing ship to pay toll or be sunk, for this fortress was built at the narrowest part of the Bosphorus.

The ruins cover a very large space of ground, and within the walls are many small houses constructed from the crumbling materials, for in the East ruins are not kept in preservation, but any one helps himself from the *débris* if he can do it conveniently.

I went very often to Roumeli-Hissar, but always by caïque or steamer. It was quite within a walk had there been one by the water-side, but this was taken up by houses hanging over the stream, and the only way was behind them by narrow stony paths and through a dirty village. The best walk by the water-side is that from Therapia to Buyukdere, which is on the coast the whole way; but then we had to take steamer or caïque to Therapia. At this latter place are the summer residences of the principal ambassadors. It is a charming breezy resort, looking up towards the Black Sea, and many degrees cooler than at Pera.

The 25th of June was the anniversary of the Sultan's accession, and from an early hour there had been a constant succession of gay boats passing down the Bosphorus,

ACCESSION FÊTE.

not the least interesting being those of the different ambassadors, who went to Constantinople to pay their respects to the Sultan. The Khédive was expected to arrive from Egypt on that day; but he did not come before evening, having stayed some hours in Constantinople to pay his respects to the Sultan. I went down the hill to the water-side at about 5 P.M. to see the arrangements for the illuminations. Carpets were spread close to the shore, and on these numbers of women had taken up their position for hours beforehand. Their bright *feridjees* and white *yashmaks* had an exceedingly pretty effect; but the Turkish *yashmak* is very different from the hideous Egyptian veil, which makes a woman look like a spectre. Most of these *yashmaks* were of the thinnest material, so that the face was not in the least concealed, but rather embellished. They did not hide the features so much as does the veil worn by an English lady. The carpets which are spread along the shore on these occasions are kept sacred to the women, and wherever there is an open space between the houses and the water, the best positions are at once taken up. The men must content themselves with standing behind. Every house along the shore contributes its quota to the illuminations, and arrangements are made for throwing up fireworks in the middle of the stream. It is a very pretty sight to see the long line of light on each side fringing the water and reflected in it. The palace of Emirghian was of course one of the most brilliant sights on the Bosphorus, as were also the steam-yachts of his Highness, which were moored in front.

A day or two after, I went in to Stamboul on an exploring expedition, and upon reaching the station found the steamer had not yet arrived. There were some Turkish ladies waiting there, escorted by a eunuch, and they would willingly have entered into conversation with me; but when one's knowledge of the language is confined to declining the personal pronouns and counting up to a hundred, conversation becomes difficult, so our efforts failed. When the boat came, I saw that it had no upper deck, and as it appeared rather crowded, I thought I would go into the part devoted to "harem," so followed my Turkish ladies. I found the part appropriated to the women was at the fore of this vessel, though generally it is at the stern, and I had to pass a great crowd to get to it. It is divided from the rest of the vessel by a screen of canvas, but when I had passed under that, I found matters much worse. Not only was every seat taken, but there was no standing-room, many being squatted on the ground, and resenting highly any pressure, which under the circumstances it was impossible to avoid. After half an hour of purgatory, I determined upon extricating myself if possible, and got out, trampling on somebody's limbs at every step, and calling forth much animadversion. These vessels are sometimes terribly crowded, particularly at certain hours of the day. They are numbered, and I got to know them all, and tried to avoid those which had not an upper deck.

I first went to the Tower of Galata, which is on the hillside between Galata and Pera, and was constructed by the Genoese as a watch-tower to give notice to the inhabitants of the outbreak of fire, an event of frightfully frequent occurrence. There are 180 steps to reach the top, several rooms in the upper part of the tower, with windows commanding views on every side, and an outer gallery, from which the view is still more extensive. Looking from this gallery upon the narrow and crooked ways leading down to the port, I saw two new streets, broad, and with some fine houses. The frequent fires do a great deal to clear out the city, and make the work of a Baron Haussman much easier. The Government decreed that no houses should be rebuilt of wood, so that large tracts desolated by fire remain untouched, until gradually wide streets and handsome houses replace the wretched tenements destroyed.

When I descended to Galata, I crossed the bridge; and remembering the tramway I had seen on a previous visit, I took one of the omnibuses, determined to see to what part of the city they went, and then to return by one of the same conveyances. The tramway had been only in use a few months; and it passed through that district which had been destroyed by the terrible fire of September 1865, which had extended from the Golden Horn across to the Sea of Marmora, and had consumed property to the value of several millions sterling. I had heard so much of the narrow alleys of Constantinople that I was astonished at the noble streets through which the tramway passed. I was in an omnibus exclusively for women, and from the windows I saw splendid views over the Sea of Marmora. The streets were well laid out; but as the new houses are all to be of brick or stone, there were as yet few built. I heard the conductor say a few words in Italian, so I addressed him in that language, which he spoke very well, though I found he was a Turk. He told me the names of all the places I passed, and said he had been a long time in Italy, and also in England. His principal recollection of the latter country was of Madame Tussaud's Exhibition.

At last the tramway terminated abruptly, the road ceased, and as it had been all a broad highway with magnificent views, I determined to walk back. I was perfectly charmed with the whole way; and as I drew near the Golden Horn, the road down to the water-side seemed so clear that I thought I would try it, and thus avoid a considerable curve to the left after passing the Mosque of St Sophia. This curve had been followed by the tramway, and I should have done better to keep to it, for what had appeared very clear looking down the road from above, became very intricate in practice, and I got into a very nasty crowded neighbourhood—near the water, it is true, but with no apparent means of reaching the bridge. I arrived there at last, however, and then thought the Turkish Government perfectly in the right not to let such dens be rebuilt when once fire had cleared them away and purified the air.

On another day we started to make the circuit of the walls of Constantinople. We had heard that a steamer left the bridge at a certain hour every morning for the Seven Towers; but although we were in very good time, we had the mortification of seeing this boat go off before we could leave the steamer, as, on account of the difficulty of approaching near enough to the bridge, we were full twenty minutes in landing. We, however, engaged a caïque to take us to the Seven Towers, and were careful to make a bargain beforehand. As soon as we got round Seraglio Point, we found the sea very rough, owing to a strong south-east wind which blew on to the shore. Our rowers pulled manfully for some time; but then stopped, and urged us to land at Yeni Kapou, about midway between Seraglio Point and the Seven Towers, refusing to take us further than that unless we paid treble the sum stipulated. When we engaged the caïque, it was quite sheltered from this wind, which was not felt until we were in the Sea of Marmora; and as we saw that the men had really worked hard, and were streaming with perspiration, we agreed to land at Yeni Kapou, though it entailed a long walk through the town in addition to that from the Sea of Marmora to the Golden Horn. We were also moved thereto by the roughness of the sea, which caused more motion than was quite agreeable. We had very much enjoyed the row hitherto, because it had given us quite a new view. Before, when seen from the deck of a steamer, our attention had always been so engrossed by the panorama on the hillside, domes and minarets rising up one above another, with the rich, dark cypress everywhere intermingling, that we had entirely overlooked the walls. But here in the caïque we were close under them, and saw nothing beyond. At short intervals rose massive towers, built to defend the walls, but, like them, crumbling away in ruins. The waves beat against them; and in imagination the memory goes back for centuries, for nothing living is to be seen. The length of the walls from Seraglio Point to the Seven Towers is six miles; from the latter to the Golden Horn (being on the land side) the distance is four miles, and on the harbour side about three.

Upon landing at Yeni Kapou we proceeded sometimes through narrow streets, sometimes through open tracts which had been desolated by fire, and where we saw a railway in process of construction—it was the line to Adrianople, a small part of which was already open. This walk was rather arduous, but at last we reached the Seven Towers, and then began the chief interest for us. The road for about four miles runs along the edge of the moat which bounds the outer wall—a scene of picturesque beauty, and at the same time of desolation, which defies description. On one side you have the walls, with the many towers, all intertwined with ivy, and every breach made in them by the frequent sieges filled up by trees. On the other hand is a vast cemetery, extending the whole length of the road, and shaded by groves of cypress-trees, before and behind the glorious views over the Golden Horn and the Sea of Marmora. Such a walk as this, taken as we did in June, with all the exquisite tints which then prevail on land, sea, and sky, can hardly be surpassed in this world. For any one who can do it, walking is on such occasions far preferable to riding or driving, as the rests under the cypress-trees and among the tombs are so delightful. Only I resolved another time to reverse the route, and go by the Golden Horn, instead of *returning* by it, as by far the finest views are towards the Sea of Marmora. There are five or six gates on the land side leading into the town, and near these gates were the only signs of life. Here were *cafés*, and generally a few persons seated. A *café* is a very simple affair in Turkey; a man wants no other capital than a few chairs and a coffee-pot, and then he sets up in business. We loitered about for nearly four hours on this road, and at last got down to the Golden Horn, and engaged a caïque. One rower sufficed for this calm water, and most refreshing it was to stretch one's self out in the caïque and glide along over the smooth surface. The water is so deep that ships of the largest size can be moored close to the shore, with their prows resting against the houses; but in the upper part of the harbour there are little bays, where the water is shallow; and I saw many buffaloes' heads just above the surface, as these creatures delight to go and stand in it. Thirty-five minutes brought us to the bridge, where we found our steamer, and returned to Emirghian.

As July advanced the weather became hotter, though frequent rain modified the temperature. We found it very difficult to keep free from cold, on account of the great transitions which occurred in the climate. Our house faced the south, and was on the hillside, so it might appear very hot when we started on one of our numerous expeditions. Arrived on the steamer, and seated on the upper deck, you found, if the wind blew from the north, that a slight wrap was desirable. Landed at the bridge, the ascent to Pera was sometimes overpowering, as no breath of wind came till you had reached the top. Later in the day you returned by steamer; the north wind was in your face, and pierced you through. There was always the alternative of descending to the main deck; but that was generally so crowded, and often screened at the side with canvas, so that it was a choice between catching cold and enduring temporary suffocation.

The Turkish money was very puzzling to us at first. In Egypt the coins of all nations pass current. Accounts are kept in piastres, of which 100 make an Egyptian sovereign, worth about £1, 0s. 6d. These piastres, small thin silver pieces, are divided into 40 paras; but as copper is very much depreciated in value, no one cares to take it, and you seldom see it. English sovereigns and napoleons are more frequently seen than Egyptian gold coins; and the shops in the new part of Cairo being all kept by Levantines or Europeans, everything is charged in francs. In the bazaars everything was by piastres, and also in the banks. All these details we had mastered; but the Turkish money perplexed us for some time. There was the gold sovereign (value about 18s. English money), which was subdivided into 100 piastres, like the Egyptian, but not of the same value; then a smaller gold piece of 50 piastres, and one still smaller of 25. We managed to class these three gold coins as 18s., 9s., and 4s. 6d.: that was easy, and so was the silver—20 beshliks made a Turkish sovereign, and 5 medjidichs made a Turkish sovereign, so that the value of a beshlik in English money was about 10¾d., and that of a medjidich about 3s. 7¼d. All this was simple and easily learned; but the difficulty was with the copper, as there was no silver piece lower than half a beshlik (5½d.) In Egypt the smallest silver coin is half a piastre, 1¼d., so you do not mind the loss of a halfpenny now and then; but in Turkey you require change for 5½d., and this you can only get in copper piastres. Nominally 5 piastres make a beshlik, but in practice it is nearly 6. This was very perplexing to us for some time, as we never seemed to get our right change.

I engaged a Turkish master, and began to take lessons.

G

The grammar is beautifully simple, but I found the characters very difficult. They have no capitals and no stops, and the letter is often written differently, according as it is in the beginning, middle, or end of the word. A book commences on the last page, and ends on the first; it is written from right to left, and not from left to right, as ours are. I got Mallouf's Grammar and Dictionaries with the phonetic pronunciation, but unfortunately no combination of letters in our European languages can adequately give the sound of some Turkish and Arabic words.

Sometimes we had two or three days of wet weather, heavy drenching rain, and at such times we missed sadly the ordinary conveniences of English life. Rain never prevented our pupils from coming. I have mentioned that there was an alley paved with smooth round pebbles, and with thick foliage arching overhead, which led from the house we inhabited down to the harem; and as it was on a rather steep slope, the wet ran off quickly, but the little garden surrounding our house was on such occasions full of pools of water, which they had to get through somehow; and as we had neither scrapers nor door-mats, the dirt brought into the house may readily be imagined. When we first saw rain we were quite delighted, but the novelty soon wore off, and then we sighed for fine weather, which came in due course; but the months of July and August are generally very hot at Constantinople, except perhaps a day or two after the rain, when it would be very pleasant.

CHAPTER X.

Picnic to the Forest of Belgrade—Sudden appearance of the cook at dinner—The Viceroy returns to Egypt—Unexpected departure of the Pasha and his household—Am at first left unprovided for—Great improvement in affairs—Weather in August—Slave children—Candili—Charming residence there—Railway from Constantinople to the Seven Towers—Miss the station—Euphrates Valley scheme.

We had a picnic to the Forest of Belgrade, which is about nine or ten miles from Emirghian. Servants were sent off the night before to make preparations in a kiosk built near one of the reservoirs. They went in carts drawn by white oxen and laden with provisions. The Forest of Belgrade contains the water-supply of Constantinople; the trees are therefore carefully watched. It is the only forest on the Thracian side of the Bosphorus. There is the fine aqueduct, consisting of twenty-one arches, built by Sultan Mahmoud in 1732, a noble structure, which spans the valley. Under this, our road led us to the kiosk situated near one of the great reservoirs. The whole way was hilly, and we had occasional lovely glimpses of the Bosphorus.

The Princess and I, with two or three others, started at once for a walk. She was as much inclined for active exercise as an English girl would have been, and was never so happy as when making one of these excursions. This was to be her last summer of liberty. What misgivings she might have had respecting the future I cannot tell, as we never spoke of her approaching seclusion. Though the day was hot, the shade of the forest was so deep that we felt neither heat nor fatigue, but wandered on until the *lalla* who attended the Princess was loud in his remonstrances, as great people in the East are supposed not to have the free use of their limbs, and he feared a scolding if his young mistress were fatigued. These picnics are expensive affairs to the Viceroy, particularly when they occur in Turkey. £30 were actually distributed in *backsheesh* among the soldiers at Bagtchekeui and the few inhabitants of the place, not one of whom did anything for us!

I have mentioned Mustapha the cook, and our disgust at finding he was appointed as our *chef*. I must describe a little his way of cooking, to account for our repugnance. The meat was cut up into square blocks, quite irrespective of joints; it was well soaked in water, and then cooked. Thus there would be many pieces of meat on the table, very sodden and tasteless; vegetables floating in water, and various sweet dishes which custom only can make palatable. This would be at luncheon, when the Pasha and the Princess were present; at dinner, in the evening, it was worse. An enormous quantity was cooked at luncheon, the greater part of which went away untouched; and this was reproduced at night, having been placed by the fire a sufficient time to make the outside skin warm, while the meat remained quite cold. As there was no change, and the same dishes appeared every day, we gave them various names, as the "inevitable," the "invariable," &c., &c. A word to his Highness would have changed all this, as was proved when it was spoken later; but there was no one to speak it. The Pasha was at the schoolboy age, when everything goes down and the palate is not critical; the Princess took no notice of it, but *we* grumbled every day. On one occasion, however, at luncheon, there was such a general chorus of complaint that I suppose one of the Arab attendants told Mustapha, for he suddenly appeared at the door (which was always open), and addressing the Pasha, asked him what there was to complain of, adding that he had four cooks under him, all employed in a room not large enough for one;

that he did his best, and he could not do more. He had on high pattens on account of the rain, which made him look a gigantic height. The Pasha was silent, and no one was disposed to get up an altercation; so when he had unburdened his mind, Mustapha returned to the kitchen. On a former occasion he had appeared once in the evening in a similar way, but something had then set us off laughing, upon which he roared aloud in concert; and this struck us as so ludicrous and so unlike European life, that we only laughed the more heartily. On the second occasion, however, Mustapha looked grave and stern, and no one replied to his oration.

The 30th of July was fixed upon for the departure of the Viceroy from Turkey. Of all his family, none were to remain but the second Princess and her two children, Zohrab Bey, and ourselves. The second Princess had been in delicate health, and the climate of Egypt was considered too hot for her and her children for the next three months. We were all very glad of the delay in our return, as we dreaded the heat of Egypt, and, moreover, had still much to see on the Bosphorus. The Viceroy was to go on board after midnight, and start at daybreak.

Before six the next morning I was looking from my window and observing that the Mahroussah was gone, when Shefket called to me from the garden below and asked me if I had heard the news. This was that the Pasha had left with his father! Seemingly a slight event, but one of great consequence to us, as it entirely broke up our party. Messrs Freeland and Michell, with Shefket and all the attendants, were to leave on that afternoon. There would be no one remaining in the house but Zohrab Bey and myself! Zohrab Bey was an old campaigner; he had his man-servant, and he could accommodate himself to any position; but what was to become of me? Of course Mrs Freeland, her children, and nurses, went with

Mr Freeland. With him they were provided for; without him, they would not have been. By-and-by the Princess and Kopsès came up, and the former told me what had occurred on the previous night. The Viceroy had settled to leave that night, but the second Princess was drinking the Broussa waters, upon which her life was said to depend, so she was to remain and her children with her. The Pasha had been rather hard worked of late; and, boylike, he longed for a little holiday. If his father would only take him also, there would be the voyage, and the illuminations in Egypt on their arrival, whereas if he stayed behind there would be nothing but lessons, lessons! This wrought so much on his feelings that he began to cry; and the Viceroy, who was tenderly attached to the boy, determined to take him with him. Then there was a general outburst of grief. The Pasha wept because his father was going; the mother wept because her son wished to leave her. The little Princess had cried for some time past to think how dull she would be when her brother and all were gone; she had only three months more of liberty, and then all social intercourse would cease for ever! The slaves all cried because everybody else did, for both crying and laughing are infectious. So the Pasha was got privately out of the room; and once on board with his father, messages were sent for his things to be packed up, and all his household to follow him in a day or two; and at daybreak the Mahroussah departed. One day was given for packing up, and on the next the educational staff, consisting of Mr Freeland (and his family), Mr Michell; Sheikh Ali and Mustapha Effendi, the Arabic and Turkish masters; and Signor Luigi, the drawing-master, sailed. Shefket had been left behind by the Pasha, and was also to accompany them.

The two little girls came up to the house as usual, but not with their customary buoyancy and merry laughter.

They went quietly through their lessons, and then loitered about, looking on at the preparations for departure, and saying little. As the time for leaving drew near, one after another of the party came to the Princess to bid her farewell. She thanked them each in turn for the kindness they had shown her, of which she said she should always have a grateful remembrance; but when Shefket came, suppressing with difficulty his own feelings, and respectfully kissed her hand, she broke out into sobs, and was some time in recovering herself. The four children had been for years companions and playmates, and that was to be over now for ever! Kopsès, who was of a different character, tried to laugh off the parting. "You will never see *us* again," she said, "but we shall see you, and hear everything concerning you; we shall often pass close to you, and you will not know us." But she felt the shock quite as much as the Princess.

I walked down the hill with our friends, and went on to the steamer with them, coming away as soon as the boat was ready to start. I watched it go down the stream, until it rounded the point of Roumeli-Hissar, when it was lost to view, and I returned slowly to the house. I felt very lonely, for there was not a creature in it but myself. The Princess and Kopsès had gone down to the harem, and the servants had all departed in the Jafferia with the masters. Zohrab Bey was to come and occupy the other end of the house on the following day. I went to the *selamlik*, which, as I have before said, was the little house in front, and routed out Pancotti, Zohrab Bey's Greek servant, asking him to find me something to eat. He brought me some bread and a little coffee, but he had nothing more. The evening passed sorrowfully enough. I had no dinner, so I went on a foraging excursion through all the rooms, and discovered some remnants of bread and wine, upon which I regaled myself. When I went to my room, I soon perceived there would be no rest for me there. A party of "wretches," as Mrs Freeland's nurse would have called them, but in plain English some of the Viceroy's Arab followers, had seized upon the little wooden house built for Mustapha the cook. They sang in full chorus a sort of demoniacal chant, varied with occasional howling and stamping. I descended in search of Zohrab Bey, who was not to be found, but I prevailed on Pancotti to go to them, and after some parley the noise ceased.

On the following day my pupil did not come, and I was quite alone. Pancotti again got me some coffee, and luncheon was sent up to me from the table kept in the palace for the different *employés*, but to which I could not go alone.

Zohrab Bey came into the house that day, and some slight improvement took place, as a man was brought in to sweep the rooms, but I could not get any dinner or any coffee. I went several times in search of Zohrab Bey, but he was never to be found. It was no part of his business to minister to my wants—he was physician to the harem; but we had got into the way of applying to him in all difficulties, and, to do him justice, he was always ready to help us when *he thought of it*. He had a great deal to do, and as he was verging towards seventy, he began to find that many of the extra duties he had, through his good-nature, taken upon himself, were too much for him. He did not like to say "No," so he would sometimes keep out of the way for days on such occasions.

On the second day after the departure of the Pasha's suite the Princess and her companion came up to me. They came early as usual (between seven and eight), expecting to breakfast with me, but no preparations whatever had been made. As Zohrab Bey was not to be found, I spoke to his servant Pancotti, and asked him to inquire about breakfast. He said there was no coffee, no milk, no charcoal, no orders, no anything! I remonstrated. He shrugged his shoulders, put his head on one side, stretched out his hands; and that was all I could get out of him, unless it was at intervals an ejaculation of "Mais, madame!" I returned to the Princess and told her how I had been situated for the last two days, begging her to go back and speak to her mother on the subject, adding that she had better have breakfast in the harem, as there was no prospect of any in the house. The Princess and Kopsès heard me quietly, and then went away without making any comment. I was amazed at their reticence; for, knowing nothing then of harem habits, except what could be gleaned from occasional visits, I was not at all aware that my pupil, though the Khédive's daughter, had not the power to give any order except to her own immediate attendants. The discipline to which all are subjected is extremely strict on this point. I had told her to go to breakfast in the harem, not knowing there was no such meal there. She had been accustomed for some years to an English breakfast, and therefore missed it as much as I did. She knew well enough she would get none in the harem, but she did not tell me so. Twice a-day regular meals were brought into the harem equivalent to our luncheon and dinner, the first about half-past eleven, and the second at about six or seven. If any one was hungry between these meals, she might perhaps get a little fruit, sweets, or a tiny cup of coffee. His Highness of course lived in the European style, and when he was there, his three wives and their children all breakfasted, lunched, and dined with him. But his Highness was away, and the regular harem habits went on. The ladies had never been taught that it was unwholesome to eat sweets or fruit all day long; so having very little to employ them, they generally did so. In about an hour the Princess came back, and told me that her mother was very much vexed that I should have been so neglected; she had inquired of Zohrab Bey, directly after the Pasha's departure, whether my wants were provided for, and he said he would see to them; and so no doubt he *meant* to do, only he forgot all about it.

All was now, however, rectified. One of the French servants of his Highness's household was charged to see that a proper table was provided for me; and M. Moulet was not a man to neglect any duty which he undertook. Breakfast, luncheon, and dinner were brought to us at fixed hours. The fare was excellent, the punctuality admirable. The Princess and Kopsès came up every morning to breakfast with me and remained until about half-past four.

Up to this time we had always given a good half-hour before luncheon, and the same time after it, to play; and the Princess was not a person to pass this time in inactivity. But just now it was very hot, and there were only three of us; consequently games were less amusing, so I was constantly urged to tell stories. I had been very anxious for a long time to get the Princess into the habit of reading for her own amusement, and just then I succeeded in doing it, to my great joy. The moment lessons were over, she and her companion ran out into the little garden in front of the house, established themselves comfortably in rocking-chairs, at a little distance from each other, and there they read half aloud. One day in our morning reading the Princess, who was always very anxious to understand thoroughly what she read, asked me some question, and I in reply added, "But that will lead me into a long story, and as I know it will interest you, I will tell you after lessons." After luncheon I remembered this, and proposed to tell her the story I had promised in the morning. In a general way she would have laid aside anything to listen, but on this occasion she said, "Oh, pray don't tell me now! I'm so interested in my book, I can think of nothing else!" Of course I was delighted, as of all things I wished her to acquire a love of reading.

The day before leaving Emirghian Mrs Freeland had kindly taken me over to Candili, on the Asiatic side of the Bosphorus, to introduce me to some friends of hers, as she justly thought I should be very lonely, and glad of some English acquaintances. The name of this family was Hanson, and Mr Hanson had been for many years one of the leading bankers of Constantinople. Candili is little promontory jutting out on the Bosphorus, with a terribly steep and stony ascent from the water-side, so uninviting that I was not at all prepared for the lovely view which awaited me after entering the house and passing a little way through the garden. It came upon me all at once while wandering among shady trees along terraces of different heights, in all of which the trees arched overhead. Suddenly I found myself on a little grassy platform, with an exquisite view of the Bosphorus, taking in Constantinople and Scutari. Other views were to the north, and commanded the upper part of the Bosphorus towards Therapia and Buyukdere. Mr Hanson told me that a short time back the Sultan had come to his house, and was astonished to find so cool a place on the Bosphorus. There was a complete colony of the Hanson family established at different heights at Candili, and the Sultan wished to purchase all the property and build a kiosk there for himself. Mr Hanson had not made up his mind whether he would sell it or not. He told me that many years before he was living at Therapia, and one of the Sultan's predecessors had taken an equal fancy to that place, and had purchased it of him at double the price he had himself given.

I have said that our table had been well arranged, thanks to the second Princess; but we were still very badly off for somebody to keep the rooms clean and in order. Domestic service is a great difficulty in the East. The natives have their slaves, and European or Levantine residents are obliged to content themselves at first with very indifferent attendance. If they get a good servant they take care to keep him, but it is rare that women-servants are to be met with. At last we got a *ferash*, or *eyewass*, as they call it in Turkish; but as we had no language in common, all efforts to come to a mutual understanding were in vain. I set him to sweep the rooms; he placed all the furniture in the centre, made an awful dust, then left the dust to settle, and me to settle the furniture. The heat for the last few days had been intense, and the wind blew mostly from the south. I mistake, however, in saying it *blew*, for not a leaf stirred; but the quarter in which it lay made all the difference to the temperature. It was 86° in the shade in the little walled-in garden in front of our house. When the wind blew from the north, however high the thermometer might be, there was always a cool breeze. After two or three days of such heat there would be thunderstorms and heavy rain. As all means of locomotion were by steamer or caïque, it was very awkward to be caught in such stormy weather, as no shelter is to be found; so I went very rarely beyond the large garden for two or three weeks. As this garden was as large as a moderate-sized park, and commanded the most exquisite views, being laid out by the best landscape-gardeners, I might think myself fortunate to have such a charming place to walk in.

The second Princess had bought a few slave children whom she was very anxious to have educated. She sent them up to the school with the Princess, to share her lessons as she said; but I discouraged their coming, as I wished as much as possible to cultivate the mind of my pupil during the short space of time she would still be under my charge, and the presence of these children much interfered with my plans. One of them was a droll little creature, about six years old, named Behrouse. I was told her price was £160; but it was quite inexplicable to me how a child could be worth so much, as there was all the trouble of bringing her up, and ultimately of providing for her for life. This purchasing of slaves is a very costly way of procuring servants, and I fully believe the Viceroy would gladly dispense with it; but in the present state of things there is no remedy. He does all he can to educate children, both male and female, and in the schools for girls which he has founded they are taught all household duties as well as mere book-learning; but the burden of all falls upon him: there is no private enterprise as in England, all must be done by the State.

This little Behrouse was not at all pretty, but a remarkably intelligent child, and exceedingly droll. When brought with several other children for inspection, the Princess was about to reject her on account of her want of beauty; but the child entreated so earnestly to be bought, and had so many funny coaxing ways, that the Princess agreed to take her.

I was now alone with my pupils for some weeks. They were both very steady and attentive, and we had long conversations. The Princess would ask me all sorts of questions about England, and whether I thought society would ever be the same in Egypt as it was with us. I told her I thought much would depend on herself. She was in a high position, and would be looked up to as an example. If she by her conduct could show that liberty was not inconsistent with modesty and innocence, there was no doubt but a few years would bring about an entire revolution in the present system with regard to women. Their seclusion was not a Mahometan doctrine—it had existed in the East long before Mahomet; but in all countries, the more civilised a state became, the higher did women rise in the social scale. She used to moralise upon all this, and speak of her past life of liberty much as an elderly lady might do of her youth; but one thing was very certain, that she dreaded the life of retirement that lay before her.

Towards the end of August there was lovely weather after nearly a week of rain, and I determined to make another excursion to the walls of Constantinople. I had seen in the newspaper that part of the railway to Adrianople was open, that the terminus was near the water-side at the Stamboul end of the bridge, and that the first station was at the Seven Towers.

A friend in the neighbourhood accompanied me. Instead of going on to the bridge as I had usually done, I left the steamer at Beshichtash to take the lovely walk between the Sultan's palaces of Beshichtash and Dolmabagtche. Then I took the omnibus to Galata, and crossing the bridge, proceeded to the terminus. I imagine the railway is on a piece of ground belonging to the Seraglio Garden, for it runs close under the walls of the city and next the gardens; from Seraglio Point it does not *follow* the sea, but takes a short cut to the Seven Towers through a district desolated by fire. I had intended getting out at the Seven Towers, and then walking along the walls to the Golden Horn as I had done before; but I had expected the station to be near the Towers, as the name of it implied.

I had become much interested in a conversation with a gentleman in the opposite seat to me. He was a Persian, and spoke French very well. He was speaking of the project then much talked of, for constructing a railway communication between England and India through Asia

Minor and the Euphrates Valley. This gentleman had been much in Europe, both in Paris and London, and seemed greatly to prefer the latter. He had been the last year in Turkey, and was on the following day going back to his own country. Like all educated Orientals, he felt the backward state of the East in comparison with the countries of Western Europe. We were in the midst of a most animated conversation when the train stopped, and I looked out to see if the Seven Towers were visible; but neither they nor any station was to be seen, so I continued the conversation. The ground on which we then were was where the fire had raged, and as nothing had been rebuilt all looked very desolate. In a minute or two, however, the train went on again, passed beyond the walls of the city, and into the open country. Then I knew we had lost our station, and had to consider what was to be done. The walk we had projected was impossible; there was nothing for it but to stop at the first pretty station we came to, and then take the next train back again to the bridge. Though a long summer day, there were very few trains went, and we had always to think of being in time to catch the last steamer from the bridge up the Bosphorus.

The next place (Macrikeui) at which the train stopped did not look very inviting, but the Persian told us that he himself was going to St Stefano, and that the next station beyond that was very pretty. So we settled to get out there, and then returned to the Euphrates Valley scheme. Soon the train stopped again, but the Persian was so intent upon explaining to me the exact line the railway was to take, that we never observed the stoppage. The train went on, and then the Persian perceived that he had passed *his* station, the same as I had done *mine*. This caused much merriment, and we made up our minds to keep a sharp look-out for the future. The next station was Kutchuk-Tchekmedjie: it looked very pretty, and was close on the Sea of Marmora, so we got out. Upon making inquiries, however, we found that a train would go back directly, and another in about three hours. We would willingly have stayed, but we might thereby lose the last boat, so we reluctantly returned by the next train, and the Persian got out at St Stefano.

From what I heard afterwards, I had reason to think it was the Persian Minister, who left Constantinople on the following day.

CHAPTER XI.

Turkish and Greek boatmen—Sudden irruption of eunuchs into our little garden—Cliff walk on the Bosphorus—Dogs—Unexpected return of the Pasha and his suite—Excursion to Eyoub—Curiosity of Turkish women—Buffaloes in the water—View from the cemetery at Eyoub—Tobacco monopoly—Candili—A Persian nurse's ideas about a bedstead—British cemetery at Scutari.

I went over one afternoon to Candili. This is on the Asiatic side of the Bosphorus, and although steamers cross zigzag from one side to the other, the only prompt way is by caïque. I engaged one myself, settled the price in Turkish, and felt rather pleased at my proficiency. When I left Mr Hanson's house it was getting near sunset, and his Greek servant escorted me down to the water-side by a short cut, which was like the rocky bed of a torrent, and in winter would probably be impassable. The Greek found me a tolerably clean boat, but as he had no knowledge of Turkish he could not settle the price, and I had been told this was an indispensable thing before engaging a caïque. I began by offering the same sum which I had paid coming over. After a glance around the boatman decidedly refused, and I went away to seek another boat. But no other was to be found, so I was obliged to return and renew my bargaining. To all my offers he briefly replied "*Akcham*" (evening), which upon consideration seemed reasonable, as it was too late to get a back-fare, so I ended with getting into the caïque on his own terms. It is a hard pull up the stream and then across the current: the man was civil and rowed well, so I ended by giving him more than he had asked me. As a rule these Turkish boatmen are not extortionate. I had much rather have to do with a Turk than with a Greek. From the former I never met with the slightest incivility; but as for the European and Levantine population of Turkey and Egypt, it seems as if the scum of all nations were there gathered together. Of course there are many highly respectable exceptions, but what I have stated is the rule.

Shaheen had a most ridiculous idea that everybody in the Khédive's service ought to pay double what was expected of other people. It looked well, he said. It was therefore some time before we found out what was the right thing to pay, for tariff there is none, except, of course, on the steamboats.

When I got back I found a telegram had arrived from his Highness to say that he should send the Mahroussah to fetch us to Egypt, as the cholera had broken out at Broussa. I suppose, however, it was a false alarm, as we heard no more of it.

One afternoon I was reading with the Princess and Kopsès, when we heard unearthly sounds proceeding from the garden below the windows. It was separated from the large garden by high walls, and these were concealed by trees, so that any one might pass close to it without being aware that a dwelling-house was within the walls. A door led out into a bypath, and some eunuchs who were amusing themselves by chasing one another about the garden had suddenly discovered this door, and looking in, saw a neat little lawn with rocking-chairs and a good swing. To rush in and take possession was the work of a moment, and they signalised their entry by whoops and yells of delight. My pupils shrieked with laughter, and I was speechless with indignation. I had not then experienced the dreary monotony of harem life, which welcomes any grotesque incident as a relief to the pent-up spirits. I felt that to reprove them for their intrusion in broken Turkish might not produce a good effect, so I stood at the window looking gravely down upon them, and they presently took their departure. These were, of course, eunuchs belonging to the Viceroy. As a rule, these men are neither good-looking nor well-made, though there are some exceptions. I saw many at Constantinople who looked more like apes than men, particularly when seen on horseback. As they only belong to great households, and implicit trust is reposed in them, they are treated with marked respect and consideration.

Mary Evans, his Highness's dairy-woman, who provided the butter for the royal table, and was consequently always in the suite at every journey, told me that many of the eunuchs were pashas. I had serious doubts on the subject; but as she told me she had repeatedly heard them addressed as such, I had no more to say. I found afterwards that the real term she had heard was *bache aga*, chief (or head) eunuch, which, pronounced rapidly, would sound like pasha, being called *bash a'a*.

During the month of August, as I had no one to join me in excursions, I confined myself to little steamboat trips, getting out wherever I saw a walk along the shore. At Yenimahallé, the last place where the steamers stop, at the north of the Bosphorus, is a charming cliff walk, which looks on to the Black Sea, and opens out many views not seen in other parts. I was obliged to go in to Pera once a-week to the post, as I had no dragoman (in the absence of Shaheen) to send, and I also had occasion to go to the Ottoman Bank; but it was in such a labyrinth of steep stony streets, so difficult to find, and when found, so difficult to get away from, that I did not care for explorations in that quarter. I discovered an omnibus that went by a circuitous route from Galata to Pera, and I thought I would try it; but the shaking and jolting was so terrible that one trial sufficed me.

I saw a funny sight one day when waiting at Beshichtash for a steamer to take me back to Emirghian. There was a little quay railed off as a landing-place; but as the steamer was not in sight, I got a chair and sat down on the shore, where I should be less crowded. A gentleman came and sat down near me, waiting also for the steamer. He had a little dog with him, and of course there were plenty of dogs lying about as usual. They appeared to be asleep, but they scented the intruder at once and surrounded him, barking violently. In a minute their barking was chorussed in every direction up and down the shore and upon the hills, and whole legions of dogs were seen hurrying to the spot to assist their companions to expel the invader. The gentleman caught his dog up in his arms, and laid about him heartily with a stick which he held in his hand, backing in the meanwhile towards the rails, and flourishing his stick with great vigour. In this way he got through the gate on to the little landing-place, and the army of dogs, after a few vain demonstrations, disappeared.

I went to pay a visit to the second Princess. She knew I had been studying Turkish for a little while, and expected I should be able to tell her what I had seen in my many excursions about Constantinople, but I could not manage it at all. I said I had learned several dialogues;

for instance, for engaging a caïque, for taking rooms at an hotel, &c., &c. She told me to repeat them to her, and I did so as well as I could remember. She laughed heartily, and was good enough to tell me that I should speak very well if I persevered. She always asked with great interest about her daughter—was she making progress? I really thought my pupil was getting on very well, and I told her mother so, at which she seemed much pleased.

At the end of August a great surprise awaited us. At a very early hour one morning the Mahroussah arrived at Emirghian, and the Pasha and his suite had all landed before any of us had seen the boat. He wanted to surprise his mother, and nothing whatever had been said or written about his return. He had had his holiday, had been present at the illuminations customary at the Viceroy's return, and then had been established with his tutors at the palace of Ras-el-Tin near Alexandria. It had been a very hot month with us on the Bosphorus, but it was much more so in Egypt, and perhaps the Pasha might have repented a little having left a cooler climate; but he became indisposed: the doctors at once pronounced Egypt as too hot for him, and recommended his immediate return to Constantinople. So the whole party came back again, with the exception of Mr Michell, who was given six weeks' leave of absence to visit England.

Very soon after their return, Mrs Freeland and I started one day for an excursion up the Golden Horn to visit Eyoub. We did not contemplate visiting the mosque of Eyoub, because it is not permitted to Europeans to enter it, as it is the holiest of all to the Moslems. It is there that each new Sultan girds on the sword of Othman, a ceremony equivalent to coronation in our country.

We went in by one of the usual steamers as far as the bridge and then parted company, agreeing to meet in an hour's time upon one of the small steamers which ply on the Golden Horn between the bridge and Eyoub.

We met at the appointed time, and took up our position in the part of the vessel appropriated to "harem." Mrs Freeland had been with Shaheen to the post, and had several letters, some of them being for me. We soon became absorbed in reading them; the boat was still stationary, and was gradually filling with passengers. I had a little packet in which was a small pocket thermometer, and I took it out and began to examine it attentively. Presently half-a-dozen hands were stretched out for it, and as I continued my examination I was tapped impatiently on the shoulder to call my attention. The thermometer went the round, and I was asked a great many questions as to the use of it, which it was quite beyond my power to explain.

Mrs Freeland had some things in her letters much more easy for them to understand. In one was a photograph; that of course was demanded, and went the round of about thirty people. When it came back again to the owner, the letter which contained it was demanded, and underwent similar inspection. In another letter were some patterns of silk, which were also required and handed about. They happened to be all quiet Quaker colours, or rather no colours but neutral tints; they did not therefore elicit approval, though duly handled and examined.

At one of the stations up the Golden Horn, where we stopped a few minutes to land passengers, I saw a head and horns projecting out of the water, and looking attentively I discovered seven or eight buffaloes, with generally only the snout visible. Now and then a back would rise for a moment, and then disappear. There was something very peculiar in this sight, and indeed in the whole scene. Some of the Turkish men-of-war ships were in the Golden Horn, but the greater part were moored in the Bosphorus near Ortakeui.

We landed at Eyoub, and bore always to the right until we came to the mosque, which having almost circumnavigated, we saw a steep path on the left hand, and this led us through the cemetery of Eyoub on the hillside, thickly planted with cypress-trees. It is one of the most picturesque and beautiful sites that can be imagined. The weather was still hot, and the shade of the cypresses was very grateful. When we reached the top of the hill we had a view quite different from any we had seen previously. The whole of Constantinople, the Golden Horn with its numerous shipping, and the opposite suburbs of Pera and Galata, were spread out before us like a map. In the background of all, the chain of Mount Olympus in Asia Minor. The mosque itself is a very striking object. We did not trouble ourselves about the steamer on our way back to the bridge, but took a caïque, which, on the Golden Horn, is particularly enjoyable, as the water is so calm, the harbour being quite shut in. On the Bosphorus it is sometimes very rough; and when on one or two occasions we missed the last steamer, and had to return to Emirghian in a caïque, we saw plainly that in rough weather such a passage would not be without some danger. Even in summer sudden gusts of wind frequently occur, and a caïque is very easily upset. Near Roumeli-Hissar the current is so strong that for some distance the boats are always towed along by men on the shore, who thus make their living.

A great sensation was occasioned about this time by the following incident: The Turkish Government, as is well known, has always been in difficulties through profuse expenditure, and it was suggested to them that a monopoly of tobacco would be a profitable speculation. Several merchants bid for it, and it was finally made over to a Greek for a term of five years; the Greek agreeing to pay the Government 20,000 Turkish pounds monthly. The Greek then formed a company, and the shares were promptly taken up. All the tobacco brought into Constantinople and its suburbs was to pass through the hands of this company, and they sold at treble the price, and adulterated the quality. I have been told that about 40,000 persons in Constantinople, Pera, Galata, and Scutari live by the sale of tobacco, which is to the Oriental what beer is to the Briton. This monopoly therefore occasioned the greatest dissatisfaction, smuggling to a large extent prevailed, and many were the conflicts which arose between the people and the excise officers. It was reported that sixteen of the latter had lost their lives. They stopped everybody in the streets and on the steamers who had a parcel in their hands, lest it should contain tobacco. They even penetrated into that part of the steamers which is appropriated to "harem," and attempted to examine pockets, which so enraged the ladies that on one occasion the offender barely escaped with his life, through the steamer stopping opportunely at Roumeli-Hissar, which gave him the chance of rushing off the vessel. I am told that among Mahometans a woman may strike a man, but that he dares not lift his hand against her unless she is his wife or slave. A great many conflicts had arisen, the people everywhere taking part against the excisemen, and matters began to look very serious.

About the fifth day the monopolist found placards posted up at his house, informing him that he would shortly be hanged at his own door, and he betook himself in great trepidation to the Vizier for protection.

"If they hang you," said the Vizier, "I'll have them all hanged."

"But that will not bring me to life again," said the Greek; "can't you protect me now?"

"No," said the Vizier; "we can only punish after the crime has been committed."

In this he exaggerated a little, but he felt that the Government was in an untenable position, and if the Greek could be worked upon by his fears to break the contract, it would be less undignified than for the Government to recede from the position it had taken. Besides, there was a penalty to be incurred by the party which broke the contract.

The Greek had then recourse to the company, urging them to withdraw from the contract; but the shareholders treated the matter with great indifference, and even taunted him with cowardice. Time passed on, smuggled tobacco was to be met with everywhere, and the Government found themselves powerless to prevent its introduction, without bringing the excisemen and the people into serious collision. But the company, which had borne with so much equanimity the threats directed against the life of the Greek, showed much greater sensitiveness on another point. Their receipts diminished day by day, and were considerably below their expenditure. The Government, seeing their advantage, no longer showed the slightest disposition to withdraw from the contract, and the company, with ruin staring them in the face, were glad to compromise the matter by forfeiting to the Government £T130,000 to be released from their contract. Nobody pitied them, and the tobacco-shops resumed their old trade amid universal satisfaction.

One day when at Candili, speaking of hotels as they are and as they used to be in the East, Mr Hanson told us that when he first settled at Constantinople, any chance traveller was always lodged at the house of some resident, if he could get an introduction through his consul. He himself had taken in a great many travellers, some of illustrious names. He related to us that once the English consul was returning from Persia to England with an infant child and its nurse. The consul had just lost his wife, and the nurse being indispensable to the life of the child, could only be induced to undertake the journey to England on condition that her husband should accompany her. Mrs Hanson put the nurse and child into a comfortable bedroom, and before going to bed herself went to see if the child was well taken care of. To her surprise she found the bedding all removed, and upon looking about to see what had become of it, and also of the nurse and child, discovered all three under the bedstead, and nurse and child fast asleep. The woman had never before slept on a bedstead, and feared that she or the baby, or perhaps both, would roll off in the night. She thought, however, the bedstead would make a good canopy.

I went one day to the British cemetery at Scutari. It was kept in excellent order by Sergeant Lyne of the Royal Engineers. The cemetery is beautifully situated on the Sea of Marmora, opposite Stamboul, and some fifty or sixty feet above the sea. There was an apparatus in the grounds for meteorological observations, and Sergeant Lyne presented me with two or three little books giving the result of those made during the years 1868, 1869, and 1870. They show the great range of temperature that takes place at Constantinople. I must add that the British cemetery is just out of the current which usually blows down the Bosphorus, and is open to the south. The thermometer is placed in the orthodox way, four feet from the ground, in the open air, and under a sort of penthouse-lid, which shields it from the sun. The highest temperature during the month of June 1869 was 103°, in July 94°, in August 99°. The lowest in the same year was, in January 13°, and in February 27°.

CHAPTER XII.

Beicos—The Giant's Mountain—The Pasha's taste for building—Greek boatmen—Leave the Bosphorus—Crowded state of the Masr—Voyage—Story of a pilgrimage to Mecca—Arrival off Alexandria—Go to the Hôtel de l'Europe—Journey to Cairo—We are sent to the New Hotel—Lessons at the harem begin, my pupil being shut up.

One of the most charming of the many delightful excursions in the vicinity of Constantinople is that to Beicos and up the Giant's Mountain. It is a very favourite resort for all classes, natives as well as foreigners. It is on the Asiatic side of the Bosphorus, and nearly opposite Buyukdere. We took a caïque across, being about three-quarters of an hour's row; and after passing through the village of Beicos, entered a broad lovely valley, in the centre of which was a road planted with trees, affording a pleasant shade. After half an hour's walk through the valley we came to a fountain under a large oak-tree, and about ten minutes' walk farther on, a road turned off sharply to the left, taking a circuitous route up the hill. The ascent was rather rough and stony, but the views were quite beautiful. The trees generally arched overhead, so that it was very lovely, even before we came to the views. When we reached the summit, we felt ourselves amply repaid for the long walk. To the north were the shores of the Bosphorus, with the picturesque ruin of Anadol Kavak in the foreground, and a large space of the Black Sea; to the south the windings of the channel were closed in by Roumeli-Hissar. But the rich vegetation, the undulating hills, and the blue waters, with the dark mass of cypresses on different heights, cannot be described. I timed our descent, which took an hour and ten minutes from the starting to reaching the boat; but, of course, we were longer going up. People usually make the excursion in bullock-carts—that is, in a kind of waggon without springs, drawn by white oxen; but we always preferred walking when we could manage it. On our way up this mountain, in a lovely, shady, but very narrow road, we met a bull coming down at a rapid pace and alone. At seeing us he shied, and we certainly shied too; but finding out, luckily, that he was afraid of us, we stood quite still, and on he went.

The Pasha, who quite inherited his father's taste for building, but was unable as yet to gratify it by constructing palaces, spent his hours of recreation in building a tiny house in a corner of our little garden. It did not add to the beauty of our surroundings, but it was an immense amusement to him. He rushed out at every interval between his lessons, and was to be seen with a trowel in his hand plastering about the mortar, and directing two or three Arab servants who were labouring for him. One day when thus engaged, the Russian Ambassador came to pay him a visit. He entered at the gate close to the little mud hut where the Pasha was at work; but, of course, he never thought of looking in that dirty corner for his Highness Ibrahim Pasha! But the Pasha saw him from his little corner; and directly the Ambassador had passed, he ran out by the same gate, and having performed his ablutions, entered calm and dignified by another door!

There were two lovely little girls on a visit at the harem. They were the children of the Viceroy's eldest daughter, who was married to Monsoor Pasha. These little creatures had an English nurse, and in their rambles about the garden, attended by their nurse and two or three eunuchs, they often met Mrs Freeland's children, with whom they were delighted to play. Tony, the youngest of the boys, was an exceedingly pretty little fellow, very small, but with pluck enough for a man; and as soon as the little girls saw him, they always ran joyfully to meet him. They spoke a little English, but very little, and so mixed in a good deal of Turkish with their prattle. But Tony, though he received their advances graciously, was a true Briton, and tolerated no foreign lingo. "Don't talk that nonsense to me," he would say rather roughly; "speak English!" so they did their best. One day as Mr Freeland was passing in front of the palace he heard cries of "Papa! papa!" proceeding from behind the lattice-work blinds. They came from these children, who, having heard Tony apply that epithet to him, supposed it to be the name by which he was generally known.

We took a caïque one day and went to visit the Turkish lady whom I had met on the Mahroussah. She lived at Courouchesme on the Bosphorus, between Arnoutkeui and Ortakeui. It was a large house by the water-side, and as is usual in Turkish houses, that for the men is separate from that for the women, no man having access to the latter but the master of the house. Our caïque stopped just in front of the harem, and we sent our dragoman Shaheen ashore to ask if the lady could receive us. He went straight to the *selamlik* (house for the men), but of course they could tell him nothing and referred him to the harem. Shaheen had been brought up under the shadow of the harem, and though he had been living for years with English people, he had a strong sense of the indecorum of making any inquiry concerning women, so he returned to us with a troubled countenance, and muttered something quite unintelligible. We pointed out to him that he had gone to the wrong door, that it was into the harem we were going, not into the *selamlik*, and told him to knock there. Thus goaded on, he went to the harem door; but I suppose the absence of a eunuch at the gate told him that it would be answered by a woman, for the moment he had knocked he shot off to some little distance, and stood with his back turned to the door.

Presently it was opened, but no one was visible. Shaheen knew, however, that one or two women were concealed behind it; so at the discreet distance at which he had placed himself, and still keeping his back turned, he made his inquiries, and the party behind the door responded.

The lady was at home, and we were admitted, and passed through several rooms, which to European eyes were unfurnished, since there was nothing in them but divans round the walls and matting on the floors; the everlasting lattice-work blinds at the windows, which turn a bright day into a dull one, and a dull day into twilight. Presently we were ushered into the room where Nafia Hanem sat, and she received us very kindly and courteously. She spoke French in the old polite style, and she had with her a lady of whom she had learnt it, a Levantine of French extraction, who had resided with her several years. First cigarettes were brought us, then coffee, and before we left, some sweet drink which was not bad.

No books lay about, no work, evidently there was no feminine employment whatever, except the indispensable household duties, from which no woman except those of the highest rank can be exempted. There was something to me inexpressibly melancholy in these harems; there was a want of air and light, of recreation and of intellectual employment.

One of my favourite walks at Constantinople was the Atmeidan, the ancient Hippodrome. There is the splendid Mosque of Sultan Ahmed (called the Ahmedyeh) with its six minarets, the only one in the Ottoman empire containing that number, as St Sophia has only four. The Hippodrome occupies a beautiful site, and in the time of the Greek empire it is said that more gods and heroes were there to be found, carved in stone or moulded in brass, than there are inhabitants in the modern city. It is now much restricted in size, as it formerly occupied part of the space taken up by the Mosque of Sultan Ahmed. It still retains the form of a circus, and the space was first planned out by the Emperor Severus. Many nations conspired at different times to rob this magnificent site of the treasures of art there accumulated. Many unrivalled masterpieces of antiquity disappeared at the time of the conquest of Constantinople by the Latins in 1204, under Baldwin and Dandolo. The rows of seats of white marble were carried off in the reign of Solyman the Magnificent, and the marble columns were used as building materials for the Mosque of Suleimanyeh. Then there was a brick column, now all dilapidated, but then covered with plates of gilt bronze and ornamented with bas-reliefs, which from the weight and value of the metal excited the cupidity of depredators, and was stripped of the bronze plates.

There is also a fine obelisk brought from Egypt, by Theodosius, and bearing an inscription in Greek and Latin on the base, to this purport—that the obelisk was raised in thirty-two days by the prætor Proclus, and the machines used in raising it are represented in bas-relief.

As I returned from one of these visits to Constantinople, I got into a steamer as usual at the bridge, and sitting on the upper deck, was amusing myself with looking at the unrivalled views on all sides. There had been a good deal of wind all day, but the atmosphere had been quite clear. As we left the bridge, four steamers started at the same time—one for Princes' Islands, one for Kadikeui, one for the Asiatic side of the Bosphorus, and one for the European side. I was on the last; and such a screaming of engines and volumes of black smoke arose as made the atmosphere suddenly appear rather like that of Newcastle or Wolverhampton than the shores of the Bosphorus. It was like a thick fog, and was, I think, occasioned partly by the great number of steamers crowded in one place, and partly by the very inferior quality of the coal used in them.

Two things would be wonderful improvements in Constantinople: one, to have a new company of steamers to destroy the monopoly of the old; and the other, to have separate quays for the different lines of steamers. At present all start from this tumble-down old bridge, which is quite inadequate to the traffic.

I went once only into the bazaars of Constantinople, which did not please me at all. They are all covered, as rain is so much more frequent in Turkey than in Egypt; but I was so persecuted by men wishing to act as guides, and had such difficulty to steer clear of the dogs that lie about, that I was rather glad to get away from them. I think the bazaars of Constantinople much less interesting than those of Cairo.

I heard a great many stories of the misbehaviour of Greek boatmen, which made me congratulate myself upon always having to do with Turks. An Englishman, an engineer in the Viceroy's service (then engaged in the Mahroussah, moored in front of the palace), told us that the evening before he had been at Bebek, and going down to the shore at about 11 P.M. to seek a caïque to take him back to the vessel, he found only one boat there, and the man to whom it belonged had so villanous a countenance that the friend who was accompanying him to the boat hesitated to leave him in such company. But the engineer said he did not mind, that he must get on board, and there was no other caïque, so his friend left him;

and having made a bargain with the boatman, they started on their voyage. They had not got far when the engineer discovered that the boatman was drunk. (He was a Greek, not a Turk.) He stood up in the boat, at the imminent risk of upsetting it, and refused to pull another stroke unless he received three medjidies instead of the one he had bargained for. (A medjidie is 3s. 7½d.) The engineer called out angrily to him to sit down; but this producing no effect, and reflecting that in case of an upset he could not swim, he thought it better to compromise, so held up two fingers to signify that he would give two medjidies, and then the Greek took to his oars again, and pulled to the Mahroussah. Arrived there, the engineer first got safely out on to the steps of the vessel; and then with one hand gave the man the medjidie he had bargained for, while with the other he soundly boxed his ears. The boatman certainly well deserved it; but the engineer was by his own account a very pugnacious fellow, and he was always telling some story the end of which was sure to be, "So I knocked him down!"

It was now the first week in October, and the weather was getting autumnal. It was something like a cool September in England, delightful for all excursions; though the days were getting shorter, which was the only drawback. We were constantly expecting the order for our return. At last it came, and we were told we were to go on board the Masr, one of the steam-yachts belonging to his Highness, which was moored in front of the palace. Our pupils were to return on the Mahroussah with the second Princess.

We went to look at the accommodation on the Masr, and were very well satisfied with it. The Mahroussah had been built (in England) expressly for his Highness and his harem, so that every possible accommodation was given to them, and the rest was little regarded, speed being the chief consideration. The Masr had also splendid harem apartments; but there were many excellent cabins all over the ship. There was no raised deck, only one from the stern to the fore; and the bulwarks were high, which rather impeded the view. The windows in the cabins were large, so I hoped to see something of the land we might pass, while dressing in the morning. We took our cabins, and our luggage was sent on board. This was on the 12th of October; but we did not start for a couple of days later. I do not know why.

On the evening of the 13th, all the harem, except the immediate attendants of the second Princess and her children, went on board. This was principally that they might not be seen, as at night no one is about, and the hour of embarkation being only known in the harem, they get on board unseen. It entails a good deal of trouble in the daytime, as soldiers or eunuchs are stationed holding up canvas, to screen them from observation. Even by this contrivance the ladies cannot be concealed from the many caïques that are on the Bosphorus, so this embarkation by night disposed of a great many difficulties.

As it was, the canvas screens would only be required for the second Princess and her train, which comprised several visitors who had been invited to pass the winter in Egypt, in order to be present at four royal marriages, which were to take place at the beginning of the new year (Gregorian calendar).

We, the educational staff, and Mrs Freeland and her children, went on board the Masr on the morning of the 14th, and were much annoyed to find that one of the cabins which we had taken had been appropriated to some one else. The disagreeable part of these journeys was that there was no one to regulate and arrange as on European ships. Numbers of people came on board who had no right whatever to be there; they knew some official, and obtained a passage by favour. The captain had no list of passengers given to him; there were so many cabins, and whoever arrived first got possession of them. He was very civil to us, and did what he could; but he had no power to expel the intruders, so we were obliged to manage as we could.

At 3 P.M. the second Princess and all her party went on board the Mahroussah. The Masr had been moored with the prow towards the Black Sea; but upon the signal being given, it turned slowly round and steamed down the Bosphorus, following the Mahroussah. At 3.30 we passed the ruined fortress of Roumeli-Hissar; at 3.50 we were off Seraglio Point; and at four we had the Seven Towers on the right, and the lovely group of Princes' Islands on our left. Then we were out in the Sea of Marmora. It was bright moonlight; but the bulwarks were so high, and the deck so encumbered, that we could only see the coast when in a standing posture.

At 4.55 the next morning we were passing the lighthouse in the Dardanelles, and at a quarter to eight we were off the southern part of Mitylene; an hour after we were between Mitylene and Scio. There is a peak near the north end, which makes it a sort of landmark; behind this is a promontory, which forms the western boundary of the Bay of Smyrna, and which stands out behind, but a little in advance of Scio: in another hour we entered the passage between the little island of Psara and Scio, and were nearly two hours coasting the latter. These islands are all mountainous and picturesque, but most of them look bare, along the coast at any rate; there may be fertile valleys between the hills, but they are not seen from the sea. At 1.30 P.M. we were nearing the island of Nicaria, and did not finally lose sight of it until sunset. It is a conspicuous object from its length and mountainous outline. After passing Nicaria, we saw several smaller islands on both sides, and one to the left was Patmos, where St John wrote the Revelation.

On the 16th when we went on deck no land was visible; we had passed Rhodes and Scarpanto in the night, and were now in the open sea. The thermometer, which I had kept hanging in my cabin, had gradually risen higher and higher. When I went on board on the Monday it was 69°, on Tuesday 74°, and on Wednesday it was 79°. This was to prepare us for Egypt, for I knew from the experience of the preceding year that October was a very hot month there.

The deck was very crowded and dirty. I wonder what an English sailor would say to their mode of washing it! They throw down a quantity of water, and then drag along a piece of flannel to wipe it up!

At half-past ten o'clock on the 16th we stopped outside the harbour of Alexandria, as it is not considered safe for any vessel to enter the port at night. I got up early next morning, and was on deck as we went in. I thought the harbour presented a much more imposing appearance than it had done the year before when I arrived in the P. & O.

We did not get off before eleven, there was so much trouble in procuring our luggage; and though Shaheen was extremely useful on these occasions, we thought it safer to verify the due arrival of our trunks before leaving the vessel. The harem boxes were all to be got up first, and there were upwards of a thousand. I stood watching them drawn up, in hopes of catching sight of my own, but I did not until nearly all were out of the hold.

I heard a curious story while on board. Some years ago one of the so-called widows of the then late Sultan conceived a strong desire to make the pilgrimage to Mecca, but she could only do it as a married woman;

and, strange as it may appear, I was told that temporary marriages are often made by rich women for that purpose. So the lady in question married a poor man, and after the pilgrimage was accomplished she departed from her temporary husband, making him a handsome present in return for his protection.

A daughter was, however, the result of the connection, who was brought up by her mother, and received a good education. In the meanwhile the repudiated husband went to Egypt, entered the service of the Viceroy, and rose to rank and dignity. The mother died; and the father, now become a great man, conceived a wish to see his daughter, who was married, and had one or more children. So the lady was in the same vessel with us, in the part devoted to the harem, on her way to Egypt to visit the father whom she had never yet beheld.

As soon as we landed we went to the Hôtel de l'Europe, where we were told we were to stay for one night, and to proceed on the next day to Cairo. At the hotel we found Mr Michell, who had arrived from England *viâ* Brindisi on the same morning, and the P. & O. not being encumbered with harem boxes, the passengers were enabled to land long before we did.

The next day we went on to Cairo. It was very hot and dusty. We had been five months absent from Egypt, and I found the mosquitoes and sand-flies as tormenting as I had thought them the year before on my first arrival.

We were ordered to go to the New Hotel, and it was said we were not to inhabit the house at Choubrah again, at any rate for the present, as it was wanted to accommodate part of the suite of the Grand Duke Nicholas, who was coming to Egypt as soon as his visit to Constantinople was over. The Grand Duke himself was to be lodged at Kasr-el-Nuss, where Lord Dudley had been the year before, and which was only a few minutes' walk from our house. We had very good rooms at the New Hotel, and as we formed a large party among ourselves, we were better provided for than one person alone would have been; but we regretted very much the house at Choubrah, which had seemed so much more homelike to us all.

My dear little pupil was now "shut up." Her last day of liberty had been that on which she left Emirghian. Henceforward I was to go to her daily to give lessons in the harem. Where the Pasha's lessons were to take place we did not know: in Eastern countries you rarely know what is in store for you from one day to another.

On the third day after our arrival at Cairo, I was summoned to go to the harem. This, of course, I was prepared for; but I did not expect a messenger to come to my room at seven in the morning telling me a carriage was waiting below for me, with the Greek *lalla* who had been in the habit of escorting the Princess to and from Choubrah every day. I sent for the *lalla* and asked him why he had not given me notice the night before—that I had not yet breakfasted, &c., &c. He said that he knew nothing about it until he was told that morning he was to go for me, and he came at once. If I was not ready, I had only to say when I should be, and he would come again. I appointed nine o'clock, and he went away, saying he would be there at nine. I felt extremely nervous about this first lesson. I had heard much of the numerous interruptions in the harem, and though determined not to tolerate them, I could not be sure that they might not proceed from a quarter where resistance on my part would be hopeless.

At nine Lalla Jani came again and took me to the harem. His introduction was necessary to enable me to pass the outer gates; but my person and business once known to the eunuchs who sat there, there would be no further difficulty.

CHAPTER XIII.

Palace of Abdeen—Difficulties with harem carriage—I remonstrate—Am provided with another—Arab weddings—We leave the New Hotel and return to Choubrah—Eunuchs—Constant interruptions from the slaves—Baïram.

The palace of Abdeen, where the Khédive resides during the winter months, is situated at the southern extremity of Cairo. There is always palace-building going on somewhere in Cairo or its vicinity; and just at this time the palace of Abdeen was being considerably enlarged. My pupil was therefore lodged for the first month in a large house adjoining, which belonged to Ismael Sadyk Pasha, *then* Mouffettish (Minister of Finance), and in high favour, but a few years after disgraced and exiled to Dongola at the period of Mr Goschen's visit to Egypt.

There was a large archway, with double gates: the outer ones were open, and two or three eunuchs sat there; my business being explained by Lalla Jani, I was admitted through the second gate, and a eunuch took me across a wide courtyard into the harem, and to the apartments of my pupil.

I found the Princess and Kopsès waiting for me, with books and everything prepared. They were very quiet, and said nothing whatever of the change that had taken place in their condition since I last saw them.

The time of my going and coming was to be fixed by myself, and the Turkish and Arabic lessons were to be arranged accordingly. We consulted for some time about the hours; the Princess no longer rose so early as she had been accustomed to do when she came to us. Then she got up briskly, knowing she was coming out to liberty and change of scene; and even if she overslept herself, her attendants, who would be blamed if she were late, would, by opening the shutters and bustling about the room, contrive that she should awake, and then hurry through the process of dressing, so as to make up for lost time.

The Khédive was a very active man, and of early habits, and if his children wished to please him, they must not indulge in idleness. His wishes were laws to the Princess, who looked upon him as the greatest man that had ever existed.

But all this was changed in the harem, as I soon had occasion to see. Perhaps the Princess might have sat up late at night, and as a growing girl, she required much sleep. In the morning the rooms were all darkened, and not a sound was to be heard until the Princess became wide awake of her own accord, and called out to her slaves to come and dress her. There was one thing which might cause the slaves to arouse her. From the time of her seclusion in the harem, she always took breakfast, luncheon, and dinner with his Highness, but the time for the first meal was not very regular. His Highness transacted much business before breakfast, so that it might be late. Some one was on the watch to give notice when he was coming, and then if the Princess was sleeping, her attendants did not hesitate to awaken her, and hurry through the toilet.

I did not find this all out, however, on the first day, so after consultation I settled that I would come every morning at half-past eight, and leave at twelve.

I would willingly have stayed longer, but at twelve his Highness took luncheon, and the Princess took it with him. After luncheon there were the Turkish and Arabic[1] masters, so my pupils could do nothing with

---

[1] The lessons with the Turkish and Arabic masters took place in an apartment just outside the harem, but within the gates. The Princess

me. When we had settled the hour at which I was to come in the morning, we calculated its equivalent according to Turkish time (beginning each day at sunset), and the carriage was ordered to fetch me from the hotel at that hour.

The next morning at ten no carriage had arrived, so I sent Shaheen on a donkey to ask the reason. He returned shortly with the carriage, but upon my inquiring why it was so late, I was told it was because I had objected to going so early the day before! So no attention was paid to the order which the Princess had given. When I arrived at the palace, I found the Princess had been waiting for me more than an hour. I was much vexed, and requested that positive directions should be given to fetch me every morning at the time named. This was done, and the next morning a *carass* came to my room-door in the hotel at seven o'clock!

I swallowed a hasty breakfast, and went to the harem, where I found the Princess not dressed, and amazed at my coming so early. The eunuch had simply told the coachman he was to go earlier, so he thought he would come in time!

After ten days' stay at the New Hotel, we were told we were to return to Choubrah. In some respects we were sorry. We had, it is true, many more comforts in the house at Choubrah; but the position of the New Hotel is very fine, and its vicinity to the opera and the French theatre made it convenient. My windows faced the east. I saw the sun rise every morning over the Mokattam Hills, and in the evening I went up to the promenade on the roof to see it set. It is impossible to imagine a more animated scene than that upon which we looked down.

---

and her companion wore the *yashmak* and the *feridjee* (veil and cloak). It is the custom for *native* masters to give lessons in this manner to girls under fifteen, but no Frank would be admitted thus.

Every day Arab weddings passed, with a long file of carriages, in the last of which the bride was seated, with large shawls or carpets thrown across the windows to conceal her from the public gaze. Let us hope she can see, though she cannot be seen!

In the poorer weddings there are no carriages. All the party walk, accompanied by the clang of instruments, and the bride is in a sort of Jack-in-the-green, which screens her from the public gaze; but there is such a throng about her, and so much dust, that I think she must be stifled!

The day of our removal to Choubrah was the first of the new moon, and troops of men were going about the streets crying out, "To-morrow, Ramadan begins!" We had seen the effects of this formidable fast the year before, and by no means looked forward to it.

It had been a very high Nile in the previous summer, and the large garden belonging to our Choubrah house had been all under water. This occasioned the most abundant vegetation, but walking in it was hardly possible, and of course the moisture had brought its full proportion of insects. The evaporation from the damp ground caused my window-shutters to be quite wet when I opened them in the morning.

The same unpunctuality with the carriage went on in spite of the repeated orders of the Princess. It sometimes came an hour before the time, and sometimes an hour after. There was the same difficulty in getting away. One day I had already been waiting more than an hour, walking up and down a little terrace outside the harem, but within the gates, when a cry arose of "Effendina!" (Highness, or, our Lord), and half-a-dozen eunuchs rushed in to clear the way. I should have stood still, according to European fashion, and bowed as his Highness passed, but my pupil appeared directly at the door of the harem, and drew me gently into an apartment just at the entrance, while she herself waited the coming of her father. As the Khédive passed the room in which I was, he caught sight of the European dress, and I heard him ask his daughter who it was.

"It is my governess, who is waiting for the carriage to take her away."

"And why don't you order it?" said his Highness.

"I have done so, but they do not come."

"What! not obey my daughter!" said the Khédive.

He walked quickly towards the door, and called loudly that a carriage was to come up immediately. It was an hour and a quarter since it had been ordered, but at his Highness's command one was at the door in two or three minutes. On ordinary occasions I got in and out of the carriage without assistance; but his Highness had deigned to order it for me, and I was almost lifted into it by two eunuchs, as if I had been a paralytic.

When I got back to Choubrah, I determined to write a letter to the second Princess, and I asked the Pasha (who came regularly to his lessons) if he would give it to his mother, and translate it to her.

After I left, the Khédive questioned his daughter as to whether this delay with the carriage had ever happened before, and was told it was of daily occurrence. I did not know this when I wrote the letter.

I said in it that it was not the personal inconvenience to myself which induced me to trouble her Highness, but the serious interruption which it caused to her daughter's studies; that a much shorter time was given to them in the harem than had been devoted before her seclusion, and that even out of that short time more than an hour was every day sacrificed. The Pasha took the letter, and promised to read it to his mother.

The next morning, at eight o'clock, I was surprised to

see a pretty open carriage at the door, and to hear that some one was waiting to speak to me from Mourad Pasha. I went down, and was told that the Khédive had given orders that a carriage should be sent for me every morning at eight, and that it was to bring me back at twelve; that I was at liberty to order it whenever I wished for a drive in the afternoon, or to go to the opera or French theatre in the evening. This was highly satisfactory, and I felt now it would be my own fault if I were not punctual with the lessons.

When I arrived at the harem, my pupil told me what his Highness had said to her afterwards, so I scarcely knew whether the new arrangement was caused by my letter or the accidental arrival of the Khédive. Probably by both.

I had often heard it said that any one who made complaints in this country, however well founded, though they might obtain temporary redress, were sure in the end to get the worst of it.

For the first week or two I had a very nice carriage, then an inferior one was substituted, and I was told it was solely to take me to and from the harem daily, though it had been distinctly said at first that I was at liberty to use it at other times. This was, however, a matter of comparative indifference to me; my great object had been to ensure punctuality in the lessons, and that I had attained.

I believe the Khédive wishes to act fairly and liberally, but there is such a jealousy existing, first, between natives and foreigners, and, secondly, between the different nationalities, that the officials manage constantly to evade the Khédive's orders; and though you may sometimes succeed in making your complaint reach his ears, so as to obtain temporary redress, the tables are sure to be turned on you in the end.

I was told by a lady who held a post about one of the princesses, that she had repeatedly asked for a box at the opera, knowing that one was frequently given to the French *femmes de chambre* in the harem. One day she thought herself sure of one, as the Princess had given orders in her presence to a eunuch to go to the director at the opera, to reserve one for her. Upon going at night with her friends, she found that no box had been ordered, and there was no remedy but to pay for one, or to go away.

When she returned to the harem, she asked the eunuch to whom the order had been given why he had not obeyed his mistress, and he told her the head eunuch had forbidden him to stir out of the house, because the order had not been given through him!

We found the mosquitoes and sand-flies at Choubrah quite as numerous as they had been the year before, but their sting was not quite so venomous to us as it had been then.

I very much enjoyed my drive every morning to the harem, but oh, how I wished that my dear little pupils could have taken it with me! It really went to my heart to see them thus caged, because they had known what liberty was, and lost it just at the age when its deprivation would be felt the most.

Some persons have said to me, "How cruel to have given the Princess her liberty in childhood, and afterwards to shut her up in the harem!" but this is an unjust judgment. The Khédive did all that lay in his power to give his daughter careful and moral training in early youth, but he could not set aside the opinion of all Mahometans, which would have been outraged by her retaining that liberty when arrived at womanhood. Besides, the young Princess would not have been surrounded with the safeguards which accompany a European lady. No mother, or persons of her own rank, would have been with her,—none but foreigners,—always an unpopular spectacle in every country. By marrying her early, and then encouraging her gradually and innocently to introduce European customs, all was done that could reasonably be attempted; and had she lived, I believe a thorough change would in a few years have taken place in female society in Egypt.

One morning I found my pupil ill in bed, suffering from the throat, an indisposition to which she was very liable. Of course she could do no lessons, and at first she seemed unwilling that Kopsès should do any, saying that Kopsès would get on before her; but I counted nine persons round her bed, and said surely she did not want ten, so she gave up with her usual sweetness of temper, and Kopsès came with me.

We were constantly interrupted in our lessons by the slaves, who came in without scruple, sometimes talked either to my pupils or among themselves, and finally, finding themselves unnoticed, went away again, generally leaving all the doors open. As a rule all doors *are* left open; my shutting them was an innovation. I would willingly have locked them, but keys invariably get mislaid in the harem, so I was unable to do so.

Every Princess has a great many attendants attached to her person, whose business it is to amuse her, and to anticipate her every want. To leave her alone would be considered a shocking neglect. They do not sit down in her presence, unless bid to do so, which only happens to a highly favoured few. Thus no place is sacred from their intrusion; they cannot understand any one wishing to be alone and undisturbed. My pupils knew this well, so they never rebuked them. I do not think my Princess could have spoken sharply to any one, or it might have been stopped.

On this occasion, when alone with Kopsès, one intruder came in after another; and at last, as we were playing a duet, the door opened again for the seventh or eighth time, and, looking round, I saw a gentleman standing in the doorway. I forgot at the moment that I was in a harem, and my near sight prevented me from distinguishing who it was; but Kopsès immediately rose, and saying to me "His Highness!" walked to the door, and I heard him ask "where Zeyneb was." Of course I rose and made a low curtsey, and his Highness made me a polite bow, but he did not come in. I was rather vexed that the Princess was not there, as I should have been so glad for him to have seen the progress she had made.

We had hardly got back to our duet when the second Princess came in, attended by a dozen slaves. We again got up, and she asked me in Turkish how I was, and I was able to reply to that question, but could not remember one of the polite speeches which I had been assiduously getting up since I began lessons. She seemed fully aware of the importance of not interrupting, and begged us to go on, which we did; and after listening a few minutes, she went away.

A day or two after, she came again, when I was engaged with the Princess. She left all her attendants in the outer room, and came in very quietly, holding up her hand as a sign that we were to go on with our studies. She stood behind her daughter's chair, and listened while the latter read, and looked at her writing, seeming much pleased with her progress.

After a month, the alterations in the palace of Abdeen being completed, my pupil was removed there. It was only a few hundred yards from where I had gone before, but the entrance was a most disagreeable one at that time. You first had to pass through an outer court, in which were soldiers, grooms, carriages, carts, &c., &c.; then into a second full of eunuchs. Here you left the carriage; but there were several doors, and you did not know which to take to enter the harem. The first time I went I was accompanied by Shaheen, lest any difficulty should be made about admitting me. Three or four eunuchs were playing some game at the farther extremity of the courtyard. I went up to them and asked them by which door I should enter to gain access to the apartments of the Princess. He to whom I spoke did not turn round, but simply jerked his head in one direction. I went that way, but soon heard a loud call after me, and turning round, found he was pointing in the opposite direction. I changed my course, and upon passing through the door, got into a labyrinth of passages. I met several girls, but they did not appear to understand my inquiries, and at any rate did not answer them. At last I emerged upon an inner court, and after crossing that, found myself in some of the best apartments. Here my inquiries after the Princess were more successful, and I was presently led to her apartments. I asked her if it was necessary that I should come into the palace by the back way, and she seemed very much puzzled by what way I had come in. Kopsès was equally unable to give me any assistance, so I applied to Zohrab Bey. He told me that he himself always went in by that entrance, as, if I went to the chief gate, I might constantly find myself much delayed by the absence of the head eunuchs, and by the gate being locked. So I continued as I had begun; though it was a daily annoyance to me all the time I gave lessons at the palace of Abdeen, and I did not meet with this annoyance in any other palace. Later on, another far better entrance was made, but I had ceased to give lessons there then.

On the 1st of December Ramadan ceased, and on the 2d the Baïram began.

We went to pay our respects to the Princesses, as we had gone the year before.

I had asked permission of the second Princess to bring

some English friends with me, as travellers are always very desirous of being present at these festivals. The Princess had graciously consented, and we took three ladies with us. The usual coffee and pipes were given. We were seated in a row opposite to the princesses, and Mdlle. O. served as our interpreter. It was rather formidable, and after the customary inquiry after the health of the ladies, and wishing them a happy Baïram, we sat perfectly mute, unable to think of anything to say. Among Orientals it is the custom on these visits of ceremony to make elaborate inquiries respecting the health of each member of the family in turn; to this the hostess makes a gracious reply, and perhaps reciprocates the inquiry; then coffee is presented, and there is a sala'am before taking it and after; then come the pipes, which occupy some time, and again the sala'am before and after smoking.

The wives of his Highness have become aware that it is not the custom in Europe for the lady of the house to ask her visitors whether they are married or single; if the latter, why they remain so, and if the former, how many children they have. Such questions are still asked when the hostess is either very young or unaccustomed to receive European visitors; but the wives of his Highness remain quiet and dignified.

We had not even the resource of the weather, an unfailing topic of interest in England. It is always fine in Egypt; and we could not touch on any of the topics of the day, because the ladies of the harem neither read the newspapers nor mixed in society. Then more visitors arrived, and we came away.

It struck me on this second Baïram visit that everything looked more European than it had done the year before. The dresses of the slaves were made more in the French fashion. As to the princesses, they were always in full European costume.

The second day of the Baïram we went to the harem of Indji Hanem, widow of the late Viceroy, Saïd Pasha. This lady is generally called the Princess Saïd among Europeans, but Indji Hanem Effendi among Mahometans. She has been known for many years among Europeans for her kind and courteous manners towards them. She has always been particularly accessible to strangers, is an admirable mistress to her own household, and is universally popular among all classes. She has been mentioned in the books of several European travellers who have had the privilege of visiting her. Miss Martineau speaks of her in 1845 as "the lovely wife of Saïd Pasha." When I first saw her in 1872, this beauty was of course on the wane; but upon seeing her, you were at once impressed with the conviction that her attractions must have been considerable, and her commanding height and dignified deportment made her still conspicuous in any assembly. She had adopted in her palace many European improvements which conduce to sanitary reform, and her table was served *à la franque;* but she, in her own person, kept to the native fashion of dressing. The material might be of the richest description, but it was worn loose, and confined at the waist by a girdle or an Indian shawl.

The Princess Saïd had a regular entertainment for us. She knew that European visitors wanted to see the amusements of harem life, and she always gratified this wish. So after the pipes and coffee a few slaves came in with musical instruments, and seating themselves on the floor, on one side of the room, began to play and sing. The instruments were all of a primitive description, the chief being the tambourine.

Then five girls came in, and danced for about a quarter of an hour. They were in pale pink silk dresses, in the Turkish fashion—that is to say, loose, confined at the

K

waist by a band, high up to the throat, and the skirt forming trousers, which, however, are not easily detected, as they are exceedingly full. They are made in this way, —suppose one of our full skirts (not gored) sewn up at the bottom like a bag, with a small opening left at each side sufficient to admit the foot. This dress is so remarkably decent, that, although the dances usually end with a somersault, there is no further display than the soles of the feet! The dance was by no means remarkable either for grace or agility. The girls followed each other in a row, the foremost deciding the step and movements, their long hair flowed down their backs, and was shaken from side to side. The inevitable somersault terminated the performance. There was a constant succession of visitors arriving and departing; but the Princess Saïd was not at all got up for the occasion, being handsomely but very plainly dressed.

CHAPTER XIV.

Opera—Four royal marriages announced as to take place during the winter—Old Cairo, Nilometer and Mosque of Amrou—Procession of the Mahmal—Mosque of Sultan Hassan—Drive to Heliopolis—Weather changes—Cold and wet—Funerals—Departure of the pilgrims for Mecca—We are told we are to leave Choubrah—Remove to the New Hotel—Arrival of two of the Princes from England—Curious instance of forgetting one's own language—Photography in the harem—Royal trousseaux—Wedding fêtes begin—Marriage contracts.

My pupil told me that she could now give me a box whenever I wished to go to the opera, so I availed myself of this offer frequently. The *mise en scène* of the opera at Cairo is really excellent, everything is so perfectly clean and fresh. The director of course manages everything, but all expenses which the general receipts do not cover are made up by the Khédive. I was told upon good authority, though I cannot pretend to vouch for the accuracy of the figures, that £75,000 came from the viceregal purse the year before. There is no expense for supernumeraries, for the Khédive's band is always in attendance, and the soldiers make up a magnificent procession in Aïda, and in other pieces. The ballet is always beautifully given, both as regards the dancing and scenic effect. Beretta Vieni was the *première danseuse* of that season. Then, in addition to the salaries and various operatic expenses, the chief *artistes* received at their departure handsome presents from the Khédive, his wives, and married daughters, as his Highness is desirous of attracting first-rate talent to Cairo.

We were told that four royal marriages were to take place during the winter, and rather a new state of things was to be inaugurated with them. Mohammed Ali had had the same kind of harem as the Sultan, consisting exclusively of slaves, and this custom had been continued by his successors down to the Khédive. But the latter in mature age wished to adopt the European law of one wife, and direct succession from father to son, instead of the old Mussulman custom of inheritance through the eldest male of the family. The second he succeeded in establishing, by fixing the succession in the person of his eldest son, Mohammed Tewfik Pasha, and the first, by restricting each of his sons to one wife of equal rank with himself.

Among the descendants of Mohammed Ali there are many to choose from. To Tewfik Pasha, the eldest son, was given Amina Hanem, the daughter of Elhami Pasha, and the great-great-granddaughter of Mohammed Ali. To Hussein Pasha, the second son, was given Ain-el-

Heiât, the daughter of Ahmed Pasha, elder brother of the Viceroy, and great-granddaughter of Mohammed Ali. To Hassan Pasha, third son of the Khédive, was given Khadija Hanem, the granddaughter of Mohammed Ali (her father bearing the same name as her grandfather). The Khédive's second daughter, Fatma Hanem, was to be married to Toussoun Pasha, son of the late Viceroy, Saïd Pasha, and grandson of Mohammed Ali. We were told that the festivities in honour of each marriage were to last a week, so that a whole month would be devoted to *fêtes* and rejoicings.

I drove one afternoon to Old Cairo to visit the island of Rhoda, and see there the palace formerly inhabited by Mohammed Ali, and also the Nilometer which is constructed on the island to mark the height which the waters attain each year. We went down a great many steps before we reached the level of the water. It had risen in the previous season to the top step, and had been considered a good Nile.

When we left the island we drove to the oldest mosque in Egypt—and indeed the most ancient monument of Islamism—that of Amrou, commenced in 620. It has the aspect of a vast cloister; round the sides are several rows of columns, and in the centre is a large open space with a fountain for ablutions. In a climate where the sky was always serene, an open temple was most appropriate: the pillars are of marble and granite; there are two so close together that the Mahometans have a tradition that only the good can pass between them. Shaheen contrived to squeeze himself through, but I do not think many Turks could do so, as they are generally fatter than the Arabs.

We went again to the procession of the Mahmal, but this time to a different spot—a little beyond the mosque of Sultan Hassan. There was the same old sheikh rolling his head; and I thought his bare neck and shoulders must have been very cold, as everybody else drew their cloaks well around them. He had thick grizzled whiskers and beard.

After the procession had passed, we went into the mosque of Sultan Hassan, one of the handsomest in Cairo. It was built in 1354, and Macrizi tells us that it was three years in construction, and that a thousand gold millikals were spent on it daily. It is falling to decay, as no one ever seems to think of repairing these monuments of past ages. There is a beautiful marble pavement in mosaic, but it is a good deal injured.

In the afternoon we drove to Heliopolis. It is a very pretty drive by Abbassieh and Kouba, through shady avenues almost all the way; but no vestige remains of the ancient city except the obelisk, which is on such low ground that it is not visible until you are close upon it. Like Memphis, its ruins have been appropriated to construct new edifices; and none of the mighty remains are to be seen which still exist in Upper Egypt.

As we drove back we came upon the procession of the Mahmal encamping in tents upon the open ground near Abbassieh. The tent in which the Mahmal was, was not high enough to cover it, and like the tree in the Exhibition of '51, it came out at the top.

For some days we had rather stormy weather—high winds and frequent rain. During the first three days the pilgrims are encamped in the neighbourhood of Abbassieh, three or four miles to the north of Cairo; then they move to a place called Birket-el-Hadj, or Lake of the Pilgrims (though no lake is there); and by that time, all stragglers being assembled, they make the final start for Mecca. It is very difficult to find out when the camp breaks up and the real departure to Mecca commences. Mr Michell was very anxious to witness it; and riding out one morning, he, after a couple of hours, came up to them just as a gun

fired and they began their march. He said there were
several thousands, and that the line of march extended
half a mile in depth. He tried to form an idea of the
numbers, and had counted two hundred camels, when he
was obliged to give up the attempt on account of their
irregular movements. There were eleven litters, which
doubtless contained women. There were no Europeans to
see the start (indeed it is very difficult to find out when it
will be); and Mr Michell told me he had made two un-
successful attempts in former years. He did not like to
go very near, as he saw many unfriendly looks cast at
him. A few years ago, if a European had thus ventured
among them, he would have been pelted at the least; but
now it is easier to see such things.[1]

On Christmas Day a grand funeral procession passed
our house at Choubrah.

I heard the noise at some distance—the hum of voices
produced by a multitude of persons, mingled with the
shrill wail of women. I looked out in time to see the
whole procession.

First came a number of Arabs on foot, and four camels
laden with large bags filled with provisions. A man rode
on each of the camels behind the bags, and distributed
from them oranges, dates, and bread to the multitude of
followers. This is always customary, as they have a long
way to walk, and require food to support them. After the
camels came a number of soldiers; and lastly, the bier,
with several women wailing and making a dismal noise;

[1] This was in the latter part of December 1872; but in the 'Times' of
December 7, 1876, is an excellent article written by Mr Michell, describing
the breaking up of the encampment, and the final departure of the pilgrims
from Birket-el-Hadj. The article is headed "Pilgrims to Mecca." Lane,
in his 'Modern Egyptians,' says it takes thirty-seven days to travel across
the desert from Cairo to Mecca; and as these travellers were using the
same means of locomotion as their forefathers, they probably took the
same time.

then immediately behind the bier were the chief mourners, and a crowd of Arabs closed the procession.

It was so long that I felt sure it must be some person of rank; and it proved to be the grandson of Mohammed Ali, and the half-brother of the young lady about to be married to Hassan Pasha.

On the 6th of January (1873) Zohrab Bey came to announce to us that his Highness wished us to move at once to the New Hotel, as the house at Choubrah was wanted for some distinguished visitors from Constantinople, who were expected shortly, and would be present at the approaching weddings. Now this packing up would give us as much trouble as if we were going to leave the country. Nothing was to be left behind: a Mahometan household was about to be established there for a time, and the probability was that all the furniture we had used would be turned out of the house.

We had capital wardrobes, book-cases, tables of all sorts and shapes—some for use, others for ornamental knick-knacks. If we left anything, Zohrab Bey told us, it was at our own risk; there would be no one responsible for it. If it were of any use it would be appropriated; if not, it would be thrown away.

This was a great trouble to us. Mrs Freeland had tables covered with all sorts of little ornaments, and I had quantities of books, which were then well arranged in an excellent book-case, and always accessible, and were now to be packed up in boxes, which renders them practically useless. Every one knows what packing is when you have to take with you everything belonging to you. We almost envied the Mahometan ladies, who keep their possessions always in boxes, and having no tables strewed with books, music, and the thousand trifles indispensable to us Europeans, are always ready for removal at an hour's notice.

Mrs Freeland had two English maids, and though they were kept tolerably occupied with the three children (the youngest of whom was about two years old), they were still able to help her to a certain degree; but I had no one, and at the end of my labours began to realise something of what a railway porter may experience after a hard day's work. We knew we should have good rooms at the New Hotel, but we could not tell how long we should stay there, and then there would be another exodus. All the rooms on the first floor at the New Hotel were occupied, so we went to the second, which I preferred, as the view was better. We had good apartments; and as we *were* to move, it was lucky we came when we did, as ten days after the hotels were all crowded, and remained so throughout the winter.

The house at Choubrah was so well built that I had never felt cold during my first winter. The second and third winters I spent mostly at the New Hotel, and that was full of draughts, and the sun never penetrated into the rooms, owing to the great balcony which surrounded both the first and second storeys on three sides of the building.

There was one great advantage, however, which I highly appreciated, and that was the promenade at the top of the house, from whence you had an extensive view for miles around, and also saw everything that passed in the road between the hotel and the Ezbekeah Gardens.

We are very apt to forget any plague after its cessation, however it may have tormented us while it lasted. I had been more than a week at the New Hotel before I remembered accidentally that the mosquitoes had disappeared. I had not felt one for nearly a month!

As my windows faced the east, I always saw the sun rise over the Mokattam Hills. On the 12th of January it rose at five minutes past seven, and I watched it set (from the top of the hotel) a little to the west of the Pyramids of Ghizeh at a quarter past five.

At the harem nothing was talked of but the approaching weddings. Prince Hassan was daily expected from England, and a surprise awaited him.

It had been said that he was to go round the world, as the Duke of Edinburgh had done; and when he arrived in Egypt, believing he was about to make the grand tour, he was informed that he was to be married! In all countries princes have very little choice in the selection of a wife, but they have probably heard something of her or seen her picture or photograph. In the reign of our present sovereign Queen Victoria princes have had a much freer choice, but that can never be among Mahometans unless their customs are completely changed and the seclusion of women abolished.

With Hassan Pasha came a younger (half) brother, Mahmoud Bey. The latter had been sent to England to be educated, and had been absent two years and two months. His mother begged the Khédive to allow her son to visit Egypt, and his Highness had given permission to have him brought with Hassan Pasha—the gentleman who had undertaken his education accompanying him. Mahmoud Bey had in the space of two years and two months acquired English, but entirely forgotten his native language (or rather languages, since Turkish is always spoken in the viceregal harems, and Arabic is the language of the country). Upon his arrival at Cairo he was taken directly to see his father; the boy ran up to him, first kissed his hand, and then threw his arms round his neck. His Highness is a very affectionate father; he was much pleased with the boy, and said something to him directly in Turkish, upon which Mahmoud Bey turned to his brother and said, "Tell him I do not understand FRENCH." This being translated amused his Highness very much, and presently after, seeing the boy standing there with his hands in his pockets gazing about on the to him unusual scene with the most perfect indifference and self-possession, he again laughed heartily, upon which Mahmoud Bey said to his brother, "If you both stand there laughing at me I shall run away." His Highness was altogether much pleased with his son; but as he was vexed at his having so entirely forgotten Turkish and Arabic, he gave orders that he should every day be sent to the palace of Kasr-el-Ali, the residence of the Queen-Mother, where the mother of Mahmoud Bey also resided, that by intercourse with his mother and her attendants he might again recover his lost mother tongue.[1]

Directly after their arrival the two brothers, Hassan Pasha and Mahmoud Bey, visited his Highness's harem and remained there for some hours. This was quite an innovation, as formerly grown-up sons would not have been admitted to their father's harem.

Prince Hassan sat in a corner with his two half-sisters, the Princesses Fatma and Zeyneb, and Mahmoud Bey finding to his great joy that Kopsès could speak English, ran about with her. His remarks were all thoroughly English, and I was so glad that my pupil should see and talk to her brothers, because his Highness not understanding English, she was apt to lay much more stress on French (which she always spoke with her father).

Mahmoud Bey lived with his brother Hassan Pasha at Kasr-el-Nuss, but everybody spoke either French, Turkish, or Arabic, not one of which languages did he understand.

---

[1] I may here incidentally mention that he never did recover it, but had to learn it as if it had been a new language to him; and, principally on that account, he never returned to England, but has remained up to the present time in Egypt.

When he went to his mother it was the same thing—nothing but Turkish spoken. "It is a jolly place," he told Kopsès, "and they let me run about as I like, but I wish you were there to talk with me."

My pupil had several photograph-books, and one contained only portraits of the ladies of the harem. Photography was quite a mania all the while I was in Egypt, and as the princesses could not be taken by any of the chief photographers of the town, women went into the harem to exercise the art. Some of the photographs thus taken were passable, but none first-rate.

The Princess was showing her photographs to her brother Hassan Pasha, and when she had done with all the public characters, she came to this particular book of the ladies of the harem. Each photograph was named, and comments made, when suddenly the Princess put her hand hastily down on one and tried to turn over the page. Hassan Pasha rightly conjectured that this photograph concerned him more nearly than any of the others; so he caught up the book and ran away to get the photograph out. His sister pursued him, laughing and calling for help, and at last got the book back again, though not before he had possessed himself of the photograph, which was, indeed, that of his intended bride, and quite pretty enough to charm any unoccupied heart.

Apropos of photographs, I must relate something which had amused me exceedingly the previous winter, when my pupil still came to me at Choubrah. Both she and her brother Ibrahim Pasha were always buying photograph-books and filling them. The Pasha's first book was occupied by the crowned heads and leading statesmen of Europe. Mr Michell had written the names under each, so that the Pasha might become familiarised with their countenances. After a time he bought a handsomer book, and the crowned heads were promoted to it, while their places were filled up by others. Each book he bought was handsomer than the last, and as he was always shifting the photos, Mr Michell had long discontinued writing their names. One day soon after my arrival I was looking over these books, when I came upon one belonging to the Pasha full of ballet-dancers. There was one of an acrobat taking a flying leap in the air, and under it was written "The Emperor William of Germany"; another of a *première danseuse* in the act of making a pirouette, with one foot on a level with her head—that was written "Prince Bismarck"; another of an actress personating a very roguish-looking page—that was "The Emperor Napoleon," &c., &c. They were all placed quite undesignedly by the Pasha, who paid no attention to the names written underneath.

We were told that our house at Choubrah was inhabited by fourteen Turks, and that one was a great personage, as he ate alone. He must have been of the old school of Turks, as none of the Khédive's family ever eat alone. Mr Michell had left his two horses in the stables, having been told by Zohrab Bey that he might safely do so; but upon going one evening to see that they were properly cared for, he found they had been turned out into the garden to make room for horses provided for the Turks!

The time for the four royal weddings was approaching, and the harem was astir with the preparations for the trousseaux. Every morning as I entered I saw no end of chests and boxes filled with the household necessaries. I had a private view of the plate and jewels for each bride, but as they were pretty much the same in each instance, I will only particularise one, which was that of the Princess Fatma, second daughter of his Highness. In a large saloon were thirty or forty women all carefully arranging the jewels on crimson velvet cushions. There were tiaras, bracelets, necklaces, brooches, medallions, clasps, buckles, butterflies, earrings, and sprays, all of gold and diamonds, a massive gold circlet for the waist with an immense diamond clasp. There were other precious stones, but diamonds greatly predominated, as being the most costly. Over each cushion was firmly fixed a wirework cover which looked like lace, and while protecting the jewels allowed them to be seen. I was then taken to two other rooms which were kept locked, and were full of stands on which were arranged the different articles of gold and silver plate for the new *ménage*. There were about sixty stands, on which were dishes, plates, looking-glasses (of silver and gold), the little jewelled filigree gold cups for coffee, amber mouthpieces for pipes, &c., &c. The plate was, like the jewels, secured by wire covers which allowed them to be seen.

The trousseau for each wedding was on a certain day carried through the town under an escort of soldiers. The streets through which it passed, and the balconies to the houses and hotels, were lined with people to witness the spectacle, which the fine wire covers guarded but did not conceal.

On Thursday, the 16th of January, the wedding *fêtes* began. The marriage-contract was signed between Mohammed Tewfik Pasha (eldest surviving son of the Khédive) and Amina Hanem, daughter of Elhami Pasha, and great-great-granddaughter of Mohammed Ali, the founder of the dynasty.

No ceremony, either religious or civil, is performed in presence of *both* the contracting parties. A large party of relations and friends on both sides are assembled in the house of the parents of the bride. The gentlemen are in the *selamlik*, the ladies in the harem. The bridegroom signs the contract in presence of witnesses, and two or three of the most influential persons (generally relatives) go into the harem to obtain from the bride's own lips authority to sign the contract in her name. These gentlemen are preceded by a couple of eunuchs crying "*Dustoor!*" which signifies "Get out of the way, attend to Mahometan customs," and all women hide themselves as the gentlemen approach. The bride is in an inner room, surrounded by her nearest relations and friends; the door is ajar, but a thick curtain is drawn before it. The gentlemen stop outside, and one of them asks the important question, "N., wilt thou have this man to be thy wedded husband?" There is a dead silence, for, willing or unwilling, it is not etiquette for the lady to be so easily won. After a pause the question is repeated, and again there is no response.

Now I have been told that if there is no reply to the third time of asking, there is an end of the business, and the parties all go home again without any marriage taking place. I don't suppose this often occurs, but there is a long pause between the second and third times of asking, to give time for the ladies to work on the bride, and induce her to pronounce the equivalent to " I will." At last it is said, and then the gentlemen go back to the *selamlik*, and the contract is signed. In the weddings I am about to describe, a royal salute in each case announced the accomplishment of the signature.

There was plenty of movement in the streets on this day, gay harem carriages flitting about, their occupants distinctly visible in their gleaming *yashmaks* and bright-coloured *feridjees;* but there were no regular *fêtes* to which Europeans were invited. The house of the bride was filled with friends, and a few European or Levantine ladies might be invited, such as the wives of the various consuls, or any one like myself connected with the household.

It happened that the annual races began on this day, and, irrespective of travellers, the hotels are always filled with Alexandrians coming to see them. I was told that

Sir George Chetwynd sent a horse to run on this occasion, but it was beaten easily—I suppose from the difference of ground and of temperature.

CHAPTER XV.

Races—Ball at Gezireh—Wedding fêtes begin—Dinners—Provisions given to the poor—Procession of the bride on the third evening—Dancing in the harem—The bride is brought out fainting—Weight of the ornaments—Christy Minstrels—Sudden death—Great difference in the treatment of Europeans during the last twenty years.

The races began on the 16th of January, the day of signing the contract. They lasted two days, a dromedary race being given on the second, very attractive from its novelty to Europeans.

On the next day, the 18th, was the anniversary of the Khédive's accession, and a ball is usually given in honour of it.

It is held at Gezireh, in the State apartments occupied by the Empress of the French during her visit to Egypt in 1869 at the opening of the Suez Canal.

They are magnificent apartments, and the position of the palace on the Nile, with the beautiful gardens all illuminated, combine to make a ball there a sort of realisation of fairyland. Invitations are ardently coveted, and liberally given—on this occasion almost too liberally, for some persons complained of being crowded. There is plenty of space, but of course if every one will rush to the ball-room, it may become rather too full for comfort.

The 19th was Sunday, kept by Europeans in the usual way; but in the afternoon the bride of Tewfik Pasha, who had remained in her mother's house since the signing of the contract on the previous Thursday, removed to Kasr-el-Ali, to the palace of the Queen-Mother, to remain there until the following Thursday, when she was to be taken to the house of her husband, whom (I believe) she had never yet seen. I mistake, however, in using the word *seen*, as these ladies in their drives out see everybody perfectly: I ought rather to have said, had never spoken to or been seen by him.

Monday, Tuesday, and Wednesday there were to be *fêtes* all day at the palace of the Queen-Mother. Mahometan visitors were staying in the palace, and others came daily. European visitors came each evening. Twelve grand dinners were to be given at this palace, three for each wedding, and forty Europeans were to be invited to each dinner. Many more had invitations for the evening.

During these three days the bride remained in retirement in her own rooms, not visible to the general visitors, though a favoured few might be admitted to her presence. On the Wednesday evening she went in procession through all the apartments, magnificently arrayed, and blazing with diamonds. She was conducted into an inner saloon, seated on a throne between the Queen-Mother and her own parent, and received there the general congratulations. After about a quarter of an hour she withdrew, in the same state as she came. To be present on the Wednesday evening was more coveted than the invitations for the Monday and Tuesday, on account of seeing the bride and the procession. On Thursday, accompanied by all her female relatives, the bride left the residence of the Queen-Mother, and proceeded to her husband's house, there to remain.

This procession was a very gorgeous one, and lasted two or three hours, as it passed through all the principal streets of the town.

On the same day the marriage-contract for the next

couple was signed, and the same round of entertainments went on, to be again repeated for the third and fourth royal pair.

While these festivities were for the upper classes, those lower in the social scale were not neglected.

During four days of every week throughout this month of weddings, his Highness paid for the under-mentioned articles, to be daily distributed to the poor: 500 sheep, 300 lambs, 200 turkeys, 800 fowls, 500 lb. of coffee, and 800 measures of bread.

Fireworks went up every night from the Ezbekeah Gardens, public buildings were illuminated, and a line of light stretched from the Ezbekeah to the palace of the Queen-Mother, a distance of upwards of two miles. In front of the palace a space of considerable extent was railed in, where entertainments went on. Admission was by ticket, which any respectable person could obtain, and the ticket included refreshment. Most of the travellers in the hotels went there, and some ladies accompanied their husbands.

Then there were dinners given at Kasr-el-Nil for gentlemen, at which his Highness was present; and concerts and theatrical entertainments, for both ladies and gentlemen.

At the harem *fêtes* only ladies were invited. I went to two each week; but as a description of one will serve as a sample of all the rest, I will relate what I saw on the Wednesday evening of the second marriage, that of the Princess Fatma, daughter of the Khédive.

The invitation-card was for dinner at seven; and as there might be impediments to progress, we—Mrs Freeland and I—left the hotel at six o'clock.

The drive to Kasr-el-Ali was crowded by carriages, pedestrians, and donkeys, the crowd increasing the nearer we approached. When we arrived, we found the whole front of the palace illuminated, as well as a large space in front, on which tents were erected, and to which admission was obtained by ticket.

At the first gate of the palace we gave our invitation-cards, and were then admitted into an inner spacious quadrangular court, where we left our carriages and were given over to the charge of eunuchs. These led us up a raised stone terrace, with trellis-work at the sides for training creepers, so as to form an arched covered-way to the palace. At intervals there were bowery walks branching off, with long rows of lights.

We entered the palace, and were received by two European ladies, whose fluency in Turkish and Arabic causes them to be engaged on these occasions to serve as interpreters between the Princesses and their European visitors. There were numbers of gorgeously dressed slaves, some clad as pages, with long wands in their hands, with which they opened a way to let us pass.

We were taken into a large room to be uncloaked, &c., and tickets were given to us, and when we left we found the corresponding number pinned on to a velvet wrapper embroidered with gold. These wrappers were arranged in chairs round the room, according to number, so that each party had no difficulty in finding her own belongings.

We were then taken into the chief saloon, to make our bow to whatever Princess might be there. Coffee and cigarettes were handed to us, and we looked round to see if there were any familiar faces among the guests.

When the Princesses had all arrived, they rose to go to dinner, and we all followed two by two. The dining-room was a splendid apartment. From the centre of the ceiling hung an enormous lustre, and at each end of the room was a tree of glass, the shape of a palm, with a very thick stem, which, like a prism, reflected every shade of colour; the lights were at the top, and the looking-glass all around the walls reflected them back again, so that there seemed to be quite a forest of crystal palms.

The dinner was served *à la franque*, and among the attendants were two or three English women, who had formerly been engaged as parlour-maids in the Khédive's harem, when Frank customs were first introduced; and these were efficient waitresses in themselves, and directed the others at the same time.

The table was shaped like a horse-shoe; the Princesses sat in the centre, and a slight space was left between them and the other guests. They were radiant with diamonds, tiaras, necklaces, earrings, and golden girdles with large clasps set in diamonds, butterflies, stars, and feathery sprays of precious stones. Their dresses were made in the last Parisian fashion, with trains two yards long at the least, trailing behind them. The latter, of course, could not be seen at the dinner-table, but they kept every one at a respectful distance in the passage to and fro.

We had taken our places near one end of the table, which was unfortunate, for we had not been seated many minutes when the musicians entered, six in number, and took up their station in our immediate vicinity. Four had tambourines, one a guitar, and another a violin; and they twanged, and banged, and strummed, and sang at the full pitch of their voices, until we were nearly deafened. An old lady, one of the Turkish visitors, sat near me. She would probably have preferred the floor, but as a chair was *de rigueur*, she compromised matters by tucking one leg under her. She also had a decided preference for using her fingers instead of a knife and fork, because these new-fangled fashions had only been introduced into the harem within the last five years, and she probably did not understand them.

When a woman is old in the East she resigns herself

to her fate, and does not think of making up; so this old lady, though richly dressed, wore a little skull-cap, and a wig under it, cut short like a boy's, and as the hair was black, and she looked old and withered, there was no attempt at deception. No flowers, no lace, a satin dress high up to the throat, and that was all.

When the dinner was over, the Princesses rose and led the way out; we following as we had come in, two by two. We went back to the same saloon where we had been before dinner; coffee was handed round, and cigarettes for those who chose them. Then we went up the grand staircase into a saloon on the first floor. It was of great size, and other apartments opened into it. At one end sat the Queen-Mother, and we were each taken up in turn to be presented to her. She had been an invalid for some time past, so that she had not been able to attend the dinner. After the presentation, dancing-girls came in, and on the different evenings gave us different dances. On one occasion it was like that at Indji Hanem's, six or eight following one another, and the leader giving the step and the measure. Another time it was a sword-dance, which was executed with great spirit and dexterity. And on another occasion they danced the mazurka, and were dressed then something as ballet-girls are on the European stage, only their dresses were not quite so short, nor so transparent. Four were as cavaliers, and looked very pretty. After that they danced the polka. At about ten o'clock the procession of the bride took place. A double line of eunuchs was formed the whole length of the vast saloon. They held in their hands branch candle-sticks, each containing six or eight candles. They stood close together, and the light was so dazzling it was difficult to see anything within the line. Through this line the bride came in the handsomest of her bridal robes, with a veil of silver threads (or gold) fastened near the back of her head, and flowing behind her. She wore as many of her jewels as could possibly be arranged on her person, or as she was able to carry. She was supported by two eunuchs, and she needed support, for I had felt the weight of the dress, ornaments, and jewels, and they were no trifle to carry. Visitors mounted on chairs and sofas to get a view of her as she passed, but the lights were so dazzling it was not easy to do so.

She passed through the saloon into an inner apartment called "the throne-room," and was led up to a raised seat under a canopy, between her mother and the *Validé* (Queen-Mother). All those who were near the doors pressed in after her, and they were immediately closed. The struggle is often great to get into this room, and for more than one reason. In the first place, all in the room obtained a good view of the bride and her costly ornaments. And in the second place, after the bride has taken her seat, the shower of coins takes place. In the throne-room it is of gold, in the large saloon of silver. These coins are all bright and new, and (besides serving as money) they make very pretty ornaments, as necklaces, earrings, and bracelets. They are to be bought in the bazaars, and travellers generally purchase them, but most persons would value the ornaments still more if it were at the same time a *souvenir* of a wedding *fête*, at which they had themselves been present. The gold coins are in value from 1s. to 5s., the silver from 2½d. to 5d. A slave carries a bag full of them, and one of the chief persons at the wedding puts her hand into the bag, and then throws them among the assembled guests. They who are nimble and quick-sighted pick up a great number, as they lie on the carpets, or on the persons of their neighbours; sometimes you will see a lady's dress covered as if with spangles, the coins falling in the folds of the trimming.

If you wish to get into the throne-room, you must take

care to be close to the folding-doors when the bride is passing down the saloon, between the double line of light held by the eunuchs. As she approaches the doors, they are thrown open, and a rush takes place. The eunuchs keep the pressure off her, but almost directly after her entrance the doors are closed. I had got close up to them when they were shut, and as I was anxious to see her, I stayed near them, hoping that some persons might come out of the room presently, and give their place to others.

A cry suddenly arose of "The bride is ill; she is coming out!" and the eunuchs began to push vigorously to make a way for her. I was jammed against the wall, and the line of eunuchs almost trod on me. The doors were thrown open, and the bride came out, and passed within two or three feet of me. She was half carried, half dragged, by two tall eunuchs. She was a remarkably handsome girl, very fair, and of middle height, but she looked more like a corpse than a living person. Her head was thrown back, and her face was deadly pale, her dress was resplendent with diamonds from head to foot, but it was a ghastly spectacle.

As I mentioned before, I had felt the weight of the tiara and veil, and the various ornaments that she would have to wear on this occasion, and had observed at the time that I should be very sorry to carry such a load. This, added to the heat of the passage through the rooms, between the blaze of so many lights, and the feeling of all eyes being upon her, no doubt overcame her, and she fainted away. I think it is a terrible ordeal that these brides have to go through.

Directly after the bride had been borne out, the Princesses rose, and the party broke up. Everybody wanted their carriages at the same time, and we had nearly an hour to wait for ours; but it was a splendid moonlight night, and the spectacle around us was so animated, and to us so novel, that we did not mind waiting. After all, compared with the dissipation of London hours, it was early, as we were back in the hotel soon after midnight.

On Thursday, at about 2 P.M., the procession of the bride, going home to her husband's house, passed the New Hotel. It consisted of, first, a band of music, then a regiment of foot-soldiers, a troop of cavalry in chain-armour, and mounted on cream-coloured horses, and a succession of state carriages, containing the female relatives of the bride,—she herself was in a carriage drawn by six horses; and, finally, a number of private carriages closed the train, which took about a quarter of an hour in passing the hotel. It had previously made the round of all the principal thoroughfares in Cairo.[1]

I went every day to the harem, notwithstanding the *fêtes*, but little was done in the way of lessons. Kopsès was very steady, but the attention of the Princess was much distracted. The valuable services which Kopsès could render, made her much in request. There was a constant arrival of boxes from Paris, containing dresses, and an influx of French *modistes*, to take orders from, or to throw temptation in the way of, the Princesses and chief ladies. Kopsès understood four languages, Turkish, Arabic, French, and English. Most persons who settle in Egypt acquire a little Arabic, but it is a foreign language to the Princesses, and they much prefer the translations into Turkish, of the various bills of the *modistes*. So Kopsès was constantly called away to serve as interpreter, and the Princess being left alone with me, would seek rather to engage me in conversation than in study. I don't know that any English girl would, under the cir-

---

[1] This bride became a widow in little more than three years after her marriage, as her husband, Toussoun Pasha, died on the 7th of July 1876, after a long and painful illness. This young Prince was highly educated, and universally beloved, both by Europeans and by natives.

cumstances, have been very studiously disposed, with the weddings of three brothers and one sister going on, and her own betrothal approaching!

This last intelligence came upon me very unexpectedly. I had known that she was some day to be married to her cousin, Ibrahim Pasha (the same name as her own brother); but she was only fourteen, and I had hoped the marriage would not take place for three or four years, as her two elder sisters, Tafita Hanem and Fatma Hanem, had not been married until they were eighteen.

One morning, when I went to the harem during the *fêtes* of the first marriage, upon entering the room where our studies took place, I saw two persons close together in the further corner, whom I took for the Princess and Kopsès. I walked straight up to them, saying, "Comment donc, vous ne venez pas à ma rencontre?" when I discovered they were strangers, and a second glance showed me they did not belong to the harem, but were evidently visitors of distinction. I apologised, and was going away to seek my pupils elsewhere, when the elder lady begged me to remain. I soon found it was mother and daughter, and that the young lady was to be the bride of Prince Hussein, the Khédive's second son. Also, what interested me still more, she was the half-sister of Prince Ibrahim, to whom my pupil was shortly to be betrothed.

The young lady spoke French extremely well, and had very nice manners. I afterwards saw a good deal of her during my residence in the harem with my pupil, as she was a frequent visitor and very much attached to her sister-in-law.

As my conversational powers in Turkish were soon exhausted, the elder lady put a good many questions to me through her daughter. "Was I married? If not, with whom did I live? Was I English or French?" and many others, which I answered.

About this time there was erected on a large open space near the entrance of the Mouskee, an equestrian statue of Ibrahim Pasha, father to the Khédive. This would not be worth mentioning, only it was quite an innovation in Mahometan customs, which prohibit statues and pictures.

His Highness had engaged a troop of Christy Minstrels out from England to perform at some of the places which were thrown open for public entertainment during the fêtes.

One day I was standing for a few minutes on the terrace in front of the hotel in company with the wife of the English chaplain, when two of these young men, accompanied by a dragoman, came up to us, and asked us where they could find the English clergyman. We knew that he was gone with Professor Owen to the Boulaq Museum, but no one else in the hotel was aware of it. We asked them what they wanted with him, and they told us it was to read the funeral service over one of their comrades who had died that morning, and was about to be buried in the English cemetery. They could not bear that he should be buried without the service being read over him; and while they were speaking to us the chaplain returned, and having heard their errand, asked why they had not come while their comrade was still alive. They replied that he had been acting four days back, and was then apparently quite well, that he was seized with fever, was quite insensible, and had died that morning. He was to be buried the same afternoon, and the hour was approaching, but his friends were anxious if possible to have the funeral service read over him by a clergyman, so Mr P. went away with them at once.

A lady who was born in Egypt and had resided in it about fifty years, told me that some five-and-twenty years ago a European lady could not go out either in Cairo or

Alexandria without the great cloak which the Egyptian
ladies wear, which completely conceals the figure, and was
formerly often drawn over the head and face. They were
sure otherwise to be insulted. Now a European may go
about without molestation; I never met with the slightest
annoyance. She told me at that time, when the Viceroy's
harem went abroad, which was a rare occurrence, any men
who might be in the streets turned their faces to the wall
immediately.

CHAPTER XVI.

*Excursion to Toura—Death in the hotel—My pupil is betrothed—Turkish
comedians brought in blindfolded—The second betrothal takes place—
Quail-shooting near the Pyramids—We return to Choubrah—Bookcase
turned into a meat-cupboard—Sprain my ankle—Court moves to
Gezireh—We are ordered to Constantinople.*

Towards the end of the *fêtes*, we made an excursion to
Toura. It was on a Friday, when we never went to
the harem.

Toura is on the east bank of the Nile, opposite Sakkara, and from the quarries of Toura the Pyramids are
said to have been built. It is about eighteen miles from
Cairo. We started at half-past eight, a party of ten
in three carriages, having sent on donkeys for the whole
party the night before.

Our way led through the Mouskee, past the Citadel,
and then out into the desert. There is no road, the
desert is as billowy as a rough sea, and it was heavy
work for the poor horses. Every now and then we had
to get out and walk, while the carriages were pushed to
get over a ridge. At last we came to the place where

the donkeys were waiting for us, and we all mounted. They were capital beasts, and away we went at a smart canter.

Our party consisted of Mr and Mrs Freeland, Mr Michell and myself, Shefket, the English chaplain and his wife, a Scottish doctor in the service, and an Irish member of Parliament (an Ulster man, *not* a Nationalist) with his wife. The Irishman played all sorts of pranks— springing to his feet on the saddle like a circus performer, then coming down suddenly with his face to the tail. He challenged Shefket to imitate him, which the latter did at once, and the two kept us in a continual roar of laughter with their antics. Sometimes in their leaps they came down on the sands, in which case they ran after their steeds and vaulted on again.

We had brought baskets of provisions with us, and they were carried up to the appointed place, for the quarries are on the hillside. They are extensively excavated, and sometimes form complete galleries. In their recesses we were not only screened from the sun, which was hot in the middle of the day, but had at the same time a beautiful view of the river and opposite shore. On each side of the Nile was a long green belt of vegetation; beyond that on the west was desert; and on the east (on which we were) the long range of Mokattam Hills. The colouring is one of the great charms in Egypt; it is so different from anything one sees in Europe. I had lately seen some pictures by an eminent artist, Mr M'Callum, which had been taken at Thebes, and gave a very good idea of the varying light. They were "Sultry Noon," "Mysterious Night," and "Ruddy Dawn." The first is quite oppressive in its pale, yellowish light, not a shadow anywhere; the air seems laden with dust. The second is strong shadow, with the silvery light of the moon in parts. The third, gorgeous sunrise, with the red glow mantling on the ruins, and seeming to increase as you gaze upon it.

We got back at about half-past six in the evening, and I always think this excursion to Toura (which I afterwards frequently made) one of the most enjoyable in the vicinity of Cairo; not for its antiquities, but for the charming views from the quarries, and the contrast presented by the desert and the green banks of the river.

But you must devote a whole day to Toura on account of the distance. If you want to make an afternoon excursion, and get a fine view over Cairo, you cannot do better than mount the Mokattams behind the Citadel. A carriage can take you a little beyond the Citadel, and then the road becomes too heavy and too steep, so you must either walk or ride; but you will be amply repaid for your trouble by the view which awaits you from the top. The road winds through hills, with quarries on each side, in which large caverns have been hollowed out, forming cool retreats where you may rest in shade should the sun prove too hot. It was here, on the top of the hill, that the observations were made on the transit of Venus.

The day after our picnic to Toura, a sad event happened in the hotel—a death! We had noticed for some time past a gentleman looking frightfully ill, and who had just returned from the Soudan. He was an English officer of Engineers, and had taken service under the Khédive. He had been two years in the Soudan, had had nineteen attacks of fever during that time, and was on his return to England. A few days after his arrival at Cairo, he had seemed a little better, and on the very day of his death he had settled to cross from Alexandria for Brindisi.

His attacks of fever had made him exceedingly deaf, so that, although everybody observed his delicate state, it was extremely difficult to enter into conversation with him. He had come down regularly to luncheon and dinner at the *table d'hôte*, but two or three days before his death there was suddenly a great stir at table: he had attempted to rise and could not. Two or three gentlemen helped him up-stairs, and every one felt it was his last appearance. The chaplain, and the Irish gentleman whom I have mentioned as accompanying us to Toura, sat up with him that night by turns, and the latter procured him a nurse on the following day, as they found he was quite unable to do anything for himself. The staff of waiters in the hotel was insufficient; the poor gentleman said his waiter had been kind to him, but the hotel was crowded, and the man's time was fully occupied. On this last day he was evidently sinking fast, his mind wandered, he talked much of his mother, imagined himself on the voyage back to England, and towards evening expired. As is customary in the hotels, the body was removed the same evening to the little chapel in the European cemetery near Cairo, and interred the following day. Six gentlemen, including the Consul, Mr Rogers, the Chaplain, Colonel Saunderson, Mr Freeland, and Dr Grant, resident physician at Cairo, attended the funeral—also the Chaplain's wife, Mrs Freeland, Mrs Saunderson, and myself. The ceremony had been fixed for 3 P.M.; but when we reached the cemetery, no grave had been dug! It being Sunday, the chaplain had to officiate at afternoon service, so we went back to the hotel (where the service was then held), and at five returned again to the cemetery. Then the body was laid in the grave—carried to it by countrymen who had known him but a few days, but who attended his funeral as reverently as if he had been a near relative.

The four weddings were now over, but there still remained two betrothals. One was between my pupil and her cousin Ibrahim Pasha, son of Ahmed Pasha (elder brother of the Khédive), accidentally drowned in the

Nile about twenty years ago. The second was between Faïk Hanem, adopted daughter of the third Princess, and Moustapha Pasha, son of the Mouffettish, then Minister of Finance.

The first betrothal took place on the 17th of February. It was at the palace of Abdeen under the Khédive's roof, not at Kasr-el-Ali the Queen-Mother's palace, where all the wedding *fêtes* had been held. The little *fiancée* was dressed in white silk, covered with Brussels point and orange flowers; and after the contract had been signed, she went through all the rooms leaning on her two married sisters, and taking her seat under the canopy, as usual with betrothed brides, received the presents of jewels brought to her. She sat there a few minutes, and then left the room, and soon after sent for me to show me her gifts. They were very costly, but she did not seem elated. She said the contract was a much more serious thing than the actual marriage, because you could *never* change your mind after that had been signed!

There were very few Europeans present, nearly all the visitors being Turkish or Egyptian ladies. There was a grand luncheon in the European style, which was indeed always used in the Khédive's harem; but the amusements were exclusively such as are common to harems. There was a troop of comedians brought in who were placed on one side of the saloon in a strong light, and then lattice-work screens were stretched across the room to separate them from the harem. Cushions were laid down in front of the screens, and there the ladies sat looking at the performance, while they themselves remained unseen. At intervals the men were led out for rest or refreshment, and it was a ridiculous sight to see them go in or out. Their eyes were bandaged, and evidently effectually, for it was done by the eunuchs; and they were led in and out thus blindfolded. A eunuch preceded them, holding one by the hand, who in turn gave his to the next, and so on through the whole troop. About every third man was grasped by the arm by a eunuch in order to keep them steady, as they were led along at a rapid rate. The eunuchs are always merciless to any men who fall into their power; and the women were all laughing as the comedians were led through. If one had been discovered peeping, what would have been his fate! However, the eunuchs took care of that; and as the men were all Mahometans, they knew better than to make any attempt at seeing what was forbidden. We came away in the afternoon, and saw the large space in front of the palace at Abdeen covered with tents: on one side a man was performing on a tight-rope. The day had been rather cold for the time of year, the thermometer not rising above 63° in the shade. It had been fine throughout the *fêtes*, which was fortunate, as so much was done in the open air.

The next morning when I went to the harem I found my pupil just out of bed. I don't know how long she had sat up the previous night, but she had had a tiring day. All the jewels she had received were spread out before her, and she took up one after another to examine, which rather retarded the process of dressing. To give me a stronger personal interest in the matter, she handed me a dark-blue velvet case, saying it was "de la part de sa belle mère." I had then never seen or spoken to this lady, so I thought she made a mistake, and I said, "You mean from your mother?"

"No," said she; "from my mother-in-law."

I was told afterwards that it was the custom at the betrothal for the mother-in-law to make presents to those about the person of the bride, and at the actual marriage for the mother to do it. I opened the case, and found it contained a gold watch, chain, and brooch. The watch was in a double case of pink enamel, set with diamonds, the brooch to match, and the chain having heavy gold tassels. There was a large rose diamond in the centre of the watch, and a similar one in the brooch.

On that day week, February 24, the betrothal of Faïk Hanem, the adopted daughter, took place. There is a Mahometan superstition that two brides or betrothed persons should not remain under one roof during the same moon, so Faïk Hanem's betrothal took place at Kasr-el-Ali, instead of at Abdeen, where she always resided.

I had the right of being in the room with the bride, but by accident I remained in the large saloon adjoining, which the Pashas would pass through when they came to ask the important question, "Wilt thou have this man," &c., &c.

There were a great many ladies of the harem in the saloon, besides a French lady, Mrs Freeland, and myself. A eunuch came in to give notice of the approach of the Pashas, upon which all the ladies hurried into the neighbouring rooms, and the doors were closed upon them. One, however, concealed herself behind Mrs Freeland and me, determined if possible to witness the ceremony. There were several eunuchs, who looked all round the saloon, and seeing no one but three European ladies, had of course nothing to say to them. We were standing, and were not aware that any one was hiding behind us; but suddenly we sat down, and then the intruder became distinctly visible. It was too late to screen her, which we would willingly have done; a eunuch caught sight of her, and walked quickly across the room. She knew her danger, and rushed to the nearest door before he got up, but I fear he had recognised her.

The Pashas came to the curtained door, and put the momentous question, which after being thrice repeated, and a due interval having elapsed, appeared to be answered in the affirmative, as they went away laughing. Then the doors were all thrown open, the slaves reappeared, and presently the *fiancée* came out, supported on each side, and holding a handkerchief up to her eyes. She went on to the throne-room, and sat there by the side of the Viceroy's mother, whilst presents were brought to her, amongst which was a diamond tiara. Then came the shower of gold, and soon after the whole party (except the betrothed) went down to luncheon. When we came up again I was sent for to the young *fiancée*, and there I found the brides of Hussein and of Hassan Pasha, the latter bride looking a mere child. After some little talk we came away.

Faïk Hanem, the second *fiancée*, and adopted daughter of the third Princess, had hitherto taken lessons in French and music from a Levantine lady, who had been engaged as governess to Fatma Hanem, the bride of the second wedding. When that lady was married, and left her father's palace for that of her husband, Toussoun Pasha, her instructress went with her as *dame de compagnie*; and as my pupil, the Princess Zeyneb, did nothing with me in the afternoon (when she had lessons in Turkish and Arabic), I was asked to give instruction during that time to Faïk Hanem. So from this period for a whole year I went to the harem regularly at about eight o'clock or soon after, returning at twelve, and then going again from two to five in the afternoon. I found Faïk Hanem very intelligent, and anxious to learn. Like the Princess Zeyneb, she had a companion to study with her, but a very different person from Kopsès. The latter would have done honour to her instructress in any country; but Irfandil was a good heavy sort of girl, with excellent intentions, but very limited capacity. She was very amiable, but instead of being an encouragement and incentive to the studies of her companion, she was rather the reverse. She had a trick of falling asleep over her

M

lessons. Poor girl! no doubt she found it trying to begin directly after her dinner, particularly as she was taught in a language which she very imperfectly understood. I would set her to copy something while I was engaged with Faïk Hanem, and when I looked at her performance I was quite amazed at the erratic movements of her pen. I did not discover at first that she dozed during the whole time, continuing her writing mechanically, but with a very indifferent result.

The 28th of February of that year (1873) was the New Year's Day of the Mahometans, the 1st of Moharrem 1290 A.H. During this month no marriages take place.

Sometimes on Fridays we drove out to the Pyramids— the chaplain, his wife, myself, and Mr Michell. The two gentlemen took guns and went shooting, while we remained in the carriage or walked about. There is excellent snipe and quail shooting after the inundation has subsided, and wherever they saw a chance for their guns they got out, and then joined us later. As they had no dogs, they of course lost a great many birds, but we always brought back a fair quantity, and they were very welcome, as our *menu* at the hotel was very limited, and very monotonous, and there was a good deal of difference in the plump little birds shot, and the poor half-starved little things which had been first snared and then sold to the hotel.

On the 20th of March we were told we were to go back to the house at Choubrah, and we left the New Hotel after a stay of ten weeks. It had been very pleasant and lively, enabling us to see much more of the *fêtes* than we should have done at Choubrah. Carriages were an exorbitant price during the month of weddings, but staying at the hotel we had found friends to share with us the expense.

When we went back to Choubrah many changes had

taken place by no means satisfactory to us. Several cherished pieces of furniture had disappeared, or were quite spoiled. A large and excellent bookcase which used to stand in the Princess's schoolroom, and which was for my use, had been removed, and after many inquiries I found it in an outhouse where it had been used for keeping meat! The greater part of the shelves had been removed and burnt, and those still left in were so stained and dirty that it was no longer fit for its original purpose. The chairs and sofas in the drawing-room had been covered with crimson SILK velvet in perfectly good condition. When we came back it had been removed, and new *cotton* velvet substituted. The springs had been taken out, and a very hard stuffing put in their place. Whenever any visitor came his Highness always gave orders that the house in which he was to be lodged should be carefully looked to, and new furniture put *where necessary*, and somehow it always was found necessary, and the new furniture was seldom an improvement on the old.

The *khamseen* winds were rather prevalent during the month of March, and I found returning from and going to the harem in the middle of the day rather trying.

On the 27th I went as usual in the morning, and found there were to be no lessons, as his Highness was going to give a grand *fête* at Gezireh to all the harem of Abdeen. The gardens were to be illuminated at night, and they were all looking forward to it immensely. The preceding day had been fresh and cool, with a north wind, and that morning had been promising; but in a few hours it veered to the south, and became one of the most oppressive days I ever remember. We kept our doors and windows closely shut all day, and towards evening the wind rose very high. At 9 P.M. I went to the door; it was like the blast of a furnace, so stifling and overpowering. This was very unlucky for the garden *fête* at Gezireh. The next two days the weather was delightful.

We were very pleased to go back to our own house-keeping, as we had again our cook of the previous winter (he was luckily disengaged), but one evening we had a little *contretemps*. Mrs Freeland had ordered some green peas, having been told they were to be bought in the market, and when they were brought up to table they were floating about in some watery fluid called melted butter, but *unshelled*, cooked in their pods!

A gentleman at Shepheard's Hotel—the Honourable Murray Finch Hatton (now Earl of Winchilsea)—who had just returned from a voyage up the Nile, had brought a young lioness cub with him, and kept it chained in the garden. He had got it at Assouan, had always fed it regularly himself, and the creature was very tame, both to him and to every one else. Its owner told me that when he had it on board the *dahabich* its great amusement was to hide behind the thing to which its chain was attached, and then suddenly spring out on some unwary passer-by, to whom, however, it did no further harm than a blow with its paw.

At the end of the month (March) I calculated that there had been since the 1st, nine days on which the thermometer had been in the shade from 80° to 87°, and seven days on which it had been from 90° to 99°. At the beginning of the month the nuisance of *fleas* had become almost intolerable; but towards the middle they disappeared, and only a stray one was seen occasionally. Their disappearance had been already foretold in the Arab calendar, and we found it quite correct. But no sooner were we rid of the fleas than the mosquitoes and sand-flies came in abundance. The latter were to me worse than the first.

I heard a curious story about this time. An Englishman had come to Cairo for his health, and suddenly decided upon joining a party just about to go up the Nile. He had, however, not money enough by him to pay the immediate expenses necessary, so he went into a shop in the Mouskee and asked the owner to lend him seventy napoleons, which the other agreed at once to do upon no other security than his note of hand, though they were previously entire strangers. The Englishman went up the Nile, but died on the return voyage. When the boat reached Cairo, his papers and effects were given up to the Consul, who found upon looking into them that he had bequeathed to the merchant two thousand napoleons in return for the seventy he had borrowed. The Consul sent for the merchant and informed him of the bequest. The latter inquired into the circumstances of the deceased's family, and hearing they were not rich, refused to accept more than one thousand napoleons, leaving the other thousand to the relatives.

I had this story from the Consul himself. Talking of this to an Irish gentleman in the hotel, Colonel Saunderson, he told me that such instances of confidence as the merchant had shown were not rare. He himself, he said, was once travelling in Moldavia, and through some mistake in sending his supplies found himself suddenly penniless. He told his case to an entire stranger, and the latter immediately took out his purse, and handing it to him begged him to help himself to what was necessary. Where London and Paris swindlers have not penetrated, confidence is rarely misplaced.

We made a great many pleasant acquaintances at the hotel among the travellers. There was one gentleman who was a universal favourite for his extreme liveliness and also for his musical talent. No picnic or party to the bazaars was complete without him. He had been bred to the Bar, and was a master in the art of "chaffing." One day, however, he got the worst of it. He went with two or three others to the bazaars. None of them had any particular intention of purchasing, but our embryo barrister amused the party by constant bargaining. He had been a long time thus employed with an old Persian, and the latter perceiving at last that there was not the slightest intention of purchasing, quietly locked up all his stores, put the key in his pocket, took out his pipe, and sat calmly smoking, apparently quite oblivious of his tormentor. The latter was not to be discouraged; he took up a piece of old iron which happened to lie near and inquired with great interest the price of that. At this moment a lad came up and handed a bag of money to the merchant. It was evidently some account which had just been paid, and the Persian began counting the money. Upon this the Englishman changed his tack, and clamoured loudly for *backsheesh*, which is the universal Arab cry. The Persian finished his counting, calmly put two pieces of gold into his tormentor's hand, and put his purse in his pocket without taking any further notice of him. The young man was in a difficulty. Of course he, a gentleman, could not take the money; his chaff had fallen harmlessly on the Oriental, so he quietly laid down the gold and walked on.

Towards the end of April, the Court removed to Gezireh. Ibrahim Pasha occupied the same apartments as he had done the year before, but my dear little pupils were now shut up in the harem. I had not been to them many days, however, before an accident happened to me. I was sitting in my room reading, with the windows shut on account of the great heat of the outer air, when I felt the sharp sting of a mosquito. My feet were crossed on a footstool, and one had gone to sleep without my being aware of it. I sprang up immediately to put some ammonia on my hand, and the foot being asleep, I rolled over on the floor and sprained my instep. I was unable to get up for some time on account of the pain, and could not walk for nearly a fortnight.

When I again went to the harem to give lessons, there were as many cries of *Hoch gueldiniz! Sefa gueldiniz!* (salutations of welcome) as if I had been a dear old friend. I do not refer to my pupils, but to the eunuchs and slaves whom I generally passed in my way into the harem. Their lives are so monotonous that they welcome any familiar face.

The treatment for my sprain was very simple and very efficacious. I had constant applications of wet bandages steeped in arnica and water (the proportion being a teaspoonful of arnica to half a pint of water). After three or four days the foot was rubbed for a quarter of an hour as often as convenient, and after ten days, cold compresses applied at night. The foot was very much swollen and discoloured, and felt weak for two or three months.

In the middle of May we received orders to go to Constantinople. We were told we were to leave Cairo by the 8 A.M. express, which reaches Alexandria at 12.30; that we were not to stop there, but to take tickets at once, and proceed by the post-boat to Constantinople, which would leave the port at 4 P.M.

We should not be the usual party, as Mrs Freeland and her three children were going to England by the next P. & O. boat, so there would be only Mr Freeland, Mr Michell, and myself. The P. & O. boat was not expected to leave Alexandria for some days (as it always depends on the arrival of the mail from India); but, as the establishment at Choubrah would be broken up at our departure, Mr Freeland decided that his wife and children should travel with us, intending to see them safely in the hotel before our departure.

CHAPTER XVII.

Departure for Alexandria—Harem travel the same day—Consequent delay—Arrive too late for the boat—Hotels crowded—Proceed in the Mahalla to Constantinople—We are ordered to Therapia—Go to the Hôtel des Ambassadeurs—Remove to Emirghian—Lessons in the harem—Fête at the palace given to the Sultane Validé.

As the orders were not countermanded, we were at the station next morning at half-past seven, with all our luggage. But before we got there, the firing of guns announced that his Highness was leaving Cairo. This occasioned our train to start half an hour later than the specified time, and very soon two special trains followed. The first contained the *Validé* (Queen-Mother) and her household; the second, the Princesses and their suite. We had started before them, but nevertheless the express had to give way to the specials, and we were always stopping at stations, and being shunted, to allow these trains to pass. Consequently, we arrived at Alexandria at 3 P.M. instead of at 12.30; our steamer was to leave at 4 P.M., and there was just a possibility of our being there in time. But the last harem train was still in the station; every carriage outside had been pressed into the service of the harem, and how were we to get to the steamer? and, above all, how were we to get our luggage?

The station was not then, as it is now, close to the end of Sheriff Pasha Street, but a long drive; and the eunuchs were rushing frantically about, seizing upon every porter, and making him bring out the harem luggage. To avoid the chance of leaving any behind, the eunuchs told them to take every trunk they could lay their hands upon; and as few of them could read, addresses were of little use under such pressure.

Under these circumstances, our dragoman, Shaheen, was

invaluable. At ordinary times he was a great admirer of the *dolce far niente*, but when travelling he came out in great force. He collected together all the luggage, and then made great efforts to impress a porter into the service. If he left it for a moment to seek a porter, some eunuch was sure to pass by, and seeing an accumulation of baggage, would order it all to be swept off with that of the harem. Then Shaheen would return with a porter, and find some of the things gone; and, leaving the porter to stand guard, would rush after the missing treasures, and rescue them. Messrs Freeland and Michell were seeking a carriage outside to convey us to the boat, and another for Mrs Freeland and her children, to take them to the hotel. At last two were found, and leaving Shaheen to look after the luggage, and bring it after us to the boat, we left the station having first found a gentleman in whose charge to place Mrs Freeland and her children. The scene during all this time at the station would have been a very singular one to anybody newly arrived from Europe. The eunuchs were so busy looking after the trunks that they had not time to guard the harem, and many of the ladies had got out of the carriages, and, with their transparent veils and brilliant *feridjees*, were standing or walking about the platform, apparently highly entertained at the, to them, unwonted spectacle. I never saw such a curious scene of confusion and deviation from all established customs, either before or afterwards.

When we had got a little way from the station, we found another empty carriage, into which Mr Freeland entered, as he had to go to the office to procure the tickets; and we thought it urgent to proceed at once to the steamer to give notice of our coming, and induce the captain, if possible, to delay the departure until we were all on board with our luggage. On his way to the office,

Mr Freeland had to pass through a narrow street, and there in another carriage he met a cousin who had just arrived in Egypt from England, and being on his way to the Mauritius, thought he would land at Alexandria, and taking Cairo on his way, rejoin his steamer at Suez. One of the principal inducements to this was, to visit his cousin at Cairo; and had they not met in this unexpected way, the cousin would have been off by the next train. As it was, he turned back with Mr Freeland, and accompanied him to the quay, expressing his intention afterwards to go to the Hôtel de l'Europe and see Mrs Freeland and her children.

In the meanwhile, Mr Michell and I hurried on board the mail-boat. We found the steam already getting up, but upon speaking to the captain were told that every berth was occupied. We were rather urgent; and the captain, calling the steward, said, after consultation, that an arrangement would be made to accommodate us. Presently Mr Freeland came on board, but had seen nothing of Shaheen nor of the luggage! The captain told us that our luggage could follow by the next boat, that we should get it in about ten days' time, and urged us to make up our minds whether we would go or stay, as the mail-bags were on board, and he was anxious to be off. We had nothing with us but the clothing upon us, and we had seen enough on our voyage last year to know that, once separated from our luggage, it was an even chance if we should ever see it again, independent of the discomfort to which we should be exposed in the meanwhile by being without it. So we came off, and the vessel began to turn slowly and get under way. We were only a few hundred yards from it when we saw Shaheen approaching it, in a large boat, with all the luggage, and making frantic gesticulations for the vessel to stop and take him and his boxes on board. We felt rather anxious lest he should succeed, and so bring about the consummation to avoid which we had left the vessel, but we were relieved presently by seeing the mail-boat slowly steam on, leaving Shaheen far behind. He, too, was not a little delighted at meeting us, as he would have been rather embarrassed at having all the luggage on his hands, and being left without a ticket or funds!

When we reached the hotel, we found it was crowded, and there was not a room to let anywhere. A gentleman had given up his room to Mrs Freeland, but it was very small, and in it were crowded her three children, two nurses, and herself. As we belonged to his Highness's service, the landlord made every effort to accommodate us, and at last induced two gentlemen to give up a large double-bedded room to Mrs Freeland and me. The arrival of his Highness always makes the hotels very full. On previous occasions the rooms had been ordered for us beforehand, so that we had found no difficulty. This time we had been told to go on board at once, and we could have done it easily but for the delay in the train, which was no fault of ours.

Mr Freeland went off immediately to Ras-el-Tin to announce that we were still at Alexandria, and should await his Highness's orders. Either the matter was misinterpreted to him, in order to screen those who were really responsible for the delay (for we learned that the Khédive himself had been quite punctual in starting a full half-hour before the express), or he thought we had not been sufficiently active in striving to execute his orders. However that might be, we were told that his Highness was displeased, and that we were to leave the next day by the Chimdi, one of the Khédive's steam-yachts, which was to be got ready for some of the officials.

We had been told that the Chimdi was to start the next day at eleven, and to avoid the crowding we had seen on the post-boat, we determined to go on board at nine and secure our berths. We were just ready to start when we were told that it was the Tanta, not the Chimdi, we were to go by; and having got down to the quay, some one came to say it was not the Tanta, but the Mahalla. So to the Mahalla we went, and early as we were, we found all the best places taken, and scraps of paper gummed or pasted on to the doors with the names of some pasha or bey. A very small end cabin, where the motion would be most felt, was marked for Mdlle. Gemila (myself!), but Mr Freeland and Mr Michell were still worse off. Ten, eleven, twelve o'clock passed, and no sign of moving; at last, at 4 P.M., the pashas and beys began to come on board, and by degrees we got up the steam.

At six we were just starting, when a signal was made that we were to stop for another passenger. This was Mary Evans,[1] his Highness's dairy-woman, who had only received one hour's intimation to prepare herself for the voyage. She was got hastily on board, and off we started. But there was no accommodation for her, and she stoutly declared she must have a cabin. They proposed (without my knowledge) to put her into mine, but this she would not hear of. She said I was a lady, and she was a servant, and she would not incommode me, but firmly maintained that she had a right to a private sleeping-place, and *must* have it. At last a good-natured bey offered to give up his cabin to Mary, and the offer was gratefully accepted. She was a respectable hard-working woman, who for good pay had accepted the post of dairy-woman to his Highness the Khédive, and, I believe, gave full satisfaction. She had lived for one year in the harem, with several other European servants, but, as was to be expected, the way of life was so different that there were continual complaints on both sides, and at last it was settled that they should

---

[1] Referred to previously.

all leave, and be boarded outside the harem. During the winter she had been in it, she had received two dresses— one a very delicate light silk, the other a black silk, with broad stripes of yellow satin; very suitable for harem *fêtes*, but not exactly so for taking a walk in the town or going to church, which were her only "outings."

The next day we were in the open sea, but I think scarcely anybody went on deck, we were all ill, and there was nothing but groaning to be heard, with other sounds unnecessary to mention. On the third day we saw the islands of Rhodes, Scarpanto, Nicaria, &c., &c. On the fourth, at a quarter past 9 P.M., we anchored off the coast between St Stefano and Constantinople.

There was no harem on board, so I knew there would this time be no impediment to my being on deck when the vessel entered the Bosphorus, and I was there next morning at 5 A.M. We had been told we were to stop at Pera at Mysseri's hotel, until his Highness arrived, and the house at Emirghian was ready for us. The Mahalla passed on, however, without stopping, until we reached Emirghian, and then we were told we were all to disembark, and take caïques to Therapia, a little higher up the Bosphorus to the north. It was 6 A.M., a lovely May morning, and Shaheen got us a couple of caïques, and followed us with the luggage to the Hôtel d'Angleterre at Therapia. But what was our consternation on arriving to find there was not a room to be had! The Hôtel d'Angleterre is admirably managed, and the position of Therapia is so delightful that rooms at the hotel are engaged months beforehand. Therapia is the summer residence of all the foreign ambassadors, and it is situated at a curve of the Bosphorus, facing the entrance to the Black Sea. There is a wide esplanade extending some distance along the shore, and in the hottest weather it is generally cool here.

We went into the hotel, and, ordering breakfast, consulted what was to be done. Should one of us go to Mysseri's at Pera, and see if there were rooms for us, as it was no trifle to take all the luggage back to Constantinople, and up the hill to Pera, if on arriving there we were to find all apartments taken? While discussing what we were to do, somebody said a new hotel was about to be opened on the opposite side of the little bay, on the northern extremity of which the Hôtel d'Angleterre is situated. Would it not be well to go and look at this first, before undertaking the troublesome transport of our luggage to Pera? So we walked round the little bay to the Hôtel des Ambassadeurs as the house was called, and were agreeably surprised by all we saw. It had been the residence of a Greek merchant; the front of the house looked on to the little bay, at the back of it was a lovely garden on the hillside, fragrant with roses, and echoing with the melodious notes of the nightingale. We broke out simultaneously with Moore's ballad, "There's a bower of roses by Bendemeer's stream," and hastened to inspect the domestic arrangements, to ascertain whether they were in keeping with the charming exterior. The large hall was of marble, the staircase ditto, the bedrooms fresh and clean. We were the first comers; we struck the bargain at once, sent Shaheen back for the luggage, and took our rooms. I chose one looking on to the bay, Mr Freeland did the same; but Mr Michell, who had had enough of water during the voyage, chose a room looking on the garden, and revelled in the roses and the nightingales. We had had such a week of turmoil and discomfort, that we seemed in a perfect haven of rest, and we went about all day with beaming countenances, quoting poetry, and thinking life was not a bad thing after all.

The *cuisine* was excellent, and at dinner there were some new arrivals, who turned out to be college friends of Mr Freeland's. They had, like ourselves, gone to the Hôtel d'Angleterre, and finding accommodation there impossible, had come on to the Hôtel des Ambassadeurs.

The next morning our satisfaction was considerably damped by hearing that one of the gentlemen of our party, who had chosen the garden apartment, had spent the whole night in the capture of B flats! This statement, and the difficulty we found in making ourselves understood by the waiters when we wanted anything, made the roses and the nightingales a little less attractive. The waiters were Greeks; they understood a little French and a little Italian, and they jumbled both together with Greek, so that with the best intentions we all found a mutual understanding very difficult.

As we who slept in the front rooms had seen no B flats, we decided upon consideration that these unwelcome visitors were to be ascribed to the bed in the garden apartment being placed in a recess with wooden supporters under it; and in this climate, wherever wood is, these insects are sure to abound, and are almost impossible to eradicate. In the other rooms the bedsteads were of iron, which served as a non-conductor. The sufferer therefore at once changed his room, and saw no more of his tormentors.

After three days we removed to Emirghian. The weather was fine and very clear. From the kiosk at the top of the garden at Emirghian, the chain of Mount Olympus, covered with snow, was distinctly visible. The day temperature in the shade ranged from 60° to 66°, delightful when compared with the heat of Egypt. We were still in May, and we remembered the 29th, not only as the anniversary of the Restoration, but as that of the taking of Constantinople by the Turks in 1453, four hundred and twenty years back. Four-and-twenty times had Constantinople been besieged, and taken six. Was the capture under Mohammed II. in 1453 to be the last? Its possession in all ages has been fiercely contested. Among the ancients, by Persians, Spartans, and Athenians. In 340 B.C. the Athenians, instigated by Demosthenes, helped to defend the city against Philip of Macedon. One dark night the Macedonians were on the point of taking the city by assault, when the new moon suddenly appeared and revealed to the sentry on the walls the danger awaiting them. This gave rise to the crescent being used as a symbol on old Byzantine coins, and the Turks finding the same, adopted the half-moon as their device.[1]

Several fires took place during the first fortnight after our arrival. One was on the Bosphorus, and we saw the flames distinctly from the top of the garden; two were in Stamboul, and one at Pera. I went through the ruins of the last three days after it occurred, and they were still smoking, and the heat was great. But it was not alone at Constantinople that fires were raging. The pretty Opera-house at Malta, where I had so often been, was burnt down in the same week. It had cost £60,000 ten years before. The tremendous conflagration at Boston was daily telegraphed.

I repeated all the excursions of the year before, finding sometimes new ways of getting to them. There was the tramway, which with a slight interruption led almost to the Yedi Koullerler Kapoussi (Seven Towers), and the railway, which lay in the same direction. Both these were available for the walk round the city walls, an excursion

[1] I met while in Egypt a lady who had had a handsome brooch given to her, shaped like a crescent, which she objected to wearing, as she considered it a symbol of Mahometanism; but upon my telling her the origin of the device, she put it on with alacrity, saying she would now have no further misgivings. Later on, when I was living in the harem, a very pretty coral cross was sent by a European lady as a present to a young lady in the harem, but the latter rejected it at once as a symbol of Christianity!

of unrivalled interest, of which I was never tired. Then the lovely Princes' Islands, for which a long day was necessary, and which amply repaid the trouble of getting to them.

We were lodged in the same house on the hillside as we had been the year before; but Mrs Freeland and her children were not there, and their rooms were taken up by others. Also my dear little pupils no longer came to me and enlivened the house with their merry laughter and sportive sallies. All that was a thing of the past, of which the memory only remained. I breakfasted early, and then walked down through the shady alley before mentioned, to the harem gates.

The rooms occupied by the Princess looked down on the harem garden, which, I have before mentioned, was enclosed by a high wall; but as the whole grounds were on the hillside, the wall could not shut out the view of the upper part of the large garden. There were venetian blinds, but as they rather darkened the room, I opened them, conceiving that as the windows looked down on the harem garden, there was no necessity for their being closed. My near-sight prevented my seeing that the windows were visible from the walks at the top of the hill; but a few days after, upon going into the room and finding the blinds closed, I was about to open them when the Princess stopped me, and said, "No; they are to remain shut." It happened to be a dull day, and the closed blinds made the room so dark, that it was difficult to read or write. I exclaimed at it, and for some time my pupils said nothing; but at last, as I repeated that it was impossible to see to read, the Princess said, "Yesterday the first Princess was out in the garden at the top of the hill, and she saw one of the slaves leaning out of the window; upon inquiry it turned out to be from this room, and the first Princess then ordered that the shutters should be kept closed." I thought only of the interruption to the lessons, and begged my pupil to remonstrate with her mother on the subject, as hitherto I had had full liberty to open or close the shutters as I thought proper, ever since I had given lessons in the harem. Besides, I had a lurking suspicion that my pupil might be thereby endeavouring to shirk her lessons, and as I considered it injurious to the eyes to read or write in so dim a light, I expected she would presently ask me to relate to her a story, instead of studying; but I was mistaken in this supposition. She repeated earnestly that she could not speak to her mother; that the first Princess had ordered the shutters to be closed, and from her order there was no appeal.

I mention this as an instance of harem discipline. Any order from the first wife is paramount throughout the household. This lady considered that harem etiquette was violated by unveiled women being seen at open windows; and so it was, according to their notions. Had it been the mother of my pupil who gave the order, I could have represented to her the injurious effect upon the lessons, and the order would doubtless have been rescinded as long as I remained in the room.

The 25th of June was the anniversary of the Sultan Abdul Aziz's accession to the throne. This was always a *fête*, but it was to be made a still greater one on this occasion, as the Viceroy had invited the Sultane Validé on a visit to Emirghian. A particular part of the palace was to be set aside for this lady and her suite, and to be newly furnished for the occasion. The gardens were to be illuminated, all the paths to be festooned with lamps, of which Ibrahim Pasha told me there were 100,000. They were small globular glasses, half full of water, with oil at the top, and the wick floating on it. It was the business of five hundred men to attend to these lamps. They commenced putting in the oil two days before, and there was such a dropping along the walks as almost to overpower the scent of the roses, and remind one of an Italian warehouse. The three fine steam-yachts that lay moored in front of the palace were also to be illuminated.

There was a rumour that all the gentlemen in our little house on the hillside would have to leave, or be locked up in the house (from whence they could see nothing); and though I was not a gentleman, it would probably have extended to me, or, if I had succeeded in getting out, I could not have got in again.

At a certain hour, the lamps being all lighted, the gardens were to be left free for the Sultan's harem to wander about as they pleased. The best place from whence to gain a view of the whole was from the Bosphorus, and numberless caïques, and even steamers, were engaged for the night.

I was invited to join a party who had taken a steamer; but I should have been obliged to remain out all night, and I thought that paying rather too dearly for the pleasure. I had seen the previous year what a crowd had lined the shore all the afternoon and evening, and the *fête* on that occasion was merely that celebrated on every anniversary of the accession. This would be something *par excellence*.

CHAPTER XVIII.

Arrival of the Sultane Validé—Illuminations—The Sultan visits Emirghian—Etiquette on the occasion—Signs of departure—Leave Turkey on the Dakahlieh—Obstructions to the view on deck—Stop at Gallipoli—At Dardanelli—Mitylene—Smyrna—Stay there twenty-four hours—Great heat—Go ashore towards evening—Leave Smyrna—Stop at Scio—At Syra—Land—Fine position of the town—Well built and well paved—Town dates only forty years back—Continue our voyage—Arrival at Alexandria.

At half-past two in the afternoon the Sultane Validé arrived. We had hoped she would come by boat, but she drove, followed by her suite in about twenty carriages, and attended by a great many eunuchs. The road led to the garden gate at the top of the hill, and there the Khédive and the Princes of his family awaited her, and led her to the palace at the foot of the hill and by the water-side. The Khédive drove, and the Princes preceded her carriage on foot.

We had been on the watch since morning for her arrival, but missed it after all. I walked through the garden down to the shore, but found it so crowded that I soon returned. People had taken up their station hours before night; benches were arranged all along the walls; women had spread their carpets, and allowed no intruders on them.

The lamps began to be lighted before sunset, because it would be a long process. At about 9 P.M. I went out with Mr Freeland to see the effect of the illuminated gardens. At the top of the hill was a belvedere, and we went up to that, as affording the finest view. The whole extent of the gardens, the palace, and the Bosphorus, with the opposite shore, was spread out before us. Every serpentine path was a line of light; the outline of the yachts was shown to perfection; and the caïques, which all bore lights, looked like fireflies darting about. The night was calm, and the lights were reflected in the water; it was altogether the most fairylike scene that could be imagined. At all the paths leading down to the palace, sentinels were placed until the eunuchs should give the signal for the gardens to be given up to the ladies. I went back into the house, and I believe the gentlemen went down to the shore.

My bedroom was rather too light to be favourable for sleep, as all the trees near were hung with Chinese lanterns; so, as sleep was impossible, I sat by the window—sometimes looking down on the water below and on the opposite coast, and sometimes reading. The trees were too thick to enable me to see the garden, but the yachts were visible, and all that passed on the water. It was near dawn before the lights died out and the crowd dispersed.

The next day we heard nothing of the movements of the Sultane Validé. She remained in the palace with all her train, until at 5 P.M. twenty carriages drove up the hill in the same state in which they had come down, preceded by the Princes of the Khédive's family and several pashas, all on foot. The day had been very hot, with a south wind; soon after they were gone, it changed to the north, and became very cloudy and threatening. Torrents of rain fell in the night. Happily the *fête* was over before the rain came.

About a fortnight after, the Sultan came to visit the Khédive, and dine with him. No, I mistake; he came to dinner, but he dined alone. He came by road, not by water. His train took up about twenty-three carriages, and we were rather anxious to see his entry; but the day was tremendously hot, and no one could tell at what time he would come.

When he arrived, he was received by the Khédive

and the Princes of his family. If the Sultan asked a question, of course he received an answer; but if he merely made an observation, it was heard in silence, with profound reverence and low salaams. Those who entered his presence kept their eyes fixed on the ground, and their arms folded lest they should by any inadvertence be betrayed into the indecorum of swinging them! He was conducted in state to the kiosk which had been fitted up for him, and there he dined. No one was present but his own attendants; and when he had finished his repast, the magnificent gold service, then used for the first time, was packed up and sent to his palace as a present!

The scenery and excursions about Constantinople are so beautiful that I repeated some of them over and over again, and was always finding fresh points of interest. Sometimes, however, I came back with disgust and disappointment. One day, after waiting nearly half an hour at the Emirghian station in a burning sun and high wind, I found, when the steamer came, that there was no upper deck, and the awnings were down on both sides, because on one side was the sun and on the other the wind; the boat was very crowded, and a great many people were smoking. Arrived at the bridge, I found some Greek *fête* was going on, and the passage of the streets of Galata up to Pera was more difficult than ever. I had heard the year before that an underground railway was about to be constructed between Galata and Pera, and that it was to be open in 1873, but funds had failed and it was still uncompleted. Omnibuses drawn by four horses took a circuitous route up the hill, and small broughams plied on the bridge ready to take you up by the same road for a beshlik (11d.) I tried each conveyance by turns, but the jolting was so frightful that I preferred walking up the usual way, in spite of the sharp pebbles, the mudholes, the *hamals* (porters), and the dogs. The two latter obstructions were dreadful. Sometimes two or four men would be met carrying long poles, which required some ingenuity and nimbleness to avoid, particularly as it was a case of Scylla and Charybdis. The dirt and refuse thrown into the streets were terrible. For the last the dogs were the scavengers, and for the first the streets were swept and watered twice a-day; but it was not pleasant to come in for that either.

On the last day of July, upon entering the harem as usual, I saw signs of departure. I knew the Khédive was about to return to Egypt, but I had taken it for granted that the second Princess and her children would remain until the middle of October, as they had done the year before. I was mistaken. The second Princess was in better health than she had been for some time, and did not approve of being left behind. In Eastern countries, to be with the sovereign is light and life, and to be away from him is banishment. The Khédive was going, so all wished to go.

Even my pupils did not seem sorry to go. They could no longer run freely about the gardens; indeed they could not go into them at all, unless with one of the Princesses towards evening. The bright spot in my pupil's life was now the short time she could spend each day in her father's presence. To be away from him was always a serious grievance to her from the time of her seclusion in the harem.

We were told we were to return to Egypt by a post-boat, the Dakahlieh, which was advertised to leave the Golden Horn at 4 P.M. on the 6th of August. Our party consisted of Messrs Freeland and Michell, Skefket, and myself. We left Emirghian by the ordinary steamboat, Shaheen being with us to look after the luggage. The Khédive and his family were still at the palace, but as they would travel faster than we, they would probably reach Egypt about the same time. The Dakahlich, being a post-boat, would touch at several places, and be at any rate six days on the voyage.

When we got out of the steamer at the bridge and had seen all our luggage safely landed, we took three caïques and went on board the Dakahlich.

We were very much pleased with the boat; it was quite new, the accommodation excellent, and there were very few passengers.

Four P.M. had been advertised as the time for starting; but four, five, six o'clock came, and no signs of moving. At last we slowly started, but to our surprise, instead of rounding Seraglio Point into the Sea of Marmora, we steamed up the Bosphorus. The Khédive's private post had not come on board, so we went to Emirghian to fetch it. It was not ready; we slowly steamed back again, and stopping near Seraglio Point, waited until half-past ten, when it was brought, and we started on our voyage. The day had been lovely and the evening bright moonlight, so we took our farewell of the Bosphorus, with all its beauties, under the most favourable circumstances.

When I looked out of my cabin window at six o'clock the next morning, I found we were just passing the nearest rocky part of the Marmora Islands. My accommodation was first-rate. I was (until we reached Smyrna) the only first-class lady passenger, so I had a large cabin to myself, with an excellent bath-room adjoining. The windows were large, and allowed of a very good view when we were near the coast.

When I went on deck, however, I was disappointed. There was an excellent upper deck for the first-class passengers, but half of it was railed off for third-class, so that standing upon it you could never see on both sides at once. There was a kind of lattice-work screen, within which women and children were put, and the men were outside it. Over this screen they hung rugs, shawls, &c., to secure to themselves a little privacy, but it disfigured the deck sadly, and made it not pleasant to remain there. There was a charming circular cabin with windows all round, but upon going up to it as soon as I was dressed, I found a number of deck passengers had taken possession of it to sleep in; and though they were turned out in an hour or two, I did not care much for sitting there after seeing the way in which it had been occupied in the night. The very close proximity of the hencoop I have mentioned, where so many women and children ate, drank, and slept during the whole voyage, was very far from pleasant or refreshing.

At 9.30 A.M. we stopped off Gallipoli, and remained there for two hours; it is the northern entrance to the Dardanelles or Hellespont. At 1 P.M. we stopped at Dardanelli, exactly opposite the Castle of Europe, and the narrowest part of the straits (the Castle of Asia is about a mile to the north on the Asiatic coast). We stayed at Dardanelli upwards of six hours. During all that time we were constantly employed in taking in bales of something (I believe of tobacco), and a good many deck passengers came on board. It was bright moonlight when we left, and we could have seen the coast beautifully from the deck but for the incumbrances that covered it. First, there was the great lattice-work cage in which the harem was enclosed; and next the crowds of Arabs, Greeks, Turks, and Levantines encamped around. The saloon on deck had not yet been appropriated, as they waited for the small hours before turning in there, but every window was blocked up by some one who had ensconced himself against it as a shelter.

I awoke at a quarter to three; the moon was still shining, so I got up to look out, and found we were stopping off Mitylene. The coast looked very bold and picturesque;

the town is on the east side of the island, just opposite the Asiatic coast, and not in the little bay to the south where I had imagined it to lie. I was on deck before four, but it was in such a state that I went back to my cabin, until others of the party joined me. At 5 A.M. we left Mitylene, and I watched the coast narrowly to find the entrance to the southern bay. A sailing-vessel was close on the coast, and was evidently making for this bay. I kept my glass fixed on it for a long time, hoping to see the entrance, but my attention was distracted for a moment, and when I looked again the vessel had disappeared!

I saw the sun rise over the mountains of Asia Minor at eighteen minutes past five (August 8th). At 10.30 we reached Smyrna. It is finely situated in an almost circular bay, with mountains all round, but they looked parched and bare. The heat was intense. We had intended going ashore directly, taking a carriage, and seeing what was to be seen; but we all with one voice agreed that it was impossible, and decided to wait on board for the five-o'clock dinner, and drive afterwards. It was full moon that night, so we thought we should have light enough to prolong our drive at pleasure.

Immediately after dinner we went ashore. The large heavy boats are very different from the light caïques of the Bosphorus, and perhaps it is well they are, for the landing-places are not very commodious, and one sometimes has to make jumps which would infallibly upset a caïque.

When we landed, we had intended taking a carriage at once, but unfortunately (not seeing one) we took the wrong turning, and found ourselves entangled in streets without hope of finding that of which we were in search. Had we gone to the right, we should have come almost immediately on a stand, but we went to the left, and after walking for some time, stopped at a little inn to ask for a carriage. At that moment one drove up with a gentleman in it, and he stopped, and told us he was going to the railway station. Should he send the carriage back for us, or would we enter it at once, and leaving him at the station, retain the carriage for ourselves? The weather was very hot, and the streets were wretchedly paved, so we thankfully accepted his offer and got in. People had before told us to be sure to see this railway station, as the Smyrniotes looked upon it as one of the sights of the town. We had not come to the East to see railway stations, but under the circumstances thought we might as well take a look at it.

It was indeed a very pretty one, and having deposited there our obliging new acquaintance, we continued our drive over a great many bridges, with the water on our left hand, gradually narrowing from a bay to a river. The road was extremely pretty, and we congratulated ourselves much upon having taken it. We first went towards Bournabat (which is on the branch line to Cassaba), and then from a northerly direction turned eastward and came round by Boojah, passing through a large cemetery (walled in), with very fine cypresses on both sides of the road. At last we got back into the town again, and for about half an hour had all our joints dislocated by jolting over the wretched pavement. We were rather under the impression that our driver took us there to show us the town, but we found afterwards that it was the regular way back. My companions (Mr Michell and Shefket) left me at the British Consulate while they went to explore further. At the Consulate I met Mr Freeland, and returned with him later to the vessel.

We remained in the Bay of Smyrna the next day until a quarter past one. The heat was overpowering; not a breath of wind was stirring. We seemed in a lake, for we were surrounded by land on all sides, but what seemed a small opening to the west. The panorama was a fine one. Before us, along the shore and on the brow of the hill, lay Smyrna, forming a large semicircle. On the heights, and on the site of the ancient acropolis, the Byzantine castle formed a prominent object; a little farther southward, lower down on the hill, was a cypress-grove of considerable dimensions. We longed to explore it all, but the heat forbade any movement,—we could only sit on deck and look at it all. While we were at anchor in the Bay of Smyrna not a breath of wind was stirring; but at 1.15, when we began to move, and made our way to the entrance of the bay, we found there was a strong head-wind, and all the port-holes were fastened down as if rough weather might be expected. But as we got well into the straits between the peninsula of Karabournou and the island of Scio, the sea again became calm, and at half-past seven in the evening we stopped at Kastro, the chief town of the island, and on the east side of it. An hour after the moon rose like a great crimson ball. We stayed two hours off Kastro, and I should like to have gone ashore, but it did not seem feasible, and perhaps, seen in the moonlight from the water, it might have looked more attractive than it really was.

I had been told that we should stop for some hours at Syra, one of the Cyclades, and that we should probably reach it early the next morning. I slept very little that night, but at last went off so soundly that I was only awoke by the stopping of the vessel at 5.30 A.M. I got up directly, and looking from my cabin window, saw we were in a lovely little bay just opposite the Lazaretto. Very soon after Mr Michell called to me outside my door to ask if I was ready to go ashore, and hearing I was not, promised to return for me in an hour. At seven I went ashore, and remained until half-past ten.

The Bay of Syra is a perfect semicircle, and the town stretches a considerable distance along the shore. It only dates back forty years, having been commenced very soon after the establishment of Greek independence. It is very well built, well paved, and picturesquely arranged. There is a mountain background to the town, and some of the hills are of a conical shape; these are covered with houses, one being surmounted by a Catholic church. We went into the church of St Nicholas, very near the Piazza, where a great many palm-trees are planted; looked at the theatre, went to a photographer's and bought several views of Syra. Then we paid a visit to a wine-seller, who, with a quantity of wine in casks round the shop, sold us two enormous bottles of wine of Syra and of Santorin at a very moderate charge. I cannot express what a relief it was to walk about the well-paved streets of Syra after the detestable pebbles of Smyrna and of Constantinople.

I forgot to say that we had the most delicious fresh figs at Smyrna, firm and sweet, green and almost hard outside, and quite different from the squashy purple figs, which are, I think, very inferior in flavour. Great quantities of fruit crops are exported to London and Liverpool from Smyrna.

We left Syra at about half-past eleven, and from that time passed continually through groups of islands; they were all bare and mountainous, and gave no sign of culture or habitation, at least on the side turned to us. Our course lay between Candia (Crete) and Caso, instead of Rhodes and Scarpanto, as on my three former voyages; but we passed them in the middle of the night, so I did not see them. The next day there was no land in sight; the sea was calm, but it was intensely hot. On the sixth day of our voyage (12th of August), at 6 A.M., we stopped to take a pilot on board, and soon after steamed into the harbour of Alexandria. No orders awaited us, so upon landing we went at once to the Hôtel de l'Europe.

CHAPTER XIX.

Arrival at Alexandria—Go to the Hôtel de l'Europe—Khédive and harem not yet come—Preparations for illuminating the town—The hotel is photographed—Khédive and harem go to Cairo—Return of my pupil—I begin lessons at Ramleh—Shaheen's story—Generosity of the second Princess—Our party diminishes—We are ordered to Cairo—Go to the New Hotel—Remove to the Palace of Gezireh—Description of it—Kiosk in the garden.

Upon reaching the hotel we found all the front rooms were bespoke. They were not only the best, but they faced the north, consequently had the cool breeze. In the back rooms, looking to the south, the air was that of a vapour-bath, so hot and damp. The hotel was full of pashas and beys awaiting the arrival of his Highness. Telegrams had come announcing that he had left Emirghian on the night of the 10th, that he did not intend coming direct, but should stop at some of the islands, and would probably reach Alexandria about the 14th or 15th.

Until the arrival of his Highness we knew nothing of our own destination. We hoped it might be either Ramleh or Ras-el-Tin, for the hotel was very hot and suffocating.[1]

Great preparations were being made for illuminating the town in honour of his Highness's return. The whole

---

[1] The palace of Ramleh is about four or five miles to the east of Alexandria, and connected by a railway with the town. Beyond the palace are numerous villa residences inhabited by the European merchants of Alexandria.

front of the hotel was hung with coloured lamps. They were at every window, and this reconciled me in some measure to having a back room, as I should have been kept awake the whole night by the glare and heat, as well as by the noise below on the Grande Place. The illuminations were to last for three nights!

The paving of the Grande Place was at last finished, and it looked very handsome. It is of great breadth, and still greater length. All down the centre is a promenade with a double row of trees on each side, and between this centre and the houses is again a broad carriage-road and excellent pavements. To the east are several handsome streets, which connect it with the roads leading to Ramleh, and to the Mahmoudieh Canal. All the chief people of Alexandria have houses either on the canal or at Ramleh.

The English colony is a large one, and we made many acquaintances. One friend introduced another, and we soon formed a large social circle, so that we hoped our stay might be prolonged, if only we could be at Ramleh and not at Alexandria. The great want of this last town is a marine promenade. It is close upon the sea, but the whole coast of the town is taken up by the backs of wretched houses. The shore is neither beach, sands, nor shingle, such as we have in England, but a loose substance in which you sink; and every opening to the sea is contaminated by bad drainage.

On the 14th, as I went down to breakfast, a prodigious firing of guns announced that the Mahroussah had entered the harbour. Presently after there was military music, and a number of soldiers passed down the Grande Place to meet his Highness at the landing-place. Then another volley told us that the Khédive had landed.

The illuminations lasted four nights instead of three, the fourth being in honour of the inauguration of a statue to Mohammed Ali. During this time the entire front of the house, with the broad balcony which stretches along the whole way, was given up to the illuminations. Altogether, including the preparations and the removal, eight or ten days were taken up, and during that interval I could not go into the balcony, the only cool spot. The streets were inconveniently crowded towards evening, and the days were far too hot for taking any exercise. I was obliged to keep the shutters closed in my room on account of the glare and heat, so that I sat in semi-darkness all day, and when I opened them at night I was kept awake by the fiddling and singing going on in two *cafés* opposite.

As is always the case on such occasions in Egypt, carriages, being much in request, were charged at an exorbitant rate, so that I had not the resource of driving. When one has to pay £1 or 30s. for a drive of a couple of hours, one is rather disposed to put it off until carriages become a little cheaper.

On the 17th his Highness went to Cairo to be present at the Khalidj, or cutting of the canal, to admit the waters of the Nile to overflow the land. A great many officials went with him, and we were enabled to secure a suite of rooms in the front, which was a great comfort.

In the course of the day I received a summons to go to Ras-el-Tin on the following morning, and I gave notice at once to Shaheen to have a carriage in readiness for me at 8 A.M.

When I went down the next morning at the appointed time, I was agreeably surprised to find the passages and doorway quite in order, and free from obstruction: it had been a work of difficulty to get in and out ever since our arrival, but now all was clear. The illumination paraphernalia had not been removed, it is true, but there was an air of order which was quite unusual. No carriage was at the door; Shaheen was not visible, nor any one belonging to the hotel. I stood for a moment in the centre of the doorway, and with my hand up to shade my eyes, looked intently at some black object at a little distance, of which I could not make out the purport. I was not long left in doubt. A gentleman came up laughing, and said in Italian, " Very well indeed, ma'am; quite a success!" and I was then aware that I had made myself the central figure in a photograph, having unwittingly taken my station just at the critical moment.

When I reached Ras-el-Tin I found my pupil just about to start for Cairo, to be present at the cutting of the canal. She had not known of this when she sent for me the day before, and she now told me she did not expect to be back for some days.

Shaheen had been very anxious, ever since our landing, to go to Cairo "to see his wife," he said; and though we thought that a natural request, we were unwilling to grant it, until our own movements were decided. As soon as the Khédive and harem went to Cairo we felt we might be secure for some days, and gave him therefore leave to go, enjoining him to be on the watch for any symptoms of removal.

Six days after the Princess returned, and it was settled that I should remain at the hotel, and drive every morning to Ramleh to give lessons, returning at about five in the afternoon. I have mentioned that there was a railway to Ramleh, which passed near the palace; but the latter stood high above the rails, with a very steep and sandy ascent, so that it was not a pleasant way for any one going there daily. The carriage-road formed a gradual curve, and landed you at the harem gate.

Just under the portal of the outer gate sat the chief eunuch in the shade, with a man standing behind fanning him. He was a great personage, and around him were a crowd of satellites, eunuchs, Arabs, and generally the Greek *lalla*, to receive any order that might be sent out from my Princess. Sentinels walked up and down in front of the gates to guard the entrance, but a nod from the chief eunuch decided everything.

The palace at Ramleh is situated very near the sea, and indeed it is several palaces, not one. The first is the harem, occupied by the wives of his Highness, with all their attendants. The next is the Khédive's own palace, with a subterranean communication to that of his wives. Then came two or three more, which have been recently added for his married daughters, the last being built for my pupil.

I was quite delighted with the palace when I entered it. Having passed the gate where the chief eunuch sat, I drove into an inner court, and then leaving the carriage, went into a sort of vestibule, where were several eunuchs. The doors were always kept locked, so that any one who might by chance have succeeded (in the absence of the chief eunuch) in passing the first gate, would here again be subjected to rigid scrutiny. I saw in this vestibule a door leading into an inner room, where lessons were given by the various Turkish and Arabic masters; and as this part of the building belonged to the eunuchs, there was sufficient surveillance. Having passed through this vestibule, another door led me into the garden and up a flight of steps to the entrance of the harem. It was upon going in here that the *coup d'œil* was so agreeable. A long and broad corridor extended the full length of the building from south to north. At the northern extremity was a very large terraced balcony, with a verandah overhead, and lattice-work screen about ten feet high on the three open sides. This balcony was full of rocking-chairs, where you might sit and listen to the ceaseless murmur of the waves breaking on the shore. The corridor was of the cruciform shape, the floors were covered with Indian matting, and the walls lined with divans; in the transepts were all sorts of easy-chairs, couches, &c., but no sign of occupation—no tables, books, or work. A great many doors opened on both sides into inner apartments, and from the transepts staircases led to an upper floor exactly similar.

My pupil, the Princess Zeyneb, had a suite of rooms on the west side, and to her and Kopsès I devoted all the mornings. Faïk Hanem's were on the east, and my afternoons were given to her.

I took luncheon with the second and third Princesses and my pupils, and after we had finished I sat studying Turkish in the large balcony overlooking the sea until it was time to go to Faïk Hanem's apartments. Sometimes, however, I remained with the second Princess while we took coffee, and I tried to talk with her. Whatever I learned, however, was by sheer study; I could not catch the language by ear as some people do.

I could not help remarking how anxious both these ladies (second and third Princesses) were respecting the education of their children, and indeed respecting the education of any of the slave children in the harem. I have already mentioned that it is common to purchase very young children, and to have them brought up in the great harems to ensure a more careful training. I never met with the slightest interruption from either of these ladies; on the contrary, they seemed much pleased with the discipline and punctuality that I maintained. Whatever interruptions I had came from the slaves, and they ceased after a time.

Shaheen returned on the same day as the Princess, but with a sad story. He had not told us why he was so anxious to go to Cairo, or we might perhaps have arranged it,—not that his presence could have altered the event.

He was expecting the birth of a child, and the mother was very young. When he reached Cairo the child was a day old, but the mother had been buried the morning of his arrival! He stayed a few days to arrange a nurse for the child, and settle other claims, and then came back to us. He was very sad, but bore it with the resignation of a Mussulman, saying "it was the will of God!"

He always accompanied me to the harem, and as I got out he said, "You tell Zeyneb Hanem; she very sorry!" I promised I would, and so I did. Both the Princess and Kopsès looked sad, heard it all, but said nothing.

When I returned, Shaheen asked me with great anxiety what the Princess had said to my communication.

"Oh," I replied, "she was very sorry!"

"Sorry! that all! I thought she help me!"

"Help you?" said I; "what can the Princess do for you? you have got a nurse!"

"Yes," said he, sadly, "but me poor man! funeral cost much! many people! much meat! much bread! cost much money!"

"Oh," I said, "I understand; you thought the Princess would give you something to help to pay the expenses?"

"Yes," said he, "she very good! I thought she help me!"

The next day I repeated the story again to the Princess, telling her that as Shaheen had been long in the service, I thought he had some claim to assistance in his trouble; that I would try and raise a subscription, if she would head it with a donation.

To this both the Princess and Kopsès objected strongly. The latter said that Zeyneb Hanem, as daughter of his Highness, could not possibly give a small sum, and that she had so many demands on her purse that she could not give what would be expected of her. To this assertion Kopsès remained firm, and her opinion on all matters of harem etiquette was final. "Well," said I, "at any rate you can ask your mother." To this the Princess readily agreed, and I then dropped the subject. At luncheon I always sat between my two pupils, and opposite the second and third Princesses. The table was elegantly served in the European style, and there was nothing in the manners or habits of these two ladies to indicate that it was new to them. If it had *once* been otherwise, that time was past.

There was a momentary lull in conversation, and I thought it a good opportunity to introduce Shaheen's story; accordingly I urged my pupil to tell her mother. Whenever I spoke to my pupils in French or English, the Princesses always asked immediately, "Ne dir?" (What does she say?) Thus urged between her mother and me, the Princess tried to render the story in Turkish. But the idiom of oriental languages is so different from that of French and English, that she hesitated a little in the translation, and became confused; upon which the second Princess turned to Kopsès for an explanation. The latter had great command of language, and as I spoke, she translated the purport into Turkish, while my dear little pupil, the burden being no longer wholly upon her, added her quota to the explanations. The second Princess heard it all silently, and when I had no more to say, the subject dropped.

I was discouraged, and thought there was an end of the matter, as I could not renew the appeal; but when we rose from luncheon, the second Princess asked me to go and take coffee with her. While doing so, I observed she said something to an attendant, who presently returned with a casket. The Princess unlocked it, and counted out twenty sovereigns, which she put into my hand, saying, "For Shaheen!" I need not say Shaheen was overjoyed at the result of my application.

About this time Mr Freeland left the service and went to England. His dismissal was very sudden, and without any fault having been found. His family were in England, but about to return shortly.

These sudden dismissals are not understood in England, but here they are very common. Plans are changed, and the parties in the way of them are at once removed. Some compensation, more or less, may be given them, and there is an end of the matter. In this case the seclusion of the Princess made a household with a family unnecessary; her governess could give her lessons in the harem, and the Pasha's establishment would henceforth be composed of gentlemen only. To me personally, this breaking up of the English household we had formed for nearly two years was a subject of great regret. We had all four lived on excellent terms, and had had as few rubs as could well be expected from persons thus thrown together without any previous acquaintance.

My pupil had asked me if I would go and live in the harem, but I was unwilling to do this for many reasons. I felt that I should be so entirely dependent on her that it would alter our relative positions, and probably make her studies merely nominal. I presume she was told to ask me; for soon after, the second Princess, during luncheon one day, asked me if I would live with her daughter when she was married, and I agreed to do so. I knew very well from her character that she was not likely to do lessons after her marriage; but I might acquire a moral influence over her that would be more important. Besides, she was so gentle and lovable that I had become very much attached to her.

I had been asked to dine and sleep at the house of some friends, two or three stations beyond the palace at Ramleh. I did so, and the next morning Mr Gisborne drove me in his waggonette to the harem gate. I sat on the front seat by him, and the *saïs* ran before, as is customary in Egypt, to clear the way. When we reached the gate, Mr Gisborne got down off the box and gave me his hand to assist me. The carriage was high, and I jumped down on the sand,—a very simple thing, and so much a matter of course with us that it seems absurd to relate it; but the moment I had done so I felt what an incongruity it was to enter a Mahometan royal harem in such a way. There sat the chief eunuch in state, an Arab standing behind him flapping a great feather fan to keep off the flies, and another in front holding a tray with coffee. I shook hands with my friend and bade him good-bye, and then walked in. How would a Mahometan lady have entered? Cloaked and veiled, she would have been lifted by two eunuchs out of the carriage like a paralytic, the others standing by with low obeisances.

The Ramleh palace was so delightfully cool and fresh, that I quite enjoyed going there every day, as much as I always disliked going into the harem at Abdeen. But the Khédive remained in Cairo, and the ladies were most anxious to join him; so on the twentieth of September I found on going to my pupil that they were all about to return to Cairo. No orders had arrived for us (Mr Michell and myself), though we knew our departure could not be long delayed. At midnight a telegram arrived to say we were to go up by the express next morning, but we were not told where to go. So we went to the New Hotel, which we found almost empty, with the exception of Sir Samuel and Lady Baker.

We heard that his Highness and the harem were all at Gezireh, and as I had now the free *entrée*, I drove there the next morning to see my pupil and to hear our plans. I found it was intended that Mr Michell and I should take up our abode at Gezireh for a time; and I was glad of it, for it was extremely hot at Cairo, and the daily transit in the heat would have been very fatiguing. We were to reside in that part of the palace where my pupil had been with Zohrab Bey in the spring of 1872, before her seclusion in the harem. Zohrab Bey had now retired, the heat of Egypt having seriously affected his health (he was living at Broussa); another doctor was there to look after the Pasha, but of course no one could fill his place. Our household was therefore composed of the Pasha (by day) and his doctor, Edward Zohrab (the nephew of Zohrab Bey), Shefket, Mr Michell, and myself. We had French servants and a French *cuisine*, so that both apartments and attendance were first-rate.

I think I have before said that the part of the palace which we inhabited was that usually devoted to illustrious visitors, except that, of course, we did not occupy the state apartments. The shape was something like this:—

WEST.

Apartments.							
Corridor.							
			Balcony.				
Apartments—South Aspect.	Corridor.	Apartments where we were—North Aspect.	Balcony.	Small Centre Garden.	Balcony—South Aspect.	Apartments.	Corridor.	State Apartments—North Aspect.
Balcony.			Steps.		Balcony.		

River Nile

EAST.

The rooms that we occupied looked northward on to the small centre garden, and opened into the balcony, which formed a promenade one-eighth of a mile in extent. We were on the first floor. This balcony formed a charming walk in the evening. The whole extent commanded everything passing on the river; but the two ends had a fine view up and down the stream. It was a great amusement to me to watch the boats as they passed, which seemed to go equally fast whether going up or down. This is caused by there being usually a strong north wind blowing up the river, and a rapid current coming down.

Of all the palaces built by the Mohammed Ali dynasty, that of Gezireh is the finest. The gardens are very extensive, with all kinds of rare plants and trees; a great many animals — lions, tigers, bears, giraffes, ostriches, gazelles, &c., &c.

The palace is not one vast block, but several distinct buildings; as, one for the Khédive himself, one for his harem, and one for illustrious visitors.

There is a beautiful kiosk in the grounds where the Princess of Wales stayed when in Egypt. It is a perfect gem. The building is in two divisions, connected by a large marble vestibule, open at two sides, one on to the garden, the other to a lake with a pleasure-boat close by, and (with a space of garden between) opposite to the chief harem entrance.

It is only one storey high, raised a few steps from the garden; the flooring all of marble, beautifully polished, chess-board pattern, with a border in mosaic. On the garden side is a long terrace walk (in marble) extending the whole length of the building. In the centre of the vestibule is a large fountain. On one side of it is the grand dining-room, with table for fifty covers, a private dining-room, and two spacious reception-rooms. In one of these are two beautiful marble tables in mosaic, wonderfully well executed. One came from Florence; the other was a present from the Pope to the Khédive. What his Highness gave in return I do not know; but, no doubt, it was something to exemplify the French saying, "On lui donne un œuf pour attraper un bœuf." It is almost impossible to believe that these tables are not paintings instead of mosaics, so exquisitely is the marble shaded to represent the figures and the borders of flowers around them.

On the other side of the vestibule is a drawing-room, in which is a beautiful Aubusson carpet, presented by Marie Amelie, Queen of the French, to Mohammed Ali. There is a second drawing-room, which was fitted up as a bedroom for the Princess of Wales, and beyond is a charming bath-room. I was told that it cost the Khédive £8000 a-year to keep this place in constant repair. The framework of the building is of iron, which gives a particularly light and elegant effect to all the pillars.

CHAPTER XX.

Harem at Gezireh—Daily lessons there—Departure of his Highness and the harem from Gezireh to Abdeen—I remain at Gezireh—Again difficulties about a carriage—October a trying month in Egypt—Ramadan begins—Sudden removal to Choubrah—French cook and Arab sentinel—Locks and keys—Mixed nationalities among us—Copper coinage—Popular superstition concerning Baïram commencing on a Friday.

The harem where my pupils now resided with the wives of his Highness was about five minutes' walk from that part of the palace which I inhabited, and which was on the banks of the Nile. All the buildings were enclosed (gardens, menageries, aviaries, &c., &c., all included) by high walls of vast extent, and any one once within these walls (by no means easy of entrance) could go about pretty freely, except that there were sentinels near the approaches to the harem to warn off intruders. I walked to the harem every morning at about eight, returning at twelve; and again in the afternoon at two, coming back at five. The walk was so pleasant and breezy that I quite enjoyed it, except that it always gave me a pang when I entered and saw my dear little pupils. I had to cross two rustic bridges and pass along shady walks, skirting the lake by the kiosk, until I came to the chief entrance of the harem. The entrance, like that to the palace at Ramleh, was thoroughly oriental in character, though otherwise very dissimilar. At Ramleh the desert came up to the gates, and the only shade to be found was in the deep archway where the chief eunuch sat. At Gezireh a broad semicircular drive was in front of the harem gates, and trees gave their thick shade all round. Several chairs were scattered under these trees, and there sat the chief eunuch and perhaps a dozen followers. Many Arab sentinels were stationed near.

I entered without opposition (as I was known) through the first gate, where some eunuchs were seated, and one took down a ponderous key and opened the heavy iron-barred door which formed the second gate. His Highness went in and out by this gate, but plenty of eunuchs were on the watch for his coming in and going out, and at such times no one could enter, but must stand aside until he had passed. When the second gate was unlocked I entered a large paved court, upon which countless windows looked drearily down, and behind which were perhaps a hundred imprisoned women. The best apartments do not look on these paved courts, but upon an inner garden surrounded by a high wall where the ladies of the harem walk. The room in which I sat with my pupils was on the ground-floor, opening on to the harem garden. It was spacious and airy, and would have been very pleasant but for one reminder. The windows had strong iron bars, so that no one could get either in or out. It might seem unnecessary to have these barred windows when the high walls and the guarded gates are considered; but men are often at work in the gardens, and these men are not eunuchs. The gardeners are engaged there a good part of the day, and during that time one or two eunuchs patrol up and down and close the venetian blinds of the apartments on the side where the men are at work. Of course if all were shut it was semi-darkness, but I always took care that *some* should be open; and though at first the eunuchs would close them, yet when I remonstrated and they saw in passing to and fro that we were always employed, they were very good-natured and took care to keep one or two open or partially so.

These daily walks through the garden to and from the harem lasted rather more than a fortnight; but one morning in October, going there as usual, I found a number of vans drawn up near the gates, and soon discovered there was a general flitting. His Highness had felt the place damp the last night or two, and had decided upon removing to Abdeen, though the palace was being altered and enlarged, and numbers of workmen were still employed upon it. When I entered the harem, I found general rejoicing at the prospect of moving. There is always rejoicing at any move, no matter where; it makes a little change in the monotony of their lives. The Pasha was to continue his lessons at Gezireh, sleeping at Abdeen, and driving out thither for some hours in the day. We (the educational staff) were therefore to continue in the same quarters for the present. For a considerable time past, a house had been building in the immediate vicinity of the palace of Abdeen, which it was rumoured was to be eventually the "school," as they called it, of Ibrahim Pasha—that is to say, he was to take his lessons there, and it was to be the abode of his (European) educational staff.

There are now two or three broad handsome streets leading to the palace of Abdeen; but a very few years ago, a thickly populated Arab quarter lay under the walls of the palace, on two sides. The Khédive has done much to clear the town, to remove the dust-heaps, to widen out the densely inhabited quarters, by planning new thoroughfares, which should run into the heart of them, and there is no doubt that this has immensely promoted the general health of the city. A great part of the ground thus reclaimed was taken in to enlarge the palace, and the walls were given a much wider sweep, but some part was devoted to the building of three or four large handsome houses, one of which was to serve as the "school," and a new gate was opened in the palace wall opposite, so that the young Pasha should be in a few minutes, from his own apartments in the palace, transferred into the school. Bodily exercise is not considered necessary among the upper classes in the East. We thought the daily drive good for the Pasha, but such was apparently not the opinion in high quarters. Whatever might be the views held concerning the desirability of this house for the Pasha, we looked upon it as decidedly objectionable for ourselves, and dreaded very much the removing thither. The house itself was then very nearly finished, but the space in front, which was intended for a garden, was a mere dust-heap, and the streets leading to it were only planned, but as yet impassable for carriages.

The loan of 1873, which had been proposed as a means of getting rid of the floating debt that had long weighed as an incubus upon the revenue of the country, had proved a total failure; and retrenchment was the order of the day. This operated unfavourably on me, for the carriage which had been given to me the previous autumn, to go to and from the harem, was taken away. There were in the Khédive's coach-houses so many carriages, and so many English grooms and stablemen, that it was a thing inexplicable to us why one of these carriages, thus lying idle, should not be ordered to come at a stated hour to take me to the harem gates, and bring me away again. These men would have received their orders, and obeyed them punctually, and there would have been an end of the matter. Instead of which an outdoor carriage was ordered for me, and when I went to the harem morning and afternoon, a napoleon a-day was charged for it. Naturally that seemed very high; so as retrenchments were being made, I found, when I had to go from Gezireh to Abdeen, that I was to return to the first plan of having a harem carriage sent for me. Now this was the inconvenience of a harem carriage. There were only a limited number which drove into the outer court of the harem at an early hour every morning. The Princesses might give a standing order (and they did do so) that a carriage was to be sent for me at a fixed hour every day; but every order was given through the eunuchs, and these latter always set aside the standing order, to execute one that might be given at the moment. One of the Princesses wanted to send for a *modiste*, or some visitor staying in the harem wanted to go to the mosque or to the bazaars, or one of the eunuchs wanted to go somewhere, having received an order from the head eunuch to get something; so a carriage that ought to have been sent for me was taken for one, two, or three hours, and then despatched for me when it returned.

During the first four days that I was supposed to go

from Gezireh to Abdeen, on two occasions no carriage whatever was sent for me. The first time that this omission occurred I managed to catch a broken-down brougham that had just brought back Martini Bey, the doctor. I arrived two hours behind time, and in a carriage of which one door was broken off and tied on with a rope. Had the Khédive known it, he would have been very angry, and have given stringent orders on the subject, which would have been obeyed for a few days, and then the same thing would have gone on again. I had to do with the harem; all orders must pass through the eunuchs, and these people have no idea of time, order, or instruction. The commands of the Princesses are heard with apparent reverence, but are virtually disregarded. The Khédive himself is the only person obeyed, and of course he cannot look into everything.

The month of October is, I think, one of the most trying in Egypt. The waters are subsiding, and the flies, mosquitoes, and sand-flies are most troublesome and venomous. There is a heavy dew night and morning, and it is unsafe to keep the windows open at night on account of the damp. Many people do it, but also many suffer from it. A few days after the harem had left Gezireh I had a feverish attack, loss of sleep and appetite, and accompanied by great weakness. We had then an excellent *cuisine*, but I took such a disgust to food I could eat nothing. For more than a week I did not go to Abdeen, and during all that time I heard (particularly at night) the barbarous sound of Arab music, which always accompanies the weddings of the lower classes. Ramadan was approaching, when no marriage can take place. The opposite side of the river (Boulak) is thickly populated, and the sounds were incessant. There had been nothing but marriages ever since we landed from Constantinople. The poor little bride, often a girl of ten or eleven, is paraded through the streets in a sort of Jack-in-the-green, where she must be nearly stifled with heat and dust. Men dance round her and play all sorts of antics.

The facilities for divorce are very great: there is no occasion for any cause—the man is tired of his wife, that is quite a sufficient reason. Can it be wondered at that the rate of infant mortality is so great?

After nine days' absence, I wrote to my pupil to tell her I was able to resume the lessons, and to ask her to order the carriage to fetch me the next day at the usual hour (eight o'clock). At five minutes past six the next morning (the sun had not risen) there were two persons at the door of my room to tell me that a carriage had been sent to take me to Abdeen. At 6.39 the driver himself came up to the door, and finding I was not to be induced to go at so early an hour, he went away, and when at eight o'clock I went down quite ready, he was gone, and no carriage to be seen! The chief eunuch had told him to fetch me and to return immediately, and the driver dared not disobey. It was so damp that the flagstones in the courtyard were as wet as if it had been raining heavily; the carriage did not come again, and I remained in the house all day. The next day was the first of Ramadan,[1] and the carriage came for me two hours later than it ought to have done.

While I was staying at Gezireh, and the harem at Abdeen, I was unable to return to luncheon as I had hitherto done, because the bridge over the Nile, which I had to cross, is open for three hours daily, from about twelve to three, to enable *dahabiehs* to pass up and down, and is consequently closed for carriages. I was obliged, therefore, to stay to luncheon at the harem. At Ramleh this had been very pleasant; I had taken it with the Princesses, and there was the charming breezy balcony to sit

---

[1] The month of fasting is called in Arabic Ramadan, and in Turkish Ramazan.

in afterwards with my book. At Abdeen it was not so. The Princesses and my pupils took their meals with his Highness, a family party where no stranger was admitted. His Highness does not fast; he is an active, energetic man, and he knows that food is necessary for those who work, so, though his table may be less luxurious in Ramadan, there is a table kept. The Princess and Faïk Hanem eat with his Highness, and Kopsès and Irfandil fasted—the first from choice; the latter had no option, but was obliged to do as the others did, and if there is one thing in which the uneducated and untravelled Mussulman is rigid, it is the fast during Ramadan. But if they had to fast, there was no necessity for their abstaining from sleep, and many indemnified themselves by dozing all day long. Luncheon was ordered for me, and difficult enough it was to get; neither slaves nor eunuchs were disposed to exert themselves to procure it, and when it came I felt ashamed to eat it while girls stood by who had taken no food since three or four o'clock in the morning, and would not have any until after sunset. This was the first year that Kopsès had fasted. She could easily have abstained from it had she chosen; indeed she was accustomed to have all her meals with the Princess, strictly as her companion. She, however, scorned to screen herself from any pain or penalty; and being bred in a Mahometan harem, shared the fast as rigidly as any, but with this difference, that she went about her daily avocations as usual, without excusing herself in any degree, and it was only by a certain feverish look towards the close of the month, that I could have discovered the privations she had imposed on herself.

At the end of October we were told one day at breakfast that we were to leave the palace immediately, to go for one night to the hotel, and on the morrow to remove to Choubrah. The cause of our sudden flitting was this:

At Gezireh the entire *cuisine* and attendance are French. A few days before our departure the cook had sent out a boy with a couple of ducks, telling him to take them back to the poulterer's, as they were unfit for cooking. This was the cook's version. The sentinel at the palace gates took the ducks from the boy, and accused him of intending to dispose of them. The cook went to the rescue. Many Arabs and Frenchmen joined, and a great altercation ensued. The Arabs said that the cook struck the sentinel, which the French denied. At any rate, his Highness took the Arab version, and the cook was dismissed on the spot; whether deservedly or not we had no means of judging. All the Frenchmen spoke of the cook as a civil, obliging man, and he had been upwards of two years in the service; but such universal peculation goes on in Egypt, that if here and there an honest man is to be found, he is not believed in.

The next day we moved into the house at Choubrah which I had inhabited on my first arrival. It was one of the handsomest and best built houses in Cairo, and the first winter of our arrival it had been provided with every comfort supposed to be necessary for English people. This was now about the fifth time of our return to it, and although at every removal the Khédive had been charged a large sum for its being refurnished, we found things worse and worse at each return. We had been provided with good, solid, and, at the same time, handsome furniture, wardrobes, dressing and writing tables, work and card tables, bookcases, &c., all fitted with good patent locks and keys. When we came back, we always found the keys lost, and the locks either broken or hampered. To the Arabs one key is the same as another; if they can only get it into the lock, they will force it, until they succeed in opening it. Locking it again is, of course, quite another matter, but that is no business of theirs.

All the good furniture that had been left in our rooms had been removed to outhouses, where it had become dirty and spoilt. If we disliked leaving our wardrobes or drawers unlocked, the only remedy was to send for a locksmith. He would charge us exorbitantly, and put the commonest things in place of the good locks broken. His keys were of no sort of use, as they would open any lock, so you might as well leave your things open. I remember the Princess had a great box in which her books, &c., were removed, whenever we went anywhere, as her things were never mixed with ours. The lock was very common and was out of order, so I sent for a locksmith, who at once said he must put a new one, to which I assented. But when he had done having put a new lock and also hinges, all of the commonest description, he had the effrontery to ask a napoleon for the job! I absolutely refused to pay it, and, after a great deal of altercation, compromised the matter for 8s. The box was quite new, a great cumbersome thing, bought in the Mouskee, but lock and hinges had both given way on the first removal. The locksmith whom I have mentioned was an Italian, not an Arab.

Our household at Choubrah was now differently composed from what it had been on my first arrival. An Armenian gentleman, Yakoub Bey, was called the Pasha's "Governor," as Mr Freeland and General Maclean had been before styled. He did not give lessons, but had the general superintendence of the household. Mr Michell, who had been originally engaged as Greek and Latin tutor to the Pasha (his Highness having then the intention of sending his son to Oxford); Martini Bey, an Italian doctor; and Shefket, the Abyssinian companion of Ibrahim Pasha. These formed the household, to which was soon after added Mahmoud Bey, the fifth son of his Highness, who had come from England on occasion of the four royal marriages, and had remained in Egypt ever since. The Pasha was at the house from about 8 A.M. to 4 P.M. Mahmoud Bey lived with us entirely. We were a strangely mixed household, composed of seven nationalities, Egyptian (or Turkish, whichever we may call the Pasha), Armenian, Abyssinian, Italian, English, and French, and Arab servants. When Mahmoud Bey joined us, he was accompanied by a Turkish gentleman, Turabi Bey, which made eight nationalities under one roof.

Turabi Bey had, many years previously, lived in England with the Turkish Embassy, and had then acquired, with the language, such an admiration of English manners and institutions, that he had actually married an English lady, and, moreover, had prevailed on her to accompany him to Egypt upon his taking service with the Viceroy. Perhaps it was a dangerous experiment for an Englishwoman to make, not only to marry a Turk, but to settle with him in a country where polygamy is the law; but I presume she had just reliance on her own attractions, and, moreover, on her excellent qualities as mistress of a household; for, with all the difficulties attendant on housekeeping in Egypt, she contrived somehow to keep up a capital table, and a very comfortable English home. As she was hospitable, and freely imparted her good things, I believe many of her husband's Mussulman friends would willingly have renounced polygamy, and its attendant discomforts, if they could only have found any like her. As to her husband, he knew when he was well off!

It is customary for all Europeans engaged in the Khédive's service to have a contract, which stipulates not only the conditions but the coin in which payment is to be made. Now copper is much depreciated in value in Egypt, and one of the gentlemen I have mentioned was complaining to me one day that about one-fifth of his monthly pay had been given to him in copper! He could not pay it away again at one-half the value at which he had received it, and then, as the weight was very great, he had to hire a man to carry it home for him! The loss thus occasioned is well understood at the *daïra;* so to make some amends for it, *backsheesh* to the amount of one and sometimes two months' pay is often given in the course of the year. As in most cases, his Highness pays for it in the end!

According to the almanack, Ramadan was to have thirty days for the year of which I am writing, and Baïram would therefore begin on a Friday. But I was told it was not the right thing for the Baïram to commence on Friday, because Friday is always a *fête,* and it was not right to have two *fêtes* on one day. The Khédive wished therefore the Baïram to begin on Thursday. The Baïram is a religious ceremony depending on the new moon, and there are sheikhs watching for its appearance all over the Mahometan empire. It may be cloudy in one place and not in another, so wherever it is first visible, it may be in Upper Egypt, or it may be in Turkey, if a telegraph wire is within reach, the news is instantly communicated. (How they managed before telegraphs were invented I do not know.) This was the sort of talk I heard around me, by persons who had lived in Egypt for years, but when I repeated it in the harem I was answered, "How can his Highness's wishes influence the Baïram? The new moon would be visible in Turkey as well as in Egypt." "But," said I, "how can such an absurd idea be gravely stated if there is no foundation whatever for it?" To this I was answered, that there was a popular superstition that if the Baïram began on a Friday, some great calamity would befall the country before the year was out. The calamity was, however, averted for that year, as in the course of the night twenty-one guns were fired to announce that the long fast was over, and the Khédive gave the usual Baïram reception at an early hour on Thursday the 20th of November.

CHAPTER XXI.

Weather—I go to the New Hotel—Customs in the harem—Different opinions of the same thing—Constant difficulties with the harem carriage—The driver is bastinadoed—Treatment of new-born infants—European servants in the harem—Invalids in the hotel—Death of one—Strange story.

On the 1st of November (1873) we had the first rain which had fallen in Egypt since the previous winter. During the month, it fell on five days; and in the course of the winter there were many which might, even in our climate, be called wet days. One inconvenience is, that no one is ever prepared for rain in Egypt. On the second day of the Baïram, when the races were held at Abbassieh, it came down in such a way that people fled for shelter in all directions, for no one is ever provided with a greatcoat or waterproof, and very few with an umbrella. The roads were soon seas of mud; and in the narrow streets where there is much traffic they remained so for several days.

On the 6th of December it was announced to us that the house at Abdeen, intended for the educational staff of Ibrahim Pasha, was ready for their reception, and I was to remove to the New Hotel, there to remain until the marriage of my pupil, when I had agreed to live with her. It was a great wrench to me leaving Choubrah, and finally breaking up the English household which had been my home since my coming to Egypt. At the hotel I soon made plenty of acquaintances; but then we had not the same interests in common which had bound me to those with whom I had hitherto resided. I continued my daily lessons at the harem; and as I had still the same trouble with the carriage, I did not come away in the middle of the day, as I had done the previous winter, but stayed to luncheon, and gave lessons to Faïk Hanem in the afternoon. When I first began to take luncheon in the harem at Ramleh, I sat at table with the Princesses; but now at Abdeen his Highness ate with them always *en famille*, so a second table was provided, where I sat with Kopsès and Charissas Hanem (a very pretty young lady who acted as amanuensis to the second Princess), and also any visitors who might happen to be staying in the palace. The table was served *à la franque*, but during Ramadan that of course ceased; and afterwards, when the regular meals began, the slaves, disliking the extra trouble which a dinner *à la franque* gave them, and having received no *fresh* orders on the subject, gave us everything *à la turque*. This service is extremely simple: a round table, on which a large circular tray is put; the dish is in the middle, and is frequently changed; and a small plate and spoon are put for each guest, with a large piece of bread; the spoon is to be used if the dish contains any liquid food, but if it is meat or anything solid, the fingers are applied. A knife and fork were put for me. I was helped, or rather I helped myself, before any one else; but when I saw each hand in turn dipped into the dish, I did not care to eat, and the next day told Kopsès that I did not want any luncheon. She asked me particularly why, upon which I said I did not feel hungry enough to eat after that fashion. She made me no reply, but the next day I found that an express order had been given that the dinner (or luncheon) should always be served *à la franque*, and this continued as long as I gave lessons in the palace. I mention this as an instance, amongst many, of the courtesy and kindness of these ladies, and their readiness to adapt their customs to European requirements.

As both the Princess and Faïk Hanem were to be married in the following February, there were naturally endless interruptions with *modistes*, &c. It is Turkish etiquette for a young lady to appear totally ignorant of the cause of these preparations. My pupil, the Princess, having been brought up among Europeans, did not observe this etiquette; but Faïk Hanem did so strictly. One day she complained of being very tired of standing. "Why have you been standing?" said I. "Oh, I have had ten dresses to try on!" she replied. "Ah, for your wedding I suppose," said I. "My wedding! I don't know what you mean!" she answered so coldly, and with so surprised a look, that I should have thought myself misinformed if I had not been so sure of the fact. Another time I mentioned something I had heard of her future husband, and she replied very quietly, "I don't know of whom you are speaking."

As I had promised to live with the Princess after her marriage, I spoke to her sometimes of the rooms I should occupy, and the way in which I should wish them to be furnished—things so matter of course with us, that it may appear unnecessary for me to trouble myself about them; but my observation in the harem had taught me that it was highly essential I should look after them myself in time. The Princess told me candidly that at present she could not move in the matter, that she was not at liberty to express any wish, that her mother had the sole management of everything.

"Well, but surely," said I, "you can speak to your own mother?" "Not even to my own mother," she replied.

Kopsès corroborated this. It was considered immodest for a young lady to allude to her approaching marriage.

But she talked to me very openly and sensibly on the subject.

I had seen that in the harem there was no such thing as privacy, and I felt and said that if I lived in it, privacy I *must* have, and also facilities for employing myself— to sit dawdling about all day would soon fit me for a lunatic asylum. I must have writing-tables, work-tables, chairs, &c.; and the ideas among Orientals of European requirements are all taken exclusively from the French, who do not excel according to our English ideas in *useful* furniture, though a great improvement upon Eastern habits.

The youngest daughter of Mohammed Ali, and great-aunt of my pupil, had come from Constantinople (where she resided with her husband Kiamil Pasha), to be present at the wedding of her grand-niece. This lady bore the same name as my pupil, being called Zeyneb Hanem Effendi. Miss Martineau, in her book upon Egypt, speaks of her marriage in 1845. She had a great many ladies in her train, and sometimes they dined at the same table with me. There were some very handsome women among them, and they had very good manners.

About the middle of December the hotels were getting very full. I made many pleasant acquaintances, and we got up several excursions. It used to amuse me very much to hear the different opinions expressed about the same thing. Some people were enthusiastic about the bazaars of Cairo, and declared they could spend whole days in visiting them—they were so quaint, so picturesque! Others saw in them nothing but dark, smelly places which they would rather avoid. Some raved about the climate of Egypt, and said it gave them new life; but these were the old stagers who came out every winter. Others, who had just arrived, and saw the rain and the mud (it being an exceptionally bad winter), declared the whole thing was a "take in" and a "sell," and wished they had remained in Europe, where, at any rate, they would have had better food and accommodation for their money.

Mr Crowfoot, a Cambridge man, who came out to search in Coptic monasteries for Biblical manuscripts, paid his first visit to the Pyramids. "What did you think of them?" said I to him on his return. "Oh, I was much disappointed in them," he replied. "A mere mass of stones, nothing more. I should never care to see them again. I was interested in the Temple of the Sphinx, but the Pyramids are nothing!"

Professor Flower, with his wife, came at the same time to winter in Egypt, and after their first visit to the Pyramids, I put the same question to them. "Oh," said he, "they are overpowering!" He and his wife started from the hotel in the early morning, as people usually do. When they got half-way, and first saw them, they stopped the carriage at once to revel in the view. "I wonder how we ever got there at all," they said to me. "Did you go inside?" "No." "Or up?" "Oh, no! we only walked round them, and stood and looked at them, and could have spent days in doing so." So they came back in the evening, with their hearts and minds full of what they had seen and felt.

There was a gentleman sat by me at the *table d'hôte*, who had just come from Constantinople, where he had been living for three years. I was talking to him one day about an article in the 'Times,' which spoke of the opening of a new railway from Haider Pasha, near Scutari, to Ismidt. The reason of its being noticed in the 'Times' was, because it might eventually become the beginning of the highroad to India. The writer dilated much on the beautiful scenery of this completed bit of railway, and its classical associations. I had looked forward much to making this excursion in the previous summer during our stay at Constantinople, but had been prevented, first by the heat, and secondly by our sudden departure. I asked this gentleman if he had been on the line, and if so, what he thought of it. He said he had made the excursion, but he did not see much to admire in it. "But," said I, "the railway skirts the sea, and you would have on your right the Sea of Marmora and the group of Princes' Islands, and on the left, in the background, the chain of Mount Olympus!" "Oh yes," he replied, "you had all that, but there is nothing particular in it that I can see." He thought Constantinople a nasty, dirty place, and the surroundings very much overpraised. A few evenings ago he had been up to the Citadel to see the sun set, and there were some people, strangers to him, who came up with the same object probably, and who stood near him. He supposed they had read that it was a fine sight, so they were in raptures, but he only saw a wide waste of sandy desert, and a great mist! He went to see the procession of the Mahmal, but he looked upon it as the same kind of thing as a Lord Mayor's show! "What kind of thing do you admire?" I asked. "Well," he replied, "I was returning once at 3 A.M. on a summer's morning from a volunteer review at Windsor, and as I crossed Waterloo Bridge, I was struck with the aspect of London at that early hour, and though very tired, I stood on the bridge half an hour looking at it. I have never seen anything to equal that."

I went very frequently to the opera, as my pupil gave me a box whenever I wished for one, and the distance from the New Hotel being only a few hundred yards, I had no occasion for the expense of a carriage. Very few people indeed used a carriage to take them to the opera—only those who lived in the outskirts of the town; but the majority of travellers, staying at the hotels in the immediate vicinity, generally walked.

This was my third winter in Egypt, and it was very different from the two preceding, and also two following winters. There were certainly many fine days worthy of Egypt, but there were also many stormy ones. Sometimes there were southerly winds (the *coldest* in winter) and clouds of dust—then nothing was to be heard but the slamming of doors and windows, and occasional breaking of glass. A few invalids, who came out hoping for a warm climate, thought they had much better have stayed at home. Those who went in a good *dahabieh* up the Nile, and came back at the end of the winter, declared it had been delightful; but for those who stayed at the hotels in Cairo, the discomfort was great. People went down to breakfast wrapped up in shawls and in greatcoats, for the draughts were terrible. There were some days on which we had torrents of rain, and the streets were almost impassable for mud. The poor Arabs complained terribly, and the old residents said the climate was undergoing an entire change, since such winters were formerly unknown in Egypt. It was all to be ascribed to the plantations which had been made in the vicinity of Cairo. A few people in the New Hotel had fires in their rooms. This hotel being one of the last built, many of the apartments were provided with fireplaces out of regard to English prejudices. I went to the harem all the same every day, though very little was done. One day, during the bad weather I have mentioned, I had occasion to go into the Mouskee, and took a carriage from the door to convey me there. There had been heavy rain on the two preceding days, but it was then fine. The Mouskee was, a few years ago, before the European element predominated so much, the chief street in Cairo, but it is a Frank and not an Arab quarter. The houses are very high, and the ground-floor occupied solely by shops. The street is about wide enough for two carriages, and the sun does not penetrate it more than an hour or two at mid-day. I could hardly have believed, without seeing, the state in which it was. I was obliged to go, but when I saw the difficulty of advancing, I would gladly have turned back, had it been possible. At last the horses stuck fast. The driver lashed in vain, but finding that useless, he got down and examined the horses. Having satisfied himself on the score of their being without any serious injury, he tried to stimulate them to exertion by thrusting the butt-end of the whip into their sides, but they never moved. I got out, and walked back through the heavy mud and deep ruts, determined never again to go to the Mouskee after such weather.

My difficulties with the harem carriage still continued. Eight A.M. was the time it was to be at the hotel door to fetch me. Sometimes it came at seven, and sometimes at nine or ten, never at the right time. I had not always the same driver, but one man, Hassan, very frequently came. Shaheen was always waiting under the portico to tell me when the carriage arrived. He accompanied me to the harem gate, and was sitting there outside when I came out again, to assist me in getting a carriage to take me back. He did what he could, but that was very little, as the eunuchs will not tolerate the slightest interference, and make a point of treating every man, gentle or simple, whose business may take him to the harem gates, with the most marked disrespect and even contumely. They thus revenge themselves for the advantages which men in the outer world have over them. This Hassan, in addition to his unpunctuality, which might not be his fault, was a very disagreeable man, noisy and blustering. He was a reckless driver, jolting and hurrying along, and keeping me in a state of continual trepidation, not for myself, but for the unfortunate donkeys who came in his way, which he would send spinning away for several yards, by coming in violent contact with the panniers with which they were laden. He considered it a point of honour, in the narrowest streets, to dart in front of any vehicle which might be before him.

As 8 A.M. was the time at which I ought to start for the harem, Shaheen was not in waiting before that hour; if, therefore, as sometimes happened, Hassan came at seven, he would leave his horses and make his way up to my room, telling me rudely (I kept the door locked) that the carriage was there, and he could not wait. On such occasions he would go away, and not return at all. It was he who came up to my room at Gezireh at 6 A.M. before sunrise. He often asked for *backsheesh*, which I did not consider myself bound to give, as he never did anything for me, and was extremely uncivil. At last I did give him a florin on two different occasions, but he was much worse after it, and would, when driving, stoop down and look through the front window of the brougham, shouting "*Backsheesh!*" He grew so insolent that, although I knew redress would only be temporary, I determined to complain to the Princesses, and did so. The next morning he did not appear until nine, but was very silent, and I was too disgusted to make any inquiry as to the cause of his being late. When I got to the harem I found out the reason. He had driven into the courtyard as usual, had been told by the eunuchs to descend from the box, had been conducted into an inner receptacle, where he well knew what awaited him, and then and there he had been bastinadoed. The next day there was a marked difference in his manner. He was quite punctual in the morning at eight, and when I came out of the harem in the afternoon, I found him waiting for me. He said something very earnestly to Shaheen, and the latter, grinning from ear to ear, explained to me, while the driver stood by watching my countenance, "that Hassan always come right time; he wait for me till I ready; he wait for me, no matter how long; he glad to wait; he do anything I want." I said "Taïb, taïb" (good, good) to this astonishing change, and there the matter ended, *for a time!*

There had been a son or daughter born of each of the royal marriages that had taken place in the beginning of 1873. An English nurse was engaged for one of these children, and she arrived about a week after the child was born. This nurse had been in Egypt before, and had made up her mind, for the sake of the high pay, to undertake a post, the discomforts of which, to an Englishwoman habituated to all the conveniences of life in our country, can hardly be exceeded. It is the custom in Egypt, when a child is born, to wash it in wine, and then bandage it up for forty days. It had been intended that the forty days should expire before the child was given up to the new nurse. I don't know whether the young mother had any misgivings, or whether she had been influenced by any one; at any rate, the child was given up at once to the new nurse. The latter immediately undressed it, and holding it over a cold bath, sponged it well from head to foot. Some old harem nurses looked on all the while, frowning much at the innovation, and auguring the direst effects to the child. Some always remained present throughout the day, going out occasionally to relieve their minds by relating what they had witnessed, and then coming back to see if the child was still alive. They were evidently astonished at his vitality, and argued that he must be a wonderfully strong infant not to succumb to such treatment. Almost all the Princesses have now

English nurses; there are a few Swiss, but the English predominate.

When first Ismael Pasha became Viceroy, and European fashions were introduced into the harem, several English, French, and Italian women were engaged to live there as parlour-maids, ironers, dressmakers, and hairdressers. The pay was high, but the terms of their contract were generally rather stringent, as it was a grave experiment to introduce free women among the inmates of the harem, taught from childhood that it was the greatest indecency to show their faces to a man. In the earliest contracts, I was told, it was inserted that they were to have free access to the harem gardens, but never to go beyond the gates, under pain of instant dismissal. This restriction was afterwards taken off, and liberty given to go out, permission having been first asked. After three or four years, most of the Europeans employed in the Viceroy's harem were dismissed, as there were constant complaints on both sides. A few still remained in the families of the married sons and daughters. One of those formerly employed as ironer in the Khédive's household told me that during Ramadan she had often been obliged to go out and purchase water for drinking. It is all filtered, and the place where the filtering goes on is kept locked. The slaves and eunuchs were either asleep or did not care to take the trouble of bringing water to a Giaour (infidel) when they were debarred the use of it themselves. This person, who was a very steady respectable woman, told me that she had sometimes ironed all day with the thermometer in the room standing at 116°! Of course this was during a *khamseen;* but the work was at all times very arduous, as in a hot climate only washing materials are worn, and the quantity was something enormous. A wardrobe-keeper of one of the Princesses told me that she had upwards of 500 dresses to keep in order, all belonging to her mistress.

Her duty was to keep these dresses, and see that all the lace, &c., was fresh, and any dress ready to put on at a minute's notice whenever it might be wanted by the Princess. Though the office is called wardrobe-keeper, there are no wardrobes; everything is kept in boxes, which are all of one size, placed round the room with a covering of shawls, so that they look like a succession of divans. According to my experience, the boxes seemed to occupy as good a room as the mistress, as they were always put in one of the chief apartments, which was kept locked.

I have said that the weather was very bad this particular winter, and unfortunately there were many invalids who had come out to seek health, and were staying in the hotel, certainly not the place to find it. Among these I soon noticed a gentleman remarkable for the extreme delicacy of his appearance. He was accompanied by a young man who was evidently no relation, but who scarcely ever left him. I will call the invalid Mr Robertson and his friend Mr Wilson. During the first few days after their arrival, they generally took a short drive in the Choubrah Road when the weather permitted, but very soon Mr Robertson took to his room and never left it. The young man came down to the *table d'hôte*, and sat next to the chaplain and me at one end of the table, always going away before the meal was over. One day I could not help being struck with the young man's countenance, he looked so ill, and I asked him if anything was the matter. He said that he had not slept for four nights, as he was so constantly watching his friend. The latter, he said, insisted upon his going down to his meals, or he would not leave him at all. In the evening I saw him again for a few minutes. The doctor had just been, and said there was no hope. "If a million could save him," said Mr Wilson, "it would be forthcoming." But riches could avail nothing; he died that night. The extraordinary thing was, that the rich man was married and had grown-up children; and yet, knowing his critical state, he preferred to come out to Egypt with only a dependant. Mr Wilson had been three years engaged in looking after some mines in Sardinia belonging to Mr Robertson, and upon landing at Southampton had received a telegram to await there the arrival of his employer. When Mr Robertson's death was approaching, Mr Wilson begged him to let his family be told of his situation; but the invalid refused, and died with only his faithful attendant. When all was over, Mr Wilson telegraphed for instructions. The answer came at once—The body was to be buried at Cairo, and Mr Wilson was to return at once to the mines!

CHAPTER XXII.

Dust-storms and rain—Unceremonious hour for paying a bill—Marriage of the Princess—Panic in the chief saloon—Intrusion of Arab women—Going home of the bride—Dine at Aurique's, and afterwards drive out to see illuminations—Meet a funeral car—Marriage of the adopted daughter—Concert at Kasr-el-Nil—First visit to the two brides.

The Kourban Baïram this year fell on the 28th of January, a very bleak and ungenial day, with a south-west wind. The south wind is the coldest in winter, but there is nothing bracing in the cold. It is so impregnated with dust that it not only nearly blinds you, but fills up all the pores of the skin. You by no means escape it by remaining indoors, as with few exceptions the houses are draughty and the windows and doors fit very badly. I had been asked to join a party to the Pyramids on the second day of the Baïram, and felt rather doubtful about accepting, but in the night such a storm of wind arose, and continued more or less throughout the day, as effectually put an end to the party. Such a day in the desert would have been one never to be forgotten; it was bad enough in the New Hotel. The air was so full of dust that the Ezbekeah Gardens opposite were not visible. The total absence of comfort in the hotel made it still more trying; there was no shutting out the wind and the dust. The only thing that could be said was, that according to the newspapers it was a very bad winter throughout Europe.

The festivities for the marriage of my pupil had been fixed to begin on the 1st of February, but they were for some reason postponed to the 8th. This was fortunate, as there are always *al fresco fêtes* on such occasions, and the weather could not have been worse than it was during the first week in February. I had had a quantity of lace sent to me from Malta, purchased for me by a lady whom I had known during my residence in the island, and I was waiting an opportunity of sending the money to pay for it. A gentleman who was just leaving by one of the P. and O. boats *viâ* Southampton, which always stop at Malta, offered to pay for me, and I accepted his offer, and gave him the money. But unluckily the steamer did not get to Malta until near midnight; and as it would leave again at 4 A.M., my friend went at once ashore and reached the Strada Mezzodi at 1 A.M. The hostess was in bed and asleep, but persistent knocking roused up the household. A parley took place from the windows, explanations ensued, and the gentleman was admitted. The money was paid, a slight account of what was going on in Egypt was given, and the gentleman took his leave and returned on board.

As the contract for the marriage of my pupil had been signed the year before, the festivities only commenced on Monday the 8th of February. On the previous day she had left her father's palace for that of her grandmother at Kasr-el-Ali, where the wedding *fêtes* had been given the preceding year. Monday, Tuesday, and Wednesday there were dinners and entertainments, as on the former occasions, but I will only particularise the Wednesday, when the procession of the bride took place. As carriages were very expensive (about £3 for the night), I had asked my pupil if she would order a harem carriage to be sent for me, and she promised that she would not forget it. The dinner was to be at seven, but as the line of carriages might be long, I wished it ordered to fetch me at six. I had just come up from luncheon at half-past one, when Shaheen came to me to say that a carriage was at the door, and that I was wanted at the harem immediately. My first impulse was to go off directly, thinking my pupil really wanted me, but a little consideration made me hesitate, and decide that the immediate urgency of my departure might be a ruse of the eunuchs who wanted the carriage. There were several ladies staying in the hotel who took the liveliest interest in the marriage of my pupil, and these surrounded me with suggestions as to why I was wanted in such haste. Now *backsheesh* is an institution in the East, and the first Europeans who were engaged in the Viceroy's harem received at the Baïram and also at other times handsome presents in jewellery, &c. Gradually it had been discovered that it was not a European fashion, and. when the new staff appointed to Ibrahim Pasha and his sister arrived from England, the practice was discontinued. With regard to weddings, however, it still held good. I had seen that all persons connected with the brides or bridegrooms of the preceding year had received presents, and I myself had, from the future mother-in-law of my pupil, received a handsome present at the signing of the contract. The ladies around me therefore argued that my pupil had sent for me in this hurry in order to give me the presents (jewels, in all probability), that I might shine with due *éclat* on this important occasion.

I dressed as fast as I could and hurried off to Kasr-el-Ali. As I entered in a harem carriage my card of invitation was not required; I was admitted without opposition and also without ceremony. The rooms through which I passed were full of company, but there were no Europeans. Theatricals were going on behind the screens, and dancing and music in different saloons. I inquired for the Princess, and was conducted to another suite of apartments, where I found her with Kopsès and a number of attendants, amongst whom was her *dada*, henceforth a person of great importance.

My pupil scanned me narrowly from head to foot, as she was anxious I should appear to advantage, and generally thought me too indifferent to dress. The inspection appeared to be tolerably favourable, and then she asked me why I had come so early, as she knew my tastes and habits, and feared I should be bored by being so long without employment or congenial companions. For herself it was not etiquette to appear in the saloons until nine or ten in the evening; she was supposed to be in strict seclusion. She had given the order, as I had asked, for a carriage to be sent for me at 6 P.M. The eunuchs, however, had followed their usual plan of sending it when it suited their convenience.

When my pupil was first "shut up" in the harem, her *dada* and other attendants had made a strong effort, by flattery and various cajoleries, to regain the influence over her which they had possessed before her long intercourse with Europeans. She was of too gentle and timid a character, even had she wished it, to dismiss them now and talk to me alone; and as I perceived that my presence was a restraint upon all, I left her and went back into the saloons to pass the two or three hours that still remained before the European visitors could arrive. There was the same monotonous music and the same dancing. One dance was by a party of nine girls, and one of them, a negress of very stout proportions, was dressed in tights, one side yellow, the other red, and a very high peaked cap—in fact, a fool's cap. This creature performed all sorts of contortions opposite to the eight girls, and the latter imitated. The dance began and ended with a somersault; and they did not do it lightly by any means, springing to their feet as I have seen boys do in England, but came down on the floor with eight distinct bumps and then rose to their feet. This dance was performed in Turkish costume, so there was not the slightest display made; but after that came the mazurka, in which the four ladies were clad in short full petticoats stopping at the knees, but with much more decorous trousers than our poor ballet-girls wear. The cavaliers were in red silk tights covered with gold spangles and embroidery, and looked very pretty. A little before seven the European visitors began to arrive, and I did not feel so lonely. Vast as were the saloons, they were crowded, and I was struck with the presence of so many Arab women of the lower class. I was told afterwards that custom has authorised the entrance of these women to either a birth, a marriage, or a death, in any great household. On occasion of the former marriages I had noticed many in the large saloon on the ground-floor where the guests took coffee immediately after dinner, but I had not observed them upstairs. On this occasion, however, they were everywhere, and in far greater numbers than at the previous weddings. As the time for the procession of the bride approached, these women began to congregate near the entrance of the throne-room where the shower of gold is scattered. The moment the doors were opened there was a rush. I happened to be close up to them and got in among the first, but so great was the crush that several eunuchs closed the doors again to shut out the numbers who were forcing an entrance. Presently the doors were reopened and the bride was brought in, pale and trembling, the eunuchs instantly shutting them after her entrance. I did not know then what had passed in the large saloon during the interval of the closed doors, but I looked in vain in the throne-room for many English ladies who I knew were at the dinner, and who would be sure to have tried to get into the throne-room. The poor little bride had evidently been much frightened by something that had happened before her entrance. She sat under the canopy holding a large fan before her face, and after a very short time was led out. When we went again into the great saloon we found very few persons there, and I heard from them, and again from English ladies afterwards, what had happened.

It appears that when the procession of the bride entered the great saloon, as numbers were mounted on chairs and couches to see her through the line of light made by the eunuchs, a crash was suddenly heard, and a cloud of dust rose from the floor at the end farthest from the throne-room. A cry arose that the floor was giving way, and the panic was terrible. The bride was hurried at a rapid rate into the throne-room, the doors of which were instantly locked to conceal from the inmates what had happened, as well as to take measures for security. There was a frantic rush to the grand staircase, and in the struggle to get away many fell, and others rolled over them. Valuable jewels were lost—at least so many said, while those belonging to the harem denied it. A lady who was in the crush told me that when she got home she missed a handsome gold bracelet, which she knew she had on at dinner, and upon going the next day to the harem with little hope of recovering it, she was overjoyed to receive it from one of the head eunuchs, who told her that an Arab woman had been seen with it in her hand, and as it was certain not to belong to her, it had been taken from her and kept until inquiry should be made.

The next day the bride was taken home to her husband's house; and, in virtue of my office, I was invited to be present to receive her there. There were no other Europeans present but Mdlle. Ott and a Greek lady who was on a visit to Fatma Hanem, one of the brides of the preceding year. I left the hotel at one o'clock. I had heard before starting that the procession was then on its way through the Mouskee; but it made such an enormous circuit that it was three before it reached the palace, where my pupil was to reside. A magnificent pile of buildings was in course of erection on the banks of the Nile, a little to the left of the fine bridge which you have to cross to go to Gezireh, or to the Pyramids. A palace belonging to Ahmed Pasha, the elder brother of the Khédive, had formerly stood on this site, but this had been pulled down to make room for a much handsomer one; only, as is always the case in Egypt, it was not ready when wanted. There were two smaller palaces in course of erection, which had been intended for other purposes, but the completion of them was hurried on; the one being destined for the temporary abode of my pupil the Princess Zeyneb, and the other for the adopted daughter, Faïk Hanem. In size, number, and disposition of rooms, they were exactly identical; each had a large garden, and each garden was surrounded by a high wall. From the chief rooms in the upper storeys it was even possible for the ladies to communicate with each other by signs, so nearly did they adjoin; in fact, on one side they were separated only by the garden wall. The entrances, however, were so wide apart, being on opposite sides, that it would have taken ten minutes or a quarter of an hour to walk out of one harem into another.

There were a number of handsomely dressed ladies walking about the saloons, waiting for the arrival of the bride and her *cortége ;* a band of twelve musicians, dressed in boys' clothes, were standing with their instruments near the entrance of the chief saloon. This band had been trained carefully with European instruments, which they played fairly, and the moment the carriages were heard to drive into the courtyard, they struck up a triumphal march. There was a large retinue with the bride, for she and all her relatives had been making the tour of the town; the bridegroom's carriage was the first to enter the courtyard, that he might be on the threshold to hand her out, as it is not the custom for bride and bridegroom to arrive in the same carriage. They entered arm in arm; he was leaning tenderly over her, and she held a large fan close to her face, so as to conceal it entirely from every one. Her features were, however, well known to him; she had been his boyish love in childhood; there was no surprise awaiting him when the unveiling should take place, only the realisation of his fondest hopes. The train passed on into an inner saloon; but after a few minutes the bridegroom came out again, and left the palace. I was told he had to go to the mosque, and pray there until sunset. The bride had retired to her own apartments, where her *dada*, and others who held the chief offices about her, had taken entire possession of her. I came away, therefore, at about five o'clock, and returned to the hotel.

I dined that night at Aurique's[1] with some friends,

---

[1] Aurique's is a restaurant at Cairo, in a narrow back street. It is of most unpretending exterior, but it is much frequented by Europeans, as they give capital dinners, proving that good food is to be obtained in Cairo, though rarely found in the hotels.

and afterwards drove out to see the illuminations and outdoor entertainments in the vicinity of Kasr-el-Ali. The whole road was a line of coloured lamps. Triumphal arches were erected near the palace of my pupil, which was very near that of her grandmother. As we were returning amidst a glare of light, fireworks going up, and Arab music on all sides, we saw a funeral car coming towards us; it was open, and on it was a coffin. A gentleman had died at the Hôtel du Nil on that day. When a death occurs in any of the hotels, the body is always removed either in the night, or, if it can be got out privately, during the evening *table d'hôte*. The position of the Hôtel du Nil made the latter time very opportune; but there was no way to the cemetery except past Kasr-el-Ali, where the fireworks and *fêtes* were going on. So the body was carried along through the illuminations to be deposited in the little chapel until the burial next day. Had I been a believer in omens, I might have looked upon this meeting a corpse on its way to burial as an evil portent—meeting it as I did just in front of my pupil's palace, and on her wedding-day! As it was, it shocked me much.

The following week was devoted to the *fêtes* for Faïk Hanem's marriage. She was to be married to Moustapha Pasha, son of the Mouffetish. The entertainments were much the same as they had been in the preceding week, but great care was taken to avoid a repetition of the scenes that had occurred on the previous Wednesday. The flooring of the saloon had been examined and strengthened. It was impossible to exclude any Mahometan woman who should present herself, but at any rate care was taken to confine such visitors to the basement floor. When, some time after dinner, the guests began to go up-stairs (for which a proper signal was given), several eunuchs were placed at the foot and at the head of the staircase, to prevent any but invited guests passing into the upper storey. At the same time, entertainments were going on below to amuse those who chose to stay there, or who had come uninvited. So all passed in easily and readily by turns, from the great saloon to the throne-room; and when the shower of gold came, there was not such a pouncing down upon it as had been at the last wedding. My near sight was always a subject of amusement in the harem; and on this occasion the second Princess, who had often thrown a handful of gold towards me, which quicker-sighted people had picked up, stretched out her hand and poured such a quantity of coins into mine that I came away richer than any.

This marriage, and the pomp attendant on it, was a singular illustration of Eastern life and manners. Here was a young lady, purchased in infancy for her beauty, adopted by a childless wife of the sovereign, tenderly reared, and educated in a palace, and finally married with the same honours as those bestowed on the Khédive's own daughter; the bridegroom the son of a man who, little more than twenty years before, was one of the poor fellaheen, but who had in that time amassed a fortune second only to that of the sovereign. Recently, as is well known, this colossal fortune has been confiscated, and he himself has been sent on exile to the Upper Nile.

On the following day I went to the house of Faïk Hanem, to await the coming home of the bride. The house itself, furniture and general arrangements, were exactly the same as what I had seen the preceding week at the marriage of the Princess Zeyneb. The bride and bridegroom entered about the same hour, and the latter went out again almost immediately to the mosque. I only observed one difference, and that was that the musicians were not attired as boys, but in the richest white satin dresses, with green sashes tied across the chest. There were a great many pretty girls among the slaves, and my attention was continually attracted to some richly dressed person, with long velvet or satin train; but upon asking who she was, I invariably received for answer, "Oh, quelque esclave!" There were two little girls richly dressed, daughters of the Mouffetish, who had European or Levantine governesses with them; but no one living in the harem could exercise *moral* training, and without that the mere acquisition of a little European knowledge would be of small avail. Turkish and Arab music was continually played, and theatricals were going on behind a screen. The day was cold, and the wind high, and every door and window in the house was open, so that the draught was terrible. I left at about six o'clock. The next evening I went to a concert and theatrical entertainment at Kasr-el-Nil, one of the Khédive's palaces on the eastern bank (Cairo side) of the Nile. This entertainment was for European ladies and gentlemen. The Khédive was at the head of the grand saloon, and each lady who arrived was led up to him, formally introduced, and his Highness shook hands with her. The ladies then passed into a side saloon, while the gentlemen walked about until all had arrived. Then the Khédive led the way to the concert-room, giving his arm to the wife of the Italian Consul, and everybody followed. The English Consul's wife was not present on this occasion, but I have understood that precedence is not given to any particular nation, but to the longest resident, and that happened to be the Italian Consul.

Everything was extremely well conducted; there was no crush or confusion whatever. First, there was a selection of music performed by the Opera company; and then, after a short interval, during which people went out and took refreshments, there was a little French *vaudeville* called "Le Bouquet." When the performance was over, all went to supper, which was laid out in the great saloon where the Khédive had received us. Everything had been cooked in his Highness's own kitchen, not provided by contract as has been sometimes the case. We were waited on by French servants in splendid liveries of crimson and gold. There was no hurry, no scramble—everything was perfectly managed. The saloon was lighted by a magnificent lustre, but there were many candelabra on the table, and girandoles on the walls. We were among the last to leave, and as we were waiting for our carriage to be announced, his Highness came out of an adjoining apartment, and seeing only two ladies, came and bade us good night, shaking hands with each. It was half-past two when I reached my room in the hotel. The temperature had been very pleasant all the evening, there being neither heat nor draught.

This *fête* closed the Mahometan year 1290 A.H., as at sunset the following day began the month of Moharrem, when no marriage is considered right. I went to pay my visit to the two brides about ten days after the first marriage. I did not go sooner, because I was told there were so many visitors in the house, for a newly married couple are not left in retirement as with us. I remained about three hours with the Princess Zeyneb, during which there was a constant succession of visitors, including the second and third Princesses. My pupil received them with all the composure and *aplomb* of a woman of the world, without the slightest *mauvaise honte* or constraint of any kind. When all the Mahometan visitors were gone, just as she was beginning to talk to me, the wife of the English Consul-General was announced, and then again the young bride behaved with the same self-possession. She took Mrs Stanton over her house, showed her jewels, her bedroom, &c., and talked as calmly of her husband as if she had been married twenty years. She spoke English, and scarcely made a mistake. I have alluded before to her jewels, which were magnificent, and comprised every ornament that can be worn; but she had also a dressing-case in which the backs of all the brushes (even the clothes-brush) were studded with diamonds. I passed on then to the house of Faïk Hanem, who had had the same concourse of visitors all day. They were, however, all gone, and after remaining some time, I also took my leave.

CHAPTER XXIII.

Visit the (so-called) school of the third Princess—Excellent arrangements—Presents received—Persian shawls—Am summoned to take up my abode in the harem—Go, but return to the hotel—Excellent police of Cairo—Burglary committed by Greeks—Finally take up my residence in the harem—My apartments—Go to the opera attended by a eunuch—Want of employment in the harem.

I had often heard of a school for girls situated near the palace of Helmire, just below the Citadel. It was founded by the Khédive, and is kept up entirely at his expense; but as he always wishes to associate his family with his undertakings, it is generally called the school of the third Princess, and is supposed to be under the patronage of that lady. It is a very large building; part of it was already standing, and had been formerly a palace, but the remainder has been added. There is a large open court in the centre, where, in the summer-time, a fountain plays. The whole building is airy, spacious, and well ventilated. At my first visit there were two hundred children boarded in the establishment, and one hundred day-scholars; but subsequently the whole number were received as boarders, going home to their parents every Friday. They were children from all classes, but put on a perfect equality.

Six years was the time fixed upon for their residence in the school; and they were not admitted after a certain age (which I think was ten). They were taught to read and write in Turkish and Arabic (later on in French also); they were instructed in arithmetic, geography and history, needlework, embroidery, worsted-work, and knitting. They were also taught to cook, to wash, to iron, and to sweep and clean their rooms. A certain number (six) were employed for a week in the kitchen under a cook, and these six girls sat for that week at the same table with their teachers, that they might be taught to eat properly, and to learn to use a knife and fork. At the end of a week they went to their books and work, and others took their places. The same rule was applied to the washing and ironing; six alternately were employed in these departments. There were many servants in the house, but the girls were nevertheless taught to do everything. On my first visit the school had only been open six months, but the progress made in that time was very satisfactory. I did not go on a visiting day, but quite unexpectedly, and I found everything in excellent working order. I inspected every part of the building—dormitories, lavatories, workroom, schoolroom, &c., and everywhere there was perfect cleanliness. There were at the beginning three Levantine and five Arabic resident teachers, and three Arabic masters came daily. There were large maps hanging on the walls of the schoolroom; and on subsequent visits I saw the girls examined in reading, writing, geography, and arithmetic. One girl was called up who wrote from the teacher's dictation on a large slate on the wall, and another was summoned to read it. One wrote the figures of a sum in addition, and another added them up. The expense of such an establishment is of course great, and it all falls on his Highness. There is as yet no public spirit in the country; everything that is done, is done by the Government. It is impossible that these girls, when they leave the school, can fall back into the degraded state from which they were taken. A girl in the East never chooses her own husband; and these will probably be bestowed in marriage by his Highness; and having been properly trained to fulfil the duties of wife and mother, a new era of things will be inaugurated for the women of Egypt.

At the end of February (1874) I calculated that we had had nine wet days since the New Year, and seventeen since the 1st of November. I may add that out of five winters passed in Egypt, it was the only one in which we had such weather.

There is perhaps no place where one sees and hears more of the vicissitudes of life than when staying in a hotel. A gentleman had for several days sat next to me at the *table d'hôte*, who had recently returned from a three months' voyage on the Nile, and was then debating within himself what to do until April, when he purposed returning to England. He at last decided that he would go to Palestine, and had arranged everything to start, when he heard by telegram that the Russian boat by which he purposed going from Port Saïd to Jaffa had somehow failed to call, and that he must wait for the next boat. Soon after, going into Robertson's (the English bookseller's), where many letters and telegrams are sent for travellers whose exact whereabout may not be known, he saw one addressed to himself, informing him of the death of a distant relation from whom he inherited a large property. It had just arrived by the Brindisi mail. Of course his plans were settled immediately; he went off to Alexandria by the next train, and caught the Brindisi boat returning on the following day.

I had had an invitation to go up the Nile directly after my pupil's marriage, and I had consulted her whether or

not I should accept it. It had been settled I should go
and live with her; but the house was full of visitors, and
as long as that was the case I could be of no use. I asked
the Princess how long the visitors would stay; she could
not tell, so I declined the invitation, and waited for the
summons. About three weeks after the marriage I was
sent for to receive the wedding presents. They were
very handsome, and were given by my pupil's mother,
by her mother-in-law, by herself, and by my other pupil,
Faïk Hanem. All persons connected with the bride receive presents—the masters mostly a sum of money and a
Persian shawl. These shawls invariably figure as presents
at a wedding, and among Orientals they are extremely
useful, as they are very warm and light. They are wound
round the loins, thus confining a loose dress. In the East
people do not seem to protect the chest; it is the loins
and the head which are wrapped up. The price of these
shawls varies from £5 to £100; they are rarely given
direct from the donor to the recipient, but pass through
the hands of eunuchs and other persons, the result of
which is, that a valuable shawl sometimes degenerates
into a very inferior one by the time it reaches its destination. I knew a gentleman attached to the person of
one of the princes at the time of the four marriages who
received an exactly similar shawl to what was given to
each of the grooms—though, from his position, there is no
doubt a superior one had been allotted to him. As the
Europeans do not wear shawls, they, if married, usually
hand them over to their wives; and if single, rush off to
the dealers to turn them into money, and knowing nothing
of their real value, are easily taken in. Thus the dealers
frequently get back at a low price the very shawls they
had just sold at a high rate, and this process is perhaps
repeated two or three times.

Towards the middle of March there were continual

sounds of Arab music passing the hotel, and upon going to the windows to see the cause, I found it was pilgrims coming from Mecca. One procession had eight carriages; the two foremost had the windows covered with shawls, showing that they contained women, who had made the pilgrimage, and thus ensured their salvation. Four or five parties passed every day.

At last, five weeks after my pupil's marriage, a summons came to me from the harem to take up my abode there. I had at first made up my mind to go and see the rooms destined for me before taking my luggage; but reflecting that I had explained all my requirements to my pupils, and that the Princess had now been her own mistress for some time, I decided upon taking everything with me. I felt exceedingly my approaching "shutting up," as it seemed to involve separation from everything which had interested me during the whole of my past life. Nothing but the great affection I felt for my pupil, and my hope of being able to influence for good her future life, could have induced me to submit to a residence in the harem. During the fifteen months in which I had given lessons there, I had seen enough to convince me of the low estimation in which Europeans were held by the eunuchs and slaves generally. How could it be otherwise? They saw the inconvenient and absurd fashions in dress in which many indulged — how for presents of dresses or jewellery the Princesses were fawned upon and flattered — and they naturally looked upon every present made to a Giaour as so much taken away from themselves. Besides, the eunuchs were the guardians of the harem, and any woman who resided in one, and was able to go in and out freely, might be engaged in intrigues. Of course, after a time they learned to discriminate.

At 3 p.m. I went away from the hotel, taking my luggage and Shaheen with me. The first thing I noticed was, that

I was taken to the back door, not that at which I had previously entered on occasion of the two or three visits I had made. Although I noted this fact, I thought it might perhaps be explained by the difficulty of getting in my luggage, which must otherwise have passed through all the chief apartments. Shaheen accompanied me into an inner court, and appeared very much scared by his position. A slave was called to the door, but was immediately ordered back by the eunuchs on account of Shaheen's presence, and I went inside, leaving him in charge of my luggage and several parcels until my return. I found myself in a perfect labyrinth of passages, where I met several black girls who only stared at me, but made no reply to my inquiries. At last I found my way into the chief apartments, and then one of the white slaves conducted me to the Princess. Two or three eunuchs were in the apartment with money-bags, and the Princess and her *dada* were busy counting out a pile of sovereigns. It seemed too important an occupation to be interrupted, and the Princess, after hastily giving me her hand, went on with her counting. I waited until it was concluded, and then asked if she would give orders for my trunks, &c., to be taken up into my rooms, and that some one should go with me to show me the way. A slave led me up the chief staircase, and then down a long passage, past the Princess's dressing-room and bath-room, to a little staircase which led to a suite of rooms set apart for me, and to which no one else was to have access. I had been told this, but as I drew near I heard some one strumming on a piano, and upon entering the apartments I saw two girls seated at the instrument, another looking out of the window and calling to some one below in one of the inner courts; and one or two others loitering about the rooms. They did not concern themselves in the least at my entrance, but seemed quite at home. I examined the room which was to serve as sleeping apartment. Many indispensable conveniences were wanting. My dear pupil had given orders for everything, but the head slaves and eunuchs had never known the use of some things ordered, and had taken no trouble about them. I knew very well that if I once entered the rooms to take up my abode without these conveniences, I should probably never have them at all, as it would be argued, if I could do without a thing for two or three days, I could do without it altogether. In the meanwhile my luggage had been brought up, and I felt I must make a decision. I went down-stairs to find Shaheen in the outer court to tell him to keep the carriage, but he was already gone. The eunuchs had hurried him off directly after I had gone into the palace. I went to the Princess and told her it was impossible for me to remain with the rooms in their present state; that she had promised me that everything should be properly arranged for me when I had agreed to live in the harem; that I should never ask anything unreasonable, but that what had been agreed upon must be done before I could live there. The Princess said she had given the orders, and appealed to her *dada*, who only laughed in reply. As my luggage was in the rooms, I locked the outer door, gave the key to Kopsès, and came away as soon as I could get a carriage, the Princess promising to send for me as soon as the necessary arrangements were completed.

Whatever there might be amiss in the life at Cairo, there was one thing which had hitherto been highly appreciated, and that was the safety to life and property. Any amount of petty pilfering might go on through leaving about money or any useful articles, but highway robbery and burglary had been unknown since the accession of the Viceroy Ismael. During this winter, however, there had been several instances. A young man going over the bridge to the railway station had been stopped by two or three men and robbed with violence. There had been two instances of burglary so cleverly planned and executed that they were evidently done by masters in the art. In each case jewellers were the sufferers, and the culprits were believed to be Greeks, certainly not Arabs. There was a story current, and generally believed, that his Highness, indignant at these robberies, had caused many persons known to be *mauvais sujets*, and strongly suspected in these cases, to be seized and conveyed on board ship, that they might be landed in their own country. But after two days the vessel came back into port without its roguish cargo, and it was left to the imagination what had become of the culprits. Certainly no consul was likely to interfere about the matter. This story was widely circulated, but I cannot vouch for the truth of it. There was always some *canard* afloat.

It was two days since I had been sent for to the harem, and had returned to the hotel, so I thought I would go again, and see if anything had been done. I got a carriage and drove to the palace with Shaheen, laying strict injunctions on him to wait for me. It was 10 A.M. when I left the hotel, and it was a drive of a quarter of an hour or twenty minutes. I had a long time to wait before I could see Kopsès, and when she came, she told me the Princess was still in bed and asleep! My rooms were in exactly the same state, nothing had been done. Kopsès thought they would be ready in a day or two, but though she did not tell me so, I saw that she had no power in the matter. The Princess was a child, and though she appeared to give orders, everything was really in the hands of the chief eunuch and the *dada*. If the Princess gave any order which pleased them, it was executed as promptly as could conveniently be. In the meanwhile my luggage was all there, which was very inconvenient. I stayed some time, as heavy rain came on directly after my arrival. The palace was exceedingly cold and draughty, the venetian blinds were all closed, but the windows and doors were open in every direction; a semi-darkness prevailed, which in the hot season might be agreeable, but on this cold wet day it was unspeakably cheerless, bleak, and gloomy. On the platform outside a eunuch walked up and down, enveloped in a thick shawl, while two or three smaller eunuchs crouched together in a corner to get out of the draught. Nothing to look upon all day but the high bare wall surrounding the enclosure, which was one day to be a garden,[1] but was then merely a bare space.

I went back to the hotel; telegrams were up announcing that five steamers were outside the port of Alexandria unable to come in; and the next morning, the 19th of March, when we went down to the large breakfast-room, a fire was lighted for the first time during the whole winter, though people had been shivering in shawls and greatcoats for more than two months past. I note this fact for the benefit of invalids with limited means who may think of wintering in Cairo, adding at the same time that this was quite an exceptional winter. The thermometer outside my window in the balcony was at 8 A.M. 40°. In an exposed place it was no doubt lower. The next day the five steamers got into port, after having been beaten about for four-and-twenty hours; and, what concerned me more nearly, a second summons came to me from the harem, to say that all was ready for my reception. I went at once, and found things were as ready as they were likely ever to be, and whatever might be wanting the Princess gave me *carte blanche* to order for myself, as the requirements of a European are so foreign to their habits that it is not to be expected they can be easily met. My rooms con-

---

[1] It was a very pretty garden a few months later: the soil of Egypt has only to be watered, and trees spring up as if by magic.

sisted of what the French would call five *pièces*—a large bedroom, two anterooms (one of which served for my boxes), bathroom, &c. I had stipulated to have keys to all the doors, and they were provided, only none of them fitted, except that to the outer door, which would lock on the outside, but not on the inside, so that I could not fasten myself in at night.

The arrangement of my rooms seemed at first fairly satisfactory, but I soon became aware of the drawbacks, which were quite insupportable. All the best part of the palace (the loftiest rooms, &c., both on the ground-floor and on the first) was appropriated to the Princess. If any visitors of distinction came to stay, beds were arranged for them in some of these rooms at night, and cleared away in the morning. These beds consisted of mattresses brought in and laid on the carpets, and *impromptu* curtains propped over them. There were lavatories all over the palace, and to them the visitors went to perform their ablutions. The Princesses had bedrooms fitted up in some measure in the European style, but that was quite an innovation, and not to be thought of for any one else. Now, if I had been lodged in the best part of the house I should have wanted my room or rooms to myself, and that would have interfered with the general harmony of the suite of apartments. All this was intelligible enough, but I soon found, as the warm weather came on, that my position was perfectly intolerable. The rooms were low, a terrible thing in a hot climate, the windows of course open at night, and the noises so great that I could not sleep. The slaves or eunuchs would call and shout to each other all day and half the night, whereas in the best apartments every sound was hushed. When we left Cairo I told the Princess I never could return to those rooms again, and during the next winter I was much better lodged in a corner of the best apartments.

The first night of my stay in the harem I never closed my eyes, partly on account of the novelty of my position, partly on account of a high wind, and the incessant slamming of a door in the courtyard below, which was like a series of thunder-claps. I did not see the Princess until the next afternoon. I was sitting with her then, and her *dada* and a number of her chief slaves were standing round, when her husband, Ibrahim Pasha, came in. The *selamlik* in which he passed his days was a separate building close by, and communicating with the harem by a private gate, which led from one garden into the other. A eunuch always sat at this gate (it was a double gate, with a small room between for bad weather) to prevent any one else but the Prince from passing. I had often heard him spoken of as a jolly good-tempered young man, and was quite prepared to be prepossessed in his favour. And here I may say that nothing could exceed his kindness and courtesy to me during the whole of my residence in the harem. He began talking to me of the opera, which was then about to close, and asked me if I were going that evening.

I replied, "How can I? I am shut up!"

"Oh no," said he, laughing, "you can go in and out when you like."

"Well, even supposing that to be the case," said I, "I have no opera box, and no carriage, and I could not go alone."

"I'll order a carriage for you, and you shall have my box."

"And where will you sit?" said I.

"Oh, I'll go into my cousin's box." (The two Ibrahim Pashas, husband and brother of my pupil, stood to each other in the double relationship of cousin and brother-in-law.)

"And as to being alone," said the Princess, "my brother

is sure to be at the opera, and all his party know you, and some will go and visit you."

I still declined, when the Princess said to me in English, "Don't refuse,—he really means to oblige you;" upon which I immediately thanked him, and accepted his offer. But as I feared the box-keeper might make some difficulty in letting me in, a eunuch was sent with me. The box was nearly opposite the stage, and the opera had already begun when I entered. I went at once to the front seat, and for some time paid great attention to the performance, when happening to cast my eyes on the looking-glass at one side of the box, I saw the eunuch, whom I believed to be gone, standing a few paces behind me, apparently following the performance with great interest. It struck me as so ludicrous for me to be seated there guarded by a eunuch, that I had the greatest difficulty to keep my countenance.

I saw very little of my pupil during the first few weeks of my stay in the harem. She was never visible in the morning, and at luncheon the musicians were always there, and made such a din that it was impossible to hold any conversation. After luncheon, if she did not go to sleep, she would play at backgammon with her *dada*, which they played with a rapidity that only long practice can give. It is the favourite game in the harem, and a great deal of time is passed in it. The *dada* of a princess is always a person of great importance in the harem, and in this case particularly so, as, on account of the extreme youth of the Princess, the general superintendence of the household devolved on her. She was a good-looking woman, but of no education, not even having acquired Arabic during all the years she had lived in Egypt. She had to a high degree the gift of talking, though I cannot pass any judgment upon the merits of her conversation, but I have heard her talk for an hour at a time, and those who had nothing else to do would sit and listen. She was a great impediment to me at first, but she ceased to be so after a time, perhaps when she found that I did not interfere with her in any way. The mother of my pupil came often to see her daughter, and always asked me if the Princess went on with her studies, to which I replied in the negative. The second Princess looked vexed, and my pupil hung her head, and afterwards I induced her to let me read to her a little, if she would not read herself, to which she consented. But the *dada* and one or two others made such a noise talking and laughing that I could not be heard. I would then ask the Princess to send them into an adjoining room, which she did hesitatingly and timidly. The *dada* would then laugh aloud, and say something disparaging as she left the room, but this was only at the beginning; after a time the Princess took more and more interest in reading, and I scarcely left her from morning till night.

CHAPTER XXIV.

Curious superstition about brides—Fantasia in the harem—Again visit the Pyramids—Photography in the harem—Summer heat begins—Amusements in the harem.

There is a popular superstition that when two brides are married from the same house, they should not meet for a period of forty days, and that the neglect of this observance entails sterility on one of them. The Princess Zeyneb, youngest daughter of Mohammed Ali (whose marriage in 1845 was described by Miss Martineau in her book on Egypt), had come expressly from Constantinople to be present at the wedding of her grand-niece and namesake, and had laid great stress on the observance of this ceremony. She herself had been married at the same time as a young companion, who had lived with her; the latter had become a mother, but the Princess remained childless, and ascribed the fact to her neglect of this observance.

I was sitting with the Princess one morning, when her *dada* came hastily in, saying, "Faïk Hanem is coming!" upon which the Princess ran into an inner room laughing. I thought this very strange conduct, and went forward to receive Faïk Hanem. She was conducted into the chief reception-room, and I sat there talking to her for some little time, when an attendant came to announce that the Princess was coming, and Faïk Hanem got up laughing, and stood in the middle of the room, with her back turned to the door at which the Princess would enter. Presently the latter appeared, led by two attendants, and walking *backwards*. The two brides were placed *dos à dos*, they intertwined each other's arms, exchanged gold coins, which they stuck on their foreheads, and then turned round and kissed each other. The ceremony being completed, they walked hand in hand to a couch, sat down there, and were soon deep in conversation, which was quite private, though there were twenty or thirty persons present; because the band formed in a line opposite to them, and struck up a deafening noise, two or three singing at the same time. The instruments were two tambourines, two fifes, two violins, and two guitars.

Some ladies may wish to know whether the due observance of this ceremony produced the desired result, to whom I reply, *It did not*.

Some dancing-girls then came in, and gave the performance which I have before described. A little wretch

of a negress, dressed as a boy in particoloured tights and
pointed cap, made the most uncouth contortions opposite
to eight girls; and here a most ridiculous scene took place.
The Princess had a pretty little dog called Fido (pets were
quite an innovation in the harem), which was an immense
amusement to all the slaves. Fido sat on the sofa by his
mistress, looking on at all that was done for her amusement; but when he saw the uncouth gestures of the
negress, he showed his disgust by barking violently, and
jumping down amongst the dancers, hoping to put an end
to such a demonstration. But at that moment all the nine
swept round in a circle, driving Fido before them, and this
chase continued throughout the whole dance. At every
halt Fido stood at bay, darting alternately upon each foot
that was jerked out, and only restrained by the doubt
which to fix upon. When the dance was over, he chased
the girls all out, and feeling then triumphant, returned to
the side of his mistress, still slightly ruffled, and venting
his feelings by occasional short barks.

One evening there was a *fantasia* (as they call any entertainment), which was very well done, and amused me
greatly. We, the persons entertained, were seated on one
side of the room; at the end of it was the band (consisting
of eight, ten, or sometimes twelve players), which of course
opened the performance. When a lull occurred in the
music, two beings entered the space before us. They were
dressed in very loose trousers, frock-coat, and broad-
brimmed wideawake; the one in black, the other nankeen.
They looked very like the *pères de famille* usually represented on the stage. One of them brought in a small
table, and the other sat down to it, and pretended to be
very busy arranging some papers. A large ape glided in
and performed all sorts of antics, of course quite unexpected by the two old gentlemen, who were ignorant of its
presence, and each absorbed in his own occupation. It

got under the table and raised it high in the air, while the old gentleman who was calmly studying looked in amazement for the motive power, which of course he never found, as the ape always got in the opposite direction to where he looked. Then the ape got behind the other old gentleman and snatched his book away, and so for a time troubled each alternately; until, thoroughly worn out, the old gentlemen rose simultaneously to make a search, and in so doing, and raising the chairs and tables to look under them, came in violent collision with each other and fell prostrate. The ape then leaped on their backs, and after performing a dance upon each in turn, darted out just as one of the old gentlemen caught sight of their tormentor, upon which they scrambled up and rushed after him, and so the performance ended.

The ape was played by a girl of about twelve years old. She wore a brown, hairy, tight-fitting skin, a long tail, and a masque representing the features of an ape. She imitated all the movements capitally, and made springs and ran along on all-fours very like the real animal. The next year she thought herself, or was thought, too old to wear such a dress, and there was no one else could do it so well. She was a bright-eyed girl, very intelligent and active, and trained as a dancer. In great harems like that of my pupil, a certain number of girls are educated as musicians, dancers, and sometimes as comedians or pantomimists; but it is solely for the amusement of their mistress and her guests. They are sometimes lent to other harems on any *fête* occasion, such as a birth or a marriage, and then generally receive handsome presents.

Although the weather was so bad this winter, there were many intervening days worthy of Egypt, and I settled one Friday to make a picnic to the Pyramids with some friends. As gentlemen would be of the party, of course they could not drive into the inner court of the harem, or indeed into the outer one either, and at that early stage of my residence in the harem I could not depend upon the eunuchs letting me know that a mixed party of ladies and gentlemen awaited me without. It was too great an outrage to all their customs and traditions to expect them to do it, so I had settled with my friends to be near the outer gate at a certain hour, and that I would be there waiting. For excursions to the Pyramids, one always put on the worst dress one had. I should have thought nothing of going out of the hotel thus clad, but felt rather ashamed of going out of the palace.

The day was delightful, 70° in the shade close to the entrance of the second Pyramid, where we climbed up and had our luncheon. We visited all the same places over again—Colonel Howard Vyse's tomb, where you can only look down, as the descent is too difficult for any but the Bedouins. We crawled into that of Leipsius to look at the hieroglyphics on the walls, and also visited the Temple of the Sphinx; but the only drawback is the constant attendance of the Bedouins, who will *not* leave you, and are all the time urging you to buy scarabeii, or some other antiquity, probably manufactured at Birmingham. But the desert air is so invigorating that with all these drawbacks one is never tired of the excursion.

When I got back to the harem I took leave of my friends outside, and walked in, but saw immediately in the outer court that some distinguished visitor was within. It proved to be the first Princess, and all were in gala costume. I was covered with dust after my day's excursion, and desirous of escaping unseen, but the band stationed in the entrance saloon caught sight of me, and (jokingly) struck up a *selam*, only given for distinguished visitors. The mother-in-law had also arrived to stay a few days, and in the evening there was a *fantasia* for her.

About six Arab musicians were led in blindfold, and placed behind one of the large lattice-screens which divide them from the rest of the company. Cushions were then placed on the ground, upon which the ladies sat, gazing through the screens, themselves unseen.

A memorable event in harem annals occurred at this time — the Princess was photographed. She had been taken two years before, and a very good likeness was produced; she was then thirteen, and now, though still a child in years, she was a woman in outward appearance, and a very pretty one. There were female photographers came to the harems, but they were not skilful, and did not produce good likenesses. The Princess saw this, and having been brought up with Europeans, she thought there would be no harm in being photographed again, as she had formerly been. There was only one drawback,— a European photographer might sell her likeness, or send it to Europe for sale, and that would violate all ideas of oriental propriety. So it was decided that an Arab photographer, said to be very good, should be introduced, and he being an Egyptian subject, could not possibly either sell or show the portraits to other persons. The man could not, however, be admitted into the harem; the business was to go on in the garden, and it was rather difficult to find a place not too sunny or too windy. The only shade was made by the walls, as there were no trees, and that was a shade which varied every half-hour, so that there was a continual shifting of the apparatus. Several eunuchs stood by, but they gave no assistance whatever. The poor man had to do everything himself, and it was evident that he felt very nervous in his unusual position. The Princess was taken standing, sitting, alone, in groups, and in several different dresses. While she went in to change them, others sat for their likenesses, and two whole days were consumed in this way.

The reason of this was that we were constantly shifting our place all over the garden; and towards the middle of the day, there being no shade at all from the walls, we were obliged to go into the palace for two or three hours.

A few days after, the proofs came, and were utter failures. Some of us looked like dwarfs, others like giantesses. The perspective was at fault in all,—some hands came out as clubs, and plump figures swelled into something Gampish. The Princess tore her own likeness into the smallest fragments, but laughed heartily at the caricatures of her friends. One of the slaves, who always expressed a great regard for me, begged the Princess to give her my photograph, which was done (I not being present); and some time after the girl showed it to me as a triumph of art. I got possession of it by ruse, destroyed the atrocious thing, and presented her instead with a very good likeness, which had been taken by Abdullah on my last visit to Constantinople.

By the help of photography two or three of the Princesses had had full-length portraits of themselves taken in oils! First a fair photograph was produced, which was sent to Paris, measures as to height and size were given, dress and ornaments added, and a few hints as to complexion, colour of eyes, &c. In one or two cases the result was not bad, in others total failure. One lady, as fanciful as she is pretty, having grey eyes of her own, but with a preference for dark blue, desired that colour to be given in the painting, which was done accordingly. One must not be too hard upon the Arab photographer for his failure, as I am afraid a first-rate European would hardly have succeeded under such circumstances. No one gave him the slightest help, and he was not allowed to have an assistant. Every time that the changing light or wind (and there was no escaping the latter) necessitated a move, there was not only his own apparatus to shift, but a complete paraphernalia around the Princess—arm-chairs, table, cushions, flower-stands, &c., besides a great canvas screen, which had to be held up every now and then.

The opera season was now over, but the French theatre continued open for a short time, and I went several times with my pupil and Kopsès to the harem boxes. It was rare that any of the Princesses were there. The weather was getting warm, and none of the ladies but my pupils understood French. I saw very fairly through the wire grating. The box was very large, with most luxurious arm-chairs; behind it was a withdrawing-room, and a passage with windows opening into an inner court, so that the box was much cooler than any other part of the house. A private door and staircase led to it, and the entrance was through a little garden at the back of the theatre, with sentinels guarding the gates. On the 15th of April the season closed, and the heat was then getting great.

My rooms became intolerable as the spring advanced, from the heat by day and the noise by night. When I left them at an early hour in the morning, I was struck with the difference of temperature in the chief apartments, and as I had nothing to employ me elsewhere, I found my time pass very tediously. For the first month or six weeks, I was very little engaged with the Princess; later on, I was never absent from her, if she was at home. For the first month or two after her marriage she would go to sleep in the afternoon for a couple of hours. She had never been accustomed to this before, but her lessons being at an end, and not knowing how to fill up the time, she, encouraged by those about her, followed the usual plan, not only in the harem, but throughout the East, of taking an afternoon siesta. As soon as she began to take an interest in reading with me, she left it off, and never again resumed it.

The Princess Ahmed, mother-in-law of my pupil, came occasionally to stay for a few days. She was the widow, and had been the sole wife, of Ahmed Pasha, elder brother of the Khédive. She was a handsome stately woman, of about six or seven and thirty, an exemplary mistress of her household, and devoted mother to her only child. She had been his nurse as well as mother, a very rare thing in high classes, according to my experience in the East. She lived a very quiet retired life, and had had little or no intercourse with Europeans. She had not adopted any of their fashions, but I never discovered that she had any prejudice against them. She was always most kind and courteous to me, and often urged my going out, which showed she saw no harm in it, as most Mahometan women would have done.

It is the custom for the mother of the husband to reside with the married couple, and she ranks *before* the wife, and is in fact the mistress of the house. According to European notions this is bad, but there is a great deal to be said for it in the East. The wife is not chosen for love, but by chance; she may or she may not (more probably the latter) be the sole mother of her husband's children, therefore the tie that binds mother and child is much stronger than that between husband and wife. Then the wife is probably, when married, a young inexperienced girl, quite unfit to be the mistress of a household. But the daughter of the Khédive, like that of the Sultan, must be sole mistress in her own house, so the usual custom was not carried out in this establishment.

During the first visit of the Princess Ahmed, a singular scene, illustrative of oriental manners, occurred one evening. The day had been very hot, with a south wind, and towards sunset we were all assembled in the large entrance-saloon, which went the entire depth of the house, opening back and front on the garden. All the windows and blinds were thrown open, and though it was still very hot, the *dada* walked out into the garden, and presently called to Kopsès to join her. There were all the symptoms of a *khamseen* wind coming on, when exercise is not very pleasant, so Kopsès declined. The *dada*, who was very fond of rough play, said she *should* come, and ran in after her. Kopsès gave her a fine chase, but as the *dada*, laughing heartily, called to others to help, she was at last captured, upon which she threw herself on the ground so as to make it as difficult as possible to drag her out. Every one was looking on laughing to see which would gain her point. The *dada* was a strong woman, and had weight on her side, while Kopsès was a little slight creature, but very muscular and active. Suddenly she sprang up with an impetus which sent the *dada* several yards forward, and threw herself at the feet of the Princess Ahmed, who had been quietly looking on. The latter immediately granted her protection, and getting up, overturned the *dada* on the carpet, and rolling her about, tickled her violently. The *dada* screamed with laughter, and defended herself as well as she could, but that was not much, as she was prevented by respect from retaliating. After a little punishment of this kind, she was allowed to get up, with her hair all down, and her dress sadly disarranged; and the Princess Ahmed passed on to an inner room, whither I followed, with Kopsès and some of the slaves. I observed an embroidered carpet placed on the floor, and I was trying to make a little conversation in Turkish with the Princess, when Kopsès said to me, "She is going to pray; will you go?" I went directly, but the doors remained open as usual, and the slaves were grouped about in the room and in the doorway.

It was the 20th of March when I went to reside in the harem, and the 23d of May when we left Cairo for Alexandria. During these nine weeks the time passed very heavily with me. My pupil would spend whole days at Abdeen at her father's palace, which was of course natural and proper, and Kopsès always accompanied her. When at home, she passed nearly all her time in receiving visits, in playing at backgammon, and in listening to interminable stories from her *dada*; also in consulting with her dressmaker about some new toilet. After the first few weeks, when the *khamseen* winds set in, it became too hot to go out, and I passed whole days in the house, with no one to talk to, no books or papers to read, and nothing but my piano for recreation. I began to doubt whether I was right to sacrifice the few remaining years of health and strength which might be in store for me, to this dreadful monotony of harem life. I took to teaching two or three of the young slaves, and they were very docile and anxious to learn, but it was simply A B C work. We had no language in common by which I could explain away difficulties, and convey to them simple information on common subjects. A person who understands two or three European languages finds the acquisition of a fourth comparatively easy, but they do not help the least in learning an oriental language. During all the time I lived in Egypt I never met with more than two or three persons who could *read* and *write* Arabic or Turkish. I speak of Europeans long resident in the country. They could talk and make themselves understood in some *patois* or other. As long as I only wanted something, I could make myself understood, but conversation was a very different thing. I used to sit about in the saloons with my Turkish books (in which the *sound* of the words was rendered in Latin characters) or at work, sometimes listening to what passed around me, and trying to understand it. The upper slaves went freely about the apartments. If their mistress was there, they stood; if she were absent, they sat on the floor in groups. There was an Arab woman called Oum Ayesha (Mother Ayesha) who was a very frequent visitor. She had been for a short time the foster-mother of the Princess, and she told me with great pride how the infant had turned away from other nurses and had clung to her. She was married to the *lalla* of Ibrahim Pasha (brother of my pupil) and had had eight children, but they were all dead. She was allowed great liberties, and was in fact the buffoon of the harem. She always passed a week or two of each month in the palace, and wandered in and out exactly where she pleased, no matter what visitor was present. She was a privileged person, and I presume had some natural drollery, since no one seemed able to help laughing at what she said,—Princes or Princesses, it was all the same. She was a good-natured creature, but very coarse, both in words and gestures. The first time I ever noticed her, I was sitting one evening in the chief saloon on a couch with my books, and a group of slaves formed a circle on the ground near me. They were at work, and they asked Oum Ayesha, who was wandering about, to come and sing to them. She began a low monotonous chant, evidently a love-song, and caught the hands of the girl next her. The latter was of a grave character, and knowing well what was coming, got out of Ayesha's way at once, who then turned to the other side. The second girl began immediately to laugh immoderately—so much so, that I could not help laughing to see her. Ayesha had cast many side glances at me, and thus stimulated to fresh exertions, she grew more and more impassioned, and at last sprang upon the girl, who was so convulsed with laughter that she was unable to defend herself, and as the others thought she was going into a fit, they dragged away Ayesha, who continued making frantic demonstrations of passion.

CHAPTER XXV.

Married life in the East contrasted with that in England—Amusements in the harem—Distinction between the white and black slaves—Sudden appearance of eunuchs in my room—Removal to Alexandria—Story of the diamond buckle—Family life on the Canal—I make a new acquaintance.

I could not help being struck even at this early stage with the different life led by a young married couple in the East and one in our country. My pupil's husband had been in love with her from a child, and was devoted to her after marriage as he had been before. Still they had no pursuits in common; they could not walk out together, ride, drive, or go to the theatre together, or have any mutual acquaintance. Any wish she might express was immediately gratified by him; he got a pretty little pony-carriage and pair of ponies and taught her to drive, but she grew weary in a few days of driving round the garden, with or without him, and gave up using it. One pet after another was given her; the poor child wanted liberty, as a bird pines in its cage, and cared for nothing else. When they went to the theatre or opera it was in separate carriages, and they sat in separate boxes. When any gentleman came to see the Prince it was at the *selamlik*, and he could not introduce them to her. If any of her brothers came they were brought in at once, and the intercourse was a great pleasure both to them and to her. Some of them had been brought up in France and England, and they highly appreciated having as sister a charming young woman, full of the light graceful *badinage* which is always so attractive in the society of young people. But after all, the visits of the brothers were only occasional; there were a great many weary hours to get through. The Princess generally drove out towards evening, and Kopsès

A HAREM JOKE. 279

went with her. She had a very elegant carriage and fine horses, two *saïs* (pronounced *syces*) preceding with long sticks, and white dress terminating at the knee, and sleeves which the wind inflated as they ran, so that they looked like wings. There were also generally a couple of outriders in handsome uniforms, and two or three eunuchs on horseback, who, however, fell behind, not riding, as a few years before was the custom, in front of the carriage-windows, with the blinds drawn down. Now, the blinds were up and the carriage was nearly all windows, and the two pretty girls, in their bright dresses and transparent *yashmaks*, were distinctly visible. The other Princesses got similar carriages and drove out in the same style, and the Choubrah or Abbassieh road presented quite a lively scene, for the hack-carriages used by travellers do not produce an elegant effect. But last winter all this had passed away, and a harem carriage driven in such a style was an unfrequent sight!

One warm evening the gates were closed and the ladies were wandering about in the garden. Two months before it had been a waste, and already it was full of plants and flowers. The Princess was seated near a little lake, which had been constructed of a serpentine shape, winding about under rustic bridges. She was laughingly scolding one of her attendants, when the girl broke away, crying out, "My mistress is angry with me! I'll drown myself!" and rushed into the water. The Princess called out, "Oh, stop her! stop her!" and three or four more followed immediately. But the first knew well enough that the water was not more than three feet deep, so she had done it for a joke, and she turned round and threw water in the faces of her pursuers. The Princess had seen the joke directly after the cry had escaped her, and now laughed heartily at the chase, and urged others to join in the capture. The general harem dress when warm weather set

in was white Indian grass-cloth, more or less fine, made
loose, and confined at the waist by a coloured sash, a
ribbon to match being usually worn round the throat, and
to tie back the hair. The dress could not hurt by the
immersion, but the ribbons might be spoiled. Some were
seen to cast a glance on their pretty ties, which was a
signal to those who saw the look to rush upon them at
once and push them in. There was nothing but screaming and laughing, several disporting themselves in the
water, others pursued all over the garden, met at the
cross-paths, turning and doubling on their pursuers. The
Princess clapped her hands with delight and laughed un-
restrainedly, and the girls themselves were so immensely
tickled with the joke that they tried to renew it on two or
three occasions, though not with the same success.

I had often heard people talk of the mystery in the
harem, and the difficulty there was in knowing what went
on within the walls, to those who lived in the outer world.
This was true enough, but I soon observed there was no
mystery amongst each other. What one knew (as a rule)
everybody knew. The mistress was never alone; there
was no place, however private, where her attendants could
not penetrate. When visitors came, the chief slaves
waited in the room, forming a semicircle at a slight distance, but within ear-shot. The only way to speak in
private appeared to me to be under cover of the band
playing, when the noise was deafening, and the voice could
only be heard by the next neighbour. Where a foreign
language was spoken, privacy was always ensured, and my
dear little Princess was not a little pleased to be able to
talk to her husband, to Kopsès, and to me, in French,
which no one else understood; and to Kopsès and me
also in English, which the Prince did not understand. I
heard an anecdote concerning this custom of the constant
presence of the attendants. A European went one day to

visit one of the married daughters of his Highness, and as the Princess understood only Turkish and Arabic, the conversation was held in one of these languages. But the visitor had something private to say, and whenever the slaves were at a little distance she broached the subject, changing it as they approached. Her visit, however, came to an end before she had an opportunity of saying what she wished, and before leaving she said in the most polite phrases which she could use, " I never could have believed that an Egyptian Princess would submit to such slavery as never to hear or to speak anything without the same being carried through the whole household." The Princess was so struck with this that she gave orders that in future, whenever any European visitor should come to her, the slaves were to remain in the anteroom. These innovations were being gradually introduced during my stay in Egypt.

Every one in the house, except the Princess and myself, were slaves, and the property of their mistress. All those, I have been told on good authority, who once enter the household of any of the Khédive's family are never sold again; they are provided for for live, and, married or single, receive the same monthly allowance until their death. Of late years they are generally bought young, and receive a certain education; there are schools within the harem in the eunuchs' department, and Turkish and Arabic masters are admitted. There was, however, a marked difference made between the white and the black slaves. To the latter all the menial work was allotted, and I observed that, although many of the white girls acted as housemaids, &c., they would always, if no *calfa* was present, try to shift their work upon any unlucky black girl who came in their way. I watched one morning from my bedroom windows, which looked down on an inner court, the daily process of cleaning it. First a row of black girls swept from end to end, driving all the dust before them. Then came another row of thirteen or fourteen black girls with mops and water, which was plentifully thrown about. Two or three white girls stood by with brooms in their hands to appear to do something, but their work was usually limited to urging on the blacks, and themselves talking to any one who happened to be looking out of the windows. Their feet were bare, and they were generally in high wooden clogs (which they left outside when they entered the house), a large thick towel, with broad red stripes, was drawn tightly round their persons, and fastened somehow behind. One had on a green satin paletot, which had probably once figured at a Baïram, but then did duty as bodice. These thick towels formed the ordinary working costume, and sometimes on grand cleaning occasions I would see a dozen in a row making an onslaught in the saloons, with the *calfa* (or overseer), a long stick in her hand with which to reach any idler, and give due admonishment. On such occasions they would be all white girls, as the furniture was too costly to be entrusted to the blacks. Indeed, wherever the *calfa* was present, the whites could not shirk their duty. The *calfa*, the *dada*, the *cahir* (housekeeper), and all the head slaves, had slaves (their own property) under them, either purchased by themselves or presents from their mistress. These "slaves of slaves" sat on the floor outside, or just within their mistresses' doors, and were as a rule much more submissive than their mistresses. Thus all the upper attendants in the harem were better served in their rooms than I, for as an Englishwoman I could not have a slave, and although the Princess appointed one to attend on me, the girl evidently looked upon it as a degradation to wait on a Giaour, and took so little pains to understand my requirements, however they might be explained to her, that I found it far less irritating to do everything for myself than to depend on her. As long as I was well this state of things, though very inconvenient, might be bearable, but if ill it became at once insupportable.

There was a black girl called Zora about the Princess who was allowed great freedom. She was the daughter of one of the many foster-mothers that the Princess had had, for Oum Ayesha was not the only person to whom this high privilege had been accorded. When a royal infant was born, more than one nurse might be procured, and the child itself made its choice; later on, the child might turn away, on which another nurse was directly procured, so that it might happen that many had been in turn promoted to the high dignity. Sometimes in the evening at sunset, the girls being all in the garden, the Princess would set them to run races with each other, she looking on, and applauding the winner. Then one of them proposed a jumping race, and after that to hop round the garden on one leg! They were all young, light and active; the gates were closed, the eunuchs standing about looking on, and, but for their presence, the whole had the effect of a girls' school out at play. Their laughter must have been heard afar off.

On the 9th of May the second and third Princesses came to tell us that we were to leave for Alexandria the next day early, by special train. There was no mention of Constantinople. We were to take up our summer residence at a new palace at Ramleh, which was being built for the Princess. I packed up everything, and was up the next morning at five, to be in readiness when called for. But no one came, and at ten I met the Prince on his way down-stairs, who told me the departure was delayed a few days. The few days were a fortnight, and on the 23d we finally started. The Prince had told me the day before, that the palace which was being built for the Princess's reception not being quite finished, they were going first on a visit to Hussein Pasha, who lived on the Mahmoudieh Canal, and that I was to go to the Hôtel de l'Europe until I could join the Princess at Ramleh. Upon hearing this, I begged that I might not be obliged to travel with the harem, because as I was not bound for the same destination, my luggage would infallibly be mixed up with that of the harem, and I should be unable to get it when I reached Alexandria. The Prince consented, though apparently quite unable to follow my reasoning, and said that his secretary, M. Eugène, should travel with me to look after me. As his house lay midway between the palace and the station, it was settled I should call for him on my way thither in the morning.

I then retired to my own apartments, and having finished my packing, and the heat being very great, I took a bath. I have before mentioned that I was furnished with a key for the outer door, which would lock on the outside, but not on the inside. I therefore usually fastened it with a string, which by no means kept out an intruder, but retarded her entry and thus gave me notice of her approach. I had just got out of the bath, and put on a dressing-gown, when I was startled by a vigorous kick which burst the door open in a moment, and two eunuchs entered the room. They did not appear in the least disconcerted at my appearance, or to consider their visit ill-timed, but one of them who spoke a little English told me that his father (!) wished to know how many boxes I had. Now it had never entered my head that a eunuch could have a father, any more than he could have a son, but that that father should be living in the harem with him was quite a revelation to me. Had he spoken in Turkish or Arabic, the oriental imagery might have suggested to me some figure of speech; but in matter-of-fact English I took the relationship as matter of fact, and could only ejaculate, "Your father!" "Yes, my father," said he.

So I communicated the number of boxes, and the two eunuchs went away, and I afterwards found that the chief eunuch held that paternal character towards all the others. The utter inefficacy of the string had discouraged me from using it again; so the next morning at half-past five, a few minutes after I had left my bed, I turned suddenly round and saw a slave within a few feet of me who had entered noiselessly, and was watching the operations of the toilet. She did not want anything, so upon being asked her business, she disappeared.

The train (ordinary) was to leave at nine, but they hurried me out of the harem at seven (having urged me strongly to go at six). Naturally I had to wait a short time for M. Eugène, who had not calculated on being called for two hours before the time. Our train started punctually, and as the harem special train was gone, there was no shunting or any stoppage; but it was a slow train, and we did not reach Alexandria till half-past 3 P.M. During the journey M. Eugène expressed great surprise that I should have preferred travelling by the ordinary slow train, which took nearly seven hours, to going with the harem, when I should have made the journey in something under four. I replied that it was on account of my luggage, as I dreaded so much its getting mixed up with that of the harem. "Oh," said he, "I took the precaution of sending mine yesterday, so that I am quite independent of everything, having only a small handbag." Nevertheless, five days after, M. Eugène had not yet got his luggage, having made several unavailing journeys to the station in quest of it. His luggage had been taken to the station on Friday, and on Saturday morning at eight the harem train went, and his luggage somehow or other got mixed up with it. A burnt child dreads the fire, and my own experience and that of others in the two preceding summers had made me dread beyond anything travelling with the harem when not bound for the same destination.

I heard a curious story just before leaving Cairo. One of the Princesses was dressing, with jewel-caskets open on the tables near her, when a little eunuch came in with some message. Among the jewels was a diamond buckle, and the boy watched his opportunity and took possession of it. He carried it to a jeweller's in the Mouskee, saying he had been sent to sell it, and asked £20 for it. The jeweller was an honest man: he examined it, and keeping it in his hands, said, "This buckle is worth more than £20; if you will take me to your harem I will find out where it was purchased, and give the value of it." The boy said his harem was a long way off; but the jeweller refusing to give up the buckle, he became frightened, and at last fairly ran away. The jeweller took the buckle to one or two of the royal harems, and at last came to the right one, and great was the joy of the slaves who had the charge of the jewels, as they were in hourly dread of a flogging when their mistress might ask for the buckle and it should not be forthcoming. The mistress was told, and she gave instant orders that the boy should be sold at any sacrifice. But the worst of the matter in my opinion was, that it was added that my Princess's establishment being then in formation, the boy was bought for her, and cautioned that if ever he stole again, he would be taken out to sea and drowned. I believe, however, my pupil would have had all her diamonds stolen before she would have ordered him to be flogged, much more drowned!

Very soon after my arrival at Alexandria, I went to the Mahmoudieh Canal to pay a visit to my pupil, who was on a visit to her half-brother Hussein Pasha. It was a double connection, as the Prince had married the half-sister of my pupil's husband. The Princess Hussein was a very amiable, agreeable person. She spoke French very well, and read a great deal. I went very early in the morning, and was shown into a room where a number of French books were lying on a table. This was quite different from Eastern habits, and presently after I heard voices in the adjoining room, mixed voices of ladies and gentlemen. The door of the room in which I sat was opened, and the Princess Hussein looked in, and seeing me, came forward, and led me into the next room, where I found Tewfik Pasha and Hussein Pasha (the two eldest sons of the Khédive), and Ibrahim Pasha (the husband of my pupil), the Princess, and Kopsès, to whom were now added the Princess Hussein and myself. They were all talking merrily together, without *gêne*, just as young people would do in Europe. The mother of Hussein Pasha was also there. She lived with her son, and was therefore, according to Eastern custom, the mistress of the house. She did not speak French, nor, as far as I could ever see, adopt European customs; but we went in to breakfast presently (*café au lait*, in the French style), and she kindly urged me to stay, and also to repeat my visit. The three Princes took their leave before we went in to breakfast, but I was told that they usually spent the evenings all together.

During my stay at the Hôtel de l'Europe at Alexandria, I visited my pupil always two or three times a-week at the Canal, and renewed acquaintance with those families I had known the previous year. I was invited one day to Ramleh to meet Miss Harris, a lady of whom I had often heard, and whose name is from that time connected in my mind with many pleasant memories. On this occasion there were several other friends, and two of them accompanied me back to Alexandria by the last train, which is (or was, for it no longer exists) called the "horse train," and conveyed to my mind the idea that it was exclusively for horses, and that the accommodation might be confined to a spare box; but I found it was a large omnibus, with a horse doing duty as locomotive. A day or two after Miss Harris called upon me, and subsequently invited me to her house, which was situated on the heights behind the town, and called Koum-el-Dikke. I was quite charmed with the position, and also with the house itself, which was very quaint, with rooms in all sorts of unexpected shapes and places, wooden balconies and terraces, commanding very extensive views. The house was full of antiquities, and also of English comforts, and the hostess was quite a character.

I will give a little outline of her. Her father was a famous Egyptologist, and also a great favourite of Mohammed Ali. She lost her mother (a native woman) at a very early age; and as her father lived frequently for months under tents or in a Nile boat, he sent the child to be educated in England, under the care of his sister, and with her children. At twenty years of age she returned to Egypt to keep her father's house, or to accompany him in his wanderings and scientific researches. She was often with him for months in the desert, living among tombs, his willing and useful assistant. All the scientific men of the day who went to Egypt visited at her father's house. After some years he was struck with paralysis, and lingered for a considerable time, leaving his daughter sole heiress of all that he possessed, including valuable antiquities, some of which are now in the possession of the British Museum.

Miss Harris was an accomplished musician, and the house in which she resided with her father (when at Alexandria) was very near the palace of the notorious Nuzzli Hanem, eldest daughter of Mohammed Ali. In this climate, where windows are almost always open, music travels far, and the sweet sounds were carried to Nuzzli Hanem. One morning, while Miss Harris was dressing, and being in her father's house, not dreaming of intrusion, three eunuchs unceremoniously entered her room, and told her that "Nuzzli Hanem wanted her." The latter did not enjoy a very good repute, and all sorts of dark deeds were related of her, so that being "wanted by Nuzzli Hanem" was not a pleasant prospect. Miss Harris was, however, of a fearless character, and thought not of after consequences, being wholly taken up by her indignation at the unceremonious intrusion of the eunuchs into her sanctum. At last, however, she routed them out, and they went into her drawing-room until her toilet was finished. When she went in to them there she found they had ordered pipes and coffee, and the room was full of tobacco-smoke; all her books were turned over, her photographs handled; in fact, all was confusion. She reprimanded them sharply upon their behaviour, and they reiterated their first speech that their mistress "wanted her." Miss Harris positively refused to go, and they went away. The next day they came again with the same message; but this time they did not come to her bedroom nor to the drawing-room, but remained below, and Miss Harris ordered pipes and coffee for them there. But the message being still of the same peremptory kind, she persisted in declining to go. After a third message, however, and a consultation with her father, it was agreed between them that she should pay the required visit, and a lady was asked to accompany her. What Miss Harris was "wanted" for was a perfect mystery to them both, and they could not divest themselves of the unpleasant idea that Miss Harris had somehow offended Nuzzli Hanem.

They went, and were introduced into a room where several slaves were standing, and one person was seated on cushions at the farther end. This was Nuzzli Hanem; but as no introduction took place, and the person seated never

T

even looked at them, Miss Harris and her friend remained immovable. So Nuzzli Hanem condescended to make a slight movement of the head, and to tell them to be seated. Now Miss Harris's companion was a very stout lady, and to sit on a cushion on the floor, and afterwards to have to get up again, was a feat to which she was not equal. Besides, Miss Harris stood out, on the ground that they were Englishwomen, and not accustomed to "squatting." So she looked about her as if for a chair, and not seeing one, kept in the same position. Nuzzli Hanem then ordered chairs to be brought, and after a little while said, "I hear you play very well; there is a piano; play." "No, I cannot," said Miss Harris. "Why not?" "Because I am not accustomed to be ordered." "Oh, please play!" "Ah, that is a different thing; when I am asked politely, I always do what I am asked." Miss Harris sat down and played for some time. "Can you play anything you have heard?" said Nuzzli Hanem. "Pretty well." Presently a number of women seated on the ground with instruments in their hands began, at a signal from their mistress, to play a native air. After a time she made a signal to them to stop, and then turning to Miss Harris, asked if she could play that. Miss Harris had an excellent ear, and she played it. Nuzzli Hanem then said, "I want you to come every day for three or four hours, to teach some of these girls to play as well as you do." "Oh, I cannot," said Miss Harris. "I have my father and my house to attend to; there's the master who taught me, send for him!" After this, Nuzzli Hanem often asked Miss Harris to come to her, and appeared to take quite a fancy to her, the more so, no doubt, from her independent behaviour, to which this lady was little accustomed, everybody around her being in the greatest awe and terror of her.

CHAPTER XXVI.

Go to reside in the palace at Ramleh—We read a great deal—Dinner-party at the harem—Am taken ill—Remove to Koum-el-Dikke—Maltese cook—Arab funeral—Corpse objects to be buried—Return to the harem—Son born to Tewfik Pasha.

About the middle of June, my pupil's palace being ready for her, she left Hussein Pasha's palace on the Canal and took up her abode at Ramleh. It had been rumoured that there would be no room for me, because I had refused to have apartments among the slaves, and none of the best rooms could be isolated and set apart for one person, unless it were the mistress, and even *her* privacy I saw on several occasions was not respected. A few days before moving, however, the Princess told me that there would be a room for me, and I had better go and see it, that I might not have objections to make when too late. I went, and felt that as the building stood, my dear pupil could not have done better for me. The palace was the last to the east, of the block of palaces at Ramleh which have been built in the present reign. It was in two distinct divisions, connected by a large square courtyard, and surrounded by a high wall. The division to the south was entirely for the slaves, the best rooms looking into the centre court, and the inferior ones into smaller courts behind. It was of two storeys. The division to the north was also of two storeys, the basement being entirely offices, and the upper floor containing the best apartments. The entrance to it was by a double flight of steps from the centre court. These led on to a terrace and an outer vestibule. Within were about fifteen apartments, exclusive of bath-room, lavatories, passages, &c. The rooms were three deep from south to north, the centre line being lighted by skylights. These rooms consisted of a large reception-saloon, the Princess's dressing-room, and so on. The rooms to the north were the Princess's bedroom, the Prince's bedroom, two saloons, and the dining-room. On the south were five rooms, all looking into the centre court, and the corner one to the east also commanded a wide view of the desert and the line of railway. The next year a further piece was enclosed, bounded by a high wall, which shut out the view; but the first summer it was very pleasant.

All these apartments communicated one with the other, and the doors being always open, there was a constant current of air, so agreeable and necessary in a warm climate. The room proposed for me was at the south-east corner; the next, to the south, was our schoolroom, fitted up much more comfortably than any other apartment—with piano, large bookcase, tables, &c., and with the most cheerful look-out, *after* my bedroom. The next room to mine, on the north, was the Princess's dressing-room, and on this side came the refreshing sea-breeze. But I saw at once that, unless this door was locked, my room would be made a constant passage by the slaves in going to and from their mistress's apartments. So I asked the Princess to allow me to lock this door, and to keep the key in my own possession. By so doing I lost the sea-breeze, but ensured privacy.

I found my pupil greatly improved by her stay at Hussein Pasha's. After her marriage she seemed to have made up her mind that, as her life was henceforth to be passed in the harem among uneducated women, it was useless for her to cultivate any of the attainments she had previously acquired. She was confirmed in this by the indolence natural to the climate, and almost inseparable from harem life, and also by the adulation of the slaves, who took complete possession of her. But her visit at the Canal had changed all this. She had for the first time in her life associated with near relatives of her own age, and educated like herself. It is true she had, up to her seclusion in the harem, always been with educated people, but they were foreigners, and she would never see them again. She had heard her brother, Prince Hussein, express his great satisfaction that his father had bestowed upon him an educated wife instead of a mere doll, and she saw herself appreciated by her own family as superior in acquirements if not in original capacity. So she came back announcing to me that she wished to go through a course of general reading, and to be well up in history, geography, and literature, and begged I would get her *all* the books necessary for such a purpose! I am afraid we never got beyond light literature; however, our readings led to a great many questions, and she always listened very patiently to the answers, and often alluded to them afterwards, showing that she had pondered them over in her mind. We read many of Sir Walter Scott's novels, Edmond About's, La Motte Fouqué's charming story of 'Undine,' and 'Les Misérables' by Victor Hugo. Those I have mentioned were her *chief* favourites, but there were a great many others,—those by Erckmann-Chatrian, Mde. Charles Reybaud, &c. She liked best for me to read to her; but after a time I would pretend to be tired when I saw an interesting part coming, and after glancing at it to see if it looked interesting, she would take the book and read for a considerable time, handing it back to me when she was tired. All the parts which she particularly liked I marked for her, and she read them over again to herself, laughing aloud with delight at anything that pleased her. She was not idle while I read, but had always some work in hand. Very soon the slaves, seeing that she was absorbed in her occupation with me, ceased to remain in the room, but would talk and laugh in an adjoining saloon, so that we spent hours alone together. When a book was finished, she spent a day or two talking about the characters in it as if they had been familiar friends, and was unwilling to begin another, as she was sure she should never be so interested again. In vain I repeated the proverb that there were as good fish in the sea as ever were caught; she would turn over the next book for some time, shaking her head, but after a day or two was just as deep in that as she had been in the preceding. She entered much more into pathos than into humour. I never could get her to take much interest in Molière, but she was very fond of the 'Cid.'

She did not care for fancy-work, but liked making little articles of millinery, bows, neckties, &c. She would send for pieces of silk and satin that her dressmaker might have remaining, and make such a litter with the cuttings as quite scandalised the head slaves that a Princess should be thus employed. One day the *calfa* ran in in a hurry to herald the approach of an important visitor. I was reading, and the Princess working, with a quantity of cuttings as usual lying about the floor. The *calfa* looked reprovingly at me, "Is this well?" said she. "*Very* well," said I; "anything is better than idleness." The *calfa* smiled and shook her head, and then called quickly to some attendants to collect the litter, while the Princess with both hands scattered on the floor everything within her reach, laughing merrily all the while.

The little dog Fido had soon been given up, and a Circassian slave child of about three years old taken instead. This child cost £125. She was a pretty little thing with a very intelligent countenance, and the Princess talked of having her brought up and educated in every possible branch. In the meanwhile she had a regular trousseau made, both as a little girl and as a boy, and one day she appeared in the first character, and soon after in the next. Half-a-dozen slaves were busy working for the child, and for a few weeks she was made quite a pet of, and then put aside. Domestic slavery is a political blunder as well as a moral wrong. It is a terrible expense, and no country can thrive financially where such an institution exists.

The Khédive often came to pay his daughter a visit. On such occasions I was always present, and he invariably did me the honour of speaking to me. The Princess Ahmed, mother-in-law of my pupil, came to Ramleh on a visit for a few days; and to signalise the event the Princess gave a dinner-party. Tewfik Pasha and Hussein Pasha came; her own brother Ibrahim Pasha, Toussoun Pasha (son of the late Saïd Pasha), who had married her sister Fatma Hanem; her younger (half) brother Mahmoud Bey, and her husband Ibrahim Pasha, made up six gentlemen. The Princess herself, her mother-in-law, myself, Kopsès, and Charissas Hanem were the ladies. The two last were pretty girls, who in any European society would have been objects of general attraction, but such mixed company was entirely new to Mussulman habits; and so, though all the gentlemen would talk freely enough to Europeans, they never looked at or addressed these two young ladies, lest by so doing they might shock their feelings of propriety. To the Princess they spoke freely enough, first because she was their hostess and near relative; and secondly, because she behaved with all the ease and self-possession of a person brought up in society. To me they also talked freely, as to a European. The Princess Ahmed sat at table between her son and Tewfik Pasha, but she spoke little, and retired directly we rose from table. The conversation was carried on in French, English, and Turkish. All the gentlemen spoke French, and most of them English. We all rose from table at the same time, and most of the gentlemen grouped themselves round the piano. The doors were all open, and the slaves stood about, looking at the unwonted spectacle of six gentlemen making themselves at home in a harem. The evening passed quickly and pleasantly, and at about half-past ten the gentlemen all rose to go. There was no moon, and the slaves stood forming a double line of light down the steps and across the courtyard to the gate. My Princess and her husband accompanied the guests to the threshold, and there the latter turned round again to take their leave, but the Princess insisted upon accompanying them to the gate. On their way down the steps, at the foot of them, and two or three times across the courtyard, one or other of the Princes turned round to disclaim the honour done to them and to stop their hostess from going further, but with much laughing and many compliments she persisted in going on as far as she could—that is, to the first door of the outer gate. Here the gentlemen all turned, and with low salaams were making their final compliments when an absurd incident illustrative of harem customs took place.

I have mentioned what great liberty, I may say licence, is allowed to a few privileged persons in the harem, such as nurses, &c. The Princess's *dada* had not been accustomed any more than others to the presence of gentlemen, but she was by no means abashed by it, and being fond of practical jokes, she thought it amusing to give a good slap on the back to a male visitor at the moment of parting. Why she singled out Hussein Pasha from all the rest I do not know, unless it was that he was a handsome young man, very light and active, and with an exceedingly glib tongue. While, therefore, making his final bow, the Prince looked narrowly round, and espied the *dada* just preparing for the usual accolade. He darted forward, gave her a hearty slap on the back, and then ran out of the gate which a eunuch held ready to open, and through which she could not follow him. I have no doubt she repaid him on his next visit, but I did not happen to be there to see. In the course of the evening, Tewfik Pasha, to show me that he understood English, though he did not (then) speak it readily, took up the 'Illustrated London News,' which lay on the table, and read a long paragraph about the Indian famine, and it was evident from his way of reading that he plainly comprehended the sense of what he read.

Two or three days after this dinner-party, I was seized with an attack of colic, and was much indisposed. It happened that Miss Harris came to pay a visit to the Princess, and seeing that I was ill, proposed that I should go to her house to be nursed. I declined, thinking I should soon be better; but a couple of days later, after a very bad night, I rose at about 6 A.M., and knocking at the door between my room and the Princess's dressing-room, called to a slave whom I heard moving there to go and ask her mistress to send at once for one of the doctors of the harem, naming one. Then knowing that my room would be invaded all day, I put everything in order, and got into bed again. Very soon the Princess came to my room and sat by me, expressing her sorrow that I was ill, and telling me she had sent for a doctor. After a time she went away, and then the Prince came and sat by me also for some time. Then three or four eunuchs came, bringing the doctor (not the one I had asked for), and I told him what I was suffering from. He told me to eat nothing but *pillau* (rice), and wrote a prescription for two powders, one of which was to be taken immediately, the other at night. In the meanwhile the eunuchs were prowling about the room, opening and looking into every-thing, examining my travelling clock, and striking the repeater, and at last all went away. After a time the eunuchs came again with the first doctor whom I had asked for. He did not approve of the powders, ordered me half-a-dozen bottles of Vichy water, said I was to begin immediately and drink a bottle a-day. I was not to eat at all, unless I felt the want of something, in which case meat was the best thing for me.

During the whole day there was an influx of visitors, the Princess Ahmed came to see me, and sent two or three times to inquire. Nothing could be kinder than she, her son, and the Princess; but no one understood anything of nursing, and nothing that the two doctors had ordered had arrived. At 6 P.M. one of the doctors came again, and finding that neither powders nor Vichy water had arrived, advised me strongly, if I had any friend to go to, to leave the harem for a few days, saying that, though there was no present danger, there was never any telling to what such things might lead. Also, that when I began to get better, nourishment would be all-important, and I could not have suitable food in the harem. There was plenty to eat, but nothing fit for me in the state in which I was. Soon after his departure, the Vichy water arrived, and I began it immediately. I had no sleep that night, was in great pain, and had continual diarrhœa. My dear pupil came in to me frequently the next day, and so did the Prince. The slaves were coming in all day long. "Are you well" (*eyisin*)? "No, very bad." "Ah, then, you will be well to-morrow, inshallah!" "Inshallah!" was all I could repeat.

I happened to be better for two or three hours in the afternoon; so when the doctor came again, I told him I thought of going to Koum-el-Dikke the next morning to be nursed, if he considered I could bear the journey. He advised me decidedly to go, and I afterwards told my dear Princess. She understood it all, but her husband did not so well, and seemed, I thought, a little vexed that I should persist in going, as it might appear a reflection on their hospitality. This was far from being the case; but I felt that in the harem the patient, no matter who she might be, was left to fight it out with nature, unassisted by remedies. So having skilful friends without, I preferred going to them. A carriage was ordered for me, and I went, dreading the journey, which, however, I got through better than I could have expected.

But my arrival at Koum-el-Dikke was extremely inopportune. My hostess had, it is true, invited me to come to be nursed; but as she had not heard from me for a week, and had seen me only at the beginning of my illness, she had taken it for granted I was quite recovered, and through the urgent persuasion of some young friends had issued invitations for an evening party and dance! Upon hearing this, I proposed to change my destination to the hospital, which was near, and where I knew I should be well cared for. My hostess would not for a moment listen to such a suggestion, so I was installed at once in an upper room, though feeling myself sadly in the way during the tumult of preparation going on in the house. The party was to take place in two days; nearly fifty invitations had been sent out (and one to me, which never got farther than the gate). Miss Harris was building a small house at the end of a little garden; it was in a very unfinished state; but it was decided that, the walls being covered with flags, and a few temporary arrangements made, it would do very well for a dance, and the house would then be free for supper-room, card-room, drawing-room, music, &c.

There was plenty to be done,—hams to boil, sirloins of beef to roast, also turkeys and fowls; pigeon-pies to make, jellies, blancmange, &c. Miss Harris was a first-rate cook and housekeeper; but there was so much to do that she required help, and a friend stopping in the house said she knew a Maltese cook, then out of place, who, she thought, would be very glad to earn a pound. He was sent for, came, and was told what was required. It was then Wednesday; the party was to be on Friday. It would take all day Thursday and Friday, he said, and he could not do it alone; but he knew a friend who could come and help him.

"Well, what would his charge be?"

"That he would rather leave to the lady."

"No; he must fix his price."

"Well, then, £5 a-day each man."

"What! £20 for the two days!"

"Yes."

Miss Harris's indignation got the better of her. "Very well, there's the door; you may go!"

"Oh, I think you had better do the cooking yourself," said the man.

Of course he was sent off. An hour or two after, he came back. He had been considering the matter, he said, and he thought it might perhaps be done in one day. He would get an assistant, and undertake the entire job for £2. The lady to whom he spoke thought that charge too high, so he came down to £1; but the matter being reported to Miss Harris, that lady said she would not engage him on any terms, because he had been overreaching and impertinent. There was no time to find any one else, so with the help of her cook, and her own unceasing exertions, she managed the whole thing herself.

I felt so much better, even in one day, through the change to more suitable food, that I looked forward to a sound sleep, which I had not had for many nights. Sunrise, however, found me still wide awake, and in a sort of despair at my position. While I was meditating on what would become of me, I fell fast asleep while there was still no sound but the twittering of sparrows. At 6 A.M. the carpenters began hammering the flags on the walls, but I slept on for three or four hours, and woke much refreshed. I saw nothing of the party the following night, as I kept entirely to my room. My illness lasted in all twelve days; and when it left me, I was so weak that I was obliged to stay some days to be nursed.

Koum-el-Dikke is on the heights behind the town of Alexandria; there are a great many houses scattered about at different elevations, and most of them command extensive views over sea and land. Miss Harris's house was one of the best, having been built by her father with every English comfort. I was standing one day by the drawing-room window, looking down the sandhills, over the town to the sea beyond, when I heard the wailing sounds of an Arab funeral. It came nearer; and as I watched, the men came staggering up with the bier, swayed backwards and forwards for some time, and at last deposited it on the ground at the corner of the house. While I was puzzling myself to know what this meant, my hostess came into the room, and I called her to the window to explain it to me. It appeared that the corpse refused to go any farther. How the body intimates this decision (for it is a common occurrence still, and was formerly much more so) is not very clear, but the bearers declare it to be unmistakable; and when once this idea is communicated, each helps no doubt to mystify the others; and a series of jerks, plunges, and dead-stops take place, until, with one accord, the bearers put down the bier and proceed to reason with the dead man. "Why does he object to that route? Is there anything he will have to pass which he does not like? Sunset is coming on; he must be buried before sunset," &c., and so they coax and wheedle him; and (if there is no way of disposing of it) they pounce upon the bier and carry it off.

But in this instance the objections of the dead man were too strong, so, after plunging about a little on the hillside, they brought him up again, and laid him down by the house. Then the persuasions began again; and the bystanders, among whom were all Miss Harris's servants, said the corpse must have been a very holy man to object so strongly to being buried. No doubt he felt that he had plenty more work to do on the earth, and was unwilling to leave it until it was accomplished. At last, whether the corpse was really mollified by the compliments paid him, or whether the bearers had become tired of the farce, is an open question, but they suddenly took up the bier, turned round two or three times, so as to puzzle him with regard to the exact points of the compass, then charged down the steepest part of the hill, and bore him triumphantly off, to the great edification of all the beholders.

I was told afterwards that the law being strict (for sanitary reasons) that all burials should take place outside the town, the idleness of the bearers caused them continually to go through this farce of pretending that the dead man refused to go on, and then burying him either in the road or in some convenient garden which might happen to be in the way. The piety or superstition of the Moslems made them think it obligatory on them to build a mosque, or at any rate a fountain, on the spot where the body was buried, which became in time such an intolerable tax on the district, that Mohammed Ali determined to try the effect of the *courbache* on the bearers. This was found to produce the desired result, but it was not always forthcoming at the moment, so the nuisance was still repeated occasionally, and Miss Harris told me that she once narrowly escaped having an old sheikh buried in her garden. She saw the *cortége* coming, and having her suspicions, ordered the garden door to be locked forthwith. The objections of the corpse were made just outside the door, and the bearers bumped against it a great many times; but as it held good, they were obliged at last to take the body up, and the old saint was finally deposited without the city gates, as he should be.

On the 14th of July, a day or two after my return to the harem, a son was born to Tewfik Pasha. There were great rejoicings, and the next day the Prince came himself to see his sister and talk of the auspicious event. He stayed a full hour, and told us he had sent for an English nurse to bring up the child. We had up to this time had gentlemen visitors on several occasions in the harem, sometimes simply calling and occasionally dining, but they were all blood relations of my Princess, as her brother-in-law Toussoun Pasha was at the same time her cousin. Now, however, we had a visit from Tafita Hanem, the Khédive's eldest daughter (usually called by Europeans the Princess Monsour), and her husband Monsour Pasha, the latter being only a connection by marriage, as he is not a descendant of Mohammed Ali. They dined and slept in the palace. These incidents would not be worth mentioning, but to show that the system of entire seclusion which has existed for so many ages among the women of the East is gradually giving way.

CHAPTER XXVII.

Return to Cairo—Nuisance of cats in the harem —Purchase of slaves —Two negresses whipped—Bézique—English groom complains of being robbed —Illness in the harem—Accident while driving—The "dada's" leg is broken—Blind doctor attends—Disastrous result—Ramadan.

The Khédive soon left Alexandria, where he never stays very long, as the climate does not agree with him. The first Princess went with him, and the third had some time before gone to Constantinople with the Queen-Mother. The second Princess was still left at Ramleh, but both she and my pupil became restless after the departure of his Highness, and were anxious to return to Cairo. I don't think the climate of Alexandria ever suited my Princess, but upon grounds of economy no journey to Constantinople (except that of the Queen-Mother, who went for health) was contemplated that year, nor during the succeeding summer. The expense of a sojourn on the Bosphorus was enormous; it was not only the money spent on the voyage, and the living in Turkey, but the *backsheesh* that was always given to the Sultan's harem and eunuchs, and the presents to the Sultan himself.

At the end of August the Queen-Mother was expected back, and it was settled that as soon as the Mahroussah came into port with her, my pupil and her mother should meet her at landing, and all should proceed to Cairo together. I obtained leave to go to Koum-el-Dikke for a few days, and was then to join my pupil in Cairo. The luggage was all sent off, and the majority of the slaves, only a very few remaining about the person of the Princess. We went to bed early, but a messenger was sent at a late hour to inform the Princess that the Mahroussah was outside the harbour, and would come in at daybreak. I was asleep, and did not know of this, but, waking about five the next morning, I was surprised at the perfect quiet that prevailed, and getting up soon, wondered that I saw none of the slaves about the courtyard, as they were generally stirring soon after daybreak. Presently Mlle. Caroline, the Princess's Italian dressmaker, who lived on the other side of the court, entered my room to ask me when I thought of going, and to tell me that everybody had left the harem—mistress, slaves, and eunuchs. They went at 4 A.M. to meet the Queen-Mother on her landing. She (Caroline) had been outside the gates, and found an Arab there whom she intended sending into the town to procure a carriage, and she wished to know if I would like one also, or whether I would share one with her. I had only just finished dressing, when I heard men's voices in the adjoining room, and I found it was some of the officials belonging to the Prince, who were left in charge of the empty palace, and were then going through it. As it would take a long time, therefore, to get a carriage from the town, I decided to go by rail; and having with some difficulty got a man to carry my carpet-bag down the hill to the station, I left the palace, and reached Koum-el-Dikke at about 7 A.M.

There were reports that the Princess would return to Ramleh, so I stayed at Koum-el-Dikke for two or three days, and then went up by the 6 P.M. express, which reached Cairo at 10.30 P.M., a very pleasant time for travelling in summer. I slept at the New Hotel, and at an early hour next morning repaired to the harem. I found that my dear Princess had changed my rooms, as I had asked her to do. My bedroom was now on the ground-floor, in an angle of the best apartments, one door leading through a sitting-room into the central saloon, and another into a lavatory and box-room communicating with the back-passages. The rooms were very lofty, and that made an immense difference to the temperature; but as the winter came on, I found that being on the ground-floor exposed me to another nuisance, that of cats! The palace garden was surrounded by high walls, and there was an outer court to pass through before entering the garden. At the outer gates the *boab* (doorkeeper) was always seated, and two or three more Arabs. Just within the gates in the large courtyard were the eunuchs' rooms, and some of these men were always standing about; within the garden were again eunuchs, either walking, or sitting, playing at backgammon, &c. The gates stood open

U

in the daytime, except an hour before sunset, when the slaves were out in the garden. Thus any authorised visitor could drive or walk in at once, up to the door of the harem. It would be difficult enough for any intruders to make their way in. But nothing could keep out cats, which ran wild about the country; and as winter came on, they would dart through the gates, hide themselves in the garden, and towards evening get into the house. Now and then the nuisance would become so serious, and the dirt made by them so great, that orders were given to chase them out, and eunuchs and slaves would join in a hunt; but that was only for a day or two; in a week they were as plentiful as ever. As the spring advanced, they began to seek out comfortable nooks for coming families; and as my windows were a convenient height from the ground, and my bedroom was less of a passage than any other apartment in the palace, the cats favoured me much more frequently than was agreeable. They were not quiet domestic animals, but frightened, rushing creatures, springing past you when you least expected it. With all my care, I had one or two families born in my room; and one day walking down the passages leading to the Princess's apartments, I found five or six parties established behind the heavy curtains which were always drawn before each door (in winter). I did not find this nuisance for a long time, however, as, when I returned to Cairo in September, the weather was too warm at night for any animals to seek the shelter of a house.

During the whole of September I scarcely went outside the harem gates. There was no one in town whom I knew. There was no divine service, except from about the middle of November to Easter. It used always to be performed in a large room at the New Hotel, but in the winter of 1875-76 the English Church was at last opened. There is, however, as yet no house for a clergyman. The chaplain is obliged to stay at one of the hotels, and as the English residents in Cairo are very few, all expenses are defrayed by contributions from travellers.

One morning the Princess was going to Gezireh to spend the day with his Highness; the carriage was already at the door, and the slaves were grouped about in the entrance-saloon awaiting her coming down. She came with her husband, and they walked through together to an inner room. I saw some reception was going to take place, and I followed them. The Prince and Princess seated themselves on a couch at one side of the saloon, and presently twelve "ladies" entered, and stood in a row opposite the young couple. They were all gaily dressed, in the half-European style which has become general among the young. They were slaves sent for inspection with a view to purchase. Now and then one of them was called up for a closer view, but no decision was made; the Princess went off to Gezireh, and the Prince to the *selamlik*, the slaves remaining for further examination. They were treated as visitors by those of the household, were taken into every part of the palace and over the garden. Four of them were musicians, and upon invitation they produced their instruments and twanged away for more than an hour for the amusement of their hosts. They paraded about the saloons all day, and the slaves of my Princess dressed themselves in their best to impress their visitors with the wealth of the establishment. It must not be supposed that the *head* slaves took the trouble of entertaining, or indeed of taking any notice of, these visitors. Those immediately about the person of the Princess were of higher rank: they aspired to be ultimately the wives of beys or pashas, and their white hands were never soiled by any menial work. But there were from ten to a dozen *sofradjis*, who waited at table; others whose business it was to carry drinking-water to the different apartments, and who kept the keys of the rooms containing the filtering machines; others, again, who held the office of upper housemaids, &c. These made up a goodly number, and when their regular work was done they lounged about in the central saloon awaiting the return of their mistress, or, if they had needlework to do, sat in groups on the floor in one of the passages adjoining. If any new white slaves were purchased they would probably fall into this class, so they met on terms of equality. The new arrivals were all about the average class, ages from sixteen to eighteen, well grown and fairly good-looking. I heard that the price demanded for the four musicians was £1000; but then, no doubt, a large margin was allowed for abatement. A very beautiful slave would cost several thousand pounds, but I never saw one of these overpowering beauties. The Khédive's two eldest daughters were the handsomest women I saw in Egypt.

I believe nothing would have induced my dear pupil to allow any of her slaves to be flogged, but she did not know all that took place under her roof. I was told one day by a looker-on of a scene that occurred in one of the inner courts. Two negresses were flogged, one at a time. Three eunuchs presided, one held the head of the victim and another the legs, the third administering the blows. The housekeeper stood by. The chastisement was administered because these two negresses had not hurried out of the way at the cry of "*Dustoor!*" raised by the eunuchs who precede the men carrying in the heavy trays for the harem meals. The cry is heard from a distance, so there is always plenty of time to get out of the way. The negresses were therefore clearly guilty of contumacy, and liable to punishment. It appeared to me that the influence of European women in the harem must have been the cause of this offence, because the Moslem women must either look upon us as the most abandoned creatures, or they must think that what we do with impunity and without shame cannot be so very heinous in them.

I was often much amused when the Princess's carriage stood outside the harem door, waiting for her. She would order it when she wished, and it waited in the outer court until she was quite ready. Then the word was given for it to drive into the garden and stop before the harem door. The entrance-saloon would be full of women, and some eunuchs stood outside by the carriage and in front of each window (all open) to take care that the venetian blinds were kept properly down. Sometimes at the last moment the Princess might be detained, and the carriage have to wait a few minutes at the door. The coachman and groom were Frenchmen, and they sat on the box during this interval like automata, never moving in the slightest degree, and staring straight forward into space. Then the door would open, and two radiant beings would come rustling out and get into the carriage. The automata knew that there were countless eyes behind every window, but they had to look as if they were absorbed in solving a problem of Euclid, or calculating the distance between the earth and one of the fixed stars.

The Princess took a great fancy to *bézique*, and before the opera season began we often spent our evenings in playing it. She first learned it for two players, then for three, and finally for four. The Prince usually came in the evening and joined us, and we all retired to rest early. The Pasha generally entered from the *selamlik* by the garden, and in that case he walked in; but sometimes he drove in at the harem entrance, and did not go out again. One evening we were sitting in the centre saloon playing at *bézique* when we heard the sound of carriage-wheels in the courtyard, and the Prince entered, and asked me if I would go with him outside the harem door to speak to his English groom, who, as well as he could understand, had lost some money and was *crying* bitterly! (The Princess had French coachmen and grooms, and the Prince English.) I went out, and found the groom with a party of eunuchs round him. The man was sobbing, and as well as he could speak, he explained to me that he had just been robbed of two hundred sovereigns, which he had kept in bags locked up in a trunk in his room (also locked), which was situated near the stables on the opposite side of the road. I asked him if he could form an idea who was the thief and when the money had been taken. He said that about a couple of hundred workmen were engaged in building a palace on the Nile, and that every evening at about sunset they passed his window. On this evening in question he had been out driving the Prince as usual, and that, unlocking his door on his return and striking a light, he had at first seen nothing amiss, but presently remarked that his box was broken in at the top and the contents turned topsy-turvy. Further examination showed him that the money-bags had been abstracted, and that the window had been broken sufficiently to admit of a slim person getting in and out again. During this narration the Prince stood by listening to the translation which I gave from time to time, and the group of eunuchs pressed sympathisingly round. I asked the groom how he could be so rash as to keep so large a sum in a detached room from which he was necessarily so many hours absent. He replied that his contract was just expiring, that he had not heard that it was to be renewed, and he had therefore preferred keeping all his savings by him, so as to be ready to start at once for England when his contract expired. All this was told me with many suppressed sobs, and was duly translated to the Prince. The latter after a little consideration said, "Tell him not to distress himself any further. I will make up the money for him." I exclaimed, "Pray, think of what you are promising, sir; you must not raise false hopes in the man; you may repent later of so hasty a promise!" "No," said he, "I shall not repent; tell him that I will make the money good." Upon this I told the groom what the Prince had said. The man touched his hat to the Prince, thanked him heartily, and went away. I told the Princess all that had passed, and referring to the approaching expiration of the contract, the Prince said, "I shall renew it. I am very well satisfied with the man, and do not wish to part with him."

Some time after, I happened to see another English groom in the Prince's service, and I asked him about Harry, and if he had heard anything of the lost money or of the thieves. The man answered me very civilly, but I saw by his manner that he did not wish to speak on the subject. I was astonished at this, and said to him, "Why, surely you do not disbelieve that he lost the money?" "I don't know anything about it, madam," said he; "he SAYS he lost it." I said no more, but at the next opportunity asked the Prince if he had renewed the contract with Harry. "Oh," said he, "it has been a very disagreeable business. When I told the *vekeel* (steward) to pay him the £200, he flatly refused to do it, saying there was no evidence that the money had been stolen, and that the man was trying to impose on me. Then when I told the *vekeel* to renew the contract, I found that the other English groom declined remaining if Harry was kept on." This looked rather suspicious, and upon asking the Prince if he had any reason himself to suspect the man had not told the truth concerning the alleged thefts, he related to me that about nine months before, Harry had complained in the same manner of having had £40 stolen from him, and that he (the Prince) had then given him the money from his own pocket. All the *employés* were of opinion that the man was imposing on the Prince, and he was naturally not exactly pleased at this view of the matter. The Prince was exceedingly good-natured and *impulsively* generous. If his wife, or even I, noticed and admired any new thing which he might be wearing, such as watch, pin, &c., he would immediately take it off and present it. This happened to me more than once, but I never would accept the gift, as it looked like asking for it, which was far from my thoughts. The Princess, however, had of course no such scruples.

A curious scene occurred in one of the great harems which was related to me by an eyewitness. The mistress had been suffering about four-and-twenty hours with a severe fit of indigestion, and was writhing in agony. Now diet is quite a minor consideration, or rather no consideration at all, in the harem. The quantity of sweets, and of unripe fruit, and crude vegetables consumed is something amazing. The whole household was convulsed by the indisposition of the mistress. Messengers were despatched to find the doctor: he was out, but at last returned, and was ushered in by several eunuchs. But the lady refused to see him, or to let him hear from her own lips what ailed her. The doctor was brought into the adjoining room; and there, the door being ajar, and a heavy curtain drawn before it, a stout middle-aged lady detailed the symptoms of the patient, two or three eunuchs standing on each side of the door to prevent the doctor from storming the passage. The medico urged much that he might see the patient, upon which he was led in, the lady being enveloped in a great black silk cloak; a hand was protruded from under the folds that he might feel the pulse, and then a tongue appeared from under the hood; and the doctor, thus enlightened, prescribed M. Purgon's remedy. The doctor was to remain to know the result. The eunuchs took a lively interest in the preparations; and finally, when the lady understood the nature of the remedy, she refused to have anything to do with it. The doctor therefore prescribed something else (which was not taken), and the patient fought it out with nature. This is the general course of medical treatment in the harems.

A serious accident happened to one of the Princess's household. My pupil and her mother returned to Cairo at the same time as the Queen-Mother, and illuminations were made in honour of the latter. My Princess drove out in the evening to see them, and took with her Kopsès and the *dada*. The Arabs are very reckless drivers, and by no means trouble themselves about the right side of the way, so an Arab coachman ran against the Princess's carriage and overturned it. Happily the Princess and Kopsès escaped without injury, but the poor *dada* had her leg broken at the ankle. It would not have been a serious fracture had she had it properly attended to immediately; but unfortunately a blind Arab doctor was called in, who was said to have performed many wonderful cures, and his blindness made him just the man to enter a harem. In about a month she was pronounced cured, and hobbled about on crutches; but unfortunately she no sooner began to use the leg than it grew much worse, and at last the poor woman kept entirely to her room on an upper floor. One day, on visiting her, she asked me if I could recommend her anything, and I replied that I would ask the English doctor. I did so on the first opportunity, but he replied that he could not possibly give an opinion without seeing the patient. The Princess heard of this, and immediately said there should be a consultation on the subject. Four doctors were therefore called in, one being my friend. They were unanimously of opinion that the leg had not been properly set; one thought it ought to be broken again and reset; but the others considered, by having a particular kind of boot made, and wearing it with a splint, the mischief might still be remedied. It was very shocking to the poor *dada* to have four men close round her in this manner, and she showed her face much more than she would otherwise have done, in her anxiety to see that they did not take possession of her foot without her consent. At last the boot and the splint were decided on, and it was settled to order it immediately. A few weeks passed; I went very often to see the *dada*, and heard that the boot and splint had not been sent, so I made a point of going to the doctor and telling him of the omission. He inquired, and assured me that it had been sent a day or two after his visit; and so it proved to have been, for after many fruitless inquiries, it turned out that the *dada* had tried it, found it extremely uncomfortable, and left it off at once, but had concealed the fact of its arrival, hoping that it would be forgotten, and that no further inquiry would be made. The consequence is that the poor woman has never recovered the free use of her leg, and probably never will. If she were a European, it could be broken under chloroform and then reset; as it is, she will doubtless be lame for life.

The new moon of the 10th of October ushered in Ramadan, and as it falls eleven days earlier every year, it was thirty-three days nearer to hot weather than the first I had passed in Egypt. October is a trying month, hot and moist. I had given lessons in the harem the previous year during Ramadan, and had found that unpleasant enough; but it was far worse to live in it. I did not fast myself, nor did the Princess, therefore I had no trouble in getting food; but it was very painful to me to see the effect produced on the poor girls.

I had noticed for some days an erection being made (opposite the harem door, and close under the wall), such as musicians are ensconced in in public gardens. I found it was intended for a sheikh to read or recite the Koran. This is begun soon after sunset, and continues for several hours. The whole day before Ramadan there was a general cleaning throughout the harem. The girls went about in bands of a dozen or more, and charged each room in succession, the *calfa* acting as overseer, with a long switch in her hand; and as the weather was very warm, they were all barefoot, and clad in the lightest of *negligées*, drawn tightly round the person, like the drapery of a statue, so as to leave no room for imagination with regard to their proportions. During Ramadan the girls cannot be called upon to do much work, so there was little more cleaning until the end of the month, when the preparations for Baïram began.

CHAPTER XXVIII.

Ramadan in the harem.

The apartments to which I had removed were so quiet by night that the unwonted sound of running about in the passages between 2 and 3 A.M. which occurred throughout Ramadan awoke me the first night, and I felt a sort of despair at what awaited me throughout the month. After two or three nights, however, I got accustomed to it, and slept through it. This was the programme of the four-and-twenty hours. Immediately after sunset some light refreshment was taken, and soon after a regular meal. About two hours before daybreak another and heavier meal was taken, and then after prayer all went to sleep. In the great houses where work is not compulsory the inmates sleep until mid-day, sometimes till two in the afternoon; the slaves and eunuchs know the habits of their masters and mistresses, and regulate their slumber accordingly. No visits are paid in the daytime, for no one is either disposed to go out or receive at home. The entire change of habits produced by thus turning day into night and night into day causes much illness; and although the poor, who are obliged to work during Ramadan the same as throughout the whole year, suffer much more *at the time*, I am not sure that they do not in the end come off better than the rich, as their food is lighter and exercise helps them to digest it.

The Khédive is a hard-working man, and knows that work cannot go on well without food and sleep, so he does not fast himself or allow his family to do so. The Princes, his sons, had all to be at their appointed posts at an early hour, so they followed their father's example; and my pupil was, I believe from constitution, physically incapable of long fasting. In such cases dispensation is given as freely as in Catholic countries. All the upper slaves had been about the Princess from her infancy, and knew how delicate she had been; how four of her brothers and sisters had died in early childhood, and how her life and that of her brother Ibrahim Pasha had been saved entirely by the care and watchfulness of Zohrab Bey. But as the Princess was now grown up and appeared strong, her *dada* was anxious, as a true believer, to impress upon her the necessity of *occasional* fasting, and had actually induced her to abstain from food one day during the Ramadan of the preceding year. Her room was darkened and she slept till mid-day, but soon after became so clamorous in her inquiries whether the sunset gun had fired that her example did not tend to edification or induce her *dada* to urge her again on the subject.

The Prince had been brought up strictly by his mother, and with exemplary regularity with regard to meals, and my dear pupil, in spite of her many amiable and endearing qualities, was, when left to herself, neither punctual nor regular. The luncheon was brought in every day at a little before twelve, and the dinner soon after sunset. These were the hours throughout the year. But the Princess had been accustomed to English breakfasts, and as soon as she became her own mistress, she and I took it regularly together. *Café au lait* was sent in by the Prince's French servants from the *selamlik*, and at my pupil's request I procured from Monferrato (the Fortnum & Mason of Egypt) all sorts of potted meats, fish, marmalade, &c. Our breakfast-hour was fixed at 8 A.M.; but if the Princess had gone to bed early, she would call for it at seven; if late, it might be nine, or even ten. In the latter case she was naturally not prepared for a heavy meal at mid-day; but it came all the same. The way of announcing luncheon or dinner is by the appearance of a slave at the door, with a gold embroidered napkin on her arm. She does not speak, but takes care to place herself where she is seen by her mistress. I generally had my back turned, and at that hour was engaged in reading to the Princess; but I was very anxious to keep up regular habits, regarding them as all-important, both for her own health and for the comfort of her household. If I saw the embroidered napkin I would presently, at a convenient break, shut the book and rise as a matter of course. If we had breakfasted early, the Princess was quite ready for luncheon; but if late, she would ask me why I was in such a hurry, was I hungry? if so, I had better go and eat, and then come back and go on with the reading. This was not my object. I would represent to her that the meal had come in, was getting cold, and there was no means of keeping it hot; that no one in the household (except she and I) had had a meal that day, and no one could eat until after she had done so. She would

hold out for some time; would say it was very hard that
she, the mistress, should be obliged to eat, whether she
liked it or not; but always finished by doing as I asked,
because, in spite of any occasional childish petulance, she
was always anxious to do right, and she did me the
justice to see that my influence was exerted solely for her
good, and not to further any end of my own. Sometimes
she was out, and then the luncheon waited for one or two
hours, sometimes even more, for her possible return; and
if she came late and then ate, the dinner would also be
deferred an hour or two. Nevertheless it was cooked at
the same hour and *sent in*, so that we had to eat it half
cold. This extreme irregularity in meals is one of the
evils of harem life. I was far less exposed to it than
most Europeans who enter the service, and this partly by
the influence I acquired with my pupil, and partly by
the great kindness and consideration with which I was
always treated by every member of his Highness's family.
It can be easily understood, however, that this irregularity in meals was not altogether pleasant to the husband
of my pupil. As the Khédive's daughter, she was supreme
mistress over all her household; and as he could give no
orders in the harem, he very wisely took his meals in the
selamlik, where he could keep up the regular hours to
which he had always been accustomed. His table was,
like the Princess's, served *à la franque* in the most elegant
style; but as he intended to keep Ramadan strictly, and
would return during that time to old Mahometan customs,
all the dinner services and plate were carefully put away
until the fast was over. The Princess and I had our
meals as usual, only with less state, and at breakfast and
luncheon we were alone. Indeed we were constantly
alone together, except when the Princess went to Abdeen
to see his Highness. We read and worked nearly all day,
her immediate attendants having entirely discontinued the

practice of waiting in the room. It was only one or two of the more privileged, such as the *dada*, who had ever ventured to interrupt us, and she had left it off, seeing it was distasteful to the Princess. If I left the room for one minute, I was sure to find several slaves lying asleep in the anterooms or on the staircase; they were obliged to be near, in case their mistress wanted them.

There was one thing that was a great relief to me, and that was, that during Ramadan we had no music at meals. After so many hours' fasting, the girls could not be called upon, when nearly fainting for want of food, either to scrape the violin, bang the tambourine, or shout to the full extent of (sometimes) very powerful lungs. I do not mean to say anything disrespectful of Turkish or Arab music, but I doubt whether anybody in our country, no matter how fond they might be of music, would care to sit at dinner every day, with the best brass band in existence thundering away within a few feet of them. If the musicians had been placed in an adjoining room, and had exerted themselves a trifle less, I might have got to like the sound, but as it was close to my ears, it was simply deafening.

On the very first day of Ramadan, I was walking up and down the central saloon with the Princess after dinner, when the quiet was disturbed by a rushing sound occasioned by the whole household giving chase to one or two girls, and presently all burst into the saloon. To my surprise, the Princess, instead of rebuking the intruders, began to laugh and clap her hands. Thus encouraged, the assembly continued to chase the fugitives until they were captured, when they were rolled over on the ground, and there was a general hissing, and cries of "*Fatra! fatra!*" I inquired with amazement what was the meaning of this, and was told it was because they had not kept the fast! I have before said that it was not difficult on the score of health to obtain a dispensation, but although winked at, it was not openly permitted, and the person thus offending had to run the gauntlet of ridicule among her companions. The life in the harem was so dull and uneventful, that a very small matter served as a joke, and a cry of "*Fatra!*" was enough to bring them all out, as ready to join in the chase as a pack of hounds to follow the fox. As Ramadan advanced, the spirits became more subdued and the non-fasters escaped better, but during the first half of the month some case would occur daily and was always hailed with enthusiasm.

On the second day we had a visit from Tewfik Pasha, the hereditary Prince. He stayed about half an hour, and just as he had taken his leave, the *calfa* came up and whispered to the Princess that one of her chief attendants, a pretty black-haired girl, then standing near her mistress, had been caught eating privately, and asked permission to give chase to her. The Princess readily agreed, and a tumultuous assemblage looking something like morris-dancers rushed in. They had a band of music, and one of them was habited something as a travelling Englishman is usually represented on the French stage, in very loose trousers and long overcoat, all of whitey-brown colour, and a slouched hat, his face powdered like a clown in a pantomime. This individual seized the girl and tried to dance with her, the band following after, and the whole assembly alternately hissing and shouting, "*Fatra! fatra!*" The victim was by no means disposed to submit quietly; they rolled over on the ground together, the girl's long black hair becoming whitened by the powder from her tormentor. At last she succeeded in darting out of the saloon, and the chase went off to another part of the palace, where it may have continued some time, but I ceased to hear it.

The next day we had again a visitor, the Princess Saïd Pasha. She of course had a dispensation: first, because she came to us in the daytime, when the rigid fasters would be either asleep or resting; and secondly, because she took a cup of coffee and smoked a cigarette. She had not long left, when, hearing great laughter from the garden, the Princess and I went thither and found a large party there. At least half-a-dozen non-fasters had been discovered, and the eunuchs had brought in a couple of donkeys; the fun being to seize on two of the non-fasters by turns, and parade them through the garden, seated on the donkeys with their faces towards the tail, everybody following, hissing, laughing, clapping their hands, and shouting, "*Fatra! fatra!*" Zora, the Princess's foster-sister, was one of the delinquents this time, and gave fine sport. She resisted so much that it took two eunuchs to hold her on. She then rolled herself up in such a way that it required their utmost efforts to keep her on the donkey. After a time she would remain so long passive that they hardly thought it necessary to do more than gently steady her so as to prevent her rolling off, and then she would suddenly spring off the donkey and dart away, while a few of the nimblest ran after her. This fun lasted until the sunset gun had fired, and then all ran in as fast as they could.

My pupil was fond of early hours, both in going to bed and getting up, except when she went to the opera or French theatre; but during Ramadan she could not go to bed early, as it is the custom to pay visits between 8 P.M. and 11 P.M. One evening five gentlemen walked in from the *selamlik*, a very ordinary thing in European houses, and a not unfrequent event in my pupil's harem, but still sufficiently so to attract observation. They were her husband and four brothers, Tewfik, Hussein, Hassan, and Ibrahim Pashas. Hassan Pasha had just returned from Berlin, and this was his first visit to his sister since her marriage. He is a handsome man, and having been educated at Oxford, speaks English well. After a little while the harem *corps de ballet* appeared, and performed before the gentlemen. They stayed an hour or two, and then left, and were succeeded by several other visitors, including one or two of the Princesses. When they were all gone the Princess and I each retired to bed.

There is one thing which a little enlivens Ramadan for the slaves, and that is the distribution of Baïram dresses, which are given very early in the month, and having to be made up, furnish useful employment. On the fourth day of the month bales of goods were brought into the harem. The Princess and her chief attendants sat in solemn conclave, and settled the dresses which were to be given to each; then the slaves were called in one by one, and received what was allotted to them. This was for each person three dresses, one being perhaps of the richest silk or satin, and the other two fine woollen. In addition to this, some of the upper slaves had also a velvet jacket, or something of the sort. Now every one of these persons had cost a good round sum as purchase-money. Each received a monthly stipend, more or less, according to her position. This would continue to be paid to her up to the end of her life. In addition were these Baïram presents, with other occasional windfalls in the course of the year. If she married there was her dower and trousseau. Will not everybody agree with me that slavery is a very costly institution, and that the country would gain much, financially as well as morally, by the emancipation of women, and the gradual introduction into households of hired female labour? Every night the saloons were brilliantly lighted up in expectation of visitors, who generally arrived between nine and eleven. We usually sat in the centre saloon because it was the coolest, or in a large reception-room facing the north, but both of these were dedicated on these evenings to visitors. The Princess was generally dead asleep at an early hour, and would yawn most demonstratively almost in the face of her visitors. She had become quite Europeanised in disliking to sit unemployed, which greatly scandalised the *dada*, who considered that a princess should never be found by visitors otherwise than seated on a divan or couch, with folded hands, perhaps condescending to listen to somebody, but certainly not *doing* anything. Nevertheless the Princess persisted in playing at *bézique*, but the moment a carriage was heard driving up, table and cards were shuffled away by the *dada's* orders, with which, as concerning Ramadan visitors, I did not pretend to interfere.

On the 16th of October I drove to the Pyramids. It had been the highest Nile on record, and great fears had been entertained of a terrible inundation. The water was subsiding, but still a vast lake stretched for miles before reaching the Pyramids. I returned at sunset, just in time for dinner; and afterwards was walking about with the Princess, when it occurred to her that there had not been a case of *fatra* for a day or two. She called the *calfa*, and inquired if no one had been discovered eating in the daytime. The latter did not know, but would go and see. Presently after visitors arrived, and we were engaged with them in the inner reception-room, when we heard a scuffle going on in the central saloon. A *fatra* had been discovered, and had allowed herself to be captured quietly; but arrived in the saloon, had suddenly darted out into the garden, and the moon being still young and giving but little light, had succeeded in hiding herself there, hoping to watch her opportunity, when she thought herself forgotten, and escape back to her own room. About two hours after we heard a great commotion without, as at the arrival of a visitor of importance. Everybody went forward to meet the personage, when in walked, supported by two eunuchs, and followed by half-a-dozen others bearing flags, the unfortunate *fatra*, for whom the eunuchs had been watching as a cat watches for a mouse, and who was at last caught in the act of escaping. The band had stationed themselves on each side of the doorway, and struck up derisive music, while the victim was paraded round the saloon; but whether she was tired and chilled by her long hiding in the garden, or thought she would get off better by remaining entirely passive, I know not, but she made no resistance, and this affording less sport, she was soon allowed to go free. Such are the amusements of the harem during Ramadan!

One evening I went to bed leaving the Princess up. She was just about to retire also when visitors arrived. The next morning I waited long for breakfast, and at last walked about through all the rooms and passages, but found nobody stirring. It was 1 P.M., yet the house was as quiet as in ordinary times at 1 A.M. No sign of any meal could I see, and I began to feel very sulky and surly. Meals were especially ordered for the Europeans, of whom there were three in the house—myself, and two Italian dressmakers—but there would have been very little chance of our ever getting any if it had not been known that the Princess ate also, and no meal was brought in unless she was there and had asked for it. Even then it was very difficult to get anything. First because all food is brought from without, and is not procurable except through the intervention of the eunuchs. The latter fast and are all hidden away asleep, and it is the most difficult thing in the world to unearth them. The doors of the harem are locked on the outside, and the eunuchs have the keys. The girls go and stand there and clap their hands—which is the signal for the eunuchs—but often stand there half an hour in vain! If this would be the case even when the Princess wanted food, how much more likely to happen when it was only I who required it! I could not find a single slave! At half-past three the Princess came down, and she then told me that her visitors had not left till past midnight, so her *dada* had persuaded her to sit up for the next meal and then fast (!) the following day. She had gone to bed at 4 A.M. and slept until 3 P.M.; she had now only about three hours to wait. I was very grumpy, and refused to read or to amuse her in any way, so the three hours hung rather heavily. At last the sunset gun fired, upon which she clapped her hands with joy, and we sat down to dinner immediately. Ramadan was not half over, but the Pasha's jovial countenance began to look less beaming. It was true he got up very late, but no one can with impunity turn night into day for any length of time without suffering for it. The eunuchs scarcely ever showed themselves in the daytime. My meals, though taken with the Princess, became more and more irregular as the month advanced. I rarely got breakfast, which was only *café au lait* and plain bread, before eleven; at about 3 P.M. perhaps I got luncheon; and at sunset, with most praiseworthy punctuality, the dinner came.

On the 17th day of Ramadan the Princess announced to me that a lady visitor was coming from Constantinople to stay with her during the remainder of the fast and for the Baïram. There is always such a mystery about women in the East, and such concealment of their names, that though actually living in the harem, I had the greatest difficulty to make out who this visitor was, and why her coming should produce such a revolution in our daily habits. I found she was the wife of the chief dervish at Constantinople, and that she was afterwards going to make the pilgrimage to Mecca. As my Princess, on account of her health, did not keep the fast, I inquired why *she* was singled out for the honour of this visit, as she was the third daughter of his Highness. To this I was told some strange incoherent story; that the mother of my pupil having lost four children, she and her offspring were under the power of this dervish, as he was somehow able to ensure eternal life for the lost ones. The first Princess had never lost a child, the third had never had one, so upon the second fell the care of entertaining the visitor. During Ramadan all who kept the fast laid aside whatever Frank habits they might have adopted, and returned to the customs of their ancestors. The Princess and I had continued to eat *à la franque;* but now, as long as this visitor remained and until the fast expired, the Princess must eat with her, and according to the ancient rigid Mahometan custom. This was the service according to the old fashion: A round tray was put upon a round table, and a dish containing food, and frequently changed, was put in the centre. From this dish all helped themselves with their fingers, using their bread as a plate, for there were neither knives, forks, spoons, nor plates. The dishes were generally either dried-up pieces of meat called *kebab* (*roti*), or sloppy dishes of vegetable floating in oil and water. Then there were sweets, and a dish of rice-milk which was not bad. For the sloppy dishes a spoon was given, never changed, and each person alternately put her spoon into the dish and then into her mouth. When dinner was over, water was brought, and each drank alternately according to rank, but from the same glass. The Princess asked me could I eat like this? If not, I must have my meals taken into my own room, where I should certainly have a knife and fork and plate; but she could neither answer for the food that would be brought to me, nor for the hours when I should have it, as she could not herself be with me. I chose the latter alternative, as I felt I could not have supported the other.

The Princess spent the next day at Abdeen with his Highness, and at about half-past one the visitor arrived— an elderly lady, quite independent of external adornment, and clad apparently in her nightgown. I must add that the Eastern nightgowns are much more decent than ours. It is a loose full dress, confined at each ankle and hanging over the feet, in no way defining the figure. A shawl is wound round the loins. The *dada* and the housekeeper received the visitor; and I did not know whether she was less rigid than I had been led to expect, or if it were merely to recover the fatigue of her voyage and subsequent railway journey, but she accepted the refreshment of a cup of coffee and a long pipe. The next day I had a little conversation with the visitor. I was sitting by the window in the chief saloon, and she was near me, when a European arrived who often procured articles from Paris for the Princess. The two last disappeared at once into an adjoining room to con over the last fashions, which seemed to be more extravagant than ever. The wife of the chief dervish looked after Madame —— in a very disparaging manner, as her costume was of the most *outré* description. She said there was a mania for everything *à la franque*, and then asked me with some hesitation if I were English or French; and upon my answer, spoke her mind very freely about the French, and by no means in their favour. Indeed nothing can be more unsuitable to the Egyptian climate than European costume as at present worn; heavy tight-fitting silks, and velvet jackets loaded with trimmings, and ever changing in cut and fashion; and those frightful high-heeled shoes or boots, rising four or five inches from the ground, on which every one tottered about. The harem costume during eight months in the year (when not expecting visitors) is the prettiest that can be imagined, and I often assured my pupil that she looked far better in that than in any other. It was of white (Indian) grass-cloth, long and flowing, shaped at the shoulders, but confined at the waist only by a coloured band. A ribbon of the same hue was worn round the neck, and another tied back the hair from off the face. It was impossible to imagine anything more simple and elegant than this costume. My pupil had magnificent hair, and thus her natural attractions were shown off to the greatest advantage, without any aid from art.

After dinner every evening during Ramadan the chief saloon would be filled with slaves, and a number of little carpets were spread at the east end for prayer. There might be twenty or thirty—the number varied; and each slave went through her stated prayers and prostrations on her own particular carpet, her face turned eastward. The windows were all open, but the venetian blinds closed, and a murmur of voices came from without. It was the sheikhs reciting the Koran. In the meanwhile, not in the least sobered down by what was going on, several girls would run in and out of the saloon, talking and laughing. One evening I was looking on at this scene, when Kopsès and the *calfa* came up and asked me for pins, as they knew I carried a pin-cushion about with me. I gave them all I had, and presently found out it was to pin all the back row of the worshippers together, which was done with such neatness and dexterity that when they finally rose to disperse they found themselves inextricably entangled together! Nobody offered to assist them; they had to struggle out as well as they could, amid universal laughter. This gave me a curious specimen of the reverence attached to their prayers and genuflections.

CHAPTER XXIX.

The Night of Power at the Mosque—Bairam—The Prince and Princess leave for a time—Candle-stealing—Discover the thief—Transit of Venus—Slight shock of earthquake.

On the Night of Power, when the Koran is supposed to have come down from heaven, I went with a party of friends to the Mosque of Mohammed Ali. This mosque is open every evening in Ramadan, but on this particular night, as we drove up to the Citadel, the effect of the illuminated minarets was extremely pretty, and so was the interior of the mosque, which was lighted in a series of circles. We reached it at 8 P.M. The gentlemen of my party walked in in their stockings, carrying their boots in their hands; but I contrived to get in without taking off mine, as so many persons were going in and out that I managed to pass unnoticed. It is true that later on I happened to be standing on some steps, and a believer asked one of my friends if I had not my *shoes* on; to which he replied in the negative, as they happened to be *boots*. My dress was luckily rather long, which hid my feet, for it would have been a great nuisance to carry my boots about for a couple of hours. The first performance we saw on entering was that of the whirling dervishes, twenty-three in number, whose gyrations continued (with occasional breaks) for twenty-three minutes. They were succeeded on the same spot by the howlers. There were many other groups in different parts of the mosque, some squatted on the ground, reading or reciting the Koran, and apparently abstracted from all sublunary considerations; others standing in a circle, bobbing and swaying alternately from side to side. There was not much reverence among the spectators. One of my companions told me that a few evenings previous he had seen a young woman chase a friend in and out of the many groups scattered about, and finding that exercise inadequate to calm her exuberant spirits, she actually turned a series of somersaults without attracting any particular attention! The tomb of Mohammed Ali was lighted up, and we went round it. It is in a little side chapel. At a few minutes before 10 P.M. the lights were being put out, and we came away.

The 10th of November was the first day of Baïram, and the Princess was off at a very early hour to breakfast with his Highness before he went to the Citadel. At ten minutes past 7 A.M. the twenty-one guns announced that he had arrived there. The Princess had given an order in my presence the preceding evening to the chief eunuch to have a carriage at the door at ten, to take me to Abdeen to pay my respects to his Highness's wives. Relying on this, I was dressed soon after eight, and waited in vain until mid-day. No carriage came! The slaves paraded about in the richest silks and satins. A dozen musicians were dressed as boys, and looked uncommonly like them. At about 3 P.M. the Princess returned from Abdeen. She was dressed in a salmon-coloured silk, trimmed with ostrich-feathers of the same hue, and the most costly lace. It had been presented to her by her husband as a Baïram gift, had been sent from Paris, and had cost, I was told, £700! She had a girdle, tiara, bracelets, earrings, and stomacher, all of diamonds, besides numerous stars that flashed all over her. Nobody concerned themselves in the least about the non-arrival of the carriage for me. It was taken as a matter of course. Soon after the return of the Princess, the gentlemen of her family began to arrive one after the other. His Highness came also, and stayed ten minutes or a quarter of an hour. The second day was for European visitors, but there are very few English residents in Cairo, and travellers seldom arrive before the end of November. The band remained in the hall each day, striking up at the arrival and departure of each visitor. The third day we had a continual stream of native visitors, which went on from 10 A.M. to 5 P.M.

There must always be a buffoon, and Oum Ayesha played that part in the Princess's harem, where she spent half her time. On the third day of Baïram, a flourish of music announcing that a visitor was driving into the court-yard, some of us went into the centre saloon to receive her. The harem doors were thrown open by the eunuchs, and somebody was supported in covered with the great black cloak worn by Arab women. This being removed, Oum Ayesha was disclosed to view in a loose white *négligée*, advancing with grotesque skips, amid general laughter. The eunuchs had taken care to send a carriage for her, and she was hurried into a side-room and a handsome satin dress put over her white gown, in which she paraded about in mock dignity for the rest of the day. This woman was kind-hearted, and had been the only person who offered to do anything for me when I was ill at Ramleh, but she was coarse and impudent in the highest degree. I should not have understood her words if they had not been accompanied by gestures which there was no mistaking. I was determined not to tolerate this, either in my presence or in that of my pupil, and I reproved her so sharply that she changed her tactics, uttered her coarse jokes in Arabic instead of Turkish, and wholly discontinued the gestures. I think this rather added pungency to the jokes, and I suppose there was a great drollery about the woman, as I often saw the face of the person talking to me quite convulsed with suppressed laughter while trying to carry on an indifferent conversation. Oum Ayesha meanwhile would walk about the saloon talking to herself aloud, and taking care always to pass frequently close to any of the Princes who might be present.

There were often *fantasias* (as they call any entertainment), regular burlesques, the characters in which were sustained by girls in the Princess's harem. If any Franks were introduced, which they usually were, they were made to play the same part assigned to the English in French plays—that is to say, they made themselves ridiculous. I have said that my apartments were in an angle on the ground-floor. Some trees had been transplanted there, and had grown so much during the year that I was anxious to have the branches pruned, as they were too near the window. One morning early I was in my room, with the blinds closed to keep out the sun, when I heard the voices of men just under the window; and knowing it to be the gardeners, I rose quickly, threw back the shutters, and called out to them, intending to show them what I wanted done. To my astonishment they darted away like thieves detected in the act of burglary, and paid no attention to my calls. There were iron bars to the window, so I could not get out, and I knew that the venetian shutters in the central saloon adjoining had not yet been unlocked by the eunuchs. The gardeners had supposed it was one of the slaves speaking to them; and as it would have been a dire offence for them to be found talking to any of the inmates of the harem, they fled at once to avoid such a catastrophe. As soon as the shutters were unlocked I went out into the garden, and having found the men, took them into the corner under my window and showed them what I wanted done, which was forthwith executed cheerfully.

The Prince's long fast had brought out upon him one of the plagues of Egypt, most of which, I am sorry to say, flourish as much in the present day as they did in the time of Pharaoh. As the Princess and all her attendants were young and knew nothing of nursing, her husband went to his mother, who lived in a large mansion in a street leading out of the Mouskee. There was nothing at all in the outward appearance of this building. There was an archway where a doorkeeper sat, and many Arabs with him. There was an outer and an inner court, the first leading into the *selamlik*, the second into the harem, but both under one roof. In the inner court were the eunuchs; and the harem was a large building with many spacious apartments, the windows of which looked down into a large garden. A high wall surrounded the whole, and close under the wall on the outside was a densely populated native quarter. The house was always cool, fresh, and orderly, with no attempt at European fashions; and both slaves and eunuchs were civil and obliging. It was evidently a well-conducted household, where there was plenty of everything, but no display. I never saw either the mistress or her slaves otherwise than simply dressed. The Prince was supposed to go for two or three days only; but his illness lasted several weeks, during which time the Princess was generally with him. My heart would have failed me quite if I had known she would be absent for so long; but *bookra* was always spoken of for the return, and I did not at first understand the nature of the illness, which is always very tedious and troublesome. The harem was unspeakably dull without my pupils (Kopsès always accompanied the Princess everywhere). I saw no one from morning to night. I always had the blinds open in my bedroom; but then it was in a corner, and trees were just in front of the windows. The eunuchs kept all the venetian blinds closed in the principal apartments, so that they were very gloomy, and offered no temptation to the slaves to hang about there. The chief attendants were with their mistress, and the *dada*, after the Baïram, kept her room entirely, as the going up and down stairs was too painful for her. This room was on the upper floor among the slaves' apartments, far away from the chief saloons, from which long passages and staircases separated them. I took all my meals alone, but in the dining-room, in the same manner as if the Princess had been there. Being winter, it was dark at five o'clock. To sit five hours alone in my room was a dreary prospect; for the sake of ventilation I must either have a door or window open. If I chose the latter, a stray cat was sure to come in and secrete herself somewhere, so as to wake me up in the night. I usually, therefore, sat with the door open, and thus looked down a long vista of saloons, which the looking-glass on the walls seemed to make interminable. To sit there, and every time I raised my head to look into a vast black space, was very spectral and unpleasant. When the Princess was at home, all the saloons were lighted up with wax candles; but in her absence all was darkness, except in the slaves' division, which was lighted by gas—rooms, passages, staircases, &c. But no gas was allowed in the best part of the palace. When I first went to live there, and occupied my original rooms, I was often struck in the evening with the strong odour of gas which pervaded the passages. The eunuchs at a certain hour turned it on, and later turned it off, but from the main; the slaves never troubled themselves about turning it off from within. Every arrangement in the harem had its inconveniences. If the eunuchs went to bed early (their movements depending entirely on those of their mistress), they turned off the gas, perhaps leaving some persons in darkness who had still employment. When they turned it on, the slaves might delay lighting it, or altogether omit some burners, the gas escaping, meanwhile, and filling the passages. If the smell became unbearable, they would go with a long pole lighted at one end, until they found the place from whence it proceeded, and quietly light the gas, at the imminent risk, as it appeared to me, of an explosion. This, however, was not so likely as I at first supposed, on account of the constant current of air that passed through these passages.

As I did not like looking into the black space, and was, besides, always in the habit of walking up and down the centre saloon for half an hour or more every evening, I asked the *cahir* (housekeeper) to let me have a couple of wax candles lighted in the adjoining room every evening, and four in the centre saloon, two at each end, that I might pursue my accustomed exercise. She agreed, and they were lighted regularly. But though I always saw them when I came out from dinner, they would suddenly disappear at about seven—by what agency I could not make out. I myself sat in a bright light at my writing-table opposite to the open door, and was visible enough to any one; though looking up into comparative darkness I could not see the thief, who might easily stand in the shade, and watching the moment when my eyes were fixed on my book or writing, noiselessly possess herself of the candles. This being repeated every evening annoyed me a great deal, and I suspected one of the black slaves rather than the white. Among the girls who had occasion to come to my room was one who brought me twice a-day a large dish containing two *goulahs*[1] of filtered water and a glass to drink from. She was a fair pleasant-looking girl, and she always lingered in the room, and at the slightest encouragement was profuse in her professions of attachment. "Seni tchoq severim," she would say (I love you very much). I did not take these professions as gospel truths, but still it was rather pleasant than otherwise to hear them, and I told her about the candles

[1] These *goulahs* are of earthenware, made up the Nile, and being exceedingly porous they preserve the water deliciously cool. They must be placed by an open window, and if it is in the shade and there is a current through the room, the water remains as fresh as if iced, and is more wholesome.

being stolen at night, and asked her who was likely to have done it. She was very sympathising, but was sure it was one of the black girls (*bou Arabdje*), as the white slaves contemptuously class all the dark-skinned, from the delicate-limbed Arab to the swarthy negro.

One evening I was sitting as usual reading opposite the open door. A minute before, I had looked up, and the rooms beyond were dimly lighted as usual. A few seconds after, I again looked, and the lights were extinguished. I rose quickly and noiselessly, for the carpets were thick and my shoes were thin, and crossing the next room arrived in the centre saloon just in time to see a girl, with her back turned to me, in the act of stretching out her hand to reach the candle, the only one still alight— the others, already extinguished, being in her left hand. I was upon her in a moment, before she was aware, and grasping her by the shoulder, while I took the lighted candle with the other hand, held it in her face that I might recognise the thief. It was my water-bearer, who had sympathised with me so much!

I never was familiar with the slaves, or put myself on a level with them. If they came to me I answered them always civilly, but allowed no liberties, as I saw it would not answer, and if treated with disrespect I either passed it unnoticed or took the law into my own hands. In this case I did the latter, for the girl was caught in the very act of theft. Presently I let her escape and went back to my room. The next day no drinking-water was brought to me. I waited until near evening, and then seeing the *cahir* (housekeeper) told her what had happened, and that no water had been brought. About a quarter of an hour after, the girl entered my room with the dish and *goulahs*, stopping before me on her way out to revile me in the choicest language. I raised my head for a moment, and then went on with my writing as before without taking the slightest notice of her. Soon after I got up to drink, and found the water was dirty! I filled a glass and carried it at once to the *cahir*, asking her if that was to be permitted. She requested me to leave it with her, and I returned to my own room. Half an hour after, the girl came again, this time with a changed manner, and, carrying another dish and *goulahs*, poured out a glass of water and asked me if that was good. I said yes, and drank it, and there the matter ended; but I don't remember that she ever renewed her professions of regard after this incident.

There were sometimes such absurd annoyances in the harem, which still did not cease to be annoyances. I had my room fairly furnished with European conveniences, and amongst them six cane-bottomed chairs. I preferred these chairs to the heavier arm-chairs, because the latter had a tendency to come to pieces when you sat on them, the heat of the climate melting the glue, so that the four legs sprawled out in different directions, and you found yourself suddenly landed on the carpet. I had seen this result in several instances, and it had also occurred to me. I preferred, therefore, the cane-bottomed chairs, as firmer and more easy to move. The slaves fully appreciated many European comforts, though they were not provided with them, and they never of their own choice sat on the floor if they could get a chair. It was by no means a rare thing for me, therefore, if I left my door unlocked for a time, to find on my return that all the chairs had disappeared from my room. Nobody knew who had taken them, nobody knew where they had gone, and it was nobody's business to bring them back. This was not pleasant; to utter complaints would only excite merriment, and be unavailing; but I contrived after a time to hold my own. Sometimes, if I happened to go down one of the passages which communicated between the best apartments and the rooms for the slaves, I would see a girl seated on the ground at work with a cane-bottomed chair near her, which served the double purpose of table and candlestick (!), a piece of candle being lighted and stuck in one of the holes formed by the plaiting of the cane. As the girls rarely troubled themselves to extinguish the candle, when it burnt low it generally ignited the cane and made a great hole. Many a candle did I put out in this way, just as it was burning low, the girl perhaps fast asleep with her head on the chair! The recklessness was frightful; the masters and mistresses were quite aware of it, but they could do nothing. It was not pleasant to think how easily a fire might occur in one of these great harems, and how impossible escape would be, with all the doors firmly locked on the outside, and every window with iron bars! I had plenty of time to think of such contingencies during these lonely weeks, when I was quite isolated from everybody else. When the Princess and her husband were in the house I did not feel quite so unprotected, as I knew the Pasha's stentorian voice could be heard a long way off. He did not relish the possibility either, and we often discussed what we should do in case of an outbreak of fire, when we talked of the extreme carelessness of the slaves. Perhaps such an event had never occurred to him before, as, when living with his mother, harem and *selamlik* had been all under one roof, communicating through a passage, so that escape by that into the *selamlik*, and from thence into the streets, would not have been difficult. But it was appalling to think what might happen in case of fire in these great isolated harems, all locked and barred!

One evening I went up to the *dada*, who kept her room and appeared to suffer a good deal. I found the *cahir* [1]

---

[1] *Cahir* and *calfa* both signify housekeeper, but there is a slight difference in their duties.

with her and one of the eunuchs named Sofian, a rather superior man of his class and not bad-looking. My entrance appeared to interrupt a serious conversation. A few compliments passed between us, and when they were exhausted, after a pause Sofian continued the discourse which I had interrupted. "Namaz bordjoudour" (Prayer is our duty), he began, and then went on to say that Allah was everywhere, and would hear us wherever we might be and whenever we called upon him, &c. I listened to him for some time, and made out his meaning perfectly, going away at last rather favourably impressed.

There was great interest at this time about the transit of Venus, many scientific men having been sent out from different capitals to various countries to watch for it. A large tent was pitched on the Mokattam Hills behind the Citadel, and astronomers were there to take observations. The greatest interest was felt in some of the harems about it, and particularly by the Princess Saïd Pasha, widow of the late Viceroy. The wives of his Highness were also very keen on the subject, and observations were, I was told, taken from the roof of the harem. They heard that expeditions had been sent out from different European Governments, and as they could see from their own housetops, they were determined not to be outdone. Everybody in the hotels was full of it, and I knew a party of seven gentlemen who started at 3 A.M. on the 9th of December, mounted on donkeys, to get a good view on the Mokattam Hills, and I was told they were repaid. I spent that evening at Shepheard's Hotel with some friends, and as we sat in one of the rooms up-stairs, the door began to rattle and the ground to shake under us. It was a slight shock of earthquake, but I did not hear of any damage done.

I had several friends about this time going up the Nile. One party, consisting of a lady, two gentlemen, maid, and courier, engaged a *dahabieh* for a month, going only as far as Thebes. For this they paid £240, exclusive of wine and *backsheesh*. They were to return by rail to save time. The other party consisted of four persons. They went as far as the Second Cataract, and were three months absent. Their expense was £180 each person, also exclusive of wine and *backsheesh*. I noted these charges, as people never seem to know what they ought to pay, and they are sure to be asked a great deal too much at first. As a rule, the longer the voyage the cheaper it is in proportion to the time, as a month's trip may prevent the boat being hired again, and is therefore charged very high.

CHAPTER XXX.

Kourban Baïram—Arab saddles—Donkey-ride to Heliopolis—Ball at Gezireh—Dinner-party at the harem—Particularly fine spring—Many donkey-rides—Readings with my pupil—Difficulty of procuring books unless specially ordered from Europe—Good disposition and unselfishness of the Princess—Cicolani's garden—" Doseh "—Am taken ill.

There was an almanac formerly published by Kauffman in the Mouskee which gave the five different computations of time, as calculated in the Arab, Coptic, Greek, Hebrew, and Gregorian calendar. Since the adoption of the latter by the Khédive for all Government payments the publication has been discontinued, as it ceased to pay, but it was a very useful little book. In this 'Calendrier de l'Orient' for 1875 the Kourban Baïram had been calculated to fall on the 17th of January. But it appeared that the sheikhs could not agree among themselves about the date; some said it would be on the 18th, others on the 19th, and when everybody had made their arrangements about carriages for the latter day, we heard that the sheikhs had announced to his Highness that it would fall on the 17th, the day which had been fixed long before in this little printed calendar. It was the gayest Baïram I had yet seen. The harem toilets were resplendent, and the number of travellers very great. H.R.H. the Duke of Connaught was among the visitors. I had many friends that winter in Egypt, and the requests to get them introductions into the harem were numerous. I went with a party to the reception in the morning; then returned to my pupil's palace, changed my dress, and proceeded to Shepheard's Hotel to lunch there with some friends, and afterwards to join them in a donkey-ride to Heliopolis. Now donkey-riding is looked upon by the upper ten in Egypt as solely for the lower classes. But they have by this time got accustomed to see that it is the first impulse of an Englishman—prince, duke, or simple tourist—to mount a donkey and career through the streets upon it. The Duke of Connaught, with all his suite, was seen scampering about in this way on the first or second morning after his arrival. A few days before, I had gone with a large party to Toura, driving a certain distance and riding on donkeys the rest. On that occasion, for the first time in my life I rode on an Arab saddle, which is used for both men and women, and has a sort of round hump in front to prevent the rider from going over the animal's head, which nevertheless often happens. These saddles were extremely hard and slippery, and made one feel very stiff afterwards. But up to this particular day of the Kourban Baïram I had always had good donkeys, and had very much enjoyed my rides. We started a party of ten, ladies and gentlemen, along the Abbassieh road to Heliopolis, thinking it would be the quietest way we could take, as everybody would be showing themselves in the Choubrah Road, which is the most frequented promenade. Eight of the party cantered gaily on, but my donkey refused to go beyond a walk, and soon showed symptoms of a desire to lie down. Mr Michell with his usual good-nature had kept near me, and he now offered, if I liked, to change donkeys with me. So we stopped and changed saddles. As the others had got considerably ahead of us during this proceeding, we hurried on our donkeys to overtake them. I soon found that it was a case of Scylla and Charybdis. There was no occasion to urge on this donkey, but his paces were so jolting and uneasy that I was obliged to hold on by the pommels of the saddle in order to keep my seat. In this undignified ride I heard a cavalcade behind me, and presently half-a-dozen harem carriages passed *en grande tenue*, with outriders and splendid liveries. It was the Princesses going to pay a visit to the Queen-Mother, who was then staying at Abbassieh. Formerly no one could have gone in black to visit a harem, and there was still a prejudice against it amongst the greater number. My pupil had, however, at this Baïram worn a black velvet dress, with no colour whatever upon her. She had, it is true, the most magnificent diamonds, which perhaps sufficiently relieved the sombre hue.

A day or two after, there was a ball at Gezireh, at which the Duke of Connaught was to be present. Balls had been given there in preceding winters, to which I had had invitations, but I had not gone for various reasons. Carriages were enormously expensive, and I never was fond of late hours. On this occasion, however, both the Princess and her husband urged me so strongly to go that I agreed to do so. They furnished me with everything that was needful, and the Prince said he would see that I was properly looked after the whole evening. He amply redeemed his promise. The invitation was for 9 P.M., but there were such stories of people spending two and three hours on the road, as they were obliged to keep the line, that I ordered the carriage at eight, and arrived at half-past. I found a great many had gone before me for the same reason, but the *coup d'œil* from the windows on the Nile and on the illuminated gardens was so beautiful that no one regretted being early. His Highness came punctually at nine o'clock, and all those who were before him went at once to make their salaam. He had some gracious little speech to make to every one. Then the Duke of Connaught arrived, and after dancing once with the wife of the English Consul-General, walked about the rooms with Prince Tewfik. Supper was at 1 A.M., and those who wished to get away early ordered their carriages immediately after. I had not taken this precaution, and only reached the harem at a little after five. I should have had some trouble to get in, but the Prince was not returned, and the eunuchs were obliged to sit up for him.

Two or three days after, my pupil gave a dinner-party. Her brother Hassan Pasha had come from Berlin about two months previous, and was now about to return. The Princess sent out several notes of invitation, some written by herself and some by Kopsès. They were written in English, French, and Turkish, according to the person addressed. I don't know who had put the idea into her head. *I* had nothing to do with it. Invitations were sent to the Princes Tewfik, Hussein, and Hassan, and to their respective wives, also to her own brother Prince Ibrahim, and her younger (half) brothers Mahmoud Bey and Fuad Bey; to her sisters, the Princesses Tafita and Fatma, to the third Princess, and the Princess Saïd, and to Faïk Hanem, the adopted daughter of the third Princess—Charissas Hanem accompanied the latter. My dear Princess busied herself all day in arranging about the dinner and giving instructions to the attendants. She settled who was to take in who, when the champagne was to be drawn, &c., and was as anxious about the success of her party as a fashionable lady in our country when she tries quite a new thing. The guests arrived punctually, with Toussoun Pasha (whom I omitted to mention among those invited), and the husband of my pupil, Prince Ibrahim. The Princess received them as naturally and gracefully as if it were a daily occurrence, and her brothers assisted her to the utmost. But the ladies were not quite so much at ease in the, to them, very novel position.[1] This feeling only showed itself *before* dinner, and that is always a dull time even with us; conversation flows much more freely afterwards. Then dinner was announced, and the Princess having requested her husband to give his arm to the Princess Saïd, and allotted to each gentleman his particular lady, quietly took the arm of one of her brothers, and waited her turn to go in. There was a momentary pause; the ladies seemed rather in doubt. Then the Princess Saïd looked round at my pupil, and laughing merrily, linked her arm with that of her cavalier, all the rest following. At dinner the example soon became infectious, and conversation was pretty general. Mahmoud Bey sat by me, and while taking wine, which, having lived in England, he did without scruple, he told me that his sister, Gemila Hanem (a girl of about thirteen, who often came to school to see him and his brother, Fuad Bey), having been urged to taste some wine, refused, saying that it would make her become a Christian!

I went to the opera a great deal this winter, as the Prince was so kind as to lend me his box very frequently. It was a very fine winter, and I joined many picnics and excursions. The Princess took great interest in hearing of them, and liked to see the ladies who had accompanied me. Her character was becoming more formed; there

---

[1] It was the first time in their lives that these ladies had been in mixed society, that is of ladies and gentlemen!

was more decision, and she was beginning to assert herself as mistress, but no further than was just and right. She had at first been so much under the influence of her head slaves and eunuchs, that her orders were not obeyed, unless entirely in accordance with their wishes. Gradually, however, this began to change. I remember one day the wife of the English Consul-General told me that she had been to call on the Princess; that at the outer gate the eunuchs had rudely told her servant to get down from the box, without coming in themselves to announce her, and assist her out of her carriage; that she had got out, and gone into the harem alone, and had then been told that the Princess was out. I repeated this to the Princess, and at the same time complained of two or three instances of disrespect to myself, which, I said, in the position in which I was, reflected on her. We were walking about in the garden then, and she immediately sent for all the eunuchs, and repeated to them what I had told her. The head eunuch was about to interrupt, but she held up her hand, and with great dignity proceeded to tell them that every visitor who came to her was to be treated with respect; that she was mistress, and the sole judge of who was to be admitted; that they were there to receive orders, and not to give them. She then said a word or two about me,—that I was also to be treated with respect, and that whatever order she gave concerning me was to be obeyed, and not put aside as of no consequence. She then dismissed them, not allowing a word in reply; and from that time I found I was better treated by them. A carriage was ordered for me every Friday and Sunday, to take me where I wished, and to fetch me back at whatever time I appointed. A eunuch always came to tell me when the carriage was ready, and the driver was punctual to the time I named.

We continued our reading very diligently. It was

always rather difficult to get books; not that there was any dearth of printed matter, but I rarely could get what I asked for. There was a good English bookseller, but his stock consisted almost entirely of guide-books and travels, and perhaps the shilling railway library, the best of which were sure to be bought up immediately. At the French booksellers' (of whom there were several) the stock also consisted mostly of travels, voyages, and guide-books, with a good sprinkling of trashy French novels. There was no circulating library; everything must be bought. I therefore made a list of books, French and English, and in about three months' time they would arrive; and it was then the Princess's great delight to look over them for two or three days to see which she would like and which she would not, for she always condemned some as looking dry. In that case I put them aside, and tried to introduce them later on as new arrivals; but she was rarely to be taken in in that way. In turning over others, she would come upon little passages which pleased her, and then those books would go on her own shelves to be read in turn. European visitors soon talked to her about her readings, and she would sometimes say that we had just finished such a book, and were uncertain what to begin next; upon which the visitor would probably propose some book which she was herself reading, and send it to the Princess. It generally turned out to be some story of the *demi-monde*. If very bad, I refused to read it altogether; but sometimes I would read a little, and then point out the evil of such works by trying to bring it home to herself as wife and mistress of a household. Though born in a harem, she had a high idea of the sanctity of marriage, and of the tie being equally binding on both parties. She was well aware of the laxity that prevailed in some of the great harems, but she never alluded to it, except by an occasional observation, "Que voulez-vous? ce ne sont que de pauvres esclaves! elles n'ont pas de choix! on n'est pas libre comme chez vous!"

One day she presented me with a beautifully bound and illustrated edition of 'L'Atmosphère,' by Flammarien. As I always got all the books for her, I wondered where she had procured it, and why she had chosen so scientific a work. This was the story of it. When my Princess went to stay at her brother's palace on the Canal, a few months after her marriage, the two young wives being both smitten with a desire to read and improve their minds, sent to a bookseller in Alexandria for a parcel of books. Among the packet were a few containing rather dry reading, and the rest trashy French novels. On my first visit my opinion was asked respecting the books, and after a slight survey I condemned some. When asked my objections, I handed one of them to the Princess Hussein, who being a year or two older than my pupil, was better able to form an opinion. She read the page, and then tore the book in two and threw it on the ground. Some time after, when we were settled in the palace at Ramleh, I was taken ill, and removed to Koum-el-Dikke to be nursed. The Princess then again in my absence wanted a NEW book, so she sent to the booksellers for one, with strict injunctions that he was to send the *best* book he had! He sent 'L'Atmosphère,' magnificently bound in crimson and gold, and beautifully illustrated. The poor dear child (for she was not sixteen) pored over it, and tried to be interested, but could not, so she settled that good books were very dry! She begged me to keep it, as she thought I should understand it, but she could not! She often went to Abdeen to breakfast and lunch with his Highness, and that was always a great pleasure to her. On her return she would talk of him, of his labours for the greatness of Egypt, and would assure me that he gave himself no rest in his anxiety for the public good.

I had always since my arrival in Egypt been in the habit of having the Fridays and Sundays to myself, and this continued after I went into the harem. One Thursday evening the Princess was mentioning rather sadly that there would be no readings on the morrow, and cried out, " Oh, je m'ennuie, je m'ennuie! mais je ne m'ennuie pas autant quand vous êtes avec moi!" I was very much touched, and at once offered to stay the next day, which offer she accepted. The next week I renewed my proposal, but she replied at once decidedly, " No ; you are accustomed to liberty, and have no recreation but what you meet with among friends on Friday and Sunday. It would not do for you to lose that." It was true these were the arguments I had myself used to her on my first residence in the harem, when she was wholly under the influence of her *dada* ; but as months had elapsed since then, it showed she had adopted them as her own sentiments, and was, I think, a proof of the unselfishness of her character.

Her anxiety *to do right* was very marked. One day a visitor was strongly recommending a book to her, and offering to send it at once, when the Princess said, " But is it pure ? " The visitor was rather out of countenance, and said to me, " It is by Dumas Fils " ! When we had finished a book, she would discuss all the characters, state what she admired, and where she considered any had failed. She liked to have the 'Almanach de Gotha,' and to look over all the sovereigns of Europe, and to know if there was any particular story connected with any of them. She was very much interested in the unfortunate Maximilian and the poor Empress Charlotte; also in the marriage of the Duke of Edinburgh, which took place only a fortnight previous to her own. I don't think there are many young ladies in Europe who in society would be thought more charming and unaffected than was my dear little Princess Zeyneb.

The spring of 1875 was the finest I had known in Egypt. There were fewer days of *khamseen* wind, and the heat never became great until quite the middle of May. The hotels continued more or less full during all this time, and many were the pleasant excursions I made. One day a party of fourteen, with a noble duke at the head, then on a visit to his Highness, started on donkeys from Shepheard's, to visit the howling dervishes at Old Cairo. After that was accomplished we returned through the town, and, slightly diminished in numbers, proceeded to Cicolani's garden, high up in the Choubrah Road, and just opposite to Kasr-el-Nuss. M. Cicolani is the Marshall & Snellgrove of Egypt, and having realised a splendid fortune, has most patriotically devoted a considerable sum to the advantage of his adopted country, by laying out a large and beautiful garden, and building in it a perfect gem of a house. The garden covers several acres; it is laid out with great taste, and there are everywhere broad firm gravel walks, a very rare thing in Egypt. Admission to this garden by ticket is to be procured by every traveller and resident in Cairo, and it is well worth visiting. All sorts of stories are current as to the ultimate destination of this garden and house, but with those stories I have nothing to do. Signor Cicolani may intend to perpetuate his name as a public benefactor; but he now enjoys seeing his work appreciated, and is there every day directing and looking into things. Of course, when he heard that a noble duke was come to the garden, he came forward in person to do the honours, but I believe he would have been equally ready had it been only a private gentleman. We went into the house, the conservatories, and over every part of the gardens, and then returned to the gates, mounted our donkeys, and cantered down the Choubrah Road. The duke was staying at the house which we had formerly inhabited, and he invited us all to go in and take tea with him. We had scarcely dismounted, and had not had time to get into the house, the duke preceding us, when a messenger hastily came up to his Grace to inform him that the Khédive was at the gates to pay him a visit. The duke went back immediately, and received his Highness, while we all formed in line to salute him as he passed. The visit was not long, and very soon the Khédive came back, saluting us as he passed, and was escorted to the gate by the duke, who remained until his Highness had driven off, and then ushered us in to tea. His Highness had been driving from the Choubrah Palace, and had given orders to call on the duke, when, as his carriage approached Cicolani's, he saw all the party emerge from the gates and mount the donkeys. His Highness then gave orders to keep at a discreet distance until the duke had gone into the house, and then to drive rapidly up to the gates, which was done.

One day, as I was going out of the harem door to drive into Cairo, one of the upper slaves, whom I had often noticed for her gentle manner, called out to me, "Oh, madam, take me with you!" I turned back directly, and went up to the couch where she was sitting. "Are you then so anxious to go out?" said I. "Oh yes," she replied, "it is so very sad here; nothing to live for day after day, year after year—nothing to live for!" I was moved, for I saw how much she felt it. "Sleep! sleep!" said she, making the gesture of laying her head on her hand—"nothing else to look forward to!" She was not very young, and I believe for some years past they had talked of marrying her; but I doubt whether she looked forward to that even, she seemed so thoroughly impressed with her melancholy lot, and she was by no means the only one who produced that effect on me.

About the middle of April I was taken with a serious illness. I had been with a party to the Pyramids, and coming back about sunset, was seized with a shivering fit and oppression at the chest, so that I felt almost choked. It did not pass off in the evening, but the next day I was as usual. Some days after, I went to the procession of the *dosch*, when a sheikh on horseback rides over a long line of prostrate human beings packed closely together across the road, so that there is not room for the horse's hoof to step between them. Whoever is killed or hurt during the passage of the horse is sure of Paradise, so that there are annually hundreds offer themselves to the sacrifice. The day was lovely, and we were on the ground at 11 A.M., but it was not until one that the line was formed and the sheikh there. We were in a very good place, and should have had an excellent view, but just before the horse came, three harem carriages drove up and placed themselves between us and the line of men. Such a thing would not have been allowed to any one else, but to a great harem strange latitude is permitted. I only saw the sheikh's head and the horse's head, and perceived that he was going as gingerly as if treading on glass. As the sheikh passed on, the crowd behind pressed forward, and if any were killed or hurt they were immediately removed by their friends, and no one was the wiser. This happened on a Friday, and it had been settled with the Princess that I should remain a few days with Miss Harris, who had taken a small house near Cairo in the Abbassieh road for the winter, and would shortly leave it and return to Alexandria. I had much difficulty in getting in and out of the carriage, which I ascribed to cold in the limbs; but in the night I suffered so much pain that I determined to call in a doctor early in the morning, and as soon as it was daylight tried to get up to go and ask Miss Harris to send for one, but found to my consternation that I had quite lost the use of my limbs! By the time Miss Harris came to my room I was unable even to raise my hand or turn in bed, so Dr Grant was sent for, who at once pronounced it to be a severe attack of rheumatic gout. As the pain was intense, he prescribed injections of morphia under the skin, which greatly soothed the pain, but produced such drowsiness that I was in a continual state of somnolence for three days. I woke up when spoken to, but fell asleep again while answering. Miss Harris sent to tell the Princess of my state, and the *cahir* came at once to see me. It was clear that I was not fit to return, so it was decided that I should remain where I was for a short time until my illness took a favourable turn.

CHAPTER XXXI.

Remove to the Hôtel d'Orient—Remain there a fortnight—Return to the palace—Three weddings in the harem—The Prince is to go to Europe—Departure—We go to Ramleh—I am taken ill.

I had been ill a week when the time expired for which Miss Harris had taken her house at Cairo; and as I was well enough to be moved, I went, with the Princess's consent, to the Hôtel d'Orient, on the Ezbekeah. I chose this hotel partly because it was within two minutes' walk of Dr Grant's house, and partly because I had just heard of an invalid who had been very well satisfied with the treatment she met with there. I stayed a fortnight, and can fully endorse the same opinion. The attendance was good, and so was the living, and the charges not out of proportion. The chief attraction to me was, however, the close vicinity of my doctor, who was doctor and nurse all in one. The morphia did not *cure* me, but it enabled me to bear the remedies, which I could not have done while the pain continued so acute, and after three weeks from the date of the first attack I was able to return to the harem. It was the 7th of May. I left a great many people at the hotel, as the heat was still quite bearable; indeed the inside of the harem was a delightful temperature.

About a week after my return, three marriages took place at Dabbassaida, the residence of the Prince's mother. They were three of the chief attendants; all received a good dower and trousseau, besides presents of jewellery. One of the brides interested me a good deal. She was a nice-looking person, with very good manners. She was in floods of tears all the day she was to go to her husband's house. When the carriage which took her thither drove into the courtyard the bridegroom was there to receive her. The eunuchs held cashmere shawls to form a sort of covered-way for her to enter the house, but she fainted directly she arrived there. She was a long time recovering, and was then led into a room where she was to receive her husband and be unveiled by him. An old woman was present to tell the bride what to do in her new position. She was perfectly aware that some persons were concealed behind the curtains—persons whose rank did not allow her to dispute their right, even had she been inclined to do so; and perhaps some rustling of silk might have betrayed their vicinity to the bridegroom, and made him feel less at home than he otherwise would have done. At any rate, he went through the prescribed etiquette on such occasions. He entered the room and took his seat; his wife stood up, brought some coffee, and remained standing before him. Sometimes the husband is too gallant to permit this, and refuses to sit unless his wife sits also. But in this case it was a very solemn affair; the bridegroom did not interfere with the prescribed etiquette, feeling probably uneasy at the unseen eyes which he suspected watched all his movements. Then the old woman conducted them into an adjoining room to give the ladies concealed behind the curtains an opportunity of escaping, of which they promptly availed themselves.

A day or two after, the bride came to pay a visit at the palace, and remained the greater part of the day. There was something that puzzled me very much in her appearance and manner. After luncheon I was seated reading in the centre saloon, and (the Princess being out) the bride was walking up and down, with six or seven of the principal slaves. She was evidently undergoing a rigid cross-examination, and her answers elicited bursts of laughter and approbation. I could not help hearing a little as they passed, and what I heard made me pay great attention to the rest. What I am going to relate is no doubt the result of intercourse with European women. First, all the slaves in the great harems insist on being the *sole* wife of the man they marry; and as it is both an honour and advantage for the man, this is always agreed to. Not only has she a dower and annuity for life, but her influence in the harem may be all-important to him in his future career. She always keeps up the connection with her former mistress, and becomes an established and recognised visitor in the house where she formerly served. Secondly, the slaves have begun to wish they could have a little choice themselves in the selection of a husband; but as that cannot be, they have determined to be *wooed* before they are *won*, and as the wooing cannot come before marriage, it shall come after it. This is therefore made a pact among themselves in all the great harems, and any one infringing it would be held to have disgraced all her companions. A day or two after the marriage the bride goes to visit the harem where she had formerly resided, and there has to undergo a strict cross-examination. If she passes it triumphantly every one feels that the position of woman has been raised by her, and she is proportionably elated.

Perhaps the man is a little astonished at this "stand off!" proceeding, which he had never anticipated, or heard of before. He may be angry or even rough—all the worse for him. He has chosen to marry into a great harem, and he must abide by their customs. He had better do the courting with a good grace and get it over, for there's no help for him.

Some months after, this person came to visit the Princess at Ramleh, and was urged to stay the night; but she said her husband was not quite well, and she would not be happy in leaving him, so preferred returning. I hope, therefore, that the marriage had turned out a happy one.

The Prince's health had never been very good since Ramadan, and his Highness (who settles everybody's movements in Egypt) had decided that he should go to Vichy for a month, from thence to England, and remain there until after Ramadan. A European princess would, of course, have accompanied her husband, but a Mahometan woman cannot go into a Christian country. It was finally settled that he should leave Cairo by special train at 4 A.M. on the 25th of May, and embark at nine for Marseilles by the Messageries *via* Naples.

The house was besieged by visitors the day preceding his departure, and he himself seemed to feel his going away as much as if he were going to the North Pole, with a doubtful prospect of ultimate return. It was the first time he had left his country and friends (except once for a short stay at Constantinople), and being of a very affectionate and domestic character, he felt much more the parting from his wife and mother than the pleasure which might await him in new scenes and countries.

It had been settled that the Princess should leave Cairo for Ramleh two days after her husband's departure; but as usual, building was going on, and her palace was not ready for her. His Highness would remain still some time in Cairo, and the first and third Princesses with him; but the second Princess could not bear heat, and she and her daughter (my pupil) were to take up their abode at his Highness's harem at Ramleh until the palace of the Princess should be ready for her reception. For myself, I had the choice of being with my pupil or with friends. As I knew she would do nothing with me while on a visit, I preferred the latter. The departure was of course, as usual, fixed two or three times, and again postponed; but as I could not change the day continually when going to friends, I kept to the third appointment. Talking with one of the Princes in the morning about my intention of leaving by that night's express at 6 P.M., he asked me when I expected to reach Alexandria. I replied that the train was due at 10.30, and that friends would be there to meet me. The Prince remarked I might think myself lucky if I got there at midnight, or even later. This was unpleasant. I knew I could rely on one friend at any rate who had promised to meet me, but I did not like the idea of anybody having to wait for me a couple of hours! It happened, however, that the train reached Alexandria ten minutes before the appointed time. There were very few passengers, so the guard had plenty of time to attend to me. I wanted to remain on the platform until the arrival of my friend, who, I felt sure, would not fail me; but I could speak no Arabic, and the guard understood no other language. He thought the right thing was to hurry me into a carriage with my luggage as quickly as could be managed, and he did so. The station was a long way out of the town, and the night very dark. As soon as the driver heard of my destination he demanded increased fare, and I had no remedy but to agree. We met a number of carriages hurrying to the station, and I felt sure I had friends in one of them; but it was too dark either to see or be seen. By the time I got into the Grand Square the horses began to require considerable persuasion to induce them to move on, but when they reached the foot of the hill nothing could prevail on them to go farther. Seeing that it was hopeless I got out, and was preparing to mount the hill on foot when I saw lights approaching, and a voice called out, " Is that you, Miss Chennells?" I knew then that a friend was at hand who had been to the station to meet me, but our carriages had crossed in the dark.

The Princess stayed about a fortnight in her father's palace at Ramleh, and then, her own being completed, removed thither, and I joined her. Our time passed rather monotonously. Her husband was in Europe. Two of her brothers also had left Egypt, Prince Hassan for Berlin and Prince Hussein for Switzerland. Her own brother, Prince Ibrahim, was also to leave shortly.

His Highness came to Alexandria in July, but chose Ras-el-Tin instead of Ramleh for his residence. Ras-el-Tin is on the west of Alexandria, and Ramleh on the east, and it is a drive of seven or eight miles between the two places. The Princess went often to spend the day at Ras-el-Tin with her father, and Kopsès always accompanied her. On other days we spent the time in reading, talking, and working. The weather was too hot for many visitors to come, so we were generally alone.

I had never thoroughly recovered my attack of rheumatic gout in the spring. The pain had quite left me, but I did not feel the same energy as before, and was disinclined for any exertion. If the Princess went to

Ras-el-Tin, I never stirred out, but sat reading the whole day in a rocking-chair on the balcony. I began to feel that a hot climate had quite changed me. I ceased to go out on the Fridays, and believe I should have given up going out altogether but for an arrangement that was made, that I should go in to Koum-el-Dikke every Saturday evening at sunset, returning early on the Monday morning. As I drove from one house to the other, that did not seem to require much exertion.

One morning the Princess went very early to Ras-el-Tin to breakfast with his Highness and spend the day, Kopsès as usual accompanying her. I sat in the balcony for hours, unable to work or to read, but listlessly rocking myself backwards and forwards. These rocking-chairs had often been the chief exercise of the slaves, but had not hitherto been mine.

The next day the same langour continued, and I could neither eat nor sleep. The Princess observed it, and said I had better go for a few days to my friend Miss Harris to be nursed, to see what change of diet would do for me.

I went, but got no better. As doctors are very expensive in Egypt, and I could not make out what was the matter with me, I thought I would see the harem doctor, and wrote to the Princess to ask her to send him to me. He came, heard my symptoms, and ordered a seidlitz-powder. This scarcely seemed to me sufficient to meet the case, and I told him so, upon which he suggested a bottle of soda-water![1]

On the 9th Ibrahim Pasha, the brother of my pupil, was to leave for Europe with all his suite. I knew this would be a great grief to my Princess, not only on account

---

[1] This was an Arab doctor. Zohrab Bey, the deservedly trusted Armenian doctor, was in England with Prince Ibrahim, the Khédive's favourite son.

of her love for her brother, and regret at parting from him, but also as a vivid reminder of her lost liberty. Formerly, wherever he went, she went too; her liberty had been as great as his. Now it was all changed, and never could be otherwise for her, she often said, and felt.

A day or two after, I went to see her. I was no better; I could neither eat nor sleep, and was very feverish; but although very much disinclined to exertion, I was not incapable of going out—at any rate, of driving out. I remained some hours with my dear pupil, and we talked together much. She seemed so thoughtful for others, and so anxious to do right, that I went away quite impressed by it. Miss Harris had taken a little house at Ramleh quite close to the sea, and was going to move into it in a day or two; and it seemed to me that if I could spend a few days there, close to the murmur of the waves, I should get back sleep and strength, and be all right again. The Princess thought so too—at any rate, she said it was worth the trial.

I had known a good many people whose strength had given way in a hot climate, and friends had said to me, "You will not feel it so much, as long as you have the change to Constantinople every year." The first two summers I had been to the Bosphorus, and had kept well. Now these same friends would say to me, "You have been two years in Egypt without leaving it, and you will not get well unless you have a complete change. Ask the Princess to give you a holiday of a couple of months, and go to Europe for that time." I began to think of this seriously, and to believe that my friends were right. But I was very unwilling to leave her, and I put off from day to day making the request. "After all," I said to myself, "what is the matter with me? I am not in pain; I can neither sleep nor eat, but I am not hungry; so what does it matter?" But at night, as I lay awake hour after hour, I felt much more despondent. The murmur of the waves did not revive me. I heard them night and day, and they did not soothe me in the least.

CHAPTER XXXII.

Illness of the Princess—Her death.

I had been about a fortnight in this state, going very often to see the Princess, when I found her one day suffering much from the throat. It was a complaint to which she had all her life been liable, an enlargement of the uvula, which would sometimes swell so much as to touch the larynx and nearly choke her. When suffering from this she could not lie down; but instead of being propped up by pillows, two or three of her chief attendants took by turns to recline behind her and support her,—a most uncomfortable position, I should say, for both, as in a hot climate the close proximity of another person for hours must be anything but agreeable. The Princess was far too gentle and unselfish to desire any one to suffer inconvenience on her account, but she had been subject to this illness from early childhood, and the slaves had always accustomed her to this propping up, so she made no resistance. Presently the doctor arrived, and gave her a gargle, which always relieved her for a time; but the swelling would only go down as the cold left her, and that often lasted for a long time. There was a remedy for all this suffering, as an instrument has been invented which, being put down the throat, cuts off this excrescence as quickly as a pair of scissors would cut a thread; but naturally she did not much like the idea of this operation. I remained with her a couple of hours, and she seemed unwilling to part with me. At sunset the carriage was announced, and I said I could not keep Miss Harris waiting for me. The Princess said she would like to see Miss Harris, so the latter came in. I had often told my female friends how much prettier my pupil looked in her simple harem costume, with her beautiful hair bound back with a ribbon, than in an elaborate tight-fitting European dress, and a scaffolding on her head of curls, plaits, and diamonds.

After this visit I did not go to the palace for four days. I felt getting worse, and was in despair what to do with myself. There seemed no complaint, but sleeplessness, total loss of appetite, and debility. Two days after I had been to the palace his Highness went to Cairo. I was told that he had left his own physician in charge of the Princess, and that the latter had said there was nothing to prevent her following his Highness to Cairo in a few days. I heard every day of the telegrams sent to Cairo. They represented the Princess's indisposition as nothing at all serious; and as she had often suffered in a similar manner, I had no reason to think this attack different from others.

After four days I went again to the palace, and was startled by the scene that met my eyes on entering. The saloons were quite full of persons, most of them seated and silent. The mother of my pupil was there, and several of her attendants, but the Princess herself was not visible. I found she was in her dressing-room, and I was going towards it when I met her in the ante-room. She was supported by two of her slaves, and was moaning pitifully. She gave me a sad look as she passed, but did not speak. In the saloons several silk mattresses were laid down for her to recline upon, and she sank down on one. Nobody spoke, glances of sympathy were exchanged, and no sound was heard but the moaning of the poor sick child. A slave knelt down with a tray to offer her food, but she turned away from it. All the windows to the north were carefully closed; it was oppressively hot, and the rooms were crowded. Kopsès passed near me, and I asked her what ailed the Princess, as I knew nothing of her being in this state. Kopsès only replied, "She is VERY ill!" Presently I inquired of some one else if the Princess was still suffering from the throat, and was told, "No; she was very feverish, and could neither eat nor sleep." These appeared exactly like my own symptoms. I sat there about an hour; the silence and heat were very oppressive. I felt I only added to the number of persons, without being able to do anything for the sufferer, so I came away. This was Tuesday morning. I heard later in the day of the telegram sent to his Highness, which was to the effect that the Princess was not seriously indisposed, and would be able to go to Cairo in a day or two.

The next day I heard that the same telegram had been sent, and as my strength seemed to be failing me, I made up my mind that I would ask for leave of absence, and go to Europe by the next boat, as I felt that if I deferred it much longer I might be too weak to bear the fatigue of travelling alone and unaided.

I thought I would go again in a day or two to the harem; and as the Princess might very soon move to Cairo, I determined to write a letter, in which I would explain all I had to say, and if she were already gone, the letter should be forwarded at once, that no time might be lost.

The next night was again sleepless, and I got up at daybreak, determined to write the letter, and to go later on to the palace, to speak to the Princess if I had an opportunity, and if not, to leave my letter with Kopsès. I was a long time dressing, and then writing my letter. Miss Harris was not an early riser, but just as I had finished she came into my room, and I told her what I had done.

"You had better wait a little," said she; "there has been another telegram sent to Cairo in the night."

"What!" exclaimed I, "you don't mean to say the Princess is in danger!"

"Worse than that, I am afraid!"

"How can it be worse," said I, impatiently, "unless she were already dead?"

"She IS dead!!!"

I sat stunned and speechless, quite unable to realise the blow.

"I must go," said I at last—"I must go to the palace directly; but how? I cannot walk! there's no getting a carriage here!"

"I will ask Mrs M'Killup to lend you hers," said Miss Harris. It was through this lady that the news had come; her husband, Admiral M'Killup, had received orders that all flags in the harbour should be hoisted half-mast high—there could be no mistake! In half an hour the carriage was at the door, and I drove to the palace. It was settled between us that Miss Harris should order a carriage from Alexandria to fetch me away from the harem. It would never be my home again; and painful as would be the task, and unfit as I was to do it, everything belonging to me must be packed up and removed from the palace within a few hours, or I should risk losing all I possessed! I knew very well that before four-and-twenty hours were over the palace would be deserted!

The carriage passed through the outer and inner courts

without opposition, and stopped at the harem gates. It was Mrs M'Killup's *saïs* who drove me, and as the horses were very spirited, he got down and stood at their heads. I was hardly able to get out, partly from weakness and partly from agitation. Half-a-dozen eunuchs sat by the gates, but not one stirred to help me. Perhaps they were as much stunned by the shock as I was. The loss was a heavy one to them also. As I passed through the double gates, such sounds from within struck my ears as harrowed me to the soul, as did also the sight which met my eyes. The Princess's slaves were all sitting or lying about, in the unrestrained grief always indulged in by untutored natures. There were no hired mourners. Their demonstrations were frantic, but genuine. They had most of them been about the person of their dear mistress from her infancy; where would they ever meet with another so kind and good? But this was not all. They knew the fate that awaited them; they knew that it was considered *unlucky* in other households to have slaves who had lost their mistress through death! All prospect of future advancement was gone; the rest of their lives would be passed in strict seclusion, without hope of change! Some tore their hair and shrieked; others sat on the floor sobbing; others, again, rolled about in agony. I spoke to one or two, but they did not answer me; their faces were swollen and distorted with grief. This was all in the entrance-saloon. I could not go farther! I sat down, hoping soon to see Kopsès. I knew the loss to her would be terrible, but she had more self-restraint than these poor girls! At last Mlle. Caroline (the Princess's Italian dressmaker) entered, and seeing me, came at once to me. She was crying, as every one else was, but had more command over her feelings than the poor slaves. She gave me an account of all that had passed, as far as she had herself witnessed.

After I left the Princess on the Tuesday, she continued in the same state, and passed a sleepless night. Still the doctor thought the illness a slight one, and that she would soon be better. On the Wednesday her mind wandered, and she fancied his Highness was still at Ras-el-Tin. Seeing Mlle. Caroline (whom she always associated with millinery), she told her to bring the last dress which she had finished and put it on the *mannequin*, that she (the Princess) might judge of its effect. She would wear it the next day, she said, when she went to see his Highness. The dress was brought, placed upon the *mannequin*, and in the dreadful change which occurred soon after, was put into *my* room, and was the first thing that struck my eyes on entering! On that evening the Princess begged for a sleeping-draught! She had not slept for three or four nights, nor had any of her immediate attendants, and she was worn out. She had a good deal of fever, and the doctor laid great stress upon perspiration coming on; she was to be kept covered, and the symptoms of perspiration were to be carefully watched. He gave the draught, and then went away. At 10 P.M. the Princess was asleep, and everybody hailed the symptom. The second Princess, who had stayed with her daughter since the departure of his Highness, went to bed in the adjoining room, desiring to be called immediately if perspiration came on. There was no thought of danger; every one rejoiced that the Princess slept. The *dada* had a mattress close by the bed, and the chief slaves were scattered about in the bedroom and the ante-rooms adjoining. Lanterns were burning in the passages and ante-rooms. In the middle of the night the *dada* rose and went to the bed to feel if perspiration was coming on. She might already have done so many times, but on this occasion there was something in the touch of that hand which startled her. She fetched a lantern, looked at the face, and saw that all was over!

She shrieked aloud, and in a moment all were around her. The poor mother was awoke by the cry; she ran to her daughter's bed, gave one look, and then rushed distracted into the harem court shrieking " Hekim! hekim!" (doctor! doctor!) The doctor was found, but he could not reanimate that prostrate form! he said the illness had turned to typhoid fever! My informant added that she was awoke by the most fearful cries, and that she got up immediately and hurried across the court to the Princess's apartments. The face was then, she said, calm and sweet as in life, but she had just heard that a terrible change had come over it within the last hour or two, and as I was weak and ill, I had better not go to see it. I felt the same, and did not go.

Mlle. Caroline told me it was about 4 A.M. when all this happened, and that directly after the doctor had pronounced all hope gone, the distracted mother had left the house with all her attendants. She had taken Kopsès with her, and they were to go to Cairo that very day. The body was to be removed in the afternoon, to be conveyed by special train to Cairo. The slaves and eunuchs would probably leave the following morning.

I asked Mlle. Caroline what she was going to do herself. She said she should go to Cairo with the harem, as she did not know what else to do for the present, and that if she could assist me with my luggage by taking care of it until I was able to take charge of it myself, she would be glad to do so.

My head was distracted; I did not feel equal to anything, but I knew there was much to do, and that it must be done. I went into my room, but found I could do nothing there. The door had been unlocked which opened from my room into the Princess's dressing-room. The body was lying in the latter, and my room was made use of as a passage. The wardrobe, drawers, trunks, &c., were all placed in the middle of the room, and the first thing that met my eyes was the *mannequin* in the dress which my dear pupil had proposed wearing for her next visit to her father! Lugubrious sounds were going on in the dressing-room, and I came out again into the saloon, feeling it quite impossible, with the presence of Death so near me, to do what I had to do.

The day wore wearily on. Men kept passing through accompanied by the eunuchs, who vainly tried to remove any slaves who might be in the way. They were past all fear of showing themselves, and sobbed and cried without intermission. At last at 4 P.M. the bier was slowly brought out, carried through the rooms, down the steps, and out of the harem gates! There was a fresh outbreak of grief, which soon gave way to utter exhaustion, and then a silence, as great as had been the previous wailing, fell on all. A eunuch came in and announced that everything was to be packed and removed to Cairo the next morning, and that then everybody would leave the harem. The slaves heard him, but they took no notice; they lay about on the ground, perfectly inanimate, and he passed on farther. I felt that I now *must* begin, and went back into my room. I heard through the closed doors the sheikhs chanting the Koran in the adjoining chamber, and was nearly maddened at the sound. What that packing was I shall never forget! Any sort of order or method was impossible. The contents of the wardrobe and drawers were thrown into the boxes and pressed down. At last I had finished, and then I began to look uneasily out for the carriage which Miss Harris had promised to send for me. I could not see it from the windows of my room, and tried to persuade a slave whom I met in the court to inquire of the eunuchs if a carriage were waiting without. She looked at me vacantly, as if not understanding me. The palace had been enlarged this summer, and after going out of the harem gates there were two courts to pass through before reaching the outer world. There was an archway at the chief entrance, and I could see that all the eunuchs were seated there, and a number of men with them. I could not bear to pass through all this concourse of men, and seeing a little eunuch, begged him to go to the gates and look if a carriage was without waiting for me. He came back presently, saying that there was no carriage there; but I had afterwards reason to believe that he had not been through the gates. I went back into the harem, and having begged Mlle. Caroline to look after my luggage and see that it was locked up in my room in the palace at Cairo, I came out again, feeling that I should die also if I stayed the night within those walls where death had so lately been.

The sun had already set, and darkness soon comes on in these latitudes. The house by the sea which Miss Harris had taken was about a mile and a half distant across the desert, but if it became too dark I might lose my way, and then I was afraid of the wild dogs. So I determined to walk along the line, which would take me to the next station, and then I could go into some friend's house, and get a guide and a donkey to take me to Miss Harris. No food whatever had entered the harem all day, but I did not feel the want of food.

When I got into the outer court of the palace and looked towards the archway, I felt an invincible repugnance to passing through the throng of men and eunuchs collected there. I saw a little door on the east side, which was used by the workmen and was half open, and I reflected that by going through that I should save a considerable detour, and get down more easily to the railway, besides getting out of the palace unobserved. I walked along the line to Bulkeley station, and then went into the house of some friends living there, and begged them to procure for me a donkey and guide to take me to Miss Harris's cottage by the sea. This was done promptly, and I arrived there safely.

About an hour after, the driver came with the carriage (which Miss Harris had ordered for me) to give her an account of what he had done, and how he had failed to find me. He said he arrived at the palace at 5 P.M.; and as he was known to the doorkeeper as being in the habit of driving me, he was about to pass through the entrance-archway, when he was stopped and told he must remain without. He was aware that it was impossible for me to know that he was there unless the eunuchs told me; and as sunset approached, he begged them to do so, but they paid no attention. Darkness came on, and the gates were about to be closed, when he again urged them so strongly that one consented to go in and tell me, but never returned; and the gates being shut, the driver went on to Miss Harris's cottage to give his account, and also to look after his day's hire.

I passed again a sleepless night, grief and anxiety being added to my previous illness. It would be impossible for me now to go away for change of air, as I had hoped to do. I was still in the service; and how in the general grief could I urge an immediate settlement of my claims? to whom could I address myself? There was no one. I must wait patiently. Then I anxiously remembered that everything I possessed was in the harem: some things in the palace at Ramleh, the rest at Cairo. Who could be responsible for their safety? That was a question I could not answer satisfactorily. Then I suddenly remembered that I had left some of my jewels, and also money, in a secret drawer belonging to a writing-table, in my room. It had a good patent-lock, and I had always carried the keys about with me. But I had an indistinct remembrance of having opened this drawer, intending to take the money and jewels out, and that I had not done so; also, that afterwards wanting the keys for some other lock, I had taken them out and left the drawer unlocked! I had been in such a state of agitation that I hardly knew what I was doing; and besides, at last the carriage had failed me and darkness had come on.

These considerations disturbed me so much that I went off soon after daybreak to the palace, and found the court-yards full of soldiers watching the transport of the luggage. Caroline was there looking after her own. I said a few hasty words to her, begging her not to allow mine to go out of the court, as I wished to keep it at Alexandria, and then went to my room. I found the drawer unlocked, as I had thought, but the money and jewels were untouched. I took possession of them, and came out again, gave orders that my trunks should be taken to Koum-el-Dikke, and not to Cairo, which order was strictly attended to; and then having begged Mlle. Caroline to look after the things I had left in the palace at Cairo, I went back to the little cottage by the sea, to think over my future plans.

CHAPTER XXXIII.

Funeral of the Princess—Conclusion.

The Princess Zeyneb had died on the 19th of August, and on the same afternoon her mortal remains were conveyed to Cairo.

On the 20th, at an early hour, the funeral *cortége* left Kasr-el-Nil (palace on the Nile) for the new mosque (still uncompleted) situated near the Citadel, and opposite to the mosque of Sultan Hassan. This was the order of the procession, as told me by eyewitnesses, for it will be remembered that I was still at Ramleh :—

1. Twenty-four buffaloes.
(To be slaughtered after the funeral, and the meat distributed to the people.)

2. Twenty-four camels.
(Laden with dates, bread, and fruit, to be thrown from time to time among the people.)

3. Six water-carts.

4. A number of porters carrying pitchers for drinking.

5. Infantry band, but not playing.

6. Infantry lining the street in two files, while the following religious and civil corporations passed between them :—
Sect of dervishes chanting, and carrying flags.
Sheikhs and Arab merchants.
Pupils of Arab schools.
More sheikhs.
Pupils of military schools.

7. Moslem sheikhs and Christian [1] priests.

8. Men and boys with incense.

9. A boy carrying the Koran.

10. THE BIER
(covered with the richest cashmere shawls, on which were sewn all the jewels belonging to the deceased).

11. Immediately behind it
the Brothers and Brothers-in-law of the deceased, and around them and behind them the chief dignitaries of the State and of the Household, with foreign consuls, merchants, chief residents, &c.

12. Eighteen harem carriages containing the female relatives of the deceased.

The newspapers of the day said that upwards of 200,000 persons followed the funeral. Whether this number was

[1] When the priests of different Christian sects asked permission of the Khédive to follow the Princess's funeral, his Highness replied, "All serve the same God, and I desire the prayers of *all* in behalf of my daughter."

over-estimated or not, I cannot tell. I know that never was mourning more general or grief more sincere. The gentle unassuming manners of the Princess, as well as her real goodness of heart, had made her universally beloved by all who approached her. Her own mother seemed almost to lose her reason in presence of this great affliction, and has never yet recovered it. The Khédive was stunned by it; but he has immense energy of character, and though he felt it as a man, he bore it also as one. He was often seen, in the intervals of business, with eyes full of tears and fixed on the ground. A gentleman repeated these words to me which the Khédive had spoken to him in alluding to his lost daughter: "She was the light of my eyes: she had a better influence over me than any one else; and that I ascribe entirely to the excellent English training she had for so many years." To the Mahometan women of Egypt the loss of this dear young lady cannot be too highly estimated. The efforts which his Highness makes to promote female education would have been doubly efficacious enhanced by the example of his daughter.

In ordinary Eastern households, when the mistress of a family dies, her slaves are probably sold, and the new mistress knows nothing of where her new purchase lived before, or with whom. In great harems, such as those belonging to the Khédive, the slaves are never, or very rarely, sold again; but if any of them are unfortunate enough to lose their mistress by death, it is very difficult for them to find another, as there is a great prejudice against them as bringing ill-luck. The Khédive himself is far too enlightened to entertain such ideas; but he cannot openly overrule strong prejudices, especially when they exist among those who are near and dear to him. So the second Princess, in her distracted grief, refused to see any one that had belonged to the household of her beloved daughter; and I am not sure that even Kopsès would have been excepted, but that after a month or so any such prejudice with regard to her was wisely overruled. She has ever since been the constant companion and devoted attendant of the desolate mother, who still lives in the strictest seclusion.[1] The rest of the Princess's household live in a large house at Abbassieh, quite apart —house and maintenance provided for them—and perhaps some day they will be married. As slaves they would always have been "shut up," but while their mistress lived they shared to a certain extent in all the *fêtes* and amusements which might be going on.

It may be asked, Where were the Princess's husband and her own brother during this time? The former was in England, and the latter in Italy; but the catastrophe was so sudden and unexpected, and her illness had been so short, that they had heard nothing of it. The births, marriages, and deaths in a Mahometan royal family are not chronicled as they are among Europeans; and although under the impulse of the moment his Highness had telegraphed to his son and son-in-law to return immediately (suppressing, however, the death of the Princess), he determined, a few hours after, that as both had gone for health, they should remain a little longer, and be kept in ignorance, in the meanwhile, of the loss which had befallen them.

They returned about a month after. All their suite were then aware of the death of the Princess, but had been charged to conceal it, and their continual movement from one place to another was given as sufficient reason for the non-arrival of letters. When they landed at Alexandria a special train awaited them to conduct them to Cairo; and there again, at the station, carriages were

[1] This was written in 1877, before the deposition of Ismael Pasha, which took place in 1879. Many changes have taken place since !

in attendance to take them to Gezireh, where, they were told, they would meet the whole family assembled. Those were his Highness's orders! that was quite enough for them. Then, when all were assembled, his Highness told them, with a breaking heart, of the loss that had befallen them! A gentleman who was much about the Prince related to me what passed, and said that the grief of the young widower was so violent that they feared for his reason! I saw him a few days after, and he was then quite calm, though sad. He inquired most minutely into every circumstance of the illness and death, and I told him all that I knew.

I remained at Ramleh a few days after my pupil's death, quite overcome with all I had gone through, and the low fever and sleeplessness continuing. I then came up to Cairo, telegraphed to Dr Grant to meet me at the station, and went at once to Shepheard's Hotel, where I kept my room for nearly a month. One of the peculiarities attending illness in a hot climate is the long time which the patient takes to rally after the attack is over.

By the time I had recovered my strength the autumn was far advanced, and the change to a colder country was no longer desirable. My contract still held good, and I waited orders. I heard that his Highness intended to employ me again, and at first the idea was insupportable to me. I felt so shattered in health, and I had been so much attached to my dear pupil, that I could not bear to undertake another. Gradually, however, I familiarised myself with the thought; but it was not to be. The loss of his beloved daughter was the beginning of the series of misfortunes which have since befallen the Khédive. They are well known to all my readers, and I need not recapitulate them.

Forty days is the longest period of mourning ever known among Mahometans. These forty days were most strictly kept. They sat in darkened rooms, mute images of woe. Then came an interval of one day, and Ramadan began, kept more strictly than ever!

Ramadan ended on the 30th of October. I had not seen the Khédive's wives, as they had lived in the strictest seclusion, so I felt I *must* go to the Baïram. I had seen the Princess Saïd several times, also the Princess Ahmed (mother-in-law of my dear pupil), as also some of the younger Princesses, but the wives had received no one hitherto.

I had heard that the Khédive had forbidden black, saying that mourning was in the heart, and not in the colour of the garments. I do not know if this were true; at any rate it made me feel very doubtful what to wear at the Baïram. I could not bear to go in colours, but did not wish to offend by wearing black, if indeed it had been forbidden. So I chose a dark-grey silk, with a black hat and white feather.

When I went into the courtyard there was not a single carriage there. The slaves were all dressed either in white with black bands, or in grey linen, or black-and-white striped cottons. Only the first Princess showed herself, very plainly dressed in white, and she wept the whole time I was there! It was the same in all the other harems, and except that it was a religious *fête*, I believe the Baïram would not have been observed at all.

At the Kourban Baïram, which began on the 6th of January (1876), I again visited all the royal harems with some European ladies. In all, the same sombre colours prevailed, an entire absence of jewels, and of *fantasia* of any description. One of the Princesses was dressed in black velvet trimmed with ermine, one or two others in black and white silks, none in gay colours. This was so entirely at variance with all former habits that I cannot but note it. Up to the 10th of January none of the Princes nor any of the harem had visited the opera. His Highness did not go, and of course none of the *employés* in his service cared to go. Then I believe a representation was made to the Khédive of the injury done to the *artistes* by this total abstention from all places of amusement, and his Highness went one night with two or three of his sons.

The hotels were very full throughout the winter, but those who came expecting to see the usual gay life of Cairo were disappointed.

I remained in Egypt a year after the death of the Princess, and then left it with deep regret. There is a fascination in the country, felt, I think, by most persons who have visited it. Its beautiful climate, its wonderful Biblical and historical associations, combine to give it an attraction surpassing that of all other countries. There is a proverb, "He who has drunk of the Nile water will long to taste it again;" and it is a proverb which I think most travellers and residents in Egypt will fully endorse.

THE END.

PRINTED BY WILLIAM BLACKWOOD AND SONS.

Catalogue

of

Messrs Blackwood & Sons' Publications

PHILOSOPHICAL CLASSICS FOR ENGLISH READERS.
Edited by WILLIAM KNIGHT, LL.D.,
Professor of Moral Philosophy in the University of St Andrews.

In crown 8vo Volumes, with Portraits, price 3s. 6d.

Contents of the Series.

Descartes, by Professor Mahaffy, Dublin.—Butler, by Rev. W. Lucas Collins, M.A.—Berkeley, by Professor Campbell Fraser.—Fichte, by Professor Adamson, Owens College, Manchester. — Kant, by Professor Wallace, Oxford.—Hamilton, by Professor Veitch, Glasgow. — Hegel, by Professor Edward Caird, Glasgow.—Leibniz, by J. Theodore Merz.—Vico, by Professor Flint, Edinburgh.—Hobbes, by Professor Croom Robertson.—Hume, by the Editor.—Spinoza, by the Very Rev. Principal Caird, Glasgow.—Bacon: Part I. The Life, by Professor Nichol.—Bacon: Part II. Philosophy, by the same Author. Locke, by Professor Campbell Fraser.

FOREIGN CLASSICS FOR ENGLISH READERS.
Edited by Mrs OLIPHANT.

In crown 8vo, 2s. 6d.

Contents of the Series.

Dante, by the Editor.—Voltaire, by General Sir E. B. Hamley, K.C.B.—Pascal, by Principal Tulloch.—Petrarch, by Henry Reeve, C.B.—Goethe, by A. Hayward, Q.C.—Molière, by the Editor and F. Tarver, M.A.—Montaigne, by Rev. W. L. Collins, M.A.—Rabelais, by Walter Besant, M.A.—Calderon, by E. J. Hasell.—Saint Simon, by Clifton W. Collins, M.A.—Cervantes, by the Editor. — Corneille and Racine, by Henry M. Trollope. — Madame de Sévigné, by Miss Thackeray.—La Fontaine, and other French Fabulists, by Rev. W. Lucas Collins, M.A.—Schiller, by James Sime, M.A., Author of 'Lessing, his Life and Writings.'—Tasso, by E. J. Hasell.—Rousseau, by Henry Grey Graham.—Alfred de Musset, by C. F. Oliphant.

ANCIENT CLASSICS FOR ENGLISH READERS.
Edited by the Rev. W. LUCAS COLLINS, M.A.

Complete in 28 Vols. crown 8vo, cloth, price 2s. 6d. each. And may also be had in 14 Volumes, strongly and neatly bound, with calf or vellum back, £3, 10s.

Contents of the Series.

Homer: The Iliad, by the Editor.—Homer: The Odyssey, by the Editor.—Herodotus, by George C. Swayne, M.A.—Xenophon, by Sir Alexander Grant, Bart., LL.D.—Euripides, by W. B. Donne.—Aristophanes, by the Editor.—Plato, by Clifton W. Collins, M.A.—Lucian, by the Editor.—Æschylus, by the Right Rev. the Bishop of Colombo.—Sophocles, by Clifton W. Collins, M.A.—Hesiod and Theognis, by the Rev. J. Davies, M.A.—Greek Anthology, by Lord Neaves.—Virgil, by the Editor.—Horace, by Sir Theodore Martin, K.C.B.—Juvenal, by Edward Walford, M.A.—Plautus and Terence, by the Editor—The Commentaries of Cæsar, by Anthony Trollope.—Tacitus, by W. B. Donne.—Cicero, by the Editor. — Pliny's Letters, by the Rev. Alfred Church, M.A., and the Rev. W. J. Brodribb, M.A. — Livy, by the Editor.—Ovid, by the Rev. A. Church, M.A.—Catullus, Tibullus, and Propertius, by the Rev. Jas. Davies, M.A. — Demosthenes, by the Rev. W. J. Brodribb, M.A.—Aristotle, by Sir Alexander Grant, Bart., LL.D.—Thucydides, by the Editor.—Lucretius, by W. H. Mallock, M.A.—Pindar, by the Rev. F. D. Morice, M.A.

Saturday Review.—"It is difficult to estimate too highly the value of such a series as this in giving 'English readers' an insight, exact as far as it goes, into those olden times which are so remote, and yet to many of us so close."

CATALOGUE

OF

MESSRS BLACKWOOD & SONS'
PUBLICATIONS.

ALISON.
   History of Europe. By Sir ARCHIBALD ALISON, Bart., D.C.L.
   1. From the Commencement of the French Revolution to
      the Battle of Waterloo.
      LIBRARY EDITION, 14 vols., with Portraits. Demy 8vo, £10, 10s.
      ANOTHER EDITION, in 20 vols. crown 8vo, £6.
      PEOPLE'S EDITION, 13 vols. crown 8vo, £2, 11s.
   2. Continuation to the Accession of Louis Napoleon.
      LIBRARY EDITION, 8 vols. 8vo, £6, 7s. 6d.
      PEOPLE'S EDITION, 8 vols. crown 8vo, 34s.
   Epitome of Alison's History of Europe. Thirtieth Thousand, 7s. 6d.
   Atlas to Alison's History of Europe. By A. Keith Johnston.
      LIBRARY EDITION, demy 4to, £3, 3s.
      PEOPLE'S EDITION, 31s. 6d.
   Life of John Duke of Marlborough. With some Account of
      his Contemporaries, and of the War of the Succession. Third Edition. 2 vols.
      8vo. Portraits and Maps, 30s.
   Essays : Historical, Political, and Miscellaneous. 3 vols.
      demy 8vo, 45s.
ACROSS FRANCE IN A CARAVAN : BEING SOME ACCOUNT
   OF A JOURNEY FROM BORDEAUX TO GENOA IN THE "ESCARGOT," taken in the Winter
   1889-90. By the Author of 'A Day of my Life at Eton.' With fifty Illustrations
   by John Wallace, after Sketches by the Author, and a Map. Demy 8vo, 15s.
ACTA SANCTORUM HIBERNIÆ ; Ex Codice Salmanticensi.
   Nunc primum integre edita opera CAROLI DE SMEDT et JOSEPHI DE BACKER, e
   Soc. Jesu, Hagiographorum Bollandianorum ; Auctore et Sumptus Largiente
   JOANNE PATRICIO MARCHIONE BOTHAE. In One handsome 4to Volume, bound in
   half roxburghe, £2, 2s.; in paper cover, 31s. 6d.
AGRICULTURAL HOLDINGS ACT, 1883. With Notes by a
   MEMBER OF THE HIGHLAND AND AGRICULTURAL SOCIETY. 8vo, 3s. 6d.
AIKMAN.
   Manures and the Principles of Manuring. By C. M. AIKMAN,
      B.Sc., F.R.S.E., &c. Lecturer on Agricultural Chemistry, West of Scotland
      Technical College ; Examiner in Chemistry, University of Glasgow. Crown 8vo.
      [*Shortly.*

AIKMAN.
Farmyard Manure: Its Nature, Composition, and Treatment.
Crown 8vo, 1s. 6d.

AIRD. Poetical Works of Thomas Aird. Fifth Edition, with
Memoir of the Author by the Rev. JARDINE WALLACE, and Portrait. Crown 8vo, 7s. 6d.

ALLARDYCE.
The City of Sunshine. By ALEXANDER ALLARDYCE. Three
vols. post 8vo, £1, 5s. 6d.

Memoir of the Honourable George Keith Elphinstone, K.B.,
Viscount Keith of Stonehaven, Marischal, Admiral of the Red. 8vo, with Portrait, Illustrations, and Maps, 21s.

ALMOND. Sermons by a Lay Head-master. By HELY HUTCH-
INSON ALMOND, M.A. Oxon., Head-master of Loretto School. Crown 8vo, 5s.

ANCIENT CLASSICS FOR ENGLISH READERS. Edited
by Rev. W. LUCAS COLLINS, M.A. Price 2s. 6d. each. For List of Vols., see p. 2.

ANNALS OF A FISHING VILLAGE. By "A SON OF THE
MARSHES." See page 28.

AYTOUN.
Lays of the Scottish Cavaliers, and other Poems. By W.
EDMONDSTOUNE AYTOUN, D.C.L., Professor of Rhetoric and Belles-Lettres in the University of Edinburgh. New Edition. Fcap. 8vo, 3s. 6d.
ANOTHER EDITION. Fcap. 8vo, 7s. 6d.
CHEAP EDITION. 1s. Cloth, 1s. 3d.

An Illustrated Edition of the Lays of the Scottish Cavaliers.
From designs by Sir NOEL PATON. Small 4to, in gilt cloth, 21s.

Bothwell: a Poem. Third Edition. Fcap., 7s. 6d.

Poems and Ballads of Goethe. Translated by Professor
AYTOUN and Sir THEODORE MARTIN, K.C.B. Third Edition. Fcap., 6s.

Bon Gaultier's Book of Ballads. By the SAME. Fifteenth
Edition. With Illustrations by Doyle, Leech, and Crowquill. Fcap. 8vo, 5s.

The Ballads of Scotland. Edited by Professor AYTOUN.
Fourth Edition. 2 vols. fcap. 8vo, 12s.

Memoir of William E. Aytoun, D.C.L. By Sir THEODORE
MARTIN, K.C.B. With Portrait. Post 8vo, 12s.

BACH.
On Musical Education and Vocal Culture. By ALBERT B.
BACH. Fourth Edition. 8vo, 7s. 6d.

The Principles of Singing. A Practical Guide for Vocalists
and Teachers. With Course of Vocal Exercises. Crown 8vo, 6s.

The Art of Singing. With Musical Exercises for Young
People. Crown 8vo, 3s.

The Art Ballad: Loewe and Schubert. With Music Illustrations. With a Portrait of LOEWE. Third Edition. Small 4to, 5s.

BAIRD LECTURES.
Theism. By Rev. Professor FLINT, D.D., Edinburgh. Eighth
Edition. Crown 8vo, 7s. 6d.

Anti-Theistic Theories. By Rev. Professor FLINT, D.D., Edinburgh. Fourth Edition. Crown 8vo, 10s. 6d.

BAIRD LECTURES.
The Early Religion of Israel. As set forth by Biblical Writers and modern Critical Historians. By Rev. Professor ROBERTSON, D.D., Glasgow. Third Edition. Crown 8vo, 10s. 6d.

The Inspiration of the Holy Scriptures. By Rev. ROBERT JAMIESON, D.D. Crown 8vo, 7s. 6d.

The Mysteries of Christianity. By Rev. Professor CRAWFORD, D.D. Crown 8vo, 7s. 6d.

Endowed Territorial Work: Its Supreme Importance to the Church and Country. By Rev. WILLIAM SMITH, D.D. Crown 8vo, 6s.

BALLADS AND POEMS. By MEMBERS OF THE GLASGOW BALLAD CLUB. Crown 8vo, 7s. 6d.

BANNATYNE. Handbook of Republican Institutions in the
United States of America. Based upon Federal and State Laws, and other reliable sources of information. By DUGALD J. BANNATYNE, Scotch Solicitor, New York; Member of the Faculty of Procurators, Glasgow. Crown 8vo, 7s. 6d.

BELLAIRS.
The Transvaal War, 1880-81. Edited by Lady BELLAIRS. With a Frontispiece and Map. 8vo, 15s.

Gossips with Girls and Maidens, Betrothed and Free. New Edition. Crown 8vo, 3s. 6d. Cloth, extra gilt edges, 5s.

BELLESHEIM. History of the Catholic Church of Scotland.
From the Introduction of Christianity to the Present Day. By ALPHONS BELLESHEIM, D.D., Canon of Aix-la-Chapelle. Translated, with Notes and Additions, by D. OSWALD HUNTER BLAIR, O.S.B., Monk of Fort Augustus. Complete in 4 vols. demy 8vo, with Maps. Price 12s. 6d. each.

BENTINCK. Racing Life of Lord George Cavendish Bentinck,
M.P., and other Reminiscences. By JOHN KENT, Private Trainer to the Goodwood Stable. Edited by the Hon. FRANCIS LAWLEY. With Twenty-three full-page Plates, and Facsimile Letter. Second Edition. Demy 8vo, 25s.

BESANT.
The Revolt of Man. By WALTER BESANT. Tenth Edition. Crown 8vo, 3s. 6d.

Readings in Rabelais. Crown 8vo, 7s. 6d.

BEVERIDGE.
Culross and Tulliallan; or Perthshire on Forth. Its History and Antiquities. With Elucidations of Scottish Life and Character from the Burgh and Kirk-Session Records of that District. By DAVID BEVERIDGE. 2 vols. 8vo, with Illustrations, 42s.

Between the Ochils and the Forth; or, From Stirling Bridge to Aberdour. Crown 8vo, 6s.

BIRCH.
Examples of Stables, Hunting-Boxes, Kennels, Racing Establishments, &c. By JOHN BIRCH, Architect, Author of 'Country Architecture,' &c. With 30 Plates. Royal 8vo, 7s.

Examples of Labourers' Cottages, &c. With Plans for Improving the Dwellings of the Poor in Large Towns. With 34 Plates. Royal 8vo, 7s.

Picturesque Lodges. A Series of Designs for Gate Lodges, Park Entrances, Keepers', Gardeners', Bailiffs', Grooms', Upper and Under Servants' Lodges, and other Rural Residences. With 16 Plates. 4to, 12s. 6d.

BLACK. Heligoland and the Islands of the North Sea. By
WILLIAM GEORGE BLACK. Crown 8vo, 4s.

List of Books Published by

BLACKIE.
Lays and Legends of Ancient Greece. By JOHN STUART BLACKIE, Emeritus Professor of Greek in the University of Edinburgh. Second Edition. Fcap. 8vo, 5s.
The Wisdom of Goethe. Fcap. 8vo. Cloth, extra gilt, 6s.
Scottish Song: Its Wealth, Wisdom, and Social Significance. Crown 8vo. With Music. 7s. 6d.
A Song of Heroes. Crown 8vo, 6s.

BLACKMORE. The Maid of Sker. By R. D. BLACKMORE, Author of 'Lorna Doone,' &c. New Edition. Crown 8vo, 6s.

BLACKWOOD.
Blackwood's Magazine, from Commencement in 1817 to December 1892. Nos. 1 to 926, forming 152 Volumes.
Index to Blackwood's Magazine. Vols. 1 to 50. 8vo, 15s.
Tales from Blackwood. First Series. Price One Shilling each, in Paper Cover. Sold separately at all Railway Bookstalls.
They may also be had bound in 12 vols., cloth, 18s. Half calf, richly gilt, 30s. Or the 12 vols. in 6, roxburghe, 21s. Half red morocco, 28s.
Tales from Blackwood. Second Series. Complete in Twenty-four Shilling Parts. Handsomely bound in 12 vols., cloth, 30s. In leather back, roxburghe style, 37s. 6d. Half calf, gilt, 52s. 6d. Half morocco, 55s.
Tales from Blackwood. Third Series. Complete in Twelve Shilling Parts. Handsomely bound in 6 vols., cloth, 15s.; and in 12 vols., cloth, 18s. The 6 vols. in roxburghe, 21s. Half calf, 25s. Half morocco, 28s.
Travel, Adventure, and Sport. From 'Blackwood's Magazine.' Uniform with 'Tales from Blackwood.' In Twelve Parts, each price 1s. Handsomely bound in 6 vols., cloth, 15s. And in half calf, 25s.
New Educational Series. *See separate Catalogue.*
New Uniform Series of Novels (Copyright).
Crown 8vo, cloth. Price 3s. 6d. each. Now ready:—

KATIE STEWART, and other Stories. By Mrs Oliphant.
VALENTINE, AND HIS BROTHER. By the Same.
SONS AND DAUGHTERS. By the Same.
MARMORNE. By P. G. Hamerton.
REATA. By E. D. Gerard.
BEGGAR MY NEIGHBOUR. By the Same.
THE WATERS OF HERCULES. By the Same.
FAIR TO SEE. By L. W. M. Lockhart.
MINE IS THINE. By the Same.
DOUBLES AND QUITS. By the Same.
HURRISH. By the Hon. Emily Lawless.
ALTIORA PETO. By Laurence Oliphant.
PICCADILLY. By the Same. With Illustrations.
THE REVOLT OF MAN. By Walter Besant.
LADY BABY. By D. Gerard.
THE BLACKSMITH OF VOE. By Paul Cushing.
THE DILEMMA. By the Author of 'The Battle of Dorking.'
MY TRIVIAL LIFE AND MISFORTUNE. By A Plain Woman.
POOR NELLIE. By the Same.
Others in preparation.

Standard Novels. Uniform in size and binding. Each complete in one Volume.

FLORIN SERIES, Illustrated Boards. Bound in Cloth, 2s. 6d.

TOM CRINGLE'S LOG. By Michael Scott.
THE CRUISE OF THE MIDGE. By the Same.
CYRIL THORNTON. By Captain Hamilton.
ANNALS OF THE PARISH. By John Galt.
THE PROVOST, &c. By the Same.
SIR ANDREW WYLIE. By the Same.
THE ENTAIL. By the Same.
MISS MOLLY. By Beatrice May Butt.
REGINALD DALTON. By J. G. Lockhart.
PEN OWEN. By Dean Hook.
ADAM BLAIR. By J. G. Lockhart.
LADY LEE'S WIDOWHOOD. By General Sir E. B. Hamley.
SALEM CHAPEL. By Mrs Oliphant.
THE PERPETUAL CURATE. By the Same.
MISS MARJORIBANKS. By the Same.
JOHN: A Love Story. By the Same.

BLACKWOOD.
Standard Novels.
SHILLING SERIES, Illustrated Cover. Bound in Cloth, 1s. 6d.

THE RECTOR, and THE DOCTOR'S FAMILY. By Mrs Oliphant.
THE LIFE OF MANSIE WAUCH. By D. M. Moir.
PENINSULAR SCENES AND SKETCHES. By F. Hardman.
SIR FRIZZLE PUMPKIN, NIGHTS AT MESS, &c.
THE SUBALTERN.
LIFE IN THE FAR WEST. By G. F. Ruxton.
VALERIUS: A Roman Story. By J. G. Lockhart.

BOLTON. Lord Wastwater. A Novel. By SIDNEY BOLTON. 2 vols. crown 8vo, 17s.

BON GAULTIER'S BOOK OF BALLADS. Fifteenth Edition. With Illustrations by Doyle, Leech, and Crowquill. Fcap. 8vo, 5s.

BONNAR. Biographical Sketch of George Meikle Kemp, Architect of the Scott Monument, Edinburgh. By THOMAS BONNAR, F.S.A. Scot., Author of 'The Present Art Revival,' 'The Past of Art in Scotland,' 'Suggestions for the Picturesque of Interiors,' &c. With Three Portraits and numerous Illustrations. Post 8vo, 7s. 6d.

BOSCOBEL TRACTS. Relating to the Escape of Charles the Second after the Battle of Worcester, and his subsequent Adventures. Edited by J. HUGHES, Esq., A.M. A New Edition, with additional Notes and Illustrations, including Communications from the Rev. R. H. BARHAM, Author of the 'Ingoldsby Legends.' 8vo, with Engravings, 16s.

BROUGHAM. Memoirs of the Life and Times of Henry Lord Brougham. Written by HIMSELF. 3 vols. 8vo, £2, 8s. The Volumes are sold separately, price 16s. each.

BROWN. A Manual of Botany, Anatomical and Physiological. For the Use of Students. By ROBERT BROWN, M.A., Ph.D. Crown 8vo, with numerous Illustrations, 12s. 6d.

BROWN. The Book of the Landed Estate. Containing Directions for the Management and Development of the Resources of Landed Property. By ROBERT E. BROWN, Factor and Estate Agent. Royal 8vo, with Illustrations, 21s.

BROWN. The Forester: A Practical Treatise on the Planting, Rearing, and General Management of Forest-trees. By JAMES BROWN, LL.D., Inspector of and Reporter on Woods and Forests. Fifth Edition, Revised and Enlarged. Royal 8vo, with Engravings, 36s.

BRUCE. In Clover and Heather. Poems by WALLACE BRUCE. New and Enlarged Edition. Crown 8vo, 4s. 6d.
A limited number of Copies of the First Edition, on large hand-made paper, 12s. 6d.

BRYDALL. Art in Scotland; its Origin and Progress. By ROBERT BRYDALL, Master of St George's Art School of Glasgow. 8vo, 12s. 6d.

BUCHAN. Introductory Text-Book of Meteorology. By ALEXANDER BUCHAN, LL.D., F.R.S.E., Secretary of the Scottish Meteorological Society, &c. Crown 8vo, with 8 Coloured Charts and Engravings, 4s. 6d.

BUCHANAN. The Shire Highlands (East Central Africa). By JOHN BUCHANAN, Planter at Zomba. Crown 8vo, 5s.

BURBIDGE.
Domestic Floriculture, Window Gardening, and Floral Decorations. Being practical directions for the Propagation, Culture, and Arrangement of Plants and Flowers as Domestic Ornaments. By F. W. BURBIDGE. Second Edition. Crown 8vo, with numerous Illustrations, 7s. 6d.

Cultivated Plants: Their Propagation and Improvement. Including Natural and Artificial Hybridisation, Raising from Seed, Cuttings, and Layers, Grafting and Budding, as applied to the Families and Genera in Cultivation. Crown 8vo, with numerous Illustrations 12s 6d.

BURROWS. Commentaries on the History of England, from the Earliest Times to 1865. By MONTAGU BURROWS, Chichele Professor of Modern History in the University of Oxford; Captain R.N.; F.S.A., &c.; "Officier de l'Instruction Publique" of France. Crown 8vo, 7s. 6d.

BURTON.
The History of Scotland: From Agricola's Invasion to the Extinction of the last Jacobite Insurrection. By JOHN HILL BURTON, D.C.L., Historiographer-Royal for Scotland. New and Enlarged Edition, 8 vols., and Index. Crown 8vo, £3, 3s.

History of the British Empire during the Reign of Queen Anne. In 3 vols. 8vo. 36s.

The Scot Abroad. Third Edition. Crown 8vo, 10s. 6d.

The Book-Hunter. New Edition. With Portrait. Crown 8vo, 7s. 6d.

BUTE.
The Roman Breviary: Reformed by Order of the Holy Œcumenical Council of Trent; Published by Order of Pope St Pius V.; and Revised by Clement VIII. and Urban VIII.; together with the Offices since granted. Translated out of Latin into English by JOHN, Marquess of Bute, K.T. In 2 vols. crown 8vo, cloth boards, edges uncut. £2, 2s.

The Altus of St Columba. With a Prose Paraphrase and Notes. In paper cover, 2s. 6d.

BUTLER. Pompeii: Descriptive and Picturesque. By W. BUTLER. Post 8vo, 5s.

BUTT.
Miss Molly. By BEATRICE MAY BUTT. Cheap Edition, 2s.
Eugenie. Crown 8vo, 6s. 6d.
Elizabeth, and other Sketches. Crown 8vo, 6s.
Delicia. New Edition. Crown 8vo, 2s. 6d.

CAIRD.
Sermons. By JOHN CAIRD, D.D., Principal of the University of Glasgow. Sixteenth Thousand. Fcap. 8vo, 5s.

Religion in Common Life. A Sermon preached in Crathie Church, October 14, 1855, before Her Majesty the Queen and Prince Albert. Published by Her Majesty's Command. Cheap Edition, 3d.

CALDER. Chaucer's Canterbury Pilgrimage. Epitomised by WILLIAM CALDER. With Photogravure of the Pilgrimage Company, and other Illustrations, Glossary, &c. Crown 8vo, 4s.

CAMPBELL. Critical Studies in St Luke's Gospel: Its Demonology and Ebionitism. By COLIN CAMPBELL, D.D., Minister of the Parish of Dundee, formerly Scholar and Fellow of Glasgow University. Author of the 'Three First Gospels in Greek, arranged in parallel columns.' Post 8vo, 7s. 6d.

CAMPBELL. Sermons Preached before the Queen at Balmoral. By the Rev. A. A. CAMPBELL, Minister of Crathie. Published by Command of Her Majesty. Crown 8vo, 4s. 6d.

CAMPBELL. Records of Argyll. Legends, Traditions, and Recollections of Argyllshire Highlanders, collected chiefly from the Gaelic. With Notes on the Antiquity of the Dress, Clan Colours, or Tartans of the Highlanders. By Lord ARCHIBALD CAMPBELL. Illustrated with Nineteen full-page Etchings. 4to, printed on hand-made paper, £3, 3s.

CAMPBELL, W. D., AND V. K. ERSKINE. The Bailie M'Phee: A Curling Song. With Illustrations, and the Music to which it may be sung. Small 4to, 1s. 6d.

William Blackwood and Sons.

CANTON. A Lost Epic, and other Poems. By WILLIAM CANTON. Crown 8vo, 5s.

CARRICK. Koumiss; or, Fermented Mare's Milk: and its uses in the Treatment and Cure of Pulmonary Consumption, and other Wasting Diseases. With an Appendix on the best Methods of Fermenting Cow's Milk. By GEORGE L. CARRICK, M.D., L.R.C.S.E. and L.R.C.P.E., Physician to the British Embassy, St Petersburg, &c. Crown 8vo, 10s. 6d.

CARSTAIRS. British Work in India. By R. CARSTAIRS. Crown 8vo, 6s.

CAUVIN. A Treasury of the English and German Languages. Compiled from the best Authors and Lexicographers in both Languages. By JOSEPH CAUVIN, LL.D. and Ph.D., of the University of Göttingen, &c. Crown 8vo, 7s. 6d.

CAVE-BROWN. Lambeth Palace and its Associations. By J. CAVE-BROWN, M.A., Vicar of Detling, Kent, and for many years Curate of Lambeth Parish Church. With an Introduction by the Archbishop of Canterbury. Second Edition, containing an additional Chapter on Medieval Life in the Old Palaces. 8vo, with Illustrations, 21s.

CHARTERIS. Canonicity; or, Early Testimonies to the Existence and Use of the Books of the New Testament. Based on Kirchhoffer's 'Quellensammlung.' Edited by A. H. CHARTERIS, D.D., Professor of Biblical Criticism in the University of Edinburgh. 8vo, 18s.

CHRISTISON. Life of Sir Robert Christison, Bart., M.D., D.C.L. Oxon., Professor of Medical Jurisprudence in the University of Edinburgh. Edited by his SONS. In 2 vols. 8vo. Vol. I.—Autobiography. 16s. Vol. II.—Memoirs. 16s.

CHRONICLES OF STRATHEDEN. A Highland Parish of To-day. By a Resident. Crown 8vo, 5s.

CHRONICLES OF WESTERLY: A Provincial Sketch. By the Author of 'Culmshire Folk,' 'John Orlebar,' &c. 3 vols. crown 8vo, 25s. 6d.

CHURCH SERVICE SOCIETY.
A Book of Common Order: being Forms of Worship issued by the Church Service Society. Sixth Edition. Crown 8vo, 6s. Also in 2 vols. crown 8vo, 6s. 6d.

Order of Divine Service for Children. Issued by the Church Service Society. With Scottish Hymnal. Cloth, 3d.

CLELAND. Too Apt a Pupil. By ROBERT CLELAND, Author of 'Barbara Allan, the Provost's Daughter.' Crown 8vo, 6s.

CLOUSTON. Popular Tales and Fictions: their Migrations and Transformations. By W. A. CLOUSTON, Editor of 'Arabian Poetry for English Readers,' &c. 2 vols. post 8vo, roxburghe binding, 25s.

COCHRAN. A Handy Text-Book of Military Law. Compiled chiefly to assist Officers preparing for Examination; also for all Officers of the Regular and Auxiliary Forces. Comprising also a Synopsis of part of the Army Act. By Major F. COCHRAN, Hampshire Regiment Garrison Instructor, North British District. Crown 8vo, 7s. 6d.

COLQUHOUN. The Moor and the Loch. Containing Minute Instructions in all Highland Sports, with Wanderings over Crag and Corrie, Flood and Fell. By JOHN COLQUHOUN. Seventh Edition. With Illustrations. Demy 8vo, 21s.

CONSTITUTION AND LAW OF THE CHURCH OF SCOTLAND. With an Introductory Note by the late Principal Tulloch. New Edition, Revised and Enlarged. Crown 8vo, 3s. 6d.

CONSTITUTIONAL YEAR BOOK. Published annually. Paper cover, 1s.; cloth, 1s. 6d.

List of Books Published by

COTTERILL. Suggested Reforms in Public Schools. By C. C.
COTTERILL, M.A. Crown 8vo, 3s. 6d.

CRANSTOUN.
The Elegies of Albius Tibullus. Translated into English
Verse, with Life of the Poet, and Illustrative Notes. By JAMES CRANSTOUN,
LL.D., Author of a Translation of 'Catullus.' Crown 8vo, 6s. 6d.

The Elegies of Sextus Propertius. Translated into English
Verse, with Life of the Poet, and Illustrative Notes. Crown 8vo, 7s. 6d.

CRAWFORD. An Atonement of East London, and other Poems.
By HOWARD CRAWFORD, M.A. Crown 8vo, 5s.

CRAWFORD. Saracinesca. By F. MARION CRAWFORD, Author
of 'Mr Isaacs,' &c. &c. Sixth Edition. Crown 8vo, 6s.

CRAWFORD.
The Doctrine of Holy Scripture respecting the Atonement.
By the late THOMAS J. CRAWFORD, D.D., Professor of Divinity in the University
of Edinburgh. Fifth Edition. 8vo, 12s.

The Fatherhood of God, Considered in its General and Special
Aspects. Third Edition, Revised and Enlarged. 8vo, 9s.

The Preaching of the Cross, and other Sermons. 8vo, 7s. 6d.

The Mysteries of Christianity. Crown 8vo, 7s. 6d.

CROSS. Impressions of Dante, and of the New World ; with a
Few Words on Bimetallism. By J. W. CROSS, Editor of 'George Eliot's Life, as
related in her Letters and Journals.' Post 8vo. [*Immediately.*

CUSHING.
The Blacksmith of Voe. By PAUL CUSHING, Author of 'The
Bull i' th' Thorn,' 'Cut with his own Diamond.' Cheap Edition. Crown 8vo, 3s. 6d.

DAVIES.
Norfolk Broads and Rivers; or, The Waterways, Lagoons,
and Decoys of East Anglia. By G. CHRISTOPHER DAVIES. Illustrated with
Seven full-page Plates. New and Cheaper Edition. Crown 8vo, 6s.

Our Home in Aveyron. Sketches of Peasant Life in Aveyron
and the Lot. By G. CHRISTOPHER DAVIES and Mrs BROUGHALL. Illustrated
with full-page Illustrations. 8vo, 15s. Cheap Edition, 7s. 6d.

DE LA WARR. An Eastern Cruise in the 'Edeline.' By the
Countess DE LA WARR. In Illustrated Cover. 2s.

DESCARTES. The Method, Meditations, and Principles of Philo-
sophy of Descartes. Translated from the Original French and Latin. With a
New Introductory Essay, Historical and Critical, on the Cartesian Philosophy.
By Professor VEITCH, LL.D., Glasgow University. Tenth Edition. 6s. 6d.

DEWAR. Voyage of the "Nyanza," R.N.Y.C. Being the Record
of a Three Years' Cruise in a Schooner Yacht in the Atlantic and Pacific, and her
subsequent Shipwreck. By J. CUMMING DEWAR, late Captain King's Dragoon
Guards and 11th Prince Albert's Hussars. With Two Autogravures, numerous
Illustrations, and a Map. Demy 8vo, 21s.

DICKSON. Gleanings from Japan. By W. G. DICKSON, Author
of 'Japan: Being a Sketch of its History, Government, and Officers of the
Empire.' With Illustrations. 8vo, 16s.

DILEMMA, The. By the Author of 'The Battle of Dorking.'
New Edition. Crown 8vo, 3s. 6d.

DOGS, OUR DOMESTICATED: Their Treatment in reference
to Food, Diseases, Habits, Punishment, Accomplishments. By 'MAGENTA.'
Crown 8vo, 2s. 6d.

DOMESTIC EXPERIMENT, A. By the Author of 'Ideala: A Study from Life.' Crown 8vo, 6s.

DOUGLAS. Chinese Stories. By ROBERT K. DOUGLAS. With numerous Illustrations by Parkinson, Forestier, and others. Small demy 8vo, 12s. 6d.

DU CANE. The Odyssey of Homer, Books I.-XII. Translated into English Verse. By Sir CHARLES DU CANE, K.C.M.G. 8vo, 10s. 6d.

DUDGEON. History of the Edinburgh or Queen's Regiment Light Infantry Militia, now 3rd Battalion The Royal Scots; with an Account of the Origin and Progress of the Militia, and a Brief Sketch of the Old Royal Scots. By Major R. C. DUDGEON, Adjutant 3rd Battalion the Royal Scots. Post 8vo, with Illustrations, 10s. 6d.

DUNCAN. Manual of the General Acts of Parliament relating to the Salmon Fisheries of Scotland from 1828 to 1882. By J. BARKER DUNCAN. Crown 8vo, 5s.

DUNSMORE. Manual of the Law of Scotland as to the Relations between Agricultural Tenants and the Landlords, Servants, Merchants, and Bowers. By W. DUNSMORE. 8vo, 7s. 6d.

DUPRÈ. Thoughts on Art, and Autobiographical Memoirs of Giovanni Duprè. Translated from the Italian by E. M. PERUZZI, with the permission of the Author. New Edition. With an Introduction by W. W. STORY. Crown 8vo, 10s. 6d.

ELIOT.
George Eliot's Life, Related in Her Letters and Journals. Arranged and Edited by her husband, J. W. CROSS. With Portrait and other Illustrations. Third Edition. 3 vols. post 8vo, 42s.

George Eliot's Life. (Cabinet Edition.) With Portrait and other Illustrations. 3 vols. crown 8vo, 15s.

George Eliot's Life. With Portrait and other Illustrations. New Edition, in one volume. Crown 8vo, 7s. 6d.

Works of George Eliot (Cabinet Edition). 21 volumes, crown 8vo, price £5, 5s. Also to be had handsomely bound in half and full calf. The Volumes are sold separately, bound in cloth, price 5s. each—viz.:
Romola. 2 vols.—Silas Marner, The Lifted Veil, Brother Jacob. 1 vol.—Adam Bede. 2 vols.—Scenes of Clerical Life. 2 vols.—The Mill on the Floss. 2 vols.—Felix Holt. 2 vols.—Middlemarch. 3 vols.—Daniel Deronda. 3 vols.—The Spanish Gypsy. 1 vol.—Jubal, and other Poems, Old and New. 1 vol.—Theophrastus Such. 1 vol.—Essays. 1 vol.

Novels by George Eliot. Cheap Edition.
Adam Bede. Illustrated. 3s. 6d., cloth.—The Mill on the Floss. Illustrated. 3s. 6d., cloth.—Scenes of Clerical Life. Illustrated. 3s., cloth.—Silas Marner: the Weaver of Raveloe. Illustrated. 2s. 6d., cloth.—Felix Holt, the Radical. Illustrated. 3s. 6d., cloth.—Romola. With Vignette. 3s. 6d., cloth.

Middlemarch. Crown 8vo, 7s. 6d.

Daniel Deronda. Crown 8vo, 7s. 6d.

Essays. New Edition. Crown 8vo, 5s.

Impressions of Theophrastus Such. New Edition. Crown 8vo, 5s.

The Spanish Gypsy. New Edition. Crown 8vo, 5s.

The Legend of Jubal, and other Poems, Old and New. New Edition. Crown 8vo, 5s.

Wise, Witty, and Tender Sayings, in Prose and Verse. Selected from the Works of GEORGE ELIOT. Eighth Edition. Fcap. 8vo, 6s.

ELIOT. The George Eliot Birthday Book. Printed on fine paper, with red border, and handsomely bound in cloth, gilt. Fcap. 8vo, 3s. 6d. And in French morocco or Russia, 5s.

ESSAYS ON SOCIAL SUBJECTS. Originally published in the 'Saturday Review.' New Edition. First and Second Series. 2 vols. crown 8vo, 6s. each.

FAITHS OF THE WORLD, The. A Concise History of the Great Religious Systems of the World. By various Authors. Crown 8vo, 5s.

FARRER. A Tour in Greece in 1880. By RICHARD RIDLEY FARRER. With Twenty-seven full-page Illustrations by Lord WINDSOR. Royal 8vo, with a Map, 21s.

FERRIER.
Philosophical Works of the Late James F. Ferrier, B.A. Oxon., Professor of Moral Philosophy and Political Economy, St Andrews. New Edition. Edited by Sir ALEXANDER GRANT, Bart., D.C.L., and Professor LUSHINGTON. 3 vols. crown 8vo, 34s. 6d.

Institutes of Metaphysic. Third Edition. 10s. 6d.

Lectures on the Early Greek Philosophy. 4th Edition. 10s. 6d.

Philosophical Remains, including the Lectures on Early Greek Philosophy. New Edition. 2 vols., 24s.

FITZROY. Dogma and the Church of England. By A. I. FitzRoy. Post 8vo, 7s. 6d.

FLINT.
The Philosophy of History in Europe. By ROBERT FLINT, D.D., LL.D., Professor of Divinity, University of Edinburgh. 3 vols. 8vo.
[*New Edition in preparation. Vol. 1.*—FRANCE. *Immediately.*

Agnosticism. Being the Croall Lecture for 1887-88.
[*In the press.*

Theism. Being the Baird Lecture for 1876. Eighth Edition, Revised. Crown 8vo, 7s. 6d.

Anti-Theistic Theories. Being the Baird Lecture for 1877. Fourth Edition. Crown 8vo, 10s. 6d.

FORBES. Insulinde: Experiences of a Naturalist's Wife in the Eastern Archipelago. By Mrs H. O. FORBES. Crown 8vo, with a Map. 4s. 6d.

FOREIGN CLASSICS FOR ENGLISH READERS. Edited by Mrs OLIPHANT. Price 2s. 6d. *For List of Volumes published, see page 2.*

FOSTER. The Fallen City, and other Poems. By WILL FOSTER. Crown 8vo, 6s.

FRANCILLON. Gods and Heroes; or, The Kingdom of Jupiter. By R. E. FRANCILLON. With 8 Illustrations. Crown 8vo, 5s.

FULLARTON. Merlin: A Dramatic Poem. By RALPH MACLEOD FULLARTON. Crown 8vo, 5s.

GALT. Novels by JOHN GALT. Fcap. 8vo, boards, each 2s.; cloth, 2s. 6d.
ANNALS OF THE PARISH.—THE PROVOST.—SIR ANDREW WYLIE.—THE ENTAIL.

GENERAL ASSEMBLY OF THE CHURCH OF SCOTLAND.
Scottish Hymnal, With Appendix Incorporated. Published for use in Churches by Authority of the General Assembly. 1. Large type, cloth, red edges, 2s. 6d.; French morocco, 4s. 2. Bourgeois type, limp cloth, 1s.; French morocco, 2s. 3. Nonpareil type, cloth, red edges, 6d.; French morocco, 1s. 4d. 4. Paper covers, 3d. 5. Sunday-School Edition, paper covers, 1d., cloth, 2d. No. 1, bound with the Psalms and Paraphrases, French morocco, 8s. No. 2, bound with the Psalms and Paraphrases, cloth, 2s.; French morocco, 3s.

Prayers for Social and Family Worship. Prepared by a Special Committee of the General Assembly of the Church of Scotland. Entirely New Edition, Revised and Enlarged. Fcap. 8vo, red edges, 2s.

Prayers for Family Worship. A Selection of Four Weeks' Prayers. New Edition. Authorised by the General Assembly of the Church of Scotland. Fcap. 8vo, red edges, 1s. 6d.

GERARD.
Reata: What's in a Name. By E. D. GERARD. Cheap Edition. Crown 8vo, 3s. 6d.
Beggar my Neighbour. Cheap Edition. Crown 8vo, 3s. 6d.
The Waters of Hercules. Cheap Edition. Crown 8vo, 3s. 6d.

GERARD.
The Land beyond the Forest. Facts, Figures, and Fancies from Transylvania. By E. GERARD. With Maps and Illustrations. 2 vols. post 8vo, 25s.
Bis: Some Tales Retold. Crown 8vo, 6s.
A Secret Mission. 2 vols. crown 8vo, 17s.

GERARD.
Lady Baby. By DOROTHEA GERARD. Cheap Edition. Crown 8vo, 3s. 6d.
Recha. Second Edition. Crown 8vo, 6s.

GERARD. Stonyhurst Latin Grammar. By Rev. JOHN GERARD. Second Edition. Fcap. 8vo, 3s.

GILL.
Free Trade: an Inquiry into the Nature of its Operation. By RICHARD GILL. Crown 8vo, 7s. 6d.
Free Trade under Protection. Crown 8vo, 7s. 6d.

GOETHE. Poems and Ballads of Goethe. Translated by Professor AYTOUN and Sir THEODORE MARTIN, K.C.B. Third Edition. Fcap. 8vo, 6s.

GOETHE'S FAUST. Translated into English Verse by Sir THEODORE MARTIN, K.C.B. Part I. Second Edition, post 8vo, 6s. Ninth Edition, fcap., 3s. 6d. Part II. Second Edition, Revised. Fcap. 8vo, 6s.

GORDON CUMMING.
At Home in Fiji. By C. F. GORDON CUMMING. Fourth Edition, post 8vo. With Illustrations and Map. 7s. 6d.
A Lady's Cruise in a French Man-of-War. New and Cheaper Edition. 8vo. With Illustrations and Map. 12s. 6d.
Fire-Fountains. The Kingdom of Hawaii: Its Volcanoes, and the History of its Missions. With Map and Illustrations. 2 vols. 8vo, 25s.
Wanderings in China. New and Cheaper Edition. 8vo, with Illustrations, 10s.
Granite Crags: The Yō-semité Region of California. Illustrated with 8 Engravings. New and Cheaper Edition. 8vo, 8s. 6d.

GRAHAM. The Life and Work of Syed Ahmed Khan, C.S.I.
By Lieut.-Colonel G. F. I. Graham, B.S.C. 8vo, 14s.

GRAHAM. Manual of the Elections (Scot.) (Corrupt and Illegal Practices) Act, 1890. With Analysis, Relative Act of Sederunt, Appendix containing the Corrupt Practices Acts of 1883 and 1885, and Copious Index. By J. Edward Graham, Advocate. 8vo, 4s. 6d.

GRANT. Bush-Life in Queensland. By A. C. Grant. New Edition. Crown 8vo, 6s.

GUTHRIE-SMITH. Crispus: A Drama. By H. Guthrie-Smith. Fcap. 4to, 5s.

HAINES. Unless! A Romance. By Randolph Haines. Crown 8vo, 6s.

HALDANE. Subtropical Cultivations and Climates. A Handy Book for Planters, Colonists, and Settlers. By R. C. Haldane. Post 8vo, 9s.

HALLETT. A Thousand Miles on an Elephant in the Shan States. By Holt S. Hallett, M. Inst. C.E., F.R.G.S., M.R.A.S., Hon. Member Manchester and Tyneside Geographical Societies. 8vo, with Maps and numerous Illustrations, 21s.

HAMERTON.
Wenderholme: A Story of Lancashire and Yorkshire Life. By P. G. Hamerton, Author of 'A Painter's Camp.' Crown 8vo, 6s.
Marmorne. New Edition. Crown 8vo, 3s. 6d.

HAMILTON.
Lectures on Metaphysics. By Sir William Hamilton, Bart., Professor of Logic and Metaphysics in the University of Edinburgh. Edited by the Rev. H. L. Mansel, B.D., LL.D., Dean of St Paul's; and John Veitch, M.A., LL.D., Professor of Logic and Rhetoric, Glasgow. Seventh Edition. 2 vols. 8vo, 24s.
Lectures on Logic. Edited by the Same. Third Edition, Revised. 2 vols., 24s.
Discussions on Philosophy and Literature, Education and University Reform. Third Edition. 8vo, 21s.
Memoir of Sir William Hamilton, Bart., Professor of Logic and Metaphysics in the University of Edinburgh. By Professor Veitch, of the University of Glasgow. 8vo, with Portrait, 18s.
Sir William Hamilton: The Man and his Philosophy. Two Lectures delivered before the Edinburgh Philosophical Institution, January and February 1883. By Professor Veitch. Crown 8vo, 2s.

HAMLEY.
The Operations of War Explained and Illustrated. By General Sir Edward Bruce Hamley, K.C.B., K.C.M.G. Fifth Edition, Revised throughout. 4to, with numerous Illustrations, 30s.
National Defence; Articles and Speeches. Post 8vo, 6s.
Shakespeare's Funeral, and other Papers. Post 8vo, 7s 6d.
Thomas Carlyle: An Essay. Second Edition. Crown 8vo, 2s. 6d.
On Outposts. Second Edition. 8vo, 2s.
Wellington's Career; A Military and Political Summary. Crown 8vo, 2s.
Lady Lee's Widowhood. Crown 8vo, 2s. 6d.
Our Poor Relations. A Philozoic Essay. With Illustrations, chiefly by Ernest Griset. Crown 8vo, cloth gilt, 3s. 6d.

HAMLEY. Guilty, or Not Guilty? A Tale. By Major-General
W. G. Hamley, late of the Royal Engineers. New Edition. Crown 8vo, 3s. 6d.

HARRISON. The Scot in Ulster. The Story of the Scottish
Settlement in Ulster. By John Harrison, Author of 'Oure Tounis Colledge.'
Crown 8vo, 2s. 6d.

HASELL.
Bible Partings. By E. J. Hasell. Crown 8vo, 6s.
Short Family Prayers. Cloth, 1s.

HAY. Arakan: Past—Present—Future. A Resumé of Two
Campaigns for its Development. By John Ogilvy Hay, J.P. ('Old Arakan'),
Formerly Honorary Magistrate of the town of Akyab, Author of 'Indo-Burmah-
China Railway Connections a Pressing Necessity.' With a Map. Demy 8vo, 4s. 6d.

HAY. The Works of the Right Rev. Dr George Hay, Bishop of
Edinburgh. Edited under the Supervision of the Right Rev. Bishop Strain.
With Memoir and Portrait of the Author. 5 vols. crown 8vo, bound in extra
cloth, £1, 1s. The following Volumes may be had separately—viz.:
The Devout Christian Instructed in the Law of Christ from the Written
Word. 2 vols., 8s.—The Pious Christian Instructed in the Nature and Practice
of the Principal Exercises of Piety. 1 vol., 3s.

HEATLEY.
The Horse-Owner's Safeguard. A Handy Medical Guide for
every Man who owns a Horse. By G. S. Heatley, M.R.C.V.S. Crown 8vo, 5s.
The Stock-Owner's Guide. A Handy Medical Treatise for
every Man who owns an Ox or a Cow. Crown 8vo, 4s. 6d.

HEDDERWICK.
Lays of Middle Age; and other Poems. By James Hedderwick, LL.D. Price 3s. 6d.
Backward Glances; or, Some Personal Recollections. With
a Portrait. Post 8vo, 7s. 6d.

HEMANS.
The Poetical Works of Mrs Hemans. Copyright Editions.
Royal 8vo, 5s. The Same with Engravings, cloth, gilt edges, 7s. 6d.
Select Poems of Mrs Hemans. Fcap., cloth, gilt edges, 3s.

HERKLESS. Cardinal Beaton: Priest and Politician. By
John Herkless, Minister of Tannadice. With a Portrait. Post 8vo, 7s. 6d.

HOME PRAYERS. By Ministers of the Church of Scotland
and Members of the Church Service Society. Second Edition. Fcap. 8vo, 3s.

HOMER.
The Odyssey. Translated into English Verse in the Spenserian Stanza. By Philip Stanhope Worsley. 3d Edition. 2 vols. fcap., 12s.
The Iliad. Translated by P. S. Worsley and Professor Conington. 2 vols. crown 8vo, 21s.

HUTCHINSON. Hints on the Game of Golf. By Horace G.
Hutchinson. Seventh Edition, Enlarged. Fcap. 8vo, cloth, 1s.

IDDESLEIGH.
Lectures and Essays. By the late Earl of Iddesleigh,
G.C.B., D.C.L., &c. 8vo, 16s.
Life, Letters, and Diaries of Sir Stafford Northcote, First
Earl of Iddesleigh. By Andrew Lang. With Three Portraits and a View of
Pynes. Third Edition. 2 vols. post 8vo, 31s. 6d.
Popular Edition. With Portrait and View of Pynes. Post 8vo, 7s. 6d.

INDEX GEOGRAPHICUS: Being a List, alphabetically arranged, of the Principal Places on the Globe, with the Countries and Subdivisions of the Countries in which they are situated, and their Latitudes and Longitudes. Imperial 8vo, pp. 676, 21s.

JEAN JAMBON. Our Trip to Blunderland; or, Grand Excursion to Blundertown and Back. By JEAN JAMBON. With Sixty Illustrations designed by CHARLES DOYLE, engraved by DALZIEL. Fourth Thousand. Cloth, gilt edges, 6s. 6d. Cheap Edition, cloth, 3s. 6d. Boards, 2s. 6d.

JENNINGS. Mr Gladstone: A Study. By LOUIS J. JENNINGS, M.P., Author of 'Republican Government in the United States,' 'The Croker Memoirs,' &c. Popular Edition. Crown 8vo, 1s.

JERNINGHAM.
Reminiscences of an Attaché. By HUBERT E. H. JERNINGHAM. Second Edition. Crown 8vo, 5s.

Diane de Breteuille. A Love Story. Crown 8vo, 2s. 6d.

JOHNSTON.
The Chemistry of Common Life. By Professor J. F. W. JOHNSTON. New Edition, Revised. By ARTHUR HERBERT CHURCH, M.A. Oxon.; Author of 'Food: its Sources, Constituents, and Uses,' &c. With Maps and 102 Engravings. Crown 8vo, 7s. 6d.

Elements of Agricultural Chemistry. An entirely New Edition from the Edition by Sir CHARLES A. CAMERON, M.D., F.R.C.S.I., &c. Revised and brought down to date by C. M. AIKMAN, M.A., B.Sc., F.R.S.E., Lecturer on Agricultural Chemistry, West of Scotland Technical College. Fcap. 8vo. [In preparation.

Catechism of Agricultural Chemistry. An entirely New Edition from the Edition by Sir CHARLES A. CAMERON. Revised and Enlarged by C. M. AIKMAN, M.A., &c. 92d Thousand. With numerous Illustrations. Crown 8vo, 1s.

JOHNSTON. Patrick Hamilton: a Tragedy of the Reformation in Scotland, 1528. By T. P. JOHNSTON. Crown 8vo, with Two Etchings. 5s.

JOHNSTON. Agricultural Holdings (Scotland) Acts, 1883 and 1889; and the Ground Game Act, 1880. With Notes, and Summary of Procedure, &c. By CHRISTOPHER N. JOHNSTON, M.A., Advocate. Demy 8vo, 5s.

KEBBEL. The Old and the New: English Country Life. By T. E. KEBBEL, M.A., Author of 'The Agricultural Labourers,' 'Essays in History and Politics,' 'Life of Lord Beaconsfield.' Crown 8vo, 5s.

KENNEDY. Sport, Travel, and Adventure in Newfoundland and the West Indies. By Captain W. R. KENNEDY, R.N. With Illustrations by the Author. Post 8vo, 14s.

KING. The Metamorphoses of Ovid. Translated in English Blank Verse. By HENRY KING, M.A., Fellow of Wadham College, Oxford, and of the Inner Temple, Barrister-at-Law. Crown 8vo, 10s. 6d.

KINGLAKE.
History of the Invasion of the Crimea. By A. W. KINGLAKE. Cabinet Edition, Revised. With an Index to the Complete Work. Illustrated with Maps and Plans. Complete in 9 vols., crown 8vo, at 6s. each.

History of the Invasion of the Crimea. Demy 8vo. Vol. VI. Winter Troubles. With a Map, 16s. Vols. VII. and VIII. From the Morrow of Inkerman to the Death of Lord Raglan. With an Index to the Whole Work. With Maps and Plans. 28s.

Eothen. A New Edition, uniform with the Cabinet Edition of the 'History of the Invasion of the Crimea.' 6s.

KNEIPP. My Water-Cure. As Tested through more than
Thirty Years, and Described for the Healing of Diseases and the Preservation of
Health. By SEBASTIAN KNEIPP, Parish Priest of Wörishofen (Bavaria). With a
Portrait and other Illustrations. Authorised English Translation from the
Thirtieth German Edition, by A. de F. Crown 8vo, 5s.

KNOLLYS. The Elements of Field-Artillery. Designed for
the Use of Infantry and Cavalry Officers. By HENRY KNOLLYS, Captain Royal
Artillery; Author of 'From Sedan to Saarbrück,' Editor of 'Incidents in the
Sepoy War,' &c. With Engravings. Crown 8vo, 7s. 6d.

LAMINGTON. In the Days of the Dandies. By the late Lord
LAMINGTON. Crown 8vo. Illustrated cover, 1s.; cloth, 1s. 6d.

LANG. Life, Letters, and Diaries of Sir Stafford Northcote,
First Earl of Iddesleigh. By ANDREW LANG. With Three Portraits and a View
of Pynes. Third Edition. 2 vols. post 8vo, 31s. 6d.
POPULAR EDITION. With Portrait and View of Pynes. Post 8vo, 7s. 6d.

LAWLESS. Hurrish: A Study. By the Hon. EMILY LAWLESS,
Author of 'A Chelsea Householder,' &c. Fourth Edition. Crown 8vo, 3s. 6d.

LEES. A Handbook of the Sheriff and Justice of Peace Small
Debt Courts. With Notes, References, and Forms. By J. M. Lees, Advocate,
Sheriff-Substitute of Lanarkshire. 8vo, 7s. 6d.

LIGHTFOOT. Studies in Philosophy. By the REV. J. LIGHT-
FOOT, M.A., D.Sc.; Vicar of Cross Stone, Todmorden. Crown 8vo, 4s. 6d.

LINDSAY. The Progressiveness of Modern Christian Thought.
By the Rev. JAMES LINDSAY, M.A., B.D., B.Sc., F.R.S.E., F.G.S., Minister of
the Parish of St Andrews, Kilmarnock. Crown 8vo, 6s.

LLOYD. Ireland under the Land League. A Narrative of
Personal Experiences. By CLIFFORD LLOYD, Special Resident Magistrate.
Post 8vo, 6s.

LOCKHART.
Doubles and Quits. By LAURENCE W. M. LOCKHART. New
Edition. Crown 8vo, 3s. 6d.
Fair to See. New Edition. Crown 8vo, 3s. 6d.
Mine is Thine. New Edition. Crown 8vo, 3s. 6d.

LOCKHART. The Church of Scotland in the Thirteenth Cen-
tury. The Life and Times of David de Bernham of St Andrews (Bishop), A.D.
1239 to 1253. With List of Churches dedicated by him, and Dates. By WILLIAM
LOCKHART, A.M., F.S.A. Scot., Minister of Colinton Parish. 2d Edition 8vo, 6s.

LORIMER.
The Institutes of Law: A Treatise of the Principles of Juris-
prudence as determined by Nature. By the late JAMES LORIMER, Professor of
Public Law and of the Law of Nature and Nations in the University of Edin-
burgh. New Edition, Revised and much Enlarged. 8vo, 18s.
The Institutes of the Law of Nations. A Treatise of the
Jural Relation of Separate Political Communities. In 2 vols. 8vo. Volume I.,
price 16s. Volume II., price 20s.

LOVE. Scottish Church Music. Its Composers and Sources.
With Musical Illustrations. By JAMES LOVE. Post 8vo, 7s. 6d

M'COMBIE. Cattle and Cattle-Breeders. By WILLIAM M'COMBIE,
Tillyfour. New Edition, Enlarged, with Memoir of the Author by JAMES
MACDONALD, of the 'Farming World.' Crown 8vo, 3s. 6d.

M'CRIE.
Works of the Rev. Thomas M'Crie, D.D. Uniform Edition.
4 vols. crown 8vo, 24s.

M'CRIE.
Life of John Knox. Crown 8vo, 6s. Another Edition, 3s. 6d.
Life of Andrew Melville. Crown 8vo, 6s.
History of the Progress and Suppression of the Reformation in Italy in the Sixteenth Century. Crown 8vo, 4s.
History of the Progress and Suppression of the Reformation in Spain in the Sixteenth Century. Crown 8vo, 3s. 6d.
Lectures on the Book of Esther. Fcap. 8vo, 5s.

M'CRIE. The Public Worship of Presbyterian Scotland. Historically treated. With copious Notes, Appendices, and Index. The Fourteenth Series of the Cunningham Lectures. By the Rev. CHARLES G. M'CRIE. Demy 8vo, 10s. 6d.

MACDONALD. A Manual of the Criminal Law (Scotland) Procedure Act, 1887. By NORMAN DORAN MACDONALD. Revised by the LORD JUSTICE-CLERK. 8vo, 10s. 6d.

MACDONALD.
History of Polled Aberdeen and Angus Cattle. Giving an Account of the Origin, Improvement, and Characteristics of the Breed. By JAMES MACDONALD and JAMES SINCLAIR, Sub-Editor 'Irish Farmer's Gazette.' Illustrated with numerous Animal Portraits. Post 8vo, 12s. 6d.
Stephens Book of the Farm. Fourth Edition. Revised and in great part Rewritten by JAMES MACDONALD of the 'Farming World.' Complete in 3 vols., bound with leather back, gilt top, £3, 3s. In Six Divisions, bound in cloth, each 10s. 6d.
Pringle's Live Stock of the Farm. Third Edition. Revised and Edited by JAMES MACDONALD. Crown 8vo, 7s. 6d.
M'Combie's Cattle and Cattle-Breeders. New Edition, Enlarged, with Memoir of the Author by JAMES MACDONALD. Crown 8vo, 3s. 6d.

MACGREGOR. Life and Opinions of Major-General Sir Charles MacGregor K.C.B., C.S.I., C.I.E., Quartermaster-General of India. From his Letters and Diaries. Edited by Lady MACGREGOR. With Portraits and Maps to illustrate Campaigns in which he was engaged. 2 vols. 8vo, 35s.

M'INTOSH. The Book of the Garden. By CHARLES M'INTOSH, formerly Curator of the Royal Gardens of his Majesty the King of the Belgians, and lately of those of his Grace the Duke of Buccleuch, K.G., at Dalkeith Palace. 2 vols. royal 8vo, with 1350 Engravings. £4, 7s. 6d. Vol. I. On the Formation of Gardens and Construction of Garden Edifices, £2, 10s. Vol. II. Practical Gardening, £1, 17s. 6d.

MACINTYRE. Hindu-Koh: Wanderings and Wild Sports on and beyond the Himalayas. By Major-General DONALD MACINTYRE, V.C., late Prince of Wales' Own Goorkhas, F.R.G.S. Dedicated to H.R.H. The Prince of Wales. New and Cheaper Edition, Revised, with numerous Illustrations. Post 8vo, 7s. 6d.

MACKAY. A Sketch of the History of Fife and Kinross. A Study of Scottish History and Character. By .E. J. G. MACKAY, Sheriff of these Counties. Crown 8vo, 6s.

MACKAY.
A Manual of Modern Geography; Mathematical, Physical, and Political. By the Rev. ALEXANDER MACKAY, LL.D., F.R.G.S. 11th Thousand, Revised to the present time. Crown 8vo, pp. 688, 7s. 6d.
Elements of Modern Geography. 55th Thousand, Revised to the present time. Crown 8vo, pp. 300, 3s.
The Intermediate Geography. Intended as an Intermediate Book between the Author's 'Outlines of Geography' and 'Elements of Geography.' Seventeenth Edition, Revised. Crown 8vo, pp. 238, 2s.

MACKAY.
Outlines of Modern Geography. 188th Thousand, Revised to the present time. 18mo, pp. 118, 1s.
First Steps in Geography. 105th Thousand. 18mo, pp. 56. Sewed, 4d.; cloth, 6d.
Elements of Physiography and Physical Geography. With Express Reference to the Instructions issued by the Science and Art Department. 30th Thousand, Revised. Crown 8vo, 1s. 6d.
Facts and Dates; or, The Leading Events in Sacred and Profane History, and the Principal Facts in the various Physical Sciences. For Schools and Private Reference. New Edition. Crown 8vo, 3s. 6d.

MACKAY. An Old Scots Brigade.
Being the History of Mackay's Regiment, now incorporated with the Royal Scots. With an Appendix containing many Original Documents connected with the History of the Regiment. By JOHN MACKAY (late) OF HERRIESDALE. Crown 8vo, 5s.

MACKENZIE. Studies in Roman Law.
With Comparative Views of the Laws of France, England, and Scotland. By Lord MACKENZIE, one of the Judges of the Court of Session in Scotland. Sixth Edition, Edited by JOHN KIRKPATRICK, M.A., LL.B., Advocate, Professor of History in the University of Edinburgh. 8vo, 12s.

MACPHERSON. Glimpses of Church and Social Life in the Highlands in the Olden Times.
By ALEXANDER MACPHERSON, F.S.A. Scot. With Illustrations. In one volume. Small 4to. [In the press.

M'PHERSON.
Summer Sundays in a Strathmore Parish. By J. GORDON M'PHERSON, Ph.D., F.R.S.E., Minister of Ruthven. Crown 8vo, 5s.
Golf and Golfers. Past and Present. With an Introduction by the Right Hon. A. J. BALFOUR, and a Portrait of the Author. Fcap. 8vo, 1s. 6d.

MACRAE. A Handbook of Deer-Stalking.
By ALEXANDER MACRAE, late Forester to Lord Henry Bentinck. With Introduction by Horatio Ross, Esq. Fcap. 8vo, with two Photographs from Life. 3s. 6d.

MAIN. Three Hundred English Sonnets.
Chosen and Edited by DAVID M. MAIN. Fcap. 8vo, 6s.

MAIR. A Digest of Laws and Decisions, Ecclesiastical and Civil,
relating to the Constitution, Practice, and Affairs of the Church of Scotland. With Notes and Forms of Procedure. By the Rev. WILLIAM MAIR, D.D., Minister of the Parish of Earlston. Crown 8vo. With Supplements. 8s.

MARSHALL.
French Home Life. By FREDERICK MARSHALL, Author of 'Claire Brandon.' Second Edition. 5s.
It Happened Yesterday. A Novel. Crown 8vo, 6s.

MARSHMAN. History of India.
From the Earliest Period to the Close of the India Company's Government; with an Epitome of Subsequent Events. By JOHN CLARK MARSHMAN, C.S.I. Abridged from the Author's larger work. Second Edition, Revised. Crown 8vo, with Map, 6s. 6d.

MARTIN.
Goethe's Faust. Part I. Translated by Sir THEODORE MARTIN, K.C.B. Second Edition, crown 8vo, 6s. Ninth Edition, fcap. 8vo, 3s. 6d.
Goethe's Faust. Part II. Translated into English Verse. Second Edition, Revised. Fcap. 8vo, 6s.
The Works of Horace. Translated into English Verse, with Life and Notes. 2 vols. New Edition, crown 8vo, 21s.
Poems and Ballads of Heinrich Heine. Done into English Verse. Second Edition. Printed on *papier vergé*, crown 8vo, 8s.

List of Books Published by

MARTIN.
The Song of the Bell, and other Translations from Schiller, Goethe, Uhland, and Others. Crown 8vo, 7s. 6d.

Catullus. With Life and Notes. Second Edition, Revised and Corrected. Post 8vo, 7s. 6d.

Aladdin: A Dramatic Poem. By ADAM OEHLENSCHLAEGER. Fcap. 8vo, 5s.

Correggio: A Tragedy. By OEHLENSCHLAEGER. With Notes. Fcap. 8vo, 3s.

King Rene's Daughter: A Danish Lyrical Drama. By HENRIK HERTZ. Second Edition, fcap., 2s. 6d.

MARTIN. On some of Shakespeare's Female Characters. In a Series of Letters. By HELENA FAUCIT, Lady MARTIN. Dedicated by permission to Her Most Gracious Majesty the Queen. New Edition, Enlarged. 8vo, with Portrait by Lane, 7s. 6d. Bound in cloth, gilt edges, 8s. 6d.

MARWICK. Observations on the Law and Practice in regard to Municipal Elections and the Conduct of the Business of Town Councils and Commissioners of Police in Scotland. By Sir JAMES D. MARWICK, LL.D., Town-Clerk of Glasgow. Royal 8vo, 30s.

MATHESON.
Can the Old Faith Live with the New? or, The Problem of Evolution and Revelation. By the Rev. GEORGE MATHESON, D.D. Third Edition. Crown 8vo, 7s. 6d.

The Psalmist and the Scientist; or, Modern Value of the Religious Sentiment. New and Cheaper Edition. Crown 8vo, 5s.

Spiritual Development of St Paul. Third Edition. Cr. 8vo, 5s.

The Distinctive Messages of the Old Religions. Cr. 8vo, 5s.

Sacred Songs. New and Cheaper Edition. Crown 8vo, 2s. 6d.

MAURICE. The Balance of Military Power in Europe. An Examination of the War Resources of Great Britain and the Continental States. By Colonel MAURICE, R.A., Professor of Military Art and History at the Royal Staff College. Crown 8vo, with a Map, 6s.

MAXWELL. Meridiana: Noontide Essays. By Sir HERBERT MAXWELL, Bart., M.P., F.S.A., &c., Author of 'Passages in the Life of Sir Lucian Elphin,' &c. Post 8vo, 7s. 6d.

MEREDYTH. The Brief for the Government, 1886-92. A Handbook for Conservative and Unionist Writers, Speakers, &c. Second Edition. By W. H. MEREDYTH. Crown 8vo, 2s. 6d.

MICHEL. A Critical Inquiry into the Scottish Language. With the view of Illustrating the Rise and Progress of Civilisation in Scotland. By FRANCISQUE-MICHEL, F.S.A. Lond. and Scot. Correspondant de l'Institut de France, &c. 4to, printed on hand-made paper, and bound in roxburghe, 66s.

MICHIE.
The Larch: Being a Practical Treatise on its Culture and General Management. By CHRISTOPHER Y. MICHIE, Forester, Cullen House. Crown 8vo, with Illustrations. New and Cheaper Edition, Enlarged, 5s.

The Practice of Forestry. Crown 8vo, with Illustrations. 6s.

MIDDLETON. The Story of Alastair Bhan Comyn; or, The Tragedy of Dunphail. A Tale of Tradition and Romance. By the Lady MIDDLETON. Square 8vo, 10s. Cheaper Edition, 5s.

MILLER. Landscape Geology. A Plea for the Study of Geology by Landscape Painters. By HUGH MILLER, of H.M. Geological Survey. Crown 8vo, 3s. Cheap Edition, paper cover, 1s.

William Blackwood and Sons. 21

MILNE-HOME. Mamma's Black Nurse Stories. West Indian Folk-lore. By MARY PAMELA MILNE-HOME. With six full-page tinted Illustrations. Small 4to, 5s.

MINTO.
A Manual of English Prose Literature, Biographical and Critical: designed mainly to show Characteristics of Style. By W. MINTO, M.A., Professor of Logic in the University of Aberdeen. Third Edition, Revised. Crown 8vo, 7s. 6d.
Characteristics of English Poets, from Chaucer to Shirley. New Edition, Revised. Crown 8vo, 7s. 6d.

MOIR. Life of Mansie Wauch, Tailor in Dalkeith. By D. M. MOIR. With 8 Illustrations on Steel, by the late GEORGE CRUIKSHANK. Crown 8vo, 3s. 6d. Another Edition, fcap. 8vo, 1s. 6d.

MOMERIE.
Defects of Modern Christianity, and other Sermons. By ALFRED WILLIAMS MOMERIE, M.A., D.Sc., LL.D. Fourth Edition. Crown 8vo, 5s.
The Basis of Religion. Being an Examination of Natural Religion. Third Edition. Crown 8vo, 2s. 6d.
The Origin of Evil, and other Sermons. Seventh Edition, Enlarged. Crown 8vo, 5s.
Personality. The Beginning and End of Metaphysics, and a Necessary Assumption in all Positive Philosophy. Fourth Edition, Revised Crown 8vo, 3s.
Agnosticism. Fourth Edition, Revised. Crown 8vo, 5s.
Preaching and Hearing; and other Sermons. Third Edition, Enlarged. Crown 8vo, 5s.
Belief in God. Third Edition. Crown 8vo, 3s.
Inspiration; and other Sermons. Second Edition, Enlarged. Crown 8vo, 5s.
Church and Creed. Second Edition. Crown 8vo, 4s. 6d.

MONTAGUE. Campaigning in South Africa. Reminiscences of an Officer in 1879. By Captain W. E. MONTAGUE, 94th Regiment, Author of 'Claude Meadowleigh,' &c. 8vo, 10s. 6d.

MONTALEMBERT. Memoir of Count de Montalembert. A Chapter of Recent French History. By Mrs OLIPHANT, Author of the 'Life of Edward Irving,' &c. 2 vols. crown 8vo, £1, 4s.

MORISON.
Æolus. A Romance in Lyrics. By JEANIE MORISON. Crown 8vo, 3s.
There as Here. Crown 8vo, 3s.
*** *A limited impression on hand-made paper, bound in vellum, 7s. 6d.*
Selections from Poems. Crown 8vo, 4s. 6d.
Sordello. An Outline Analysis of Mr Browning's Poem. Crown 8vo, 3s.
Of "Fifine at the Fair," "Christmas Eve and Easter Day," and other of Mr Browning's Poems. Crown 8vo, 3s.
The Purpose of the Ages. Crown 8vo, 9s.
Gordon: An Our-day Idyll. Crown 8vo, 3s.
Saint Isadora, and other Poems. Crown 8vo, 1s. 6d.
Snatches of Song. Paper, 1s. 6d.; Cloth, 3s.

MORISON.
Pontius Pilate. Paper, 1s. 6d.; Cloth, 3s.
Mill o' Forres. Crown 8vo, 1s.
Ane Booke of Ballades. Fcap. 4to, 1s.

MOZLEY. Essays from 'Blackwood.' By the late ANNE
MOZLEY, Author of 'Essays on Social Subjects'; Editor of 'The Letters and Correspondence of Cardinal Newman,' 'Letters of the Rev. J. B. Mozley,' &c. With a Memoir by her Sister, FANNY MOZLEY. Post 8vo, 7s. 6d.

MUNRO. On Valuation of Property. By WILLIAM MUNRO, M.A., Her Majesty's Assessor of Railways and Canals for Scotland. Second Edition, Revised and Enlarged. 8vo, 3s. 6d.

MURDOCH. Manual of the Law of Insolvency and Bankruptcy: Comprehending a Summary of the Law of Insolvency, Notour Bankruptcy, Composition-contracts, Trust-deeds, Cessios, and Sequestrations; and the Winding-up of Joint-Stock Companies in Scotland; with Annotations on the various Insolvency and Bankruptcy Statutes; and with Forms of Procedure applicable to these Subjects. By JAMES MURDOCH, Member of the Faculty of Procurators in Glasgow. Fifth Edition, Revised and Enlarged. 8vo, £1, 10s.

MY TRIVIAL LIFE AND MISFORTUNE: A Gossip with no Plot in Particular. By A PLAIN WOMAN. Cheap Edition. Crown 8vo, 3s. 6d.
By the SAME AUTHOR.
POOR NELLIE. Cheap Edition. Crown 8vo, 3s. 6d.

NAPIER. The Construction of the Wonderful Canon of Logarithms. By JOHN NAPIER of Merchiston. Translated, with Notes, and a Catalogue of Napier's Works, by WILLIAM RAE MACDONALD. Small 4to, 15s. *A few large-paper copies on Whatman paper, 30s.*

NEAVES.
Songs and Verses, Social and Scientific. By An Old Contributor to 'Maga.' By the Hon. Lord NEAVES. Fifth Edition. Fcap. 8vo, 4s.
The Greek Anthology. Being Vol. XX. of 'Ancient Classics for English Readers.' Crown 8vo, 2s. 6d.

NICHOLSON.
A Manual of Zoology, for the use of Students. With a General Introduction on the Principles of Zoology. By HENRY ALLEYNE NICHOLSON, M.D., D.Sc., F.L.S., F.G.S. Regius Professor of Natural History in the University of Aberdeen. Seventh Edition, Rewritten and Enlarged. Post 8vo, pp. 956, with 555 Engravings on Wood, 18s.
Text-Book of Zoology, for the use of Schools. Fourth Edition, Enlarged. Crown 8vo, with 188 Engravings on Wood, 7s. 6d.
Introductory Text-Book of Zoology, for the use of Junior Classes. Sixth Edition, Revised and Enlarged, with 166 Engravings, 3s.
Outlines of Natural History, for Beginners: being Descriptions of a Progressive Series of Zoological Types. Third Edition, with Engravings, 1s. 6d.
A Manual of Palæontology, for the use of Students. With a General Introduction on the Principles of Palæontology. By Professor H. ALLEYNE NICHOLSON and RICHARD LYDEKKER, B.A. Third Edition, entirely Rewritten and greatly Enlarged. 2 vols. 8vo, £3, 3s.
The Ancient Life-History of the Earth. An Outline of the Principles and Leading Facts of Palæontological Science. Crown 8vo, with 276 Engravings, 10s. 6d.
On the "Tabulate Corals" of the Palæozoic Period, with Critical Descriptions of Illustrative Species. Illustrated with 15 Lithographed Plates and numerous Engravings. Super-royal 8vo, 21s.

NICHOLSON.
Synopsis of the Classification of the Animal Kingdom. 8vo, with 106 Illustrations, 6s.

On the Structure and Affinities of the Genus Monticulipora and its Sub-Genera, with Critical Descriptions of Illustrative Species. Illustrated with numerous Engravings on Wood and Lithographed Plates. Super-royal 8vo, 18s.

NICHOLSON.
Communion with Heaven, and other Sermons. By the late MAXWELL NICHOLSON, D.D., Minister of St Stephen's, Edinburgh. Crown 8vo, 5s. 6d.

Rest in Jesus. Sixth Edition. Fcap. 8vo, 4s. 6d.

NICHOLSON.
A Treatise on Money, and Essays on Present Monetary Problems. By JOSEPH SHIELD NICHOLSON, M.A., D.Sc., Professor of Commercial and Political Economy and Mercantile Law in the University of Edinburgh. 8vo, 10s. 6d.

Thoth. A Romance. Third Edition. Crown 8vo, 4s. 6d.

A Dreamer of Dreams. A Modern Romance. Second Edition. Crown 8vo, 6s.

NICOLSON AND MURE.
A Handbook to the Local Government (Scotland) Act, 1889. With Introduction, Explanatory Notes, and Index. By J. BADENACH NICOLSON, Advocate, Counsel to the Scotch Education Department, and W. J. MURE, Advocate, Legal Secretary to the Lord Advocate for Scotland. Ninth Reprint. 8vo, 5s.

OLIPHANT.
Masollam : A Problem of the Period. A Novel. By LAURENCE OLIPHANT. 3 vols. post 8vo, 25s. 6d.

Scientific Religion ; or, Higher Possibilities of Life and Practice through the Operation of Natural Forces. Second Edition. 8vo, 16s.

Altiora Peto. Cheap Edition. Crown 8vo, boards, 2s. 6d. ; cloth, 3s. 6d. Illustrated Edition. Crown 8vo, cloth, 6s.

Piccadilly. With Illustrations by Richard Doyle. New Edition, 3s. 6d. Cheap Edition, boards, 2s. 6d.

Traits and Travesties ; Social and Political. Post 8vo, 10s. 6d.

Episodes in a Life of Adventure ; or, Moss from a Rolling Stone. Fifth Edition. Post 8vo, 6s.

Haifa : Life in Modern Palestine. Second Edition. 8vo, 7s. 6d.

The Land of Gilead. With Excursions in the Lebanon. With Illustrations and Maps. Demy 8vo, 21s.

Memoir of the Life of Laurence Oliphant, and of Alice Oliphant, his Wife. By Mrs M. O. W. OLIPHANT. Seventh Edition. 2 vols. post 8vo, with Portraits. 21s.
POPULAR EDITION. With a New Preface. Post 8vo, with Portraits. 7s. 6d.

OLIPHANT.
Katie Stewart. By Mrs OLIPHANT. Illustrated boards, 2s. 6d.

Katie Stewart, and other Stories. New Edition. Crown 8vo, cloth, 3s. 6d.

Valentine and his Brother. New Edition. Crown 8vo, 3s. 6d.

Sons and Daughters. Crown 8vo, 3s. 6d.

OLIPHANT.
Diana Trelawny: The History of a Great Mistake. 2 vols. crown 8vo, 17s.

Two Stories of the Seen and the Unseen. The Open Door —Old Lady Mary. Paper covers, 1s.

OLIPHANT. Notes of a Pilgrimage to Jerusalem and the Holy Land. By F. R. OLIPHANT. Crown 8vo, 3s. 6d.

ON SURREY HILLS. By "A SON OF THE MARSHES." See page 28.

OSSIAN. The Poems of Ossian in the Original Gaelic. With a Literal Translation into English, and a Dissertation on the Authenticity of the Poems. By the Rev. ARCHIBALD CLERK. 2 vols. imperial 8vo, £1, 11s. 6d.

OSWALD. By Fell and Fjord; or, Scenes and Studies in Iceland. By E. J. OSWALD. Post 8vo, with Illustrations. 7s. 6d.

PAGE.
Introductory Text-Book of Geology. By DAVID PAGE, LL.D., Professor of Geology in the Durham University of Physical Science, Newcastle, and Professor LAPWORTH of Mason Science College, Birmingham. With Engravings and Glossarial Index. Twelfth Edition, Revised and Enlarged. 3s. 6d.

Advanced Text-Book of Geology, Descriptive and Industrial. With Engravings, and Glossary of Scientific Terms. Sixth Edition, Revised and Enlarged. 7s. 6d.

Introductory Text-Book of Physical Geography. With Sketch-Maps and Illustrations. Edited by Professor LAPWORTH, LL.D., F.G.S., &c., Mason Science College, Birmingham. Twelfth Edition, Revised. 2s. 6d.

Advanced Text-Book of Physical Geography. Third Edition, Revised and Enlarged by Professor LAPWORTH. With Engravings. 5s.

PATON.
Spindrift. By Sir J. NOEL PATON. Fcap., cloth, 5s.

Poems by a Painter. Fcap., cloth, 5s.

PATON. Body and Soul. A Romance in Transcendental Pathology. By FREDERICK NOEL PATON. Third Edition. Crown 8vo, 1s.

PATRICK. The Apology of Origen in Reply to Celsus. A Chapter in the History of Apologetics. By the Rev. J. PATRICK, B.D. Post 8vo, 7s. 6d.

PATTERSON.
Essays in History and Art. By R. HOGARTH PATTERSON. 8vo, 12s.

The New Golden Age, and Influence of the Precious Metals upon the World. 2 vols. 8vo, 31s. 6d.

PAUL. History of the Royal Company of Archers, the Queen's Body-Guard for Scotland. By JAMES BALFOUR PAUL, Advocate of the Scottish Bar. Crown 4to, with Portraits and other Illustrations. £2, 2s.

PEILE. Lawn Tennis as a Game of Skill. With latest revised Laws as played by the Best Clubs. By Captain S. C. F. PEILE, B.S.C. Cheaper Edition. Fcap., cloth, 1s.

PETTIGREW. The Handy Book of Bees, and their Profitable Management. By A. PETTIGREW. Fifth Edition, Enlarged, with Engravings. Crown 8vo, 3s. 6d.

PHILIP. The Function of Labour in the Production of Wealth. By ALEXANDER PHILIP, LL.B., Edinburgh. Crown 8vo, 3s. 6d.

William Blackwood and Sons. 25

PHILOSOPHICAL CLASSICS FOR ENGLISH READERS.
Edited by WILLIAM KNIGHT, LL.D., Professor of Moral Philosophy, University of St Andrews. In crown 8vo volumes, with Portraits, price 3s. 6d.
[For list of Volumes published, see page 2.]

POLLOK. The Course of Time: A Poem. By ROBERT POLLOK, A.M. Cottage Edition, 32mo, 8d. The Same, cloth, gilt edges, 1s. 6d. Another Edition, with Illustrations by Birket Foster and others, fcap., cloth, 3s. 6d., or with edges gilt, 4s.

PORT ROYAL LOGIC. Translated from the French; with Introduction, Notes, and Appendix. By THOMAS SPENCER BAYNES, LL.D., Professor in the University of St Andrews. Tenth Edition, 12mo, 4s.

POTTS AND DARNELL.
Aditus Faciliores: An Easy Latin Construing Book, with Complete Vocabulary. By A. W. POTTS, M.A., LL.D., and the Rev. C. DARNELL, M.A., Head-Master of Cargilfield Preparatory School, Edinburgh. Tenth Edition, fcap. 8vo, 3s. 6d.

Aditus Faciliores Graeci. An Easy Greek Construing Book, with Complete Vocabulary. Fifth Edition, Revised. Fcap. 8vo, 3s.

POTTS. School Sermons. By the late ALEXANDER WM. POTTS, LL.D., First Head-Master of Fettes College. With a Memoir and Portrait. Crown 8vo, 7s. 6d.

PRINGLE. The Live-Stock of the Farm. By ROBERT O. PRINGLE. Third Edition. Revised and Edited by JAMES MACDONALD. Crown 8vo, 7s. 6d.

PUBLIC GENERAL STATUTES AFFECTING SCOTLAND from 1707 to 1847, with Chronological Table and Index. 3 vols. large 8vo, £3, 3s.

PUBLIC GENERAL STATUTES AFFECTING SCOTLAND, COLLECTION OF. Published Annually, with General Index.

RADICAL CURE FOR IRELAND, The. A Letter to the People of England and Scotland concerning a new Plantation. With 2 Maps. 8vo, 7s. 6d.

RAE. The Syrian Church in India. By GEORGE MILNE RAE, M.A., Fellow of the University of Madras; late Professor in the Madras Christian College. With 6 full-page Illustrations. Post 8vo, 10s. 6d.

RAMSAY. Scotland and Scotsmen in the Eighteenth Century. Edited from the MSS. of JOHN RAMSAY, Esq. of Ochtertyre, by ALEXANDER ALLARDYCE, Author of 'Memoir of Admiral Lord Keith, K.B.,' &c. 2 vols. 8vo, 31s. 6d.

RANKIN.
A Handbook of the Church of Scotland. By JAMES RANKIN, D.D., Minister of Muthill; Author of 'Character Studies in the Old Testament,' &c. An entirely New and much Enlarged Edition. Crown 8vo, with 2 Maps, 7s. 6d.

The Creed in Scotland. An Exposition of the Apostles' Creed. With Extracts from Archbishop Hamilton's Catechism of 1552, John Calvin's Catechism of 1556, and a Catena of Ancient Latin and other Hymns. Post 8vo, 7s. 6d.

The Worthy Communicant. A Guide to the Devout Observance of the Lord's Supper. Limp cloth, 1s. 3d.

The Young Churchman. Lessons on the Creed, the Commandments, the Means of Grace, and the Church. Limp cloth, 1s. 3d.

First Communion Lessons. 23d Edition. Paper Cover, 2d.

RECORDS OF THE TERCENTENARY FESTIVAL OF THE UNIVERSITY OF EDINBURGH. Celebrated in April 1884. Published under the Sanction of the Senatus Academicus. Large 4to, £2, 12s. 6d.

ROBERTSON. The Early Religion of Israel. As set forth by Biblical Writers and Modern Critical Historians. Being the Baird Lecture for 1888-89. By JAMES ROBERTSON, D.D., Professor of Oriental Languages in the University of Glasgow. Third Edition. Crown 8vo, 10s. 6d.

ROBERTSON. Orellana, and other Poems. By J. LOGIE ROBERTSON, M.A. Fcap. 8vo. Printed on hand-made paper. 6s.

ROBERTSON. Our Holiday among the Hills. By JAMES and JANET LOGIE ROBERTSON. Fcap. 8vo, 3s. 6d.

ROBERTSON. Essays and Sermons. By the late W. ROBERTson, B.D., Minister of the Parish of Sprouston. With a Memoir and Portrait. Crown 8vo, 5s. 6d.

RODGER. Aberdeen Doctors at Home and Abroad. The Story of a Medical School. By ELLA HILL BURTON RODGER. In one volume, demy 8vo. *[In the press.*

ROSCOE. Rambles with a Fishing-rod. By E. S. ROSCOE. Crown 8vo, 4s. 6d.

ROSS. Old Scottish Regimental Colours. By ANDREW ROSS, S.S.C., Hon. Secretary Old Scottish Regimental Colours Committee. Dedicated by Special Permission to Her Majesty the Queen. Folio, £2, 12s. 6d.

RUSSELL. The Haigs of Bemersyde. A Family History. By JOHN RUSSELL. Large 8vo, with Illustrations. 21s.

RUSSELL. Fragments from Many Tables. Being the Recollections of some Wise and Witty Men and Women. By GEORGE RUSSELL. Crown 8vo, 4s. 6d.

RUTLAND.
Notes of an Irish Tour in 1846. By the DUKE OF RUTLAND, G.C.B. (Lord JOHN MANNERS). New Edition. Crown 8vo, 2s. 6d.

Correspondence between the Right Honble. William Pitt and Charles Duke of Rutland, Lord-Lieutenant of Ireland, 1781-1787. With Introductory Note by JOHN DUKE OF RUTLAND. 8vo, 7s. 6d.

RUTLAND.
Gems of German Poetry. Translated by the DUCHESS OF RUTLAND (Lady JOHN MANNERS). [*New Edition in preparation.*

Impressions of Bad-Homburg. Comprising a Short Account of the Women's Associations of Germany under the Red Cross. Crown 8vo, 1s. 6d

Some Personal Recollections of the Later Years of the Earl of Beaconsfield, K.G. Sixth Edition, 6d.

Employment of Women in the Public Service. 6d.

Some of the Advantages of Easily Accessible Reading and Recreation Rooms, and Free Libraries. With Remarks on Starting and Maintaining them. Second Edition. Crown 8vo, 1s.

A Sequel to Rich Men's Dwellings, and other Occasional Papers. Crown 8vo, 2s. 6d.

Encouraging Experiences of Reading and Recreation Rooms, Aims of Guilds, Nottingham Social Guide, Existing Institutions, &c., &c. Crown 8vo, 1s.

SCHILLER. Wallenstein. A Dramatic Poem. By FRIEDRICH VON SCHILLER. Translated by C. G. N. LOCKHART. Fcap. 8vo, 7s. 6d.

William Blackwood and Sons. 27

SCOTCH LOCH FISHING. By "BLACK PALMER." Crown 8vo, interleaved with blank pages, 4s.

SCOUGAL. Prisons and their Inmates; or, Scenes from a Silent World. By FRANCIS SCOUGAL. Crown 8vo, boards, 2s.

SELLAR. Manual of the Education Acts for Scotland. By the late ALEXANDER CRAIG SELLAR, M.P. Eighth Edition. Revised and in great part rewritten by J. EDWARD GRAHAM, B.A. Oxon., Advocate. With Rules for the conduct of Elections, with Notes and Cases. 8vo.
[*New Edition in preparation.*
[SUPPLEMENT TO SELLAR'S MANUAL. Being the Acts of 1889 in so far as affecting the Education Acts. 8vo, 2s.]

SETH.
Scottish Philosophy. A Comparison of the Scottish and German Answers to Hume. Balfour Philosophical Lectures, University of Edinburgh. By ANDREW SETH, M.A., Professor of Logic and Metaphysics in Edinburgh University. Second Edition. Crown 8vo, 5s.

Hegelianism and Personality. Balfour Philosophical Lectures. Second Series. Crown 8vo, 5s.

SETH. Freedom as Ethical Postulate. By JAMES SETH, M.A., Brown University, Providence, Rhode Island. 8vo, 1s.

SHADWELL. The Life of Colin Campbell, Lord Clyde. Illustrated by Extracts from his Diary and Correspondence. By Lieutenant-General SHADWELL, C.B. With Portrait, Maps, and Plans. 2 vols. 8vo. 36s.

SHAND.
Half a Century; or, Changes in Men and Manners. By ALEX. INNES SHAND, Author of 'Against Time,' &c. Second Edition. 8vo, 12s. 6d.

Letters from the West of Ireland. Reprinted from the 'Times.' Crown 8vo, 5s.

Kilcarra. A Novel. 3 vols. crown 8vo, 25s. 6d.

SHARPE. Letters from and to Charles Kirkpatrick Sharpe. Edited by ALEXANDER ALLARDYCE, Author of 'Memoir of Admiral Lord Keith, K.B.,' &c. With a Memoir by the Rev. W. K. R. BEDFORD. In 2 vols. 8vo. Illustrated with Etchings and other Engravings. £2, 12s. 6d.

SIM. Margaret Sim's Cookery. With an Introduction by L. B. WALFORD, Author of 'Mr Smith: A Part of his Life,' &c. Crown 8vo, 5s.

SKELTON.
Maitland of Lethington; and the Scotland of Mary Stuart. A History. By JOHN SKELTON, C.B., LL.D., Author of 'The Essays of Shirley.' Demy 8vo, 2 vols., 28s.

The Handbook of Public Health. A Complete Edition of the Public Health and other Sanitary Acts relating to Scotland. Annotated, and with the Rules, Instructions, and Decisions of the Board of Supervision brought up to date with relative forms. Second Edition. With Introduction, containing the Administration of the Public Health Act in Counties. 8vo, 8s. 6d.

The Local Government (Scotland) Act in Relation to Public Health. A Handy Guide for County and District Councillors, Medical Officers, Sanitary Inspectors, and Members of Parochial Boards. Second Edition. With a new Preface on appointment of Sanitary Officers. Crown 8vo, 2s.

SKRINE. Columba: A Drama. By JOHN HUNTLEY SKRINE, Warden of Glenalmond; Author of 'A Memory of Edward Thring. Fcap. 4to.
[*Immediately.*

SMITH. For God and Humanity. A Romance of Mount Carmel. By HASKETT SMITH, Author of 'The Divine Epiphany,' &c. 3 vols. post 8vo, 25s. 6d.

SMITH.
Thorndale ; or, The Conflict of Opinions. By WILLIAM SMITH,
Author of 'A Discourse on Ethics,' &c. New Edition. Crown 8vo, 10s. 6d.

Gravenhurst ; or, Thoughts on Good and Evil. Second Edition. With Memoir and Portrait of the Author. Crown 8vo, 8s.

The Story of William and Lucy Smith. Edited by GEORGE MERRIAM. Large post 8vo, 12s. 6d.

SMITH. Memoir of the Families of M'Combie and Thoms, originally M'Intosh and M'Thomas. Compiled from History and Tradition. By WILLIAM M'COMBIE SMITH. With Illustrations. 8vo, 7s. 6d.

SMITH. Greek Testament Lessons for Colleges, Schools, and Private Students, consisting chiefly of the Sermon on the Mount and the Parables of our Lord. With Notes and Essays. By the Rev. J. HUNTER SMITH, M.A., King Edward's School, Birmingham. Crown 8vo, 6s.

SMITH. Writings by the Way. By JOHN CAMPBELL SMITH, M.A., Sheriff-Substitute. Crown 8vo, 9s.

SMITH. The Secretary for Scotland. Being a Statement of the Powers and Duties of the new Scottish Office. With a Short Historical Introduction and numerous references to important Administrative Documents. By W. C. SMITH, LL.B., Advocate. 8vo, 6s.

"SON OF THE MARSHES, A."
Within an Hour of London Town : Among Wild Birds and their Haunts. By "A SON OF THE MARSHES." Edited by J. A. OWEN. Second Edition. Crown 8vo, 6s.

On Surrey Hills. Third Edition. Crown 8vo, 6s.

Annals of a Fishing Village. New and Cheaper Edition. Crown 8vo, 5s. Illustrated Edition. Crown 8vo, 7s. 6d.

SORLEY. The Ethics of Naturalism. Being the Shaw Fellowship Lectures, 1884. By W. R. SORLEY, M.A., Fellow of Trinity College, Cambridge, Professor of Logic and Philosophy in University College of South Wales. Crown 8vo, 6s.

SPEEDY. Sport in the Highlands and Lowlands of Scotland with Rod and Gun. By TOM SPEEDY. Second Edition, Revised and Enlarged. With Illustrations by Lieut.-General Hope Crealocke, C.B., C.M.G., and others. 8vo, 15s.

SPROTT. The Worship and Offices of the Church of Scotland. By GEORGE W. SPROTT, D.D., Minister of North Berwick. Crown 8vo, 6s.

STARFORTH. Villa Residences and Farm Architecture : A Series of Designs. By JOHN STARFORTH, Architect. 102 Engravings. Second Edition. Medium 4to, £2, 17s. 6d.

STATISTICAL ACCOUNT OF SCOTLAND. Complete, with Index. 15 vols. 8vo, £16, 16s.

STEPHENS.
Book of the Farm ; detailing the Labours of the Farmer, Farm-Steward, Ploughman, Shepherd, Hedger, Farm-Labourer, Field-Worker, and Cattle-man. Illustrated with numerous Portraits of Animals and Engravings of Implements, and Plans of Farm Buildings. Fourth Edition. Revised, and in great part Rewritten by JAMES MACDONALD, of the 'Farming World,' &c. Complete in Six Divisional Volumes, bound in cloth, each 10s. 6d., or handsomely bound, in 3 volumes, with leather back and gilt top, £3, 3s.

The Book of Farm Implements and Machines. By J. SLIGHT and R. SCOTT BURN, Engineers. Edited by HENRY STEPHENS. Large 8vo, £2, 2s.

Catechism of Agriculture. [*New Edition in preparation.*

William Blackwood and Sons.

STEVENSON. British Fungi. (Hymenomycetes). By Rev. JOHN STEVENSON, Author of 'Mycologia Scotia,' Hon. Sec. Cryptogamic Society of Scotland. Vols. I. and II., post 8vo, with Illustrations, price 12s. 6d. net each.

STEWART.
Advice to Purchasers of Horses. By JOHN STEWART, V.S. New Edition. 2s. 6d.

Stable Economy. A Treatise on the Management of Horses in relation to Stabling, Grooming, Feeding, Watering, and Working. Seventh Edition. Fcap. 8vo, 6s. 6d.

STEWART. A Hebrew Grammar, with the Pronunciation, Syllabic Division and Tone of the Words, and Quantity of the Vowels. By Rev. DUNCAN STEWART, D.D. Fourth Edition. 8vo, 3s. 6d.

STEWART. Boethius: An Essay. By HUGH FRASER STEWART, M.A., Trinity College, Cambridge. Crown 8vo, 7s. 6d.

STODDART. Angling Songs. By THOMAS TOD STODDART. New Edition, with a Memoir by ANNA M. STODDART. Crown 8vo, 7s. 6d.

STORMONTH.
Etymological and Pronouncing Dictionary of the English Language. Including a very Copious Selection of Scientific Terms. For use in Schools and Colleges, and as a Book of General Reference. By the Rev. JAMES STORMONTH. The Pronunciation carefully revised by the Rev. P. H. PHELP, M.A. Cantab. Eleventh Edition, Revised throughout, with Supplement. Crown 8vo, pp. 800. 7s. 6d.

Dictionary of the English Language, Pronouncing, Etymological, and Explanatory. Revised by the Rev. P. H. PHELP. Library Edition. Imperial 8vo, handsomely bound in half morocco, 31s. 6d.

The School Etymological Dictionary and Word-Book. Fourth Edition. Fcap. 8vo, pp. 254. 2s.

STORY.
Nero; A Historical Play. By W. W. STORY, Author of 'Roba di Roma.' Fcap. 8vo, 6s.

Vallombrosa. Post 8vo, 5s.

Poems. 2 vols., 7s. 6d.

Fiammetta. A Summer Idyl. Crown 8vo, 7s. 6d.

Conversations in a Studio. 2 vols. crown 8vo, 12s. 6d.

Excursions in Art and Letters. Crown 8vo, 7s. 6d.

STRICKLAND. Life of Agnes Strickland. By her SISTER. Post 8vo, with Portrait engraved on Steel, 12s. 6d.

STURGIS.
John-a-Dreams. A Tale. By JULIAN STURGIS. New Edition. Crown 8vo, 3s. 6d.

Little Comedies, Old and New. Crown 8vo, 7s. 6d.

SUTHERLAND (DUCHESS OF). How I Spent my Twentieth Year. Being a Record of a Tour Round the World, 1886-87. By the DUCHESS OF SUTHERLAND (MARCHIONESS OF STAFFORD). With Illustrations. Crown 8vo, 7s. 6d.

SUTHERLAND. Handbook of Hardy Herbaceous and Alpine Flowers, for General Garden Decoration. Containing Descriptions of upwards of 1000 Species of Ornamental Hardy Perennial and Alpine Plants; along with Concise and Plain Instructions for their Propagation and Culture. By WILLIAM SUTHERLAND, Landscape Gardener; formerly Manager of the Herbaceous Department at Kew. Crown 8vo, 7s. 6d.

TAYLOR. The Story of my Life. By the late Colonel
Meadows Taylor, Author of 'The Confessions of a Thug,' &c., &c. Edited by
his Daughter. New and Cheaper Edition, being the Fourth. Crown 8vo, 6s.

THOLUCK. Hours of Christian Devotion. Translated from
the German of A. Tholuck, D.D., Professor of Theology in the University of
Halle. By the Rev. Robert Menzies, D.D. With a Preface written for this
Translation by the Author. Second Edition. Crown 8vo, 7s. 6d.

THOMSON. A History of the Fife Light Horse. By Colonel
Anstruther Thomson. With numerous Portraits. Small 4to. 21s.

THOMSON.
Handy Book of the Flower-Garden: being Practical Directions for the Propagation, Culture, and Arrangement of Plants in Flower-Gardens all the year round. With Engraved Plans. By David Thomson, Gardener to his Grace the Duke of Buccleuch, K.T., at Drumlanrig. Fourth and Cheaper Edition. Crown 8vo, 5s.

The Handy Book of Fruit-Culture under Glass: being a
series of Elaborate Practical Treatises on the Cultivation and Forcing of Pines, Vines, Peaches, Figs, Melons, Strawberries, and Cucumbers. With Engravings of Hothouses, &c. Second Edition, Revised and Enlarged. Crown 8vo, 7s. 6d.

THOMSON. A Practical Treatise on the Cultivation of the
Grape Vine. By William Thomson, Tweed Vineyards. Tenth Edition. 8vo, 5s.

THOMSON. Cookery for the Sick and Convalescent. With
Directions for the Preparation of Poultices, Fomentations, &c. By Barbara Thomson. Fcap. 8vo, 1s. 6d.

THORNTON. Opposites. A Series of Essays on the Unpopular
Sides of Popular Questions. By Lewis Thornton. 8vo, 12s. 6d.

TOM CRINGLE'S LOG. A New Edition, with Illustrations.
Crown 8vo, cloth gilt, 5s. Cheap Edition, 2s.

TRANSACTIONS OF THE HIGHLAND AND AGRICULTURAL SOCIETY OF SCOTLAND. Published annually, price 5s.

TRAVEL, ADVENTURE, AND SPORT. From 'Blackwood's
Magazine.' Uniform with 'Tales from Blackwood.' In 12 Parts, each price 1s. Handsomely bound in 6 vols., cloth, 15s.; half calf, 25s.

TRAVERS. Mona Maclean, Medical Student. A Novel. By
Graham Travers. 3 vols. crown 8vo, 25s. 6d.

TULLOCH.
Rational Theology and Christian Philosophy in England in
the Seventeenth Century. By John Tulloch, D.D., Principal of St Mary's College in the University of St Andrews; and one of her Majesty's Chaplains in Ordinary in Scotland. Second Edition. 2 vols. 8vo, 16s.

Modern Theories in Philosophy and Religion. 8vo, 15s.

Luther, and other Leaders of the Reformation. Third Edition, Enlarged. Crown 8vo, 3s. 6d.

Memoir of Principal Tulloch, D.D., LL.D. By Mrs Oliphant,
Author of 'Life of Edward Irving.' Third and Cheaper Edition. 8vo, with Portrait, 7s. 6d.

TURNBULL. Othello: A Critical Study. By W. R. Turnbull.
Demy 8vo, 15s.

TWEEDIE. The Arabian Horse: his Country and People.
With Portraits of Typical or Famous Arabians, and numerous other Illustrations; also a Map of the Country of the Arabian Horse, and a descriptive Glossary of Arabic words and proper names. By Colonel W. Tweedie, C.S.I., Bengal Staff Corps, H.B.M.'s Consul-General, Baghdad, and Political Resident for the Government of India in Turkish Arabia. [In the press.

William Blackwood and Sons. 31

VEITCH.
Institutes of Logic. By JOHN VEITCH, LL.D., Professor of Logic and Rhetoric in the University of Glasgow. Post 8vo, 12s. 6d.
History and Poetry of the Scottish Border. In One Volume. Demy 8vo. [*In the press.*
The Feeling for Nature in Scottish Poetry. From the Earliest Times to the Present Day. 2 vols. fcap. 8vo, in roxburghe binding, 15s.
Merlin and other Poems. Fcap. 8vo. 4s. 6d.
Knowing and Being. Essays in Philosophy. First Series. Crown 8vo, 5s.

VIRGIL. The Æneid of Virgil. Translated in English Blank Verse by G. K. RICKARDS, M.A., and Lord RAVENSWORTH. 2 vols. fcap. 8vo, 10s.

WACE. The Christian Faith and Recent Agnostic Attacks. By the Rev. HENRY WACE, D.D., Principal of King's College, London; Preacher of Lincoln's Inn; Chaplain to the Queen. In one vol. post 8vo. [*Shortly.*

WALFORD. Four Biographies from 'Blackwood': Jane Taylor, Hannah More, Elizabeth Fry, Mary Somerville. By L. B. WALFORD. Crown 8vo, 5s.

WARREN'S (SAMUEL) WORKS:—
Diary of a Late Physician. Cloth, 2s. 6d.; boards, 2s.
Ten Thousand A-Year. Cloth, 3s. 6d.; boards, 2s. 6d.
Now and Then. The Lily and the Bee. Intellectual and Moral Development of the Present Age. 4s. 6d.
Essays: Critical, Imaginative, and Juridical. 5s.

WARREN. The Five Books of the Psalms. With Marginal Notes. By Rev. SAMUEL L. WARREN, Rector of Esher, Surrey; late Fellow, Dean, and Divinity Lecturer, Wadham College, Oxford. Crown 8vo, 5s.

WEBSTER. The Angler and the Loop-Rod. By DAVID WEBSTER. Crown 8vo, with Illustrations. 7s. 6d.

WELLINGTON. Wellington Prize Essays on "the System of Field Manoeuvres best adapted for enabling our Troops to meet a Continental Army." Edited by General Sir EDWARD BRUCE HAMLEY, K.C.B., K.C.M.G. 8vo, 12s. 6d.

WENLEY. Socrates and Christ: A Study in the Philosophy of Religion. By R. M. WENLEY, M.A., Lecturer on Mental and Moral Philosophy in Queen Margaret College, Glasgow; Examiner in Philosophy in the University of Glasgow. Crown 8vo, 6s.

WERNER. A Visit to Stanley's Rear-Guard at Major Barttelot's Camp on the Aruhwimi. With an Account of River-Life on the Congo. By J. R. WERNER, F.R.G.S., Engineer, late in the Service of the Etat Independant du Congo. With Maps, Portraits, and other Illustrations. 8vo, 16s.

WESTMINSTER ASSEMBLY. Minutes of the Westminster Assembly, while engaged in preparing their Directory for Church Government, Confession of Faith, and Catechisms (November 1644 to March 1649). Edited by the Rev. Professor ALEX. T. MITCHELL, of St Andrews, and the Rev. JOHN STRUTHERS, LL.D. With a Historical and Critical Introduction by Professor Mitchell. 8vo, 15s.

WHITE.
The Eighteen Christian Centuries. By the REV. JAMES WHITE. Seventh Edition, post 8vo, with Index, 6s.
History of France, from the Earliest Times. Sixth Thousand. Post 8vo, with Index, 6s.

32 Books Published by William Blackwood and Sons.

WHITE.
Archæological Sketches in Scotland—Kintyre and Knapdale. By Colonel T. P. WHITE, R.E., of the Ordnance Survey. With numerous Illustrations. 2 vols. folio, £4, 4s. Vol. I., Kintyre, sold separately, £2, 2s.

The Ordnance Survey of the United Kingdom. A Popular Account. Crown 8vo, 5s.

WILLIAMSON. The Horticultural Exhibitor's Handbook. A Treatise on Cultivating, Exhibiting, and Judging Plants, Flowers, Fruits, and Vegetables. By W. WILLIAMSON, Gardener. Revised by MALCOLM DUNN, Gardener to his Grace the Duke of Buccleuch and Queensberry, Dalkeith Park. Crown 8vo, 3s. 6d.

WILLIAMSON. Poems of Nature and Life. By DAVID R. WILLIAMSON, Minister of Kirkmaiden. Fcap. 8vo, 3s.

WILLIAMSON. Light from Eastern Lands on the Lives of Abraham, Joseph, and Moses. By the Rev. ALEX. WILLIAMSON, Author of 'The Missionary Heroes of the Pacific,' 'Sure and Comfortable Words,' 'Ask and Receive,' &c. Crown 8vo, 3s. 6d.

WILLS AND GREENE. Drawing-room Dramas for Children. By W. G. WILLS and the Hon. Mrs GREENE. Crown 8vo, 6s.

WILSON.
Works of Professor Wilson. Edited by his Son-in-Law, Professor FERRIER. 12 vols. crown 8vo, £2, 8s.

Christopher in his Sporting-Jacket. 2 vols., 8s.

Isle of Palms, City of the Plague, and other Poems. 4s.

Lights and Shadows of Scottish Life, and other Tales. 4s.

Essays, Critical and Imaginative. 4 vols., 16s.

The Noctes Ambrosianæ. 4 vols., 16s.

Homer and his Translators, and the Greek Drama. Crown 8vo, 4s.

WITHIN AN HOUR OF LONDON TOWN. Among Wild Birds and their Haunts. By "A SON OF THE MARSHES," *See page 28.*

WORSLEY.
Poems and Translations. By PHILIP STANHOPE WORSLEY, M.A. Edited by EDWARD WORSLEY. Second Edition, Enlarged. Fcap. 8vo, 6s.

Homer's Odyssey. Translated into English Verse in Spenserian Stanza. By P. S. Worsley. Third Edition. 2 vols. fcap., 12s.

Homer's Iliad. Translated by P. S. Worsley and Prof. Conington. 2 vols. Crown 8vo, 21s.

YATE. England and Russia Face to Face in Asia. A Record of Travel with the Afghan Boundary Commission. By Captain A. C. YATE, Bombay Staff Corps. 8vo, with Maps and Illustrations, 21s.

YATE. Northern Afghanistan; or, Letters from the Afghan Boundary Commission. By Major C. E. YATE, C.S.I., C.M.G. Bombay Staff Corps, F.R.G.S. 8vo, with Maps, 18s.

YOUNG. A Story of Active Service in Foreign Lands. Compiled from letters sent home from South Africa, India, and China, 1856-1882. By Surgeon-General A. GRAHAM YOUNG, Author of 'Crimean Cracks.' Crown 8vo, Illustrated, 7s. 6d.

YULE. Fortification: For the use of Officers in the Army, and Readers of Military History. By Colonel YULE, Bengal Engineers. 8vo, with Numerous Illustrations, 10s. 6d.

11/92.

www.ingramcontent.com/pod-product-compliance
Lightning Source LLC
Chambersburg PA
CBHW030552300426
44111CB00009B/948